£8 LIT 23/24 RW

Drawing on the Victorians

Series in Victorian Studies

Series editors: Joseph McLaughlin and Elizabeth Miller

Drawing on the
Victorians

The Palimpsest of Victorian and Neo-Victorian Graphic Texts

EDITED BY **Anna Maria Jones and Rebecca N. Mitchell**

WITH AN AFTERWORD BY Kate Flint

OHIO UNIVERSITY PRESS ATHENS

Ohio University Press, Athens, Ohio 45701
ohioswallow.com
© 2017 by Ohio University Press
All rights reserved

To obtain permission to quote, reprint, or otherwise reproduce or distribute
material from Ohio University Press publications, please contact our rights and
permissions department at (740) 593-1154 or (740) 593-4536 (fax).

Printed in the United States of America
Ohio University Press books are printed on acid-free paper ⊗ ™

27 26 25 24 23 22 21 20 19 18 17   5 4 3 2 1

Library of Congress Cataloging-in-Publication Data available upon request.

Contents

CONTENTS

Illustrations

ILLUSTRATIONS

Acknowledgments

A collection about visual culture like this one depends on the reproduction of images; *Drawing on the Victorians: The Palimpsest of Victorian and Neo-Victorian Graphic Texts* could not have been realized without the kind assistance of myriad individuals at libraries, archives, presses, and museums around the world. The Cadbury Research Library at the University of Birmingham provided essential support in procuring the images that are at the heart of this collection; we thank the staff there, especially Library Support Assistant Catherine Martin, for their assistance. Cartoons from *Punch* that remain in copyright appear courtesy of the *Punch* Cartoon Library, London; special thanks are due to Andre Gailani there. We are grateful to Bryan Talbot for allowing us to reproduce images from *Alice in Sunderland*. Diana Schutz at Dark Horse Comics helped secure permissions for the images from works by Talbot and by Will Eisner; images from Eisner's *Fagin the Jew* in chapter 5 are reproduced with permission. Images from Jerzy Szyłak and Mateusz Skutnik's *Alicja* appear courtesy of Timof i cisi wspólnicy, and images from Nicholas Mahler's *Alice in Sussex* were reproduced with permission from Suhrkamp Verlag. Portions of chapter 3 appear in "10 April 1818: John Cleves Symmes's 'No. 1 Circular'" in *BRANCH: Britain, Representation, and Nineteenth-Century History*. Michael Dahl's portrait of Edmond Halley appears thanks to the Royal Society. Olivia Plender graciously allowed the reproduction of illustrations from *A Stellar Key to the Summerland*. Thanks to Roman Dirge and Titan Books for granting permission to include images from *Lenore* in chapter 6. The Royal Photographic Society generously allowed us to reproduce Henry Peach Robinson's "Fading Away." We are grateful to Elisabet Paredes at Donadio and Olson for facilitating permission to reproduce three images by Edward Gorey. Thanks to Mark Samuels Lasner and his assistant, Ashley Gail Rye, for scans of six illustrations in chapter 7. The picture of Dr. Barnardo's street waifs is reproduced with kind permission of the British Newspaper Archive (www.britishnewspaperarchive.co.uk). Images from Alan Moore and Kevin O'Neil's *The League of Extraordinary Gentlemen* and

Grant Morrison and Steve Yeowell's *Sebastian O* appear thanks to DC Comics. Victorian valentines in chapter 9 are reproduced with permission from the Picture Library at the Museum of London. Marilyn Meeker at ProQuest was helpful in facilitating our use of images from *British Periodicals*. Images from *Lady Victorian* appear thanks to the generosity of Moto Naoko; thanks also to Fujii Hiro at Akitashoten for facilitating the permissions. The fashion plate from *Blackwood's Lady's Magazine* in chapter 10 is reproduced by kind permission of the Syndics of Cambridge University Library; thanks to Grant Young, head of digital content, and Jo Turnbull, administrative assistant for digital content, at Cambridge University Library. Yinka Shonibare's work appears in the afterword with the generous permission of the artist; thanks to Pete Woronkowicz at DACS for assistance with the arrangements. Clare Strand and Grimaldi Gavin graciously allowed us to reproduce a print from *Gone Astray Portraits, 2001/2*.

We would also like to thank Joseph McLaughlin and Rick Huard at Ohio University Press, who supported our project with enthusiasm. We are grateful as well to the two anonymous readers whose helpful feedback shaped this volume. Finally, our sincere thanks to Kate Flint for providing the afterword to our collection.

Reading the Victorian and Neo-Victorian Graphic Palimpsest

ANNA MARIA JONES AND REBECCA N. MITCHELL

In *Through the Looking-Glass and What Alice Found There* (1871), Lewis Carroll and his famous illustrator John Tenniel revisited (the latter with some reluctance, as the story goes) their ingénue, sending her this time to Looking-Glass House. As with any reunion tour, the second trip both did and did not replicate the first. Whereas the seven-year-old heroine of *Alice's Adventures in Wonderland* (1865) encounters the King and Queen of Hearts and the royal soldiers, who are "nothing but a pack of cards,"[1] during her later adventures she meets the Black and White Kings and Queens, who are governed (more or less) by the rules of chess. In the former, the Cheshire Cat, Bill the Lizard, the Caterpillar, and the Mock Turtle feature. In the latter, Tweedledee and Tweedledum, Humpty Dumpty, and the White Knight make appearances. Yet two characters recur: the Hatter and the March Hare. Alice initially meets these two at the tea party, which has been persisting indefinitely because, as the Hatter explains, he has quarreled with Time: "And ever since that . . . [Time] wo'n't do a thing that I ask! It's always six o'clock now."[2] By the second novel, the pair has been transformed into the White King's "queer Anglo-Saxon Messengers," Hatta and Haigha.[3] Even though the written names are different from their *Wonderland* counterparts, readers would recognize these familiar characters if they were to sound out the names. The narrator encourages readers to do just this when he remarks paren-thetically that the King pronounced Haigha's name "so as to rhyme with 'mayor.'"[4] Even more obvious allusions occur in the illustrations. The first reference to the Hatter precedes his textual appearance; in an earlier illustration the as-yet-unnamed King's Messenger, clearly recognizable as the Hatter, languishes in prison for a crime he has yet to commit, so readers attentive to the interplay of text and image would have already been alerted to the fact that the Hatter has re-turned, still with a problematic relationship to time. Hatta's second graphic appearance, in the later scene with the White King, shows him looking like the Hatter of *Alice's Adventures in Wonderland,* com-plete with oversized, price-tag-bedecked hat (see fig. I.1); also, the image's composition echoes the iconic image Tenniel produced for that earlier volume (see fig. I.2): In the *Wonderland* image, Alice, the March Hare, the Dormouse, and the Hatter are seated at the tea table. The March Hare and the Hatter face one another, with the sleeping Dormouse squeezed between them. In the *Looking-Glass* image, Alice, Haigha, the White King, and Hatta are standing in a group. As with the *Wonderland* image, Alice occupies the leftmost position, in partial pro-file, while Haigha and Hatta again face one another, partially obscur-ing the King, just as they obscure the Dormouse in the earlier image. Viewed together, the two illustrations create an uncanny layered effect, as though we are looking through one to another that is still visible beneath it: as though we were viewing a palimpsest, in other words.

Carroll's *Through the Looking-Glass* both gratifies and thwarts the reader's desire for a return to the "original." Likewise, Tenniel's illus-trations create tension, both with Carroll's text and with one another, thus highlighting the complexity of image-textual interactions. Taken in toto, Carroll and Tenniel's collaboration in the *Alice* books troubles any assumption of the priority of the written word over graphic rep-resentation. The double-yet-single nature of *Alice in Wonderland,* as the two novels together are commonly called, likewise underscores what Gérard Genette calls in *Palimpsests* (1982) "transtextuality," that is, "all that sets the text in a relationship, whether obvious or concealed, with other texts."[5] After Genette, critics have found the palimpsest a useful conceptual device for understanding this layered aesthetic in postmodern fiction; however, as works like *Alice in Wonderland* demonstrate, Victorian graphic texts were already doing the layered

FIG. I.I   Alice with Hatta and the White King. John Tenniel for Lewis Carroll, *Through the Looking-Glass* (London: Macmillan, 1873), 148. Image courtesy of Cadbury Research Library: Special Collections, University of Birmingham.

FIG. I.2   Mad Tea Party. John Tenniel for Lewis Carroll, *Alice's Adventures in Wonderland* (London: Macmillan, 1874), 97. Image courtesy of Cadbury Research Library: Special Collections, University of Birmingham.

self-referential, metatextual, and image-textual work that has become the signature of "the neo-Victorian" in our contemporary moment. The chapters in this collection, *Drawing on the Victorians: The Palimpsest of Victorian and Neo-Victorian Graphic Texts,* explore Victorian as well as neo-Victorian manifestations of this interplay.

M uch neo-Victorian scholarship takes its cue from theories of postmodern fiction deriving from Genette's work, such as Linda Hutcheon's oft-cited delineation of "historiographic metafiction," which, she writes, "offers a sense of the presence of the past, but this is a past that can only be known from its texts, its traces—be they literary or historical."[6] Christian Gutleben's dichotomization, following from Genette's and Hutcheon's work, has likewise been influential. He claims, "In many ways establishing the difference between a subversive and [a] nostalgic reworking of Victorianism can be achieved by determining whether the contemporary novels favour the derisive quality of parody or the mimetic quality of pastiche."[7] Ann Heilmann and Mark Llewellyn, similarly, define the term *neo-Victorianism* as "a series of metatextual and metahistorical conjunctions [that] interact within the fields of exchange and adaptation between the Victorian and the contemporary."[8] To be neo-Victorian, as they conceive of it, "texts (literary, filmic, audio/visual) must in some respect be *self-consciously engaged with the act of (re)interpretation, (re)discovery and (re)vision concerning the Victorians.*"[9] Others, however, have challenged the dichotomy between nostalgic attachment and postmodern detachment that these critics use to privilege particular kinds of neo-Victorian texts. Kate Mitchell argues that nostalgia "does not preclude sustained, critical engagement with the past," thereby opening up space to consider a broader range of texts under the umbrella of "neo-Victorian."[10] Cora Kaplan, too, usefully reminds us that "there is a high degree of affect involved in reading and writing about the Victorians."[11] Inter- and metatextuality are not, to be sure, postmodern inventions grafted onto Victorian texts. Likewise, modes of reading—then and now—combine sentimental and self-consciously critical engagements with the text.

In forwarding analyses of neo-Victorian metatexts, critics have proffered various metaphorical schemata for understanding our postmodern (or post-postmodern) attachments to the Victorians: Rosario Arias and Patricia Pulham use haunting and spectrality as the organizing metaphors for their 2010 collection; Kate Mitchell suggests the photographic afterimage as conceptual framework in her *History and Cultural Memory in Neo-Victorian Fiction* (2010); Marie-Luise Kohlke and Christian Gutleben build their essay collection, *Neo-Victorian Tropes of Trauma* (2010), around the notion that contemporary culture continues to bear the traces of the Victorian past as trauma.[12] Elizabeth Ho employs a similar metaphor in her 2012 *Neo-Victorianism and the Memory of Empire:* "Neo-Victorianism becomes an opportunity to stage the Victorian in the present as a means of recovery of and recovery *from* the memory of the British Empire that impedes the imagination of a post-imperial future."[13] Simon Joyce gives us the notion of the "Victorians in the rearview mirror"—that is, receding in the distance but also closer than they appear: "The image usefully condenses the paradoxical sense of looking forward to see what is behind us. . . . It also suggests something of the inevitable distortion that accompanies any mirror image."[14] As this growing body of scholars has explored, the contemporary fascination with "the Victorian" comprises both desires for and anxieties about our connections to the historically and culturally distant Other. We may wish to explore a nineteenth-century "wonderland" peopled by more or less fantastic inhabitants, yet we may also dread finding ourselves reflected in the looking glass of those retrograde Victorians.

The neo-Victorian boom encompasses all manner of media: numerous Man Booker prize short-listers, such as Matthew Kneale's *English Passengers* (2000), Sarah Waters's *Fingersmith* (2002), and Julian Barnes's *Arthur & George* (2005); video games like *American McGee's Alice* (2000) and *American McGee's Alice: Madness Returns* (2011); film and television reboots such as *Sherlock Holmes* (2009) and *Sherlock Holmes: A Game of Shadows* (2011), both directed by Guy Ritchie, and the BBC's runaway hit series *Sherlock* (2010–); and the professional and amateur art, costumes, and artifacts that feature at steampunk conventions worldwide.[15] But nowhere has the engagement with the Victorians been more striking than in contemporary image-texts. In a *New York Times* 2007 article, "More than Words: Britain Embraces the Graphic Novel," Tara Mulholland notes Britain's history of "visual satire" and "celebrated social and political cartoonists," including

Victorians George Cruikshank and George Du Maurier, and the recent financial and critical successes of works like Bryan Talbot's *Alice in Sunderland* (2007).[16] She also cites the 2005 recognition of graphic novelist Posy Simmonds by Britain's Royal Society of Literature and tells readers to look forward to the single-volume publication of Simmonds's *Tamara Drewe* (2007), a loose adaptation of Thomas Hardy's *Far from the Madding Crowd,* which had run as a weekly comic strip in the *Guardian* and has since been turned into a film by Stephen Frears.[17] Mulholland does not mention, but might, the popular and critical attention to "Victorian" comics like Alan Moore and Eddie Campbell's contribution to Ripperology, *From Hell* (1989–96); Moore and Kevin O'Neill's *The League of Extraordinary Gentleman* (2000), which offers a mash-up of Victorian literary characters (such as Mina Harker, Allan Quatermain, and Dr. Jekyll) as superheroes in a steampunk nineteenth century; or Grant Morrison and Steve Yeowell's *Sebastian O* (1993), which reprises the Wildean dandy as a countercultural action hero.[18]

Whereas the *New York Times* article focuses on Britain's embrace of the graphic novel, the influence of nineteenth-century visual culture on graphic texts worldwide is likewise noteworthy. French *bande dessinée* artists Joann Sfar and Emmanuel Guibert's *The Professor's Daughter* (1997) features an unlikely Victorian romance between revived mummy Imhotep IV and Lillian Bowell, daughter of a prominent Egyptologist.[19] Neo-Victorian manga (Japanese comics) and anime (animation)— for example, Mori Karou's story of an upwardly mobile maid, *Emma* (2002–6); Mochizuki Jun's fantasy series *Pandora Hearts* (2006–15), based loosely on the characters of Carroll's *Alice in Wonderland*; and Toboso Yana's Faustian gothic adventure, *Black Butler* (2007–)—are enjoying worldwide popularity.[20] Singaporean comics artist Johny Tay's webcomic, *Seven Years in Dog-Land* (2009–11) reworks Alice's journey to Wonderland as a darker adventure in which Alice becomes trapped in a "gritty and cruel kingdom" where dogs are masters and humans are pets, in order to explore "humans' relationship with nature and the human condition itself."[21] These examples are a fraction of the many neo-Victorian graphic texts in circulation today. However, the bulk of neo-Victorian studies scholarship focuses on novels and film and television adaptations and how these hark back to the Victorian novel. There has been no sustained examination of the connections between Victorian and neo-Victorian graphic texts.[22] And until recently, there has been very little critical attention paid to neo-Victorianism as a global phenomenon. As Llewellyn and Heilmann note, "Neo-Victorian critics have largely awaited the appearance of the cosmopolitan and international on our own literary and critical shores."[23] Even in nuanced treatments of neo-Victorianism, there is an inherent danger in using "the Victorian" to signify a single, stable set of referents or, conversely, to serve as a conveniently broad catchall term.

It is with these lacunae in mind that *Drawing on the Victorians* takes up the notion of the palimpsest as a conceptual framework: one that operates at several levels simultaneously. The palimpsest—a manuscript in which one text overwrites the imperfectly erased traces of previous writings, which themselves reemerge over time, thus altering the subsequent layers—has been an important figure employed by poststructuralist thinkers to challenge the fixity of textual meaning and the linearity of historical progress. Linda Hutcheon argues in *A Theory of Adaptation* that "to deal with adaptations *as adaptations* is to think of them as . . . inherently 'palimpsestuous' works, haunted at all times by their adapted texts. If we know that prior text, we always feel its presence shadowing the one we are experiencing directly."[24] Looking back to Genette's *Palimpsests,* which also employs the neologism *palimpsestuous,*[25] Christian Gutleben argues similarly that the palimpsest highlights the importance of the Victorian to backward-looking postmodern fiction: "The postmodern text is the sum of its various sub-texts and their ideologies; it superimposes the contemporary, the mock-Victorian and the Victorian texts in order to combine their perspectives and messages and to take stock of both anarchy and harmony, to suggest both disorientation and sources of plenitude."[26] The palimpsest offers a compelling image of the presence of a ghostly, partially legible past bleeding through contemporary textual productions. It also speaks to the layers of meaning that accrue in the process of transnational adaptation and appropriation, as Monika Pietrzak-Franger's and Anna Maria Jones's contributions to this volume demonstrate. The Victorian/neo-Victorian palimpsest acquires multiple layers of signification in the "translation" of Victorian graphic texts across linguistic, geohistorical, and temporal boundaries.

Sarah Dillon argues evocatively that the palimpsest as a concept (as opposed to palimpsests as literal objects) is a Victorian invention. Dillon credits Thomas De Quincey's 1845 essay "The Palimpsest" with inaugurating the palimpsest as a metaphor though which to understand abstract notions of time, memory, and selfhood.[27] De Quincey imagines the mind as a "natural and mighty palimpsest" upon which "everlasting layers of ideas, images, [and] feelings" have fallen.[28] And while "each succession has seemed to bury all that went before," he insists that "in reality not one has been extinguished."[29] As Dillon claims, "De Quincey was not the first writer to use palimpsests in a figurative sense. However, his inauguration of the concept of the palimpsest marks the beginning of a consistent process of metaphorization of palimpsests from the mid-nineteenth century (the most prolific period of palimpsest discoveries) to the present day."[30] In fact, fifteen years before De Quincey's essay, Thomas Carlyle, in "On History" (1830), described history thusly:

> Let us search more and more into the Past. . . . For
> though the whole meaning lies far beyond our ken; yet
> in that complex Manuscript, covered over with formless
> inextricably tangled unknown characters,—nay, which
> is a *Palimpsest,* and had once prophetic writing, still
> dimly legible there,—some letters, some words, may be
> deciphered; and if no complete Philosophy, here and there
> an intelligible precept, available in practice, be gathered.[31]

To deploy the palimpsest as a metaphor for understanding contemporary neo-Victorianism is, thus, to use Victorian tools to undertake our intellectual labor. When we do the imaginative and critical work of relating to the Victorians, in many ways, we replicate the Victorians' own modes of self-representation and engagement with culture. The figure of the palimpsest speaks to the combined visuality and textuality—the complex overlayering of words, images, and texts—that the Victorians themselves developed through their illustrated books and periodicals and cartoons.

——◆——

Scholars embracing the so-called visual turn in Victorian studies have become increasingly attuned to the ways in which the Victorians understood themselves in relation to (and as) layered image-textual productions. However, visual cultural studies have tended to develop around separate disciplinary nexuses, which often remain distinct from one another. From an overtly art historical (and high culture) perspective, scholars such as David Peters Corbett and Elizabeth Prettejohn have traced the development of movements in nineteenth-century painting (modernism and Pre-Raphaelitism, respectively), considering only tangentially the degree to which these movements influence and are influenced by print culture outside of the fine arts.[32] For Corbett, that focus is intentional. Even as he acknowledges that "the Victorian cultural scene and its attitudes towards language and the visual are enormously complex," his study turns expressly to painting, the medium in which the prevailing "mental climate about the visual arts" was "expressed most forcefully in the manipulation of pigment on a surface."[33] Others explore more directly the interrelations of the visual arts and the written word: Rachel Teukolsky and Elizabeth Helsinger, for example, argue that print culture, in particular the burgeoning field of art criticism, was an integral part of shaping formal and thematic trends in painting. Teukolsky introduces her study by locating "aesthetic history not only in the visual arts, but in the prismatic assemblage of texts, spaces, institutions, and practices that shaped Victorian critical discourse more broadly."[34] Nonetheless, the bulk of nineteenth-century art historical scholarship privileges the arts that were in turn privileged in nineteenth-century galleries and art criticism.

On the opposite end of the cultural spectrum is popular print culture—illustrated magazines and newspapers, gift books, fashion plates, children's literature, playbills and posters, and so forth—which in recent decades has received increased scholarly attention.[35] Lorraine Janzen Kooistra's *Poetry, Pictures, and Popular Publishing: The Illustrated Gift Book and Victorian Visual Culture* (2011), for example, shines a light on a "middlebrow artifact" long relegated to the margins of Victorian studies but one that, as Kooistra argues, forms a unique locus that connects "the 'high art' of painting and exhibition culture with the mass art of wood engraving and print culture."[36] Such scholarship is part of a larger movement of interest in periodical and ephemera studies. Supported by the establishment of the *Victorian Periodicals Review* in 1968, this push has more recently been encouraged by the digitization of nineteenth-century ephemera and periodicals, which has opened up access to works formerly viewable only in archives and has given scholars the ability to scan across the vast quantities of media, thereby allowing patterns and networks to emerge.[37] In his 2005 essay "Googling the Victorians," which remains one of the most cogent assessments of the effect of digitization on the study of the nineteenth century to date, Patrick Leary describes a revolution in textual scholarship occasioned by the "extraordinary power, speed, and ubiquity of online searching."[38] Leary is careful, though, to balance the "optimism about these expanding resources" with "a recognition of how much remains to be done" in terms of digitization; further, he emphasizes that training and "close prior acquaintance with nineteenth-century prose" are necessary complements to any search engine.[39] What is more, the brisk pace of additions to the online archive means that conclusions derived from online searches are necessarily unstable. When the present volume was being written, for example, a Google search of occurrences of the word *palimpsest* in digitized books indicated that between 1820 and 1980, the word reached peak frequency in 1896, supporting the argument that (English-speaking) Victorians indeed had a special relationship with the concept. As more books are digitized, though, especially books from the late eighteenth and early nineteenth centuries, that result might change. We would add another caution, one immediately relevant to this volume: while digitization has fundamentally altered the way we access and understand texts, especially those that were previously beyond the reach of many readers, limitations in the documentation and coding of images mean that the visual realm is not open to the same search strategies that we have developed for text, at least not yet.

Another strain of Victorian visual studies seeks to bridge the gap between the study of the rarefied and the popular by addressing the role and function of visuality in nineteenth-century culture at large. If early theorists laid the foundations for these inquiries—among them the still-influential Walter Benjamin on the importance of modes of production in framing our engagement with art and Michel Foucault on the hegemonic social control that inheres in surveillance—much important work over the subsequent decades has created a more nuanced understanding of the incredible variety of Victorian visual modalities outside of the fine arts and print genres.[40] In his exploration of Victorian exhibitions, for instance, Richard Altick provocatively suggests that these "public nontheatrical entertainments" did not merely "[run] parallel to and sometimes [mingle] with . . . the printed word" but rather were "an alternative medium of print, reifying the word."[41] For Kate Flint, the connection between specularity and textuality is less stable; indeed, the vexed nature of the relationship between text and image, between the organic eye and vision, gives rise to her argument that, for the Victorians, the visual was "a heavily contested category," and seeing involved "a whole matrix of cultural and social practices."[42] Nancy Armstrong notes similarly the pervasive effects of visual technology: "[T]he rapid production and wide dissemination of photographic images permanently altered not only what novels represented when they referred to the real world, but also how readers experienced life outside the novel."[43] What is perhaps surprising, then, is not the upswing of scholarship on visual culture in relation to major Victorian literary, political, and scientific figures but rather that the attention to these connections—which now appear central to a comprehensive understanding of the nineteenth century—is so belated.[44]

From among these many visual modes, this collection focuses on the graphic text, broadly conceived to include illustrated stories and poems, books and periodicals, comics, cartoons, and other ephemera. Three aspects of Victorian graphic-textual production are especially relevant for understanding the Victorian and neo-Victorian texts examined in this collection: the prominence of revival movements; self-referential practices in popular media; and the negotiation of the image/narrative relationship in many high-art and popular arenas. First, nineteenth-century artists, writers, and illustrators were themselves steeped in constant revivals of earlier authors, writers, artists, and representational styles, which served as one way of negotiating the Victorian self in relation to history, of recuperating the past to perform modernity. The medieval iconography that appears in illustrated magazines such as *Once a Week* is—as Linda Hughes argues in chapter 7—one example of this trend. Printers also turned to anachronistic technologies: rejecting fin-de-siècle advances in printing, the founders of art journals (such as the *Century Guild Hobby Horse*) and artistic presses (such as Shannon and Ricketts's Vale Press and William Morris's Kelmscott Press) instead adopted antiquated methods that foregrounded handcraftsmanship. The opening page of the 1896 Kelmscott Chaucer (see fig. I.3)—with borders designed by Morris and a woodcut illustration by Edward Burne-Jones—mixes medieval-esque illuminated characters with a flattened picture plane and early Roman font; yet at the same time, its effect is archetypically Victorian. The Pre-Raphaelite, neo-Gothic, neo-medieval, and neo-Carolinian, and neo-Romantic impulses (to name only a few movements) that shaped nineteenth-century graphic texts establish a pattern of self-conscious revivals that is itself revived in neo-Victorian graphic texts.

Second, referentiality and intertextuality were ever present in Victorian graphic texts. The *Alice in Wonderland* and *Through the Looking-Glass* examples that open this introduction demonstrate this allusive image-textual interplay, which depends not only on content but also on form. Consider the function of the cartoon in the popular satirical magazine *Punch, or the London Charivari:* in order to work, the parody and satire that define many of the cartoons in *Punch* depended on reaching a public that was aware of the current state of politics and trends in art and literature. And newspapers and magazines were the primary source through which the public could gain this awareness. Further, with its stable of staff illustrators producing a steady flow of images for the weekly magazine, *Punch* helped educate the public (consciously or unconsciously) in the recognition of pictorial style— the heaviness of lines, repetition of facial types, idiosyncrasies of depth or perspective, and so forth—that is to say, in the formal qualities of the image. A reader could be expected to recognize the work of an illustrator, and journals could leverage that familiarity to any number of ends. In other words, the success of *Punch's* cartoons depended on readers who were trained to read periodicals generally and to read *Punch* in particular. Moreover, *Punch* cultivated the development of a visual vocabulary of signifiers that could be taken up by readers and reproduced outside the pages of the magazine, in ways that might exceed the original satirical aims of author, illustrator, or editor.

George Du Maurier's pseudofamily of aesthetic fops provides a useful example: the group includes a Mrs. Cimabue Brown (patron), Postlethwaite (poet), and Maudle (painter), recurring characters whose very forms instantly call to mind Du Maurier's longstanding (if playful) critique of the Aesthete (see fig. I.4). Du Maurier was an adept at deploying the visual shorthand that he developed to comedic

FRUSTRATED SOCIAL AMBITION.

COLLAPSE OF POSTLETHWAITE, MAUDLE, AND MRS. CIMABUE BROWN, ON READING IN A WIDELY-CIRCULATED CONTEMPORARY JOURNAL THAT THEY ONLY EXIST IN MR. PUNCH'S VIVID IMAGINATION. THEY HAD FONDLY FLATTERED THEMSELVES THAT UNIVERSAL FAME WAS THEIRS AT LAST.

(above) FIG. I.3 Opening page of *The Works of Geoffrey Chaucer* (London: Kelmscott Press, 1896). Image courtesy of Cadbury Research Library: Special Collections, University of Birmingham.

(left) FIG. I.4 George Du Maurier, "Frustrated Social Ambition," *Punch*, 21 May 1881, 229. Image courtesy of Cadbury Research Library: Special Collections, University of Birmingham.

effect: the high-Aesthete dress of Mrs. Cimabue Brown, the vase of lilies and *Japonisme* décor in the background, the overwrought emotion telling on their faces and bodies were all common tropes in his oeuvre. But rather than putting an end to what Du Maurier viewed as a risible fad, his cartoons helped to codify the Aesthetic style of dress and objects of fascination, making them more—not less—appropriable by a middle-class reading public. In his 1881 cartoon "Frustrated Social Ambition," Du Maurier humorously addresses this blurring of the lines between art and life as his trio of Aesthetes faces the limits of their own existence as cartoon characters. The caption reads "Collapse of Postlethwaite, Maudle, and Mrs. Cimabue Brown, on reading in a widely-circulated contemporary journal that they only exist in *Mr. Punch*'s vivid imagination. They had fondly flattered themselves that universal fame was theirs at last."[45] With one figure clutching a crumpled newspaper in one hand, and the other two figures in grief-stricken postures, the cartoon not only mocks the ubiquity of the Aesthetes in the periodical press but also reinscribes it. *Punch*'s readers experience Aestheticism thrice removed; they read a cartoon depicting characters reading comments about their own status as ephemera. It is postmodern transtextuality *avant la lettre*.

Finally, Victorian graphic texts constantly addressed the relationship of image to narrative, whether by embracing it or by protesting it. William Hogarth's enormously popular eighteenth-century engravings—series of sequential images that depict a chronological narrative—were foundational in establishing a British consumer primed to understand images as telling a story, and a story with a moral, at that.[46] As Brian Maidment's contribution (chapter 1) to this volume shows, such narrativization of images could (and did) inspire the creation of new texts: the text/image relationship, in other words, is not unidirectional, with an originary text-based story providing the impetus for illustration. The proliferation and popularity of increasingly affordable illustrated books and magazines throughout the nineteenth century would further encourage the view that illustration and text (narrative text, in particular) were necessarily complementary.[47] In fact, this desire to attach or impose a narrative on an image was so strong for both audience and critic that entire artistic movements arose to counter it. James McNeill Whistler's libel trial against John Ruskin (1877–78) was a media sensation and brought the matter into the public arena, pitting Whistler's advocacy of the purely artistic against Ruskin's insistence that art must edify.[48] The quarterly art magazine *The Yellow Book*, launched in 1894 and inspired by the French *l'art pour l'art* dictum, insisted that the many illustrations it contained must stand alone, untethered to any textual context.[49] In its very protests, the journal underscored the point that the default mode of engagement with the printed image was to superimpose a narrative on it.

This self-conscious awareness of how images are read—that is to say, attention to the image's potential to make narrative or epistemological meaning—is evident in myriad Victorian graphic texts. Indeed, by the 1890s, a magazine like *The Strand*, likely best known for Arthur Conan Doyle's stories detailing Sherlock Holmes's deductive feats, could depend on readers' abilities to understand both for the narrative and for the "scientific" significance of images. For example, *Zig Zags at the Zoo*, a graphic-textual series in *The Strand*, required reading sequential images as narrative but also demanded fairly complex analogical and metacritical reasoning to deliver combined didactic and comedic messages (see fig. I.5). In a page from Arthur Morrison and J. A. Shepherd's collaboration, a playful sequence of scenes of anthropomorphized bugs—a bluebottle fly and a black beetle—demonstrates the truth of the accompanying textual comment, that "to acquaintances of his own size," the bluebottle "must be an intolerable nuisance."[50] The fly pesters his newspaper-reading acquaintance to join him on the town, ignoring his friend's protests and apparent discomfort (the beetle seems to be under the weather). Morrison underscores the human quality of the bugs' interactions, comparing the bluebottle to "those awful stout persons who . . . take you forcibly by the arm and drag you out for promenades when you are anxious to be left alone," detailing precisely the actions of the jaunty bluebottle in Shepherd's series of illustrations.[51] The endearing images combine with the text to encourage readers to identify with the characters, which—given that those characters are bugs—is alone an impressive feat.

A cartoon like *Zig Zags at the Zoo* also plays on readers' familiarity with illustrated natural history texts. Twenty years earlier, Edward Lear established a precedent by adopting the taxonomic mode of the illustrated botany, pairing absurd Latinate titles and whimsical illustrations of imaginary species of plants: the flower of "Piggiawiggia Pyramidalis," for example, features tiny pigs arranged by size (see mine," and pass by on the other side. But he doesn't. He flies into it again and burns his other wing, or, more probably, roasts himself completely. Thousands of generations of scorched and roasted moths have passed away without developing the least knowledge of the properties of fire in their descendants. The moth remains consistent, and a fool.

There are few things of its size more annoy-

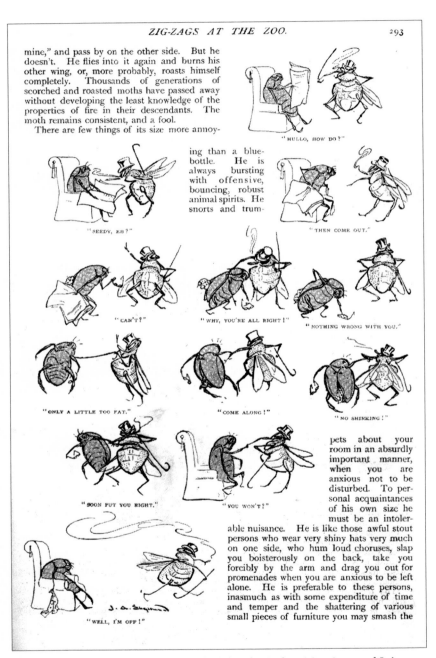

"HULLO, HOW DO?"

ing than a blue-bottle. He is always bursting with offensive, bouncing, robust animal spirits. He snorts and trum-

"SEEDY, EH?"

"THEN COME OUT."

"CAN'T?"

"WHY, YOU'RE ALL RIGHT!"

"NOTHING WRONG WITH YOU."

"ONLY A LITTLE TOO FAT."

"COME ALONG!"

"NO SHIRKING!"

"SOON PUT YOU RIGHT."

"YOU WON'T?"

pets about your room in an absurdly important manner, when you are anxious not to be disturbed. To personal acquaintances of his own size he must be an intolerable nuisance. He is like those awful stout persons who wear very shiny hats very much on one side, who hum loud choruses, slap you boisterously on the back, take you forcibly by the arm and drag you out for promenades when you are anxious to be left alone. He is preferable to these persons, inasmuch as with some expenditure of time and temper and the shattering of various small pieces of furniture you may smash the

"WELL, I'M OFF!"

FIG. I.5   Bluebottle fly pestering black beetle. Arthur Morrison and J. A. Shepherd, *Zig Zags at the Zoo, Strand* 6 (July 1893): 293. Image courtesy of Cadbury Research Library: Special Collections, University of Birmingham.

fig. I.6), and the "Manypeeplia Upsidownia" looks like a Lily-of-the-Valley with people (hanging upside down, naturally), in place of white flowers.[52] The resulting visual gags, aimed at young readers, depend not on narrative sequence but on the pleasure of sending up the serious work of science. The *Zig Zags* cartoon maintains the whimsy of Lear's illustrations but adds, in its textual component, a more complicated critique of comparative and taxonomic studies of the natural world that purported to explain human types and human behavior. The article opens by noting that "entomology is a vast, a complicated,

and a bewildering thing" and cautions that the "illustrative moralist" who might turn to nature for life lessons should note that "the insect world is the most immoral sphere of action existing."[53] By offering the playful visual narrative of the bluebottle fly, combined with textual commentary, the cartoon invites simultaneously the reader's investment in the narrative, identification with the bugs and contemplation of familiar social types by way of entomological characteristics, and self-conscious critique of that same analogical exercise.

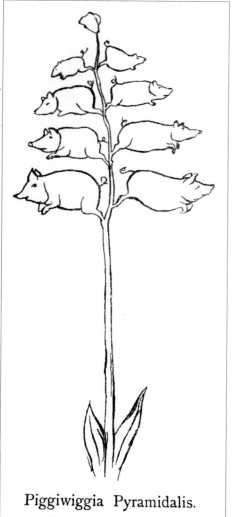

Piggiwiggia Pyramidalis.

FIG. I.6   Edward Lear, "Piggiawiggia Pyramidalis," from *Nonsense Songs, Stories, Botany, and Alphabets* (Boston: James R. Osgood, 1871), 88.

All of these acts of self-referentiality, inscription and reinscription, narrativization, and resuscitation of earlier art forms demonstrate that Victorian visual culture was already deeply enmeshed in palimpsestuous modes of creation. Thus, the Victorians offer to their neo-Victorian successors not just a rich resource of appropriable, adaptable content but also highly nuanced ways of engaging with that content. In a similar fashion, this volume is committed to layering critical perspectives, rather than proceeding from taxonomic separations. Instead of carefully separating the illustrated book from the development of the comics form, for example, or nostalgic homage to the Victorians from ironic parody, the contributions to *Drawing on the Victorians,* taken together, highlight the points of imbrication and the blurring of categories. This methodological mandate may be said to extend to the volume's theoretical commitments as well, where there is much to be gained, for instance, from layering comics theory with historicist approaches to Victorian periodicals. Thinking structurally about how graphic texts function can offer a means of conceptualizing Victorian culture's relationship to contemporary neo-Victorianism more broadly.

As the foregoing discussion of visual culture scholarship suggests, a vast array of approaches to the Victorians reside under the designation "Victorian studies." Nonetheless, it is fair to say that the field has been since the 1980s dominated by cultural studies and New Historicism. Recent debates about "surface" versus "symptomatic" reading and the so-called new formalism have sought to return to formal concerns in a sustained way and to offer various challenges to the "hermeneutics of suspicion." Whereas critics employing Marxian, Freudian, and Foucauldian models of analysis seek for "something latent or concealed" in the text, other critics, such as Stephen Best and Sharon Marcus, advocate attention to surface as "what, in the geometrical sense, has length and breadth but not thickness, and therefore covers no depth. A surface . . . insists on being looked *at* rather than what we must train ourselves to see *through*."[54] In this suggestion, they echo Whistler, who bemoaned that his contemporary art viewers and critics had "acquired the habit of looking . . . not *at* a picture, but *through* it, at some human fact."[55] Caroline Levine's "strategic formalism" likewise seeks to complicate cultural studies modes of analysis: "Form itself emerges in my own account as . . . an apparatus that operates on the levels of both method *and* object."[56] Rather than thinking of these theoretical modes as antithetical—"surface reading" versus "deep reading" or "strategic formalism" versus cultural analysis—our attention to the graphic text foregrounds the convergence of cultural context and form.

Comics studies in its major branches (Anglo-American, Franco-Belgian, Japanese) might be characterized, broadly speaking, as pursuing structuralist aims more frequently than does Victorian studies, perhaps in part because many of the prominent theorists of graphic texts are or were also practitioners.[57] The range of important sociohistorical scholarship on graphic texts notwithstanding, the field has focused less on what cultural messages might be hidden in the depths of the image-text and more on how any message at all might be conveyed through the juxtaposition of images and text.[58] Yet as Hillary Chute and Marianne DeKoven argue, this attention to form is the very thing that enables comics to engage with the social, cultural, and political effectively: the frames of comics function as "boxes of time," creating "a representational mode capable of addressing complex political and historical issues with an explicit, formal degree of self-awareness."[59] We suggest that comics theory offers one avenue for rethinking the Victorians and our abiding fascination with them, not by jettisoning historicist concerns, which continue to be relevant, but in taking the form of the palimpsest, to borrow Levine's language, as "an apparatus that operates on the levels of both method *and* object."[60]

The groundbreaking work of Thierry Groensteen, for instance, presents a suggestive view of comics as a spatial rather than temporal medium. Arguing against the easy equivalence of sequential panels with narrative progress, he stresses that "comics panels, situated relationally, are, necessarily, placed in relation to space and operate on a share of space."[61] This spatial conception allows Groensteen to explore how comics are organized by what he calls "iconic solidarity": "[I]nterdependent images[,] . . . in a series, present the double characteristic of being separated . . . [and] plastically and semantically over-determined by the fact of their coexistence *in praesentia*."[62] Natsume Fusanosuke gets at a similar idea when he describes the ability of a manga panel layout to produce in the reader "a multi-layered reception of the infinite space and the characters as located both in the same temporality and apart at the same time," thereby "turning the limitations of the printed page into advantage."[63] Attending to this interrelation of temporal movements and spatial relationships offers a useful corrective to the tendency to read (only) for the plot in any given graphic narrative, but even more than this, it suggests a model for reading juxtaposed Victorian and neo-Victorian texts (graphic or otherwise) palimpsestuously rather than genealogically—that is to say, rather than tracing connections and developments historically through time, we might take our cue from Thomas Carlyle and read our (literary) history as "that complex Manuscript, covered over with formless inextricably-tangled unknown characters," a palimpsest.[64] In fact, if we take these Victorian and neo-Victorian texts on the palimpsestuous terms in which they offer themselves, we cannot avoid viewing spatial juxtapositions overlaying historical trajectory.

This "spatialization" of historical (and historiographical) concerns can be seen, for example, in Bryan Talbot's 2007 graphic narrative, *Alice in Sunderland,* an immense, multifaceted project that undertakes a sweeping history of Sunderland, interwoven with literary biography of Lewis Carroll, exhaustive cataloging of *Alice in Wonderland* adaptations, and formal analysis of graphic narrative. Talbot uses hectically crowded pages, a wandering narrative style, and layered images—photographs, black-and-white and color drawings, and facsimile reproductions of maps, books, playbills, and newspapers—to demonstrate that our present does not just follow from the past but coexists with it and the future. As the Performer, the narrator and authorial stand-in, explains, "You may have noticed that I've been telling these stories in the *present tense*—as if they're all happening simultaneously. . . . . . and, in a way, they *are!* They're *all* happening **right now**—but in **the past!**"[65] The text also plays with the roles of reader/viewer, author, and character, as these positions morph into and out of one another through the graphic narrative's relationship to its hypotext, Carroll's *Alice in Wonderland* (see fig. I.7). Explaining Carroll's original intention for the layout of the images of Alice going through the looking glass, the Performer stands before reproductions of Tenniel's mirror(ed) illustrations: "He designed this bit so that *Alice* passes through the page to emerge into *Looking Glass Land* on the other side" (191).[66] The Performer then proceeds to draw a frame of a Moroccan street scene, from his memory of a recent trip. He, like Alice, will pass through this image to arrive on the following page in a full-color version of the same scene, with the background and himself both drawn in the manner of Belgian comic Hergé's *Tintin* adventures. And from

FIG. I.7 The Performer discusses Tenniel. Bryan Talbot, *Alice in Sunderland* (Milwaukie, OR: Dark Horse Comics, 2007), 191. © Bryan Talbot. Reproduced with permission.

FIG. I.8 The Performer discusses Hogarth. Bryan Talbot, *Alice in Sunderland* (Milwaukie, OR: Dark Horse Comics, 2007), 190. © Bryan Talbot. Reproduced with permission.

thence the Performer travels back to his own dining room, where he discusses the history and formal composition of William Hogarth's *Gin Lane* and *Beer Street,* explaining how the different compositions of Hogarth's two scenes convey their respective messages about the evils of gin and the virtues of beer (see fig. I.8). Talbot's graphic narrative self-consciously trains its readers how to read it (and how to read ourselves reading it).

For *Alice in Sunderland*'s reader, layers of international comics history become indistinguishable from Talbot's autobiography, from Carroll's biography, from literary history, and from the history of Sunderland and of England more generally. In his retelling of the medieval legend of the Lambton Worm (which originates in Sunderland), for example, Talbot literally inserts book history into the landscape of Sunderland. The Performer, drawn in black and white, wanders through a photographic, color landscape; holding a thick, leather-bound volume (drawn in color), he describes the local history and geography as prologue to the legend. In the final frame, the Performer opens the volume to the reader's gaze: "Ladies and gentlemen. . . . . . I give you . . ." (231). On the following page, the Performer's volume seems to have transferred to the reader's hands, as the reader faces a full-page rendering of the manuscript pages from the previous frame: Talbot's homage to William Morris's neo-medieval Kelmscott Chaucer (see fig. I.9). As the medieval past (or at least a legendary version thereof) has been drawn through the layers of its nineteenth-century adaptations into the reader's present, so too has the reader been inserted into the space of Sunderland's landscape through the pages of Talbot's graphic novel. The reader can only experience the past of Sunderland, Victorian book history, and the present as "interdependent images . . . over-determined by the fact of their coexistence *in praesentia*," to return to Groensteen's turn of phrase.[67] Thus, the graphic narrative form of *Alice in Sunderland* realigns the reader's sense of history, textuality, even of self, through its spatialization of relationships.

Drawing on the Victorians offers a similar set of "interdependent images" of Victorian and of neo-Victorian visual culture, inviting palimpsestuous readings of the volume's chapters, which are arranged in thematic

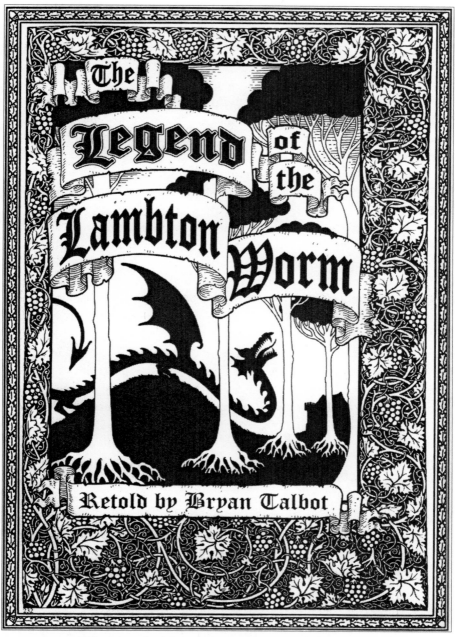

FIG. I.9   "The Legend of the Lambton Worm." Bryan Talbot, *Alice in Sunderland* (Milwaukie, OR: Dark Horse Comics, 2007), 232. © Bryan Talbot. Reproduced with permission.

pairs. In the first section, "Adaptations," the authors consider what is lost and gained in the process of adapting texts and images across different mediums and across national and linguistic boundaries. The two chapters in "Graphic Epistemologies" examine the use of iconography to convey radical scientific theories and heterodox Spiritualist doctrines. In "Refigured Ideologies," chapters explore the power of graphic texts to shape and to challenge hegemonic social categories. Authors in "Temporal Images" discuss the graphic representations of historical progress and of the passage of time. And in "Picturing Readers," the final two chapters investigate the ways that Victorian and neo-Victorian graphic texts both represent and address their readers.

In the first pairing, chapters by Brian Maidment and Monika Pietrzak-Franger consider the terms of adaptation and appropriation of Victorian primary materials. A decade ago, Thomas Leitch challenged the primacy of the text in studies of text-to-film adaptations, by far the predominant focus in adaptation studies.[68] These chapters further complicate the relationship between source and adaptation. Maidment considers Robert Seymour's *Sketches* (1831–34) and Kenny Meadows's *Heads of the People* (1841) as examples of Victorian image-to-text adaptation that invert the usual text-to-image progression, which places the graphic always after (chronologically and in terms of significance) the textual. Tracing the post-Hogarthian lineage of graphic texts, Maidment argues that Charles Dickens's *Pickwick Papers* is indebted to Seymour's *Sketches*. He further documents the ways that Meadows's work was taken up as the basis for multiple narrativizations: Meadows's work provides a compelling instance in which the image preceded textual narrativization and gave rise to multiple textual adaptations. Taken together, these works demonstrate how open visual representations were to textual superscription. Pietrzak-Franger's study participates in the movement in neo-Victorian studies to investigate the transnational and transmedial character of graphic texts, exploring the global reproduction and translatability of the Victorian era and its problems. With particular focus on one Swiss/German and two Polish graphic adaptations of Lewis Carroll's *Alice,* Pietrzak-Franger considers how the global Alice industry enables rethinking local histories. Localized graphic wonderlands, she argues, challenge the global-local continuum, pointing to "the constructed and palimpsestuous nature of identities that are as much affected by global trends as they are rooted in local geographies."

As Lear's *Nonsense . . . Botany* and Morrison and Shepherd's *Zig Zags at the Zoo* demonstrate, the alliance of graphic representation with scientific epistemology was creatively adapted to diverse ends in the nineteenth century. Even the most fantastical supernatural romances exploited this alliance; for example, H. Rider Haggard's novels *King Solomon's Mines* (1885) and *She* (1887) included illustrations of fictitious maps and artifacts to create the illusion of empirical evidence. Similarly, Edwin Abbott's mathematical satire *Flatland* (1884) provided explanatory geometric diagrams to accompany its narrative. "Graphic Epistemologies," the second pairing of chapters in this volume, addresses more earnest applications of illustration to educate or persuade readers. Peter W. Sinnema and Christine Ferguson consider the ways that graphic representations of metaphysical concepts and natural (and supernatural) phenomena push their readers to explore unconventional worldviews. Sinnema traces the influence of Enlightenment iconography on nineteenth-century alternative cosmological paradigms. His chapter explores the influence of seventeenth-century astronomer Edmond Halley's hollow-earth hypothesis on the works of transatlantic nineteenth-century novelists and (eccentric) thinkers, such as the pseudonymous Captain Adam Seaborn's 1820 scientific romance *Symzonia: A Voyage of Discovery* and Cyrus Reed Teed's 1898 religious manifesto *The Cellular Cosmogony,* both of which included detailed drawings of the earth as a hollow "cosmic egg"; Sinnema shows how these images "experimented with, challenged, or abandoned altogether the heliocentric foundations of the Copernican universe," reimagining infinite space as the finite—and therefore knowable and even habitable—interior of the earth. As Ferguson notes, twentieth-century graphic novelists have been drawn to nineteenth-century images as a means of negotiating contemporary scientific and spiritual concerns: this "proof of spiritual survival," she argues, can "make the inquirer see anew." Ferguson shows that Olivia Plender's 2007 graphic novel *A Stellar Key to the Summerland* reframes Andrew Jackson Davis's similarly titled illustrated book, *A Stellar Key to the Summer Land* (1867), resurrecting "the forgotten iconography and visual ephemera of nineteenth-century transatlantic Spiritualism . . . to track, probe, and then ultimately undo the movement's seeming complicity with the subsequent cultures of New Age libertarianism and neoliberal capitalism." Both chapters demonstrate the transnational reach (and longevity) of their respective alternative graphic epistemologies.

Our next section, "Refigured Ideologies," explores two figures that carried (and continue to carry) enormous sociocultural freight: the Jew and the child. Visual representations of these figures in the nineteenth century—for example, illustrations of the sinister Fagin and the tragic Little Nell—condensed and consolidated cultural stereotypes and narrative tropes. And as Heidi Kaufman and Jessica Straley demonstrate, neo-Victorian graphic texts harness these iconic figures to challenge readers' attachments to stereotype and trope alike. Kaufman's study focuses on Will Eisner's *Fagin the Jew* (2003), which takes Dickens's *Oliver Twist* (1837–39) as a point of departure for its consideration of the otherness embodied in the figure of Fagin. Eisner's work, Kaufman argues, does not attempt "to revive the story of Oliver Twist's adventures" or to recover "an idealized Victorian world"; rather, the graphic novel seeks "to expose and correct a critical silence and a dangerous injustice lurking in Dickens's novel." Eisner uses comics conventions to wrestle with the possibilities and limits of historical recovery and literary (re)invention. Straley takes seriously Oscar Wilde's quip that "one must have a heart of stone to read the death of Little Nell without laughing" and asks how the Victorians' attempts to represent an event of unspeakable sadness—the death of the child—have in fact produced a seemingly infinite resource for twentieth- and twenty-first-century ridicule. Through analysis of works by Dickens (and George Cattermole, his illustrator), Edward Gorey, and Roman Dirge, Straley suggests that for the Victorians, the dying, beautiful, innocent girl became not merely a hackneyed cliché but a signifier overburdened with multiple and paradoxical meanings. The resurrection of the "dead metaphor of the dead girl" in twentieth- and twenty-first-century parodies like Gorey's and Dirge's enables us to examine the "limitations of our aesthetic practices" and thus to become implicated in the joke.

Central to the figure of the palimpsest is the visual demarcation of the passage of time, traces of the past bleeding into the present. For the neo-Victorian author or artist, the changing styles of Victorian iconography—or the changes that nineteenth-century images document—can function as a chronometer. Yet as the two chapters in

"Temporal Images" show, the Victorians' representations of the passage of time were themselves often highly stylized and self-conscious. Linda K. Hughes considers the long underexplored archive of illustrated poems that appeared in illustrated periodicals ranging from the 1860s through the turn of the twentieth century. Hughes examines the preponderance of medieval iconography in poem illustration, arguing that repeated revivals of earlier artistic modes established a Victorian paradigm for later neo-Victorian works. She suggests that by considering the poem and illustration as inseparable—as "poetic-graphic texts"—we are alerted to the disputed grounds or social fissures underlying this Victorian body of work. Working in a similar register, Rebecca N. Mitchell uses the Diamond Jubilee issue of *Punch* as a case study of historicizing typology. Noting that the Victorians used graphic forms to reflect on the changes documented in their own time, Mitchell argues that nineteenth-century graphic texts consolidated a series of symbols and iconographic modes that became aligned with specific cultural moments and ideologies. These distilled images, then, become the familiar, even clichéd, visual tropes of "the Victorian" in contemporary neo-Victorian graphic texts, particularly in steampunk works, which are founded on anachronistic juxtapositions. By self-consciously employing anachronism or historicized iconography established by the Victorians, these neo-Victorian works further the palimpsestuous attachments that, as Hughes notes, were established in the nineteenth century.

Having considered various modes of graphic meaning-making, the volume concludes by turning to the reader. It is a turn demanded by Victorian and neo-Victorian graphic texts themselves, which do not simply solicit readers' engagement but, rather, construct theories about the act of reading and the role of the reader. In the final section, "Picturing Readers," authors Jennifer Phegley and Anna Maria Jones explore how Victorian and neo-Victorian serials, marketed to women readers, articulate self-reflexive and sophisticated theories of their relationships to their readers. They thus challenge the view—prevalent in the nineteenth century and still in circulation today—that pleasure reading is an addictive and dangerous pastime, particularly for readers perceived as susceptible or naïve (such as women, children, and the working class). Phegley argues that for Victorian working-class women readers of the magazine *Bow Bells,* reading was "social and

active," as readers were "pulled into intrigue, sensation, and even tragedy" through their investments in the illustrated narratives. Focusing
especially on Valentine's Day issues, and building on her reading of
actual Victorian valentines, Phegley contends that the valentine—
present both textually as narrative device and visually as illustration—
becomes an iconic stand-in for a host of social and personal desires
and anxieties. In the collection's tenth chapter, Anna Maria Jones
considers the ways that a neo-Victorian manga mediates its own readers' desires through its depiction of Victorian girl readers' investments
in serial fiction. The plot of Moto Naoko's serial *Lady Victorian* (*Redī
Vikutorian*) caters to readerly desires for adventure and romance, even
as it also offers a self-reflexive account of how reading constructs
those very desires. Further, Moto playfully invokes fin-de-siècle *Japonisme,* inviting readers to consider how nineteenth-century transnational cultural exchanges continue to shape contemporary modes
of cultural consumption.

Finally, in her afterword, "Photography, Palimpsests, and the
Neo-Victorian," Kate Flint extends the discussion to photography,
the transformative technology that, by the end of the nineteenth century, was as ubiquitous as the drawn image. As Flint shows, the medium's potential both to tell a story and to interrogate history was
exploited fully by Victorian photographers. Moreover, photography's metareferential quality—the ability to capture "temporal complexities"—is precisely what recommends it to contemporary artists
such as Yinka Shonibare, Clare Strand, and Tracey Moffatt, who invoke eighteenth- and nineteenth-century visual conventions "to think
about connections not only between the experience of the past and
now but also between earlier and current practices of representation."

Through these chapters, *Drawing on the Victorians* brings together
a variety of formal, historical, and theoretical concerns under the umbrella of "Victorian and neo-Victorian graphic texts." By necessity,
any edited collection presents a multilayered rather than unified vision of its topic, and this one seeks to cultivate rather than forestall
its topical and methodological multiplicity. Indeed, it is precisely in
this multiplicity that, like Carlyle's palimpsest, this collection delivers
a methodological guide to future study: perhaps not a "complete philosophy" but "here and there an intelligible precept, available in practice."[69] To take seriously the palimpsestuous nature of these Victorian

and neo-Victorian texts is to be willing to conceive of "the Victorian" as belonging to a much broader field and longer historical trajectory than the traditional boundaries of Victorian studies, devoted to the study of British literature and culture of the nineteenth century, have recognized. Moreover, to appreciate the complex intertextual play that the figure of the palimpsest suggests, one must be prepared to seek "the Victorian" in a wide range of visual and textual contexts, to embrace unlikely juxtapositions, and even to value the distortions and entanglements that those juxtapositions entail.

Notes

1. Lewis Carroll, *Alice's Adventures in Wonderland,* in *The Annotated Alice: The Definitive Edition,* ed. Martin Gardner (London: Norton, 2013), 124.

2. Carroll, *Alice's Adventures in Wonderland* (2013), 74.

3. Lewis Carroll, *Through the Looking-Glass and What Alice Found There,* in *The Annotated Alice: The Definitive Edition,* ed. Martin Gardner (London: Norton, 2013), 233.

4. Carroll, *Through the Looking-Glass,* 223.

5. Gérard Genette, *Palimpsests: Literature in the Second Degree,* trans. Channa Newman and Claude Dubinsky (Lincoln: University of Nebraska Press, 1997), 1. First published in French in 1982. Genette first introduces this definition in *Introduction à l'architexte* (Paris: Editions du Seuil, 1979), 87. He equates *transtextuality* with "literariness itself" and uses it as a blanket term comprising several "aspects of textuality": intertextuality, hypertextuality, paratextuality, metatextuality, architextuality (2, 8).

6. Linda Hutcheon, "Historiographic Metafiction: Parody and the Intertextuality of History," in *Intertextuality and Contemporary American Fiction,* ed. Patrick O'Donnell and Robert Con Davis (Baltimore, MD: Johns Hopkins University Press, 1989), 4.

7. Christian Gutleben, *Nostalgic Postmodernism: The Victorian Tradition and the Contemporary British Novel* (Amsterdam: Rodopi Press, 2001), 7–8.

8. Ann Heilmann and Mark Llewellyn, *Neo-Victorianism: The Victorians in the Twenty-First Century, 1999–2009* (Basingstoke, UK: Palgrave Macmillan, 2010), 4.

9. Ibid., 4. Emphasis in the original.

10. Kate Mitchell, *History and Cultural Memory in Neo-Victorian Fiction: Victorian Afterimages* (Basingstoke, UK: Palgrave Macmillan, 2010), 6.

11. Cora Kaplan, *Victoriana: Histories, Fictions, Criticism* (New York: Columbia University Press, 2007), 5.

12. Rosario Arias and Patricia Pulham, eds., *Haunting and Spectrality in Neo-Victorian Fiction: Possessing the Past* (Basingstoke, UK: Palgrave Macmillan, 2010); Mitchell, *History and Cultural Memory;* Marie-Luise Kohlke and Christian Gutleben, eds., *Neo-Victorian Tropes of Trauma: The Politics of Bearing After-Witness to Nineteenth-Century Suffering* (Amsterdam: Rodopi Press, 2010).

13. Elizabeth Ho, *Neo-Victorianism and the Memory of Empire* (New York: Continuum, 2012), 171.

14. Simon Joyce, *The Victorians in the Rearview Mirror* (Athens: Ohio University Press, 2007), 4.

15. Matthew Kneale, *English Passengers: A Novel* (New York: Anchor, 2000); Sarah Waters, *Fingersmith* (New York: Riverhead, 2002); Julian Barnes, *Arthur & George* (New York: Vintage, 2005); *American McGee's Alice* (Electronic Arts, 2000) and *American McGee's Alice: Madness Returns* (Electronic Arts, 2011); *Sherlock Holmes,* directed by Guy Ritchie (2009; DVD, Warner Home Video, 2009) and *Sherlock Holmes: A Game of Shadows,* directed by Guy Ritchie (2011; DVD, Warner Home Video, 2012); *Sherlock,* created by Mark Gatiss and Steven Moffat (Hartswood Films and BBC Wales for Masterpiece Theatre, 2010–); a Google search for "steampunk convention" returns hundreds of thousands of hits for conventions all over the world.

16. Tara Mulholland, "More than Words: Britain Embraces the Graphic Novel, *New York Times,* 22 August 2007; Bryan Talbot, *Alice in Sunderland: An Entertainment* (Milwaukie, OR: Dark Horse Comics, 2007).

17. Posy Simmonds, *Tamara Drewe* (New York: Houghton Mifflin, 2007); *Tamara Drewe,* directed by Stephen Frears (2010; DVD, Sony Pictures Classics, 2011).

18. Alan Moore and Eddie Campbell, *From Hell* (Marietta, GA: Top Shelf, 1989–96); Alan Moore and Kevin O'Neill, *The League of Extraordinary Gentlemen,* vol. 1 (La Jolla, CA: America's Best Comics, 2000); Grant Morrison and Stephen Yeowell, *Sebastian O* (New York: DC Comics, 1993).

19. Joann Sfar and Emmanuel Guibert, *The Professor's Daughter,* trans. Alexis Siegel (New York: First Second, 1997).

20. Mori Kaoru, *Emma,* 10 vols. (2002–2006; New York: CMX Comics, 2006–2009); Mochizuki Jun, *Pandora Hearts,* 24 vols. (2006–15; New York: Yen Press, 2009–16); Toboso Yana, *Black Butler,* 23 vols. to date (2006–; New York: Yen Press, 2010–). Here as throughout we maintain Japanese naming convention, with family name listed first, for authors writing in Japanese.

21. Johny Tay, "*Seven Years in Dog-Land*: An Overview," *All My Things: The Website for Johny Tay's Stuff,* http://johnytay.net/2013/10/overview-seven-years-in-dog-land/.

22. There are, however, some very interesting articles on individual neo-Victorian graphic texts. See Ellen Crowell, "Scarlet Carsons, Men in Masks: The Wildean Contexts of *V for Vendetta*," *Neo-Victorian Studies* 2, no. 1 (2008/2009): 17–45; Christine Ferguson, "Victoria-Arcana and the Misogynistic Poetics of Resistance in Iain Sinclair's *White Chappell Scarlet Tracings* and Alan Moore's *From Hell*," *LIT: Literature, Interpretation, Theory* 20, nos. 1–2 (2009): 45–64; Monika Pietrzak-Franger, "Envisioning the Ripper's Visions: Adapting Myth in Alan Moore and Eddie Campbell's *From Hell*," *Neo-Victorian Studies* 2, no. 2 (2009/2010): 157–85.

23. Mark Llewellyn and Ann Heilmann, "The Victorians Now: Global Reflections on Neo-Victorianism," *Critical Quarterly* 55, no. 1 (2013): 24–42. Recent works have begun to address this gap. See, e.g., Ho, *Neo-Victorianism and the Memory*; Antonija Primorac and Monika Pietrzak-Franger, eds., "Neo-Victorianism and Globalisation: Transnational Dissemination of Nineteenth-Century Cultural Texts," special issue of *Neo-Victorian Studies* 8, no. 1 (2015): 1–206. In particular, there have been some interesting articles on Japanese manga appropriations of Victorian hypotexts. See, e.g., Elizabeth Ho, "Victorian Maids and Neo-Victorian Labour in Kaoru Mori's *Emma: A Victorian Romance*," *Neo-Victorian Studies* 6, no. 2 (2013): 40–63; Tsugumi Okabe, "From Sherlock Holmes to 'Heisei' Holmes: Counter Orientalism and Post Modern Parody in Gosho Aoyama's *Detective Conan* Manga Series," *International Journal of Comic Art* 15, no. 1 (2013): 230–50.

24. Linda Hutcheon, *A Theory of Adaptation,* 2nd ed., with contributions by Siobhan O'Flynn (London: Routledge, 2013), 6 (emphasis in the original).

25. Following these critics, we use the term *palimpsestuous* to denote the quality of the palimpsest-as-concept, as opposed to *palimpsestic,* which might be taken more literally to describe qualities of real palimpsests. For a useful discussion of the distinction, see Sarah Dillon, "Reinscribing De Quincey's Palimpsest: The Significance of the Palimpsest in Contemporary Literary and Cultural Studies," *Textual Practice* 19, no. 3 (2005): 244–45.

26. Christian Gutleben, "Palinodes, Palindromes and Palimpsests: Strategies of Deliberate Self-Contradiction in Postmodern British Fiction," *Miscelánea: A Journal of English and American Studies* 26 (2002): 16.

27. Dillon, "Reinscribing De Quincey's Palimpsest," 243.

28. Thomas De Quincey, "The Palimpsest," in *Suspiria de Profundis: Being a Sequel to the Confessions of an English Opium Eater*, pt. 1, *Blackwood's Edinburgh Magazine* 57, no. 356 (June 1845): 742.

29. Dillon, "Reinscribing De Quincey's Palimpsest," 243.

30. Ibid.

31. Thomas Carlyle, "On History," in *Historical Essays*, ed. Chris R. Vanden Bossche (Berkeley: University of California Press, 2003), 8 (emphasis in the original).

32. David Peters Corbett, *The World in Paint: Modern Art and Visuality in England, 1848–1914* (Manchester: Manchester University Press, 2004); David Peters Corbett and L. Perry, eds., *English Art, 1860–1914: Modern Artists and Identity* (Manchester: Manchester University Press, 2001); Elizabeth Prettejohn, *Art for Art's Sake: Aestheticism in Victorian Painting* (New Haven, CT: Yale University Press, 2007) and *After the Pre-Raphaelites: Art and Aestheticism in Victorian England* (Manchester: Manchester University Press, 1999).

33. Corbett, *World in Paint*, 11.

34. Rachel Teukolsky, *The Literate Eye: Victorian Art Writing and Modernist Aesthetics* (Oxford: Oxford University Press, 2009), 3; Elizabeth Helsinger, *Poetry and the Pre-Raphaelite Arts: Dante Gabriel Rossetti and William Morris* (New Haven, CT: Yale University Press, 2008).

35. Examples include Richard Maxwell, ed., *The Victorian Illustrated Book* (Charlottesville: University of Virginia Press, 2002); Paul Goldman and Simon Cooke, eds., *Reading Victorian Illustration, 1855–1875: Spoils of the Lumber Room* (Farnham, UK: Ashgate, 2012); Brian Maidment, *Reading Popular Prints, 1790–1870* (Manchester: Manchester University Press, 1996); John Hewitt, "The Poster in England in the 1890s," *Victorian Periodicals Review* 35, no. 1 (Spring 2002): 37–62; Mary Elizabeth Leighton and Lisa Surridge, "The Plot Thickens: Toward a Narratological Analysis of Illustrated Serial Fiction in the 1860s," *Victorian Studies* 51, no. 1 (2008): 65–101 and "The Transatlantic *Moonstone*: A Study of the Illustrated Serial in *Harper's Weekly*," *Victorian Periodicals Review* 42, no. 3 (2009): 207–43, among their other works.

36. Lorraine Janzen Kooistra, *Poetry, Pictures, and Popular Publishing: The Illustrated Gift Book and Victorian Visual Culture, 1855–1875* (Athens: Ohio University Press, 2011), 3.

37. The *Victorian Periodicals Review* is the organ of the Research Society for Victorian Periodicals (RSVP). This group of scholars is largely responsible for the major currents in Victorian periodical research. See Patrick Leary, *The* Punch *Brotherhood: Table Talk and Print Culture in Mid-Victorian England* (London: British Library, 2010); Laurel Brake, *Print in*

Transition, 1850–1910: Studies in Media and Book History (Basingstoke, UK: Palgrave, 2011); Laurel Brake and Marysa Demoor, eds., *Dictionary of Nineteenth-Century Journalism in Great Britain and Ireland* (Ghent, Belgium: Academia Press, 2009); Brake, "'Time's Turbulence': Mapping Journalism Networks," *Victorian Periodicals Review* 44, no. 2 (Summer 2011): 115–27. *VPR's* summer 2012 special issue, "Teaching and Learning in the Digital Humanities Classroom" (edited by Jim Mussell, with articles by Linda K. Hughes, Natalie Houston, and Mussell, among others), offers an excellent snapshot of the ways that digitization has affected current pedagogical and scholarly endeavors.

38. Patrick Leary, "Googling the Victorians," *Journal of Victorian Culture* 10, no. 1 (Spring 2005): 73.

39. Ibid., 82, 81.

40. Benjamin's "The Work of Art in the Age of Mechanical Reproduction" is especially important (in Walter Benjamin, *Illuminations: Essays and Reflections,* ed. Hannah Arendt [London: Fontana, 1986], 217–52. See Michel Foucault, *The History of Sexuality,* vol. 1, trans. Robert Hurley (New York: Vintage, 1990). Jonathan Crary's work, especially *Techniques of the Observer: On Vision and Modernity in the Nineteenth Century* (Cambridge, MA: MIT Press, 1992), for instance, takes up the Foucauldian mantle.

41. Richard Altick, *The Shows of London* (Cambridge, MA: Harvard University Press, 1978), 1. See also Tony Bennett, *The Birth of the Museum: History, Theory, Politics* (London: Routledge, 1995); Patricia Anderson, *The Printed Image and the Transformation of Popular Culture, 1790–1860* (Oxford, UK: Clarendon Press, 1991); and Judith Walkowitz, "Urban Spectatorship," in *City of Dreadful Delight: Narratives of Sexual Danger in Late Victorian London* (Chicago: University of Chicago Press, 1992), 15–40.

42. Kate Flint, *The Victorians and the Visual Imagination* (Cambridge: Cambridge University Press, 2000), 39, 25.

43. Nancy Armstrong, *Fiction in the Age of Photography: The Legacy of British Realism* (Cambridge, MA: Harvard University Press, 2002), 38. See also Jennifer Green-Lewis, *Framing the Victorians: Photography and the Culture of Realism* (Ithaca, NY: Cornell University Press, 1996); and Daniel Novak, *Realism, Photography, and Nineteenth-Century Fiction* (Cambridge: Cambridge University Press, 2008).

44. Examples include Jim Cheshire, ed., *Tennyson Transformed: Alfred Lord Tennyson and Visual Culture* (Aldershot, UK: Lund Jeffries, 2009); Jonathan Smith, *Charles Darwin and Victorian Visual Culture* (Cambridge: Cambridge University Press, 2006); Anselm Heinrich, Katherine Newey,

and Jeffrey Richards, eds., *Ruskin, the Theatre, and Victorian Visual Culture* (Basingstoke, UK: Palgrave Macmillan, 2009); Barbara Jean Larson and Fae Brauer, eds., *The Art of Evolution: Darwin, Darwinisms, and Visual Culture* (Hanover, NH: Dartmouth College Press, 2009); and Kimberly Rhodes, *Ophelia and Victorian Visual Culture: Representing Body Politics in the Nineteenth Century* (Aldershot, UK: Ashgate, 2008).

45. George Du Maurier, "Frustrated Social Ambition," *Punch,* 21 May 1881, 229.

46. The opening volume of William Makepeace Thackeray's *Cornhill Magazine* ran an extended essay on Hogarth's life and work, titled "William Hogarth: Painter, Engraver, and Philosopher," which remarks that the artist "ever preached the sturdy English virtues that have made us what we are.... For this reason it is that ... cheap and popular editions of his works have been multiplied, even in this fastidious nineteenth century; that in hundreds of decorous family libraries a plump copy of Hogarth may be found," *Cornhill* 1, no. 2 (February 1860): 180. See also Frederick Antal's discussion in *Hogarth and His Place in European Art* (London: Routledge and Kegan Paul, 1962).

47. Deviation from this formula often drew rebuke. A review of Gustave Doré's illustrated *Don Quixote* in *All the Year Round*, for example, bemoaned the fact that illustrators were beginning to "produce a set of drawings which shall redound to [their] own credit, rather than to help the author whose work [they] illustrate[] to make himself understood." The critic much preferred illustrators like George Cruikshank and Hablot Brown (Phiz), who aspired "to put the more remarkable scenes described by the author, before the reader's eyes," and to "select as subjects all the most dramatic situations, whether of a comic or tragic sort, which were treated of in the narrative." "Book Illustrations," *All the Year Round,* 10 August 1867, 151. Sacherevell Sitwell's study *Narrative Pictures: A Survey of English Genre and Its Painters* (London: B. T. Batsford, 1936) remains a foundational text on this subject.

48. See Linda Merrill, *A Pot of Paint: Aesthetics on Trial in Whistler v. Ruskin* (Washington, DC: Smithsonian, 1993).

49. The publisher's prospectus insisted, "The pictures will in no case serve as illustrations to the letter-press, but each will stand by itself as an independent contribution." "Prospectus for *The Yellow Book* 1," April 1894, Mark Samuels Lasner Collection, on loan to the University of Delaware Library, Newark, in *The Yellow Nineties Online,* ed. Dennis Denisoff and Lorraine Janzen Kooistra, Ryerson University, 2011, www.1890s.ca/HTML.aspx?s=YBV1_prospectus.html.

50. Arthur Morrison, *Zig Zags at the Zoo*, illus. J. A. Shepherd, *Strand Magazine* 6 (1893): 293.

51. Ibid., 293.

52. Edward Lear, *Nonsense Songs, Stories, Botany, and Alphabets* (Boston: James R. Osgood, 1871), 88, 90.

53. Morrison, *Zig Zags*, 288–89.

54. Stephen Best and Sharon Marcus, "Surface Reading: An Introduction," *Representations* 108, no. 1 (2009): 3, 8 (emphasis in the original). See also the other contributors to this special issue of *Representations,* titled "The Way We Read Now."

55. James McNeill Whistler, *Mr. Whistler's Ten O'Clock* (Cambridge, MA: Riverside Press, 1896), 9 (emphasis in the original).

56. Caroline Levine, "Scaled Up, Writ Small: A Response to Carolyn Dever and Herbert F. Tucker," *Victorian Studies* 49, no. 1 (2009): 104. (emphasis in the original).

57. Scott McCloud, Will Eisner, Natsume Fusanosuke, Benoît Peeters, and Neil Cohn, to name just a few.

58. Indeed, a fair amount of scholarship has been devoted to defining the very parameters of "comics," arguing for and against more or less restrictive definitions. Scott McCloud, for example, begins his now-classic *Understanding Comics* by arguing against too-restrictive definitions, preferring instead an all-encompassing one: "Juxtaposed pictorial and other images in deliberate sequence, intended to convey information and/or to produce an aesthetic response in the viewer." McCloud, *Understanding Comics: The Invisible Art* (New York: HarperCollins, 1993), 8. For a useful summary of the state of the field, see Hillary Chute, "Comics as Literature? Reading Graphic Narrative," *PMLA* 123, no. 2 (2008): 452–65.

59. Hillary Chute and Marianne DeKoven, "Introduction: Graphic Narrative," special issue of *MFS: Modern Fiction Studies* 52, no. 4 (Winter 2006): 769.

60. Levine, "Scaled Up, Writ Small," 104. (emphasis in the original).

61. Thierry Groensteen, *The System of Comics,* trans. Bart Beaty and Nick Nguyen (Jackson: University Press of Mississippi, 2007), 21.

62. Ibid., 18.

63. Natsume Fusanosuke, "Pictotext and Panels: Commonalities and Differences in Manga, Comics and BD," trans. Jessica Bauwens-Sugimoto, in *Comics Worlds and the World of Comics: Towards Scholarship on a Global Scale,* ed. Jaqueline Berndt (Kyoto: Kyoto Seika University Press, 2010), 44–45.

64. Carlyle, "On History," 8.

65. Talbot, *Alice in Sunderland*, 55. Hereafter cited in text. Here and in subsequent quotations, ellipses and emphases are reproduced as in the original.

66. Not all of the editions with Tenniel's illustrations place these illustrations back to back, but the original Macmillan's did.

67. Groensteen, *System of Comics,* 18.

68. Thomas Leitch, "Twelve Fallacies in Contemporary Adaptation Theory," *Criticism* 45, no. 2 (Spring 2003): 149–71.

69. Carlyle, "On History," 8.

I.

Adaptations

ONE

The Explicated Image

Graphic "Texts" in Early Victorian Print Culture

BRIAN MAIDMENT

The overwriting of graphic or visual "texts" by the verbal in the early
Victorian period is a process allied to, if not exactly enacting, the
mechanisms of accretion and overlay that characterize the palimpsest. Such overwriting can be best described by using a range of ugly
participles such as *verbalizing, narrativizing,* and *novelizing.* The deploy-
ment of these processes of augmentation and rewriting clearly suggests something complex about the relationships between text and
image during a historical phase in which both literary genres and
reprographic technologies were undergoing radical change. The publication from the period that most obviously embodies this complex
of accretion and remaking is Charles Dickens's illustrated serial *The
Pickwick Papers,* first published between 1836 and 1837.[1] *Pickwick* is for
many reasons a seminal symbolic event in the history of print culture,
the moment when serialized illustrated fiction became established as
a hugely significant commodity, when the author stepped up to take
command of his or her intellectual property, and when the generic
formulation of fiction began to take shape as what we know as the
"Victorian novel."

Two further issues raised by the publication of *Pickwick* are important for this analysis. The first is the complex involvement of the

draftsman Robert Seymour in the genesis of the novel. The extensively discussed ambiguities of Seymour's presence as a possible source or origin for *Pickwick* are not examined here; however, other published works of his, especially the *Humorous Sketches* (better known as *Sketches by Seymour*), provide extensive and complicated evidence of the relationship between word and image in the Victorian period.[2] In particular, Seymour's early death allowed his images to become available for refashioning in the many modes and formats of print genres accessible to mid-Victorian publishers, and the posthumous history of his work offers an important case study of the extent to which mid-nineteenth-century readers privileged the verbal over the graphic.

This discussion of the history of the verbalizing of Seymour's images is situated within considerations of two other print occasions that suggest the continuing dialogue between the word and the image in the mid-nineteenth century. The first concerns the extensive republication of William Hogarth's works in various mass circulation venues; the second addresses the reworkings of a series of Kenny Meadows's images, originally intended as extra illustrations to Dickens's *Nicholas Nickleby*, as, firstly, decorative elements in periodicals and, secondly, the origins for a series of commissioned sketches in which Meadows's plates become representations of social "types."[3] The textual history of all three publications reverses or renders complex the traditional role of illustration as something essentially derived from, and thus subordinate to, the text. The struggle to establish and maintain their autonomy as images against the recurring depredations of text is the central unifying element of the following discussion.

Pickwick's publication raises a broader issue about the effects that Dickens's triumphant transformation of a sequence of graphic images into a long and generically complex text had on the development of primarily visual narratives in the Victorian period. A mere glance at David Kunzle's *History of the Comic Strip,* for example, reveals how little space Kunzle devoted to the British contribution in developing what he regards as a major strand of nineteenth-century cultural production.[4] The emergence of the comic strip as a hugely popular and inventive literary mode elsewhere in Europe and in the United States had little influence on the British tradition until late in the nineteenth century. As Kunzle has noted elsewhere, the protonarrative elements that were beginning to emerge in the sets of oblong folio plates on similar themes produced by caricaturists like Henry Alken, Henry Heath, and Seymour in the late 1820s never matured into sustained graphic narratives.[5] In looking beyond the detailed discussion of the burden on particular images to retain their individuality in the face of a verbal assault most obviously represented by the serialized novel, this chapter begins to describe the extent to which an emergent tradition of visual narrative was smothered by an early Victorian devotion to words.

This is the context within which I want to consider more generally why an extended narrative with illustrations might have been more successful both with its readers and as a commercial commodity in the early Victorian period than a publication that was conceived exclusively as a sequence of visual images and almost entirely comprising graphic elements. The commonsense argument is that written texts "say more" than graphic images. It is worth thinking what "saying more" might mean. "More" has both a temporal and a spatial dimension. In temporal terms, the argument might be made that reading the image is instantaneous, or at least rapid, when compared to the prolonged pleasure of the verbal. Thus, a potential line of argument might run that the gratifications of instant visuality are shallower and more ephemeral than the satisfactions offered by the verbal. One could argue that the layers of everyday use and depth of allusion coded in language take longer to unravel than do the cultural references of the graphic image, although, of course, the reverse might be true: that it takes more time and requires a more educated sensibility to decode the allusiveness of the visual image. In spatial terms, the book as a physical object is bulkier than a single print and better able to withstand daily use. Books, perhaps, fit more easily into the domestic space than do prints, especially unframed images. Such material considerations have evident commercial implications. The serialized novel, presented in a cheap and attractive form in weekly or monthly parts, was nonetheless ultimately extremely expensive for readers, especially given the sometimes-generous layout of the text on the page. The term *illustration* implies a secondary function, suggesting images that exist primarily as dependents on a text. Similarly, there are, and were, differences in the status of the novelist and the illustrator. The aesthetic limitations of illustration were further publicized by the necessity of the intervention of an engraver between the production of the original image by the draftsman and its realization and reproduction on the page. Simply put, by the 1830s, the illustrator had already been situated in a less prestigious place in an aesthetic and cultural hierarchy than a novelist, and such differences clearly must have influenced the ways in which illustrations and texts were read and consumed.

Beyond all these rather wild generalizations about cultural practices, there are also issues concerning illustration that derive from what might be called the fear of being misread, the notion that visual information was, and is, more open to diverse interpretations than are meanings constructed in language. The opposite possibility is also important for the discussion that follows: that the verbalizing of graphic images entails reconstructing their meanings to serve changed sociopolitical understandings of society or new ideological purposiveness. Such a process would inevitably be complex and could be managed in many ways—through the re-engraving of images to highlight or repress particular details, for example, or through the addition of expository notes and explanations that directed the viewer's attention to particular aspects of the image at the expense of others. This analysis suggests how the full range of the suppositions described above may have influenced early Victorian reluctance to leave visual texts without annotation or forms of restructuring that replaced their potential ambiguities with clear verbal instructions to the reader about how the visual should be read.

One paradigmatic example from the early Victorian period of how graphic texts might be verbalized and textualized into new social purposiveness and unambiguous meaningfulness is provided by the republication, especially in mass circulation periodicals, of Hogarth's prints, most obviously the narrative sequences like *A Harlot's Progress* (1732), *The Rake's Progress* (1735), *Marriage à la Mode* (1745), and *The Idle and Industrious Apprentice* (a 1747 sequence almost always referred to later as *Industry and Idleness*). Hogarth's prints always demonstrated a complex relationship between the verbal and the visual. The twelve prints that make up *Industry and Idleness,* for example, carry a heavy freight of metatext, both verbal and graphic, around the central engraved image. Each image is presented in a brick-like framing surround that emblematically suggests that the viewer is looking through a window into the image.[6] The surround is embellished with decorative flourishes in both the bottom corners. At the top of the image, and apparently poking out from behind the image's frame, there is on one side a representation of a mace and on the other leg irons, thus emblematically prefiguring the fates of the two apprentices. These two emblems shift sides through the sequence, being attached to the relevant apprentice located nearby through the composition of the print. Above each image Hogarth placed an engraved summary of the narrative being enacted below. In the brickwork at the base of the image, the artist introduced scriptural quotations located in carved frames or cartouches that might have come from a church memorial plaque or gravestone.

In various ways, then, Hogarth's prints combine text and image with literary elements. Hogarth used the idea of the "progress" or emblematic biography to structure his sequences of images into an essentially narrative form derived from literary genres such as parables or fables. He constructed several layers of verbal presence that, while not overlaying or obtruding onto the image, nonetheless frame it with words. One might almost say that Hogarth "illustrated" many of his images with texts, perhaps in the belief that the elaborate visual texture constructed in his images might need verbal simplification to be understood by the broad range of customers that his business practices sought to reach. Further, through the obvious presence of mace and leg irons as representations of the two apprentices, he made it clear that his images should be read with the care and attention to detail that was more usually associated with verbal texts. His images insist, by their strenuous and scrupulous depiction of small things, on being "read" and interpreted as one might read and interpret a biblical text. Detail in Hogarth's prints forms a crucial form of exposition but not always one available to the casual glance of the viewer seeking immediate visual gratification or drawn only to the decorative surface of the image.

Given Hogarth's close engagement with the verbal and his constant suggestion to the viewer that his images needed to be "read" like a book, we should not be surprised by the extent to which his work was vulnerable to a verbalizing compulsion that began to emerge immediately after his death. The key book for understanding the ways in which Hogarth's original visual projects were overwritten by later commentators is the Reverend John Trusler's *Hogarth Moralized,* first published at the behest of Hogarth's wife, Jane, in serial form between 1766 and 1768.[7] The work was frequently reprinted in various forms, ranging from large quarto two-volume versions to relatively modest single volumes. The original 1768 edition published by S. Hooper made innovative use of small-scale copperplate versions of Hogarth's plates dropped into the text (see fig. 1.1). Whereas *Hogarth Moralized* retained all the verbal and decorative metatext to be found in the original engravings, the shift to small-scale reproductions within a mass of circumambient text represents a major shift in the balance of power between image and text, with the tiny images becoming visual traces of or prompts to recall their large-scale original publication. The verbal elements, so prominent a part of many of Hogarth's original prints, were frequently relegated by Trusler and his publishers to footnotes, thus forming another assertive typographical element in his text. Editions of *Hogarth Moralized* were published in (at least) 1821, 1824, 1827, 1831, 1833, and 1841, and in addition to Trusler's commentary, the book accumulated an introductory essay by one of its later publishers, John Major, on its sustained journey through print culture (see fig. 1.2). As with Seymour's *Sketches,* the addition of explanatory and expository editorial material was important in suggesting the contemporary relevance of a text produced for a different previous reading public. The popularity of *Hogarth Moralized* in its various forms established the moral usefulness and educative potential of Hogarth's works as the overwhelmingly most relevant and valuable way of responding to his work in the early Victorian period. In this blatant remaking of the sociocultural meanings inscribed in Hogarth's prints, much, of course, had to be omitted or repressed for an emergent mass readership.

Licensed by Trusler's confidence in the primacy of moral education as the central factor in Hogarth's stature as an artist, as well as by their sense of ideological purpose, many cheap illustrated early Victorian periodicals that aimed at a mass readership incorporated Hogarth's prints into their quest to improve their readers' minds. Inevitably, this meant resetting his images in a miniaturized wood-engraved form that eliminated much of the rich detail that characterized his work, giving

(left) FIG. 1.1 Plate 3 of William Hogarth, *The Rake's Progress,* from John Trusler, *Hogarth Moralized* (London: S. Hooper, 1768), 24.

(below) FIG. 1.2 Plate 3 of William Hogarth, *The Rake's Progress,* from John Trusler, *Hogarth Moralized* (London: John Major, 1831), 28–29.

cautious editors a chance to excise elements of London low life that would offend against decency. But it also meant, using the technology that wood engraving made possible, immersing the images in a new sea of textual exposition. The many magazines that made use of extended and highly annotated sequences of Hogarth images drawn from his narrative series spanned a wide range of potential readers. *Saturday Night,* one of many cheap weekly miscellanies from the late 1820s dedicated to gathering together diverse "information," serialized both *Industry and Idleness* and *Marriage à la Mode* for an implied readership from the lower, middle, and artisan classes keen to improve their stock of general knowledge (see fig. 1.3).[8] The celebrated *Penny Magazine,* run by Charles Knight on behalf of the Whig-inspired Society for the Diffusion of Useful Knowledge and firmly aimed at offering artisans secularized information free from ideological bias, devoted consider-able space to a long run of images drawn from Hogarth's prints (see fig. 1.4).[9] The *London Journal,* which depended on a hugely successful investment in the kinds of illustrated serialized fiction popular with lower-class readers, reprinted the images from *Marriage à la Mode* in eight installments between 1847 and 1849, while another of G. W. M. Reynolds's several major journals, *Reynolds's Miscellany,* ran across al-most a full year an illustrated novel called *The Days of Hogarth,* which derived its narrative from a range of the artist's prints.[10] Children, too, could be addressed by carefully edited and textualized versions of Ho-garth's images, as suggested by the inclusion of a highly abbreviated and simplified *Idle and Industrious Apprentice* in *Cottager's Monthly Visi-tor.* Other magazines from this period that printed Hogarth sequences include the *London Spy* and *The Thief.*[11]

Apart from the rather more complicated gothic fictions of *The Days of Hogarth,* all of these publications united in propagating a vision of Hogarth's work as essentially moralistic and didactic, even though such a view frequently required omitting the artist's evident aesthetic fascination with the details of London low life. The illustrations, pri-marily small-scale wood engravings dropped into the text, inevitably simplified Hogarth's detail, and the accompanying texts offered some-times crudely moralistic commentary. The introduction to the most prominent reprinting of Hogarth's work in a popular periodical, the *Penny Magazine,* offers a characteristic response. Using Charles Lamb as its authority, in 1834 the *Penny Magazine* declared that Hogarth's art

FIG. 1.3 Plate 1 of William Hogarth, *Industry and Idleness*, "The Idle Apprentice," from *Saturday Night* 1, no. 13 (1824): 193.

FIG. 1.4 Plate 5 of William Hogarth, *Industry and Idleness*, "The Industrious Apprentice in the Confidence of His Master," from *Hogarth and His Works*, *Penny Magazine* monthly supplement, vol. 3 (1834): 216.

was essentially narrative and was thus available to be "read" like a literary text. As Lamb put it, Hogarth's "graphic representations are indeed books: they have the teeming, fruitful, suggestive meaning of *words*."[12] The magazine article goes on to stress the moral functions of Hogarth's work and to preempt criticism of reproducing images of low-life dissipation by underlining the editorial policy of reproducing only "unexceptionable" images. The chosen prints act out this moral vision: only one plate from *Marriage à la Mode* and two plates from *The Rake's Progress* fulfilled the magazine's moral purposes and standards, and plates 7, 8, 11, and 12 from *Industry and Idleness* were also discarded.

Commentators on the history of mass print have widely acknowledged Hogarth's presence in mass culture in the 1830s as unsurprising evidence of the moral imperative that underwrote the production and dissemination of visual images to a reading public. Patricia Anderson argues that the reasons for Hogarth's appeal "are fairly obvious: he was English, his works reproduced easily, and their openly moralistic subjects . . . were 'made to order' for the purpose of civilizing by negative example."[13] Anderson proposes that the use of Hogarth's images, and of art reproductions more generally, in the *Penny Magazine* was not merely a function of the magazine's ideological purpose but also alluded to "an established aesthetic tradition: that body of thought which equated art with intellectual and moral elevation and advanced civilization, and artists with virtue and industriousness."[14] In her study of Charles Knight, the publisher of the *Penny Magazine,* Valerie Gray argues that the ideological purposes of the *Penny Magazine*'s use of images can be overstated and that the meanings of the pictures by Hogarth and others were available to all and "innocent" of hidden meanings.[15] Nevertheless, the reproductions of Hogarth's works in the *Penny Magazine* offered accessible and simplified versions of the moral elements to be found in his prints and supported the wider ideological purposes of cheap periodical literature aimed at an artisan readership.

I could pursue such reworkings of Hogarth's prints more extensively through nineteenth-century periodicals to show how widely his work was rewritten according to the moral imperatives and limits of good taste that were emerging in mass print culture in the early Victorian period. But for the remainder of this chapter, I turn to subtler albeit equally dramatic verbalizations of a major graphic publication in which the moral and ideological imperatives of rewriting the visual were a less central preoccupation. Indeed, the extensive wordiness that was used to overwrite other graphic texts may be best understood as primarily commercial in its aims. The graphic image as a print commodity proved entirely amenable to the opportunism of the marketplace in the 1830s and 1840s, and the accretion of textual elements meant that relatively cheap single prints or sequences of prints could be turned into illustrated books, thus gaining an enhanced material presence and improved commercial potential.

One fascinating example of such commercial opportunism is provided by the publishing history of a set of extratextual illustrations to Dickens's part-issue novel *Nicholas Nickleby* (1838–39) drawn by a youngish and aspiring comic artist, Kenny Meadows, to cash in on Dickens's immense celebrity and popularity (see fig. 1.5). Extra illustrations depended on the lengthy process of part issue for their

FIG. 1.5   Title page to part issue of Kenny Meadows, *Heads from Nicholas Nickleby* (London: Robert Tyas, 1839).

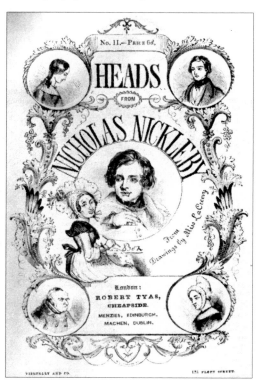

commercial appeal and allowed the reader to bind extended interpretative or decorative elements into the accumulated text alongside the "original" illustrations provided by the publisher. Meadows's set of plates for *Nicholas Nickleby* offers an object lesson in the ways in which illustrations might float not just from text to text but also from meaning to meaning.[16] Working initially under the defensive pseudonym of "Miss La Creevy" (the name of a portrait painter who appears in the novel), Meadows was astutely aware of commercial opportunity in what he offered to accompany Dickens's texts. In creating a series of quite detailed portraits of leading characters, drawn against little or no explanatory background, and refusing all elements of narrative, Meadows found a genre somewhere between caricature and character sketch that was a form of illustration quite distinct from Phiz's illustrations, which were drawn to provide detailed responses to the narrative. Meadows's illustrations offer no expository or explanatory visualizations of Dickens's text, despite the publisher, Tyas, advertising that the portraits would be "selected at the period where their very actions define their true characters, and exhibit the inward mind by its outward manifestations."[17] Tyas's claims notwithstanding, the illustrations offer little insight into character, especially in comparison with the psychological complexity of Dickens's text. They form, rather, a decorative addition to the pleasures of the text, saving the reader the trouble of having to imagine visually a physiognomy and appearance constructed verbally, if at all. They might be called, damningly, "likenesses." Meadows's plates, detached as they were from narrative function, make sense only in decorative terms, and to gain a meaning that continued to influence and interest the Victorian reading public required the development of a text that could assimilate them into a quite distinct and different project.

Was Meadows aware as he drew these illustrations of their potential for use beyond extra illustrations to Dickens's serialized novel? It certainly did not take long for the images to turn up in a new context. The editor of a new edition of a part-issued miscellany, *The Scrapbook of Literary Varieties,* announced in a somewhat disingenuous preface that he had "availed himself of some literary and graphic sketches from the inimitable Boz" that "much enhance[d] the interest of the whole."[18] The textual extracts were, of course, shamelessly pirated, but the implication that Meadows's *Heads* were somehow the

FIG. 1.6   Kenny Meadows, "The
Lounger," from *The Scrapbook of
Literary Varieties* (London: Edward
Lacey, n.d.), 209.

THE LOUNGER.

proper illustrations to Dickens's
novel was equally shameless.
However, a subsequent undated
edition of *The Scrapbook of Literary Varieties,* this time published
by Edward Lacey, continued to
use Meadows's *Nickleby* "heads"
but instead of presenting them as
Dickensian subjects, transformed
their meaning by the introduction of new captions that, at a
stroke, turned the images into
representations of a variety of
social "types." Thus, Mr. Man-
talini became "The Lounger" (see fig. 1.6), Crummles became a
"Country Theatre Manager," and the Cheeryble Brothers became,
much less distinctively, "Philanthropists." A simple renaming of the
images, then, broke the particularity of Meadows's portraits as illustrations tied to a particular text. Tyas's claim that they "exhibit the
inward mind by its outward manifestations" seems lame given this
shift from the individual to the type.

Somewhere along this chain of publication and republication,
Meadows and his publisher must have come up with the idea for
what was to become an important and generically significant book,
Heads of the People, published in two volumes in 1840 and 1841 (see
fig. 1.7).[19] Many of Meadows's *Nickleby* portrait "Heads" were re-
packaged here with the accompaniment of commissioned articles by
prominent journalists and writers to form, as the subtitle of the two
volumes suggests, "Portraits of the English." *Heads of the People* was
extremely influential in giving an enhanced status to the hastily written sketches of urban types with equally rapidly produced illustrations
that had become a staple component of magazines in the late 1830s
and early 1840s. Despite the crudely, and often humorously, drawn

FIG. 1.7   Title page spread from Kenny Meadows, *Heads of the People*, vol. 1 (London: Robert Tyas, 1841).

generalizations inherent in the urban sketch, the roots of sustained social observation and investigation are to be found in such works.[20] *Heads of the People* rather shockingly demonstrates the openness of images to commercial reinvention and reinterpretation in the volatile and entrepreneurial marketplace for print culture in the early Victorian period and suggests that the meaning of graphic images was entirely dependent on the text they accompanied.

Quite aside from its importance for book history, the narrative of Meadows's images thus raises major issues to do with the remaking of meanings for readers through newly textualized, subsequent reworkings of original graphic texts. In the case of the book considered in detail here, *Sketches by Seymour*, such shifts in meanings depended on transforming a primarily picaresque and celebratory vision of the urban scene as a theatrical space best depicted through the tropes of

Regency caricature into a more naturalistic, if still primarily comic, investigative impulse in which the lives of low or middling urban dwellers become the focus of social scrutiny and, to a limited extent, analysis.

Seymour's Sketches were originally issued as *Seymour's Humorous Sketches* between 1834 and 1836 by Richard Carlile as single plates costing threepence each.[21] They could also be purchased as short series of plates gathered into paper covers. The complete run eventually issued by Carlile comprised 197 separate images. Seymour's original lithographic stones were then sold to the entrepreneur Henry Wallis. Wallis, in a canny move characteristic of a burgeoning awareness of how to work the market for graphic publications, sold the stones to G. S. Tregear, who reissued 180 of Seymour's images in five volumes along with new title pages, probably in 1837. These works, along with the same artist's *New Readings of Old Authors* (1832–34), formed one of the defining visual accounts of Victorian London. But Wallis was aware of the new potential of the visual/verbal interrelationship, and, having kept the copyrights to Seymour's images, he redrew 86 of the images on steel, brought in "Crowquill" (Albert Forrester) to write a connecting narrative for the sequence of plates, and reissued the resulting volume as *Seymour's Humorous Sketches* in 1841. It was this version of Seymour's plates, with an emphasis on the narrative potential of the adventures of a gauche urbanite at large in the countryside, playing at pursuits such as fishing and shooting, that continued to please later Victorian readers. Henry Bohn issued a second edition of this book in 1841 which was reprinted in 1843. Later Bohn editions of this text issued from 1866 on added a biographical notice about Seymour and some quite detailed notes on each plate, written by the publisher. The final Bohn version of the book—including 86 plates, the Crowquill text, the Bohn descriptive list and biography, and the single title page and frontispiece rather than the five found in the Tregear volumes—was then reprinted successively in (at least) 1872, 1878, 1880, and 1888. Another, completely different rival text by R. B. Peake, built around 92 of Seymour's original plates, was issued in 1846, making clear in its title—*An Evening's Amusement; or, The Adventures of a Cockney Sportsman*—the transformation of Seymour's original series of plates into something far more Pickwickian than Seymour had initially imagined. Thus, *Sketches by Seymour* existed in the nineteenth century in essentially three formats: a series of social and sporting caricatures often loosely organized into volume format but also to be found floating about the marketplace as single sheets; a selection from the original images heavily annotated with a commentary by a professional and reasonably well known hack writer (Forrester) and poised somewhere in genre between disparate "sketches" and the picaresque novel; and a more thoroughly "novelized" version with a text by another seasoned hack writer and dramatist, which emphasizes the rural misadventures of Cockney sportsmen, a topic that had secured Seymour's original celebrity with Regency readers.

The publishing history of *Seymour's Sketches* is complicated by the artist's suicide in 1836 while illustrating the first parts of Dickens's *Pickwick Papers*. His death was variously regarded as a family tragedy, with several publishers rallying around his widow, Jane, in an attempt to realize money from his work to support his family, and as a commercial opportunity, with at least one publisher undertaking a new edition of his work that used his death as a marketing tool. The original owner of Seymour's plates, Henry Wallis, could barely contain his excitement at the commercial opportunity given him by Seymour's widely reported sudden death: "The premature and unfortunate death of ROBERT SEYMOUR has imported a value to his productions—too often the case with works of art and genius—far beyond what they enjoyed even during the life of their highly gifted and mirth-inspired author. Everyone at all acquainted with passing events must have heard of 'Seymour,' even whilst living; but now that death has claimed him as its own, and Momus is in mourning for the loss of his favourite son, everyone is eager to possess some relic of 'departed genius.'"[22] But Wallis's tough-minded commercial instincts would be offset by the efforts of other publishers, notably William Spooner, who tried to help Jane Seymour to bring out previously unpublished drawings by her husband.[23]

Nonetheless, Seymour's death seems to have made his large output of sketches widely available to opportunistic and unscrupulous commercial interests. Such commercial interests were instrumental in making a more thematically coherent selection from the nearly two hundred available *Sketches,* adding text that treated the images as a protonarrative rather than autonomous caricatures, and assembling images and texts into a bound volume that might also contain metatexts in a variety of forms, most obviously biographical accounts of

Seymour's career and explanatory notes to the images. In its clumsiest forms, the reworking of the *Sketches* was made simply to exploit Seymour's posthumous reputation as a "sporting artist," who, along with Henry Alken, had used the comic image to explore the rural misadventures of urban tradespeople and artisans in their newfound interest in field sports. While unease at the changing aspirations of social classes just becoming wealthy and secure enough to enjoy leisure interests may have underpinned the widespread consumer interest in humorous sporting images at this time, it is also obvious that confusion, dislocation, and embarrassment formed part of the stock in trade of the Regency comic artist.[24]

If images of shooting, hunting, fishing, and other rural pursuits provided one key strand of Seymour's output, much of his work nonetheless occupied the "humorous" category, a category that might be best described as a prolonged scrutiny, using grotesque iconography and comic tropes drawn from Regency caricature, of the lives of the urban lower and middling classes both in their public street presence and in their domestic lives. Images of urban social interaction form roughly a third of the prints originally published by Carlile in the *Humorous Sketches.* Seymour's other sustained serial publication, *New Readings of Old Authors* (1832–34), further suggests the centrality of the everyday life of the metropolitan middling and lower classes to his satirical project. Each monthly issue contained ten small lithographs that comically reinterpreted Shakespearian quotations to form commentaries on the quotidian events of street and domestic life in the poorer areas of Regency London.

To some extent, the textualized reprints of *Seymour's Sketches* directed attention away from his original sociopolitical enterprise, with its troubling interest in class conflict, urban confrontation, and the aspirational impulses of the vulgar, by predominantly anthologizing his less controversial sporting images and thus reinforcing the commercial potential of his reputation in this field. For early Victorian sensibilities, the sight of the socially ambitious urban middling classes in ignorant pursuit of traditional rural pleasures remained an endlessly satisfying source of humor, and one that frequently appeared, for example, in *Punch* cartoons in the 1840s. But the textualizing of Seymour's images of social relationships and urban manners among the lower classes is what best suggests the nature of early Victorian anxiety over the dangers of permitting comic images from a previous generation to be reprinted without annotation or explanation. To suggest how such a process of reinterpretation and republication worked, I focus on a few of the images from *Seymour's Sketches* that center on the most frequently used compositional trope for the comic graphic formulation: the street encounter between differing social types in which "difference" is analyzed and expressed.

As would be expected from their widespread presence in Regency caricature, there are several images of sweeps' boys in the original *Sketches*. Perhaps the most revealing image occurs as number 30 of volume 4 of the five-volume Tregear edition (see fig. 1.8). Two sweeps' boys, laden with the accoutrements of their trade (soot bags, brushes, and shovels), have been ushered out of the back door of a genteel house by a black servant carrying a covered silver dish. The assumption is that the servant has paused in his task of taking up breakfast to the household to see the boys off the premises; sweeps worked early in the mornings before domestic fires were lit and were thus frequently encountered during the day on the streets, where they were perceived as idle nuisances. The black servant is represented through the characteristic visual tropes accorded to his class. His portly form is just about contained in the confines of his livery, and he is centrally depicted through his broad and vacuous grin and two white eyes. His geniality and implied slowness of wit are offset against the knowingness of the dialogue exchanged between the two sweeps' boys. The first boy asks his companion, "Bob, arnt you glad you aint a Black-emoor?" to which his companion replies, "I should think so, they're sich ugly varmints, Master's daughter wot's come from boarding school, says, the sight of 'em is enough to frighten one into conwulsions!!"[25]

An immediate response to the image would be to say that it forms a graphic racial slur on the black servant, confirmed by the ignorant verbal annotations of the two sweeps' boys. But such one-dimensional readings are undermined by considerable complexity in both the visual and the verbal elements that make up the print. First of all, the sweeps' boys are themselves "ugly varmints." Their caricatured physiognomy is in many ways more animalistic and threatening than

FIG. 1.8   Robert Seymour, "Bob, arnt you glad . . ." from *Sketches by Seymour*, vol. 4, no. 30 (London: G. S. Tregear, ca. 1836).

that of the servant. Their "blackness" offers the threat of immediate physical contamination on contact. Perhaps most damning of all is the cheerful and unquestioning ignorance displayed by the boys, an ignorance that is the product of transposed judgments derived from the social prejudices of their semieducated "Master's daughter." In short, although the crude racial stereotype accorded to the representation of the servant here is undeniable, the central focus of satire is the un-self-aware bigotry of the sweep's boys in failing to see themselves as uglier, more threatening, and potentially more socially undesirable than their street companion. A further dimension to the visual dialogue between servant and sweeps here is the ambiguity accorded to the viewer: how far did the print challenge the prejudices and assumed attitudes of its original purchasers and viewers? In posing the question of whether a genially portrayed black servant is less amenable to satiric commentary than two physically threatening, dirty, and ignorant boys who have been exposed to the social prejudices of the aspiring working classes, Seymour's image contains considerable complexity, a complexity that requires only a short verbal annotation to construct its full satiric depth. Additionally, for Seymour's contemporaries, such an image would resonate powerfully with the many other depictions of sweeps' boys to be found in contemporary caricature. Their distinctive appearance (with brass cap-badges, a brush, a sack, and a shovel, as well as their perpetual sootiness), the dangerous and exploitative nature of their trade, their implied link with the particular kinds of filth derived from the involvement of sweeps in the removal of night soil, and their widespread presence on the streets during daytime served to remind Regency society of elements of everyday urban life that challenged genteel values. The recognition and satirical exploitation of the kinds of social anxieties and taboos represented by sweeps' boys by Regency caricaturists was widespread and brought together anxieties about class, race, violence, and masculinity.

How could such visual and verbal complexity be translated into a narrative illustrated by this image? In the case of Forrester's ("Crowquill's") 1843 *Seymour's Humorous Sketches,* accomplishing this posed considerable difficulty. Indeed, Forrester's text shows the essential incompatibility between a developed narrative coherence and the attempt to use Seymour's images as the basis for a sustained work of fiction. Here is the opening of chapter 13:

> Having to deliver a letter . . . to one of Mr. Timmis's
> clients . . . in crossing through one of the fashionable
> squares, I observed a flat-faced negro servant in livery,
> standing at the door of one of the houses.
>
> Two chimney-sweepers who happened to be
> passing, showed their white teeth in a contemptuous
> grin at the African.
>
> "Bob," I overheard one remark, "arn't you glad you
> ain't a black-a-moor?"
>
> "I should think so," replied his sooty brother, "they're
> sich ugly warmints. Master's daughter, wots come from
> boarding school! Says the sight of 'em's enough to
> frighten one into conwulsions!"
>
> Alas! For the prejudice of the world! How much
> this ignorant remark reminded me of my patron's
> unfounded hatred of all "forriners." It was precisely the
> same sentiment, differently expressed, that actuated the
> thoughts and opinions of both.[26]

Forrester's rather desperate allusion to his accompanying illustration here suggests that the need to refer to the image hampered the narrative drive of his text and served only as an occasion for sententious comment. Forrester's commentary on the image is, in other words, a crude misreading as the author attempts to incorporate visual elements into his text. The chimney sweeper's boys do not "show their white teeth" in a "contemptuous grin," although the liveried servant is grinning and showing his white teeth. By my reading of the image, the boys do not "happen to be passing" but are instead being ushered out of the house by the back door: why else would a liveried servant be standing at the door with a covered tray unless interrupted in his task of serving breakfast? The language used by the boys has been tidied up considerably to conform to standard written English while retaining some vernacular elements.

But what has been centrally omitted from this narrative incident is the possibility that the sweeps' boys are an ironic counterpart to the black servant and that the image constructed a wide range of potential satirical viewpoints. Instead, the author offers us what seems at first like an admirable if sententious warning against racial or nationalistic prejudice. Yet such an apparently liberal sentiment immediately follows the description of the servant as "flat-faced." In this instance, then, the "novelization" of Seymour's image reduces it to a disconnected incident that disrupts the flow of the narrative. In no sense is any attempt made to use the text as a serious commentary on the image it accompanies. The illustration becomes merely a decorative addendum to Forrester's narrative, and it has been purged of its considerable weight of satiric intensity for a readership more interested in comic diversion than social commentary.

R. B. Peake's novelization of Seymour's *Sketches,* variously called *An Evening's Amusement; or, The Adventures of a Cockney Sportsman* and *Snobson's Seasons,* was, in many ways, more successful than Forrester's. Peake's title suggests that the work was deliberately episodic, a sequence of sketches rather than a sustained narrative. He also created a helpful literary voice—"Snobson"—through which to speak his narrative. Snobson is an embodiment of a genteel Regency world contemporary with, and appropriate to, Seymour's images, providing a garrulous and nostalgic anecdotal sequence of long-remembered incidents from the hunting field and London life. In short, Peake acknowledged Seymour's images as anachronistic to the knowledge and taste of his early Victorian readers and described them through a misty lens of nostalgia. He did, however, accept that Seymour's images were capable of complexity and might provide and provoke an interest in social commentary.

The extent of Peake's ability to acknowledge the sophistication of Seymour's caricatures can be gauged by looking at another image of sweeps from the *Sketches.* This image, reprinted on page 54 of *An Evening's Amusement,* depicts two older and more-established sweeps conversing on the street in front of a police office (see fig. 1.9). A frieze of sweeps' boys lines the railing of the office, and a matronly lady and a policeman are glimpsed at the door. The caption runs, "Vel I dos'nt think it can be blasphemy for us to sing out—Laws ha' mercy upon us" "No, sure its not nothing at all o' the sort, and ve ought to know, seeing as how they calls us clargymen."[27] The image is one of many caricatures from the 1830s and 1840s commenting on the increasing regulation of street trades, especially concerning street noise. For caricaturists, of course, the decline of picturesque street sellers was also a major loss of potential topics for humorous comment. Although drawn in caricature idiom, Seymour's image is a serious one.

FIG. 1.9 Robert Seymour and R. B. Peake, "Vel I dos'nt think it can be blasphemy . . ." from *An Evening's Amusement; or, The Adventures of a Cockney Sportsman* (London: privately printed, 1846), 54.

Increasingly, legislation in the 1830s and 1840s had limited the ability of London tradespeople, with the special exclusion of dustmen, to advertise their services by means of cries, bells, or other noisy ways of calling attention to their presence. Largely the outcome of a middle-class campaign to instill urban order and quietude, laws against street cries brought particular anguish to sweeps, who were simultaneously losing their right to send climbing boys up chimneys.[28] In this image, the harassed sweeps have been brought to the police office on public order charges relating to their street cries. The first sweep dolefully recounts that his despairing cry of "laws ha' mercy upon us" has been considered blasphemous, a sardonic comment by Seymour about the rigor of the new legislation, while his companion, citing the nickname given to sweeps because of their blackened clothes, argues that if they are called "clergymen" they should surely be the best guides as to what might be considered blasphemy. Their plight is further emphasized by the line of unemployed sweeps' boys lounging on the police office railings.

This image that Peake elected to include in *An Evening's Amusement* is in many ways as arbitrary a decorative intrusion into the narrative as are the similar images that Forrester drew from Seymour's social satires, but Peake gave his commentary on the illustration at least some semblance of thematic unity by reverting to the self-consciously punning mode that formed a staple element of Regency humor:

> At the Battle-bridge races, an unusual number of clergymen congregate. But be it remembered that they are of that order of clergy who are accustomed to *sackcloth and ashes*. The races are generally for *sweep-stakes*—and formerly, a *handy-cap,* with the owner's name thereon, was conspicuous; [*sic*]
> Everything, even to the cleansing of chimneys, is now going through so extensive a revolution, that the employment of the ascending youths is abolished, and climbing boys summon their black-looking masters to the police office for *not* making creep through narrow flues, crawl over smoke jacks and fill their eyes ears, nostrils, and stomachs, with soot. The art of sweeping has devolved to a mere machine; but there must still be much money earned, for there is scarcely a public-house without its "DERBY SWEEP," from £500 to £2 10s.[29]

Peake has caught something of Seymour's sense of social irony, pathos, and recognition of distress in his commentary on the image. He has also tried to capture something of a Regency sensibility in the rueful acknowledgement of the apparent absurdities brought about by social change, although his exploitation of a series of rather heavy-handed and outdated puns as a means of tempering his sense of loss and disruption is less successful.

These few examples indicate that the "verbalization" of Seymour's prints in narrative form does little to solve the problems of how to build a fictional text out of a sequence of images. The allusiveness and complexity of Seymour's images are difficult to reproduce in an extended work of fiction, and the images have an autonomy and framework of reference that could be spelled out only by extensive verbal explanation that would be inimical to the forward drive of the narrative. The formal problems posed by the narrativizing of Seymour's *Sketches* are considerable, and the hybridized books produced by Forrester and Peake are not aesthetic successes, despite their commercial value. In carrying Seymour's graphic work into the nineteenth century, both *Sketches by Seymour* and *An Evening's Amusement* performed a valuable act in maintaining the presence of Regency social satire in Victorian consciousness, however diluted by deference to Seymour's reputation as a primarily sporting artist. Nonetheless, the refashioning of Seymour's images involved in the textualizing of his work denied his prints much of the allusiveness and complexity that they had carried for their original audience.

—◆—

Insofar as any conclusion can be drawn, it seems fair to say that images struggled to maintain their autonomy and fullness when subjected to extensive narrativization and explication. For early Victorian readers, such subordination of the visual to the verbal seems to have satisfied a complex of aesthetic, commercial, and sociocultural motives. Yet in the later refusal to allow graphic images to speak for themselves, a considerable level of simplification and misrepresentation was introduced through the typeset pages that accompanied or surrounded the visual content of the reprinted publications. In the cases studied here, the explicated image, however socially useful and entertaining it may have been to early Victorian society, becomes something less rich and complex than its unexplicated predecessor.

How far the publications studied here might begin to explain the wider absence of the comic strip from British nineteenth-century cultural history is difficult to establish. In contradistinction to France, eighteenth-century caricature and comic art in Britain had remained largely unhampered by any legislative and legal inhibition, and publishers had been free to produce any material, constrained only by modes of self-censorship (usually driven by self-interest). But by the time of the accession of Queen Victoria, some element of anxiety about unannotated images on sociocultural themes had taken hold of the marketplace for print. Whether such anxiety was predominantly the result of social tensions created by the urban environment and emergent class consciousness or, rather, the outcome of the demands of commercial instinct or changing tastes in visual comedy is hard to establish. To my mind, the continuing and extensive annotation of images shown by the history of the publications discussed above is part of a wider, early Victorian worry about the effects of publishing graphic images, especially satirical and comic images, without the mediating presence of textual explication. Early in this chapter, I argue that "the verbalizing of graphic images [is] an aspect of reconstructing the meanings of the images concerned to serve changed sociopolitical understanding of society or new ideological purposiveness." The republication of Hogarth's work as a means of reinforcing certain Victorian moral imperatives clearly exemplifies such a process of reconstruction. The "verbalizing" of Meadows's *Heads of the People* and Seymour's *Sketches* is less obviously tied to "ideological purposiveness" or "changed sociopolitical understanding." Yet the verbalizing and narrativizing of these images subsequent to their first publication clearly act as an inhibiting force on their original graphic statements, making them something less, although perhaps something safer, than they were once were. For early Victorian publishers, writers, and possibly even readers, unannotated graphic satirical images concerning sociocultural topics that had been inherited from earlier times remained dangerously open to alternative, and possibly transgressive, readings, an openness that could be neutralized by the intervention of the explicatory text.

Notes

1. The most recent detailed account of the genesis and publication of *The Pickwick Papers* can be found in Robert L. Patten, *Charles Dickens and "Boz": The Birth of the Industrial Age Author* (Cambridge: Cambridge University Press, 2012).

2. Seymour's *Humorous Sketches* were first published between 1831 and 1834. A detailed discussion of the publishing history of the work can be found later in this chapter.

3. [Joseph] Kenny Meadows's images were first published in response to the serialization of *Nicholas Nickleby* in 1838–39. In their reprinted form as *Heads of the People,* they were first issued in 1840–41.

4. David Kunzle, *The History of the Comic Strip: The Nineteenth Century* (Berkeley: University of California Press, 1990).

5. David Kunzle, "Between Broadsheet Caricature and *Punch:* Cheap Newspaper Cuts for the Lower Classes in the 1830s," *Art Journal* 43, no. 4 (Winter 1983): 339–46. For an overview of these issues, see also Brian Maidment, *Comedy, Caricature and the Social Order, 1820–1850* (Manchester: Manchester University Press, 2013), 47–112.

6. William Hogarth, *Hogarth:The Complete Engravings,* ed. Joseph Burke and Colin Caldwell (London: Alpine Fine Arts Collection, 1989), 203–14.

7. John Trusler, *Hogarth Moralized* (London: S. Hooper, 1768).

8. Hogarth's images, encompassing *The Idle and Industrious Apprentices, The Harlot's Progress,* and *The Rake's Progress,* appeared in *Saturday Night* beginning in issue 13 of volume 1 (1824) and were published mainly on a fortnightly basis.

9. *Hogarth and His Works* was published as a sixteen-part monthly supplement to *Penny Magazine* between March 1834 and May 1835.

10. Andrew King, *The London Journal, 1845–83* (Aldershot, UK: Ashgate, 2004); chapters 2 and 3 provide an overview of the *London Journal.* On *Reynolds's Miscellany,* see Brian Maidment, "The Mysteries of Reading: Text and Illustration in the Fiction of G. W. M. Reynolds," in *G. W. M. Reynolds: Nineteenth-Century Fiction, Politics, and the Press,* ed. Ann Humpherys and Louis James (Aldershot, UK: Ashgate, 2008), 227–46.

11. Originally published in *Cottager's Monthly Visitor,* this version of *Industry and Idleness* was reprinted in George Davys, *A Volume for a Lending Library,* 2nd ed. (London: J. G. F. and J. Rivington, 1840). *The Thief: A London, Edinburgh and Dublin Journal of Literature and Science* was published in London by W. Strange from 1832 to 1833.

12. "Hogarth and His Works," *Penny Magazine,* monthly supp. (March 1834): 122 (emphasis in the original). The statement appeared originally in Charles Lamb, "On the Genius and Character of Hogarth, with some Remarks on a Passage in the Writings of the Late Mr. Barry," *Reflector 2,* no. 3 (March 1811): 61–77.

13. Patricia Anderson, *The Printed Image and the Transformation of Popular Culture, 1790–1860* (Oxford, UK: Clarendon Press, 1991), 64.

14. Ibid., 67.

15. Valerie Gray, *Charles Knight: Educator, Publisher, Writer* (Aldershot, UK: Ashgate, 2006), 157.

16. Kenny Meadows, *Heads from Nicholas Nickleby* (London: Robert Tyas, 1839–40).

17. Advertisement taken from the March 1839 part issue of *Nicholas Nickleby* (issue 12) and quoted by Michael Slater in *The Composition and Monthly Publication of Nicholas Nickleby* (Menston, UK: Scolar Press, 1973), appendix.

18. Preface to *The Scrapbook of Literary Varieties* (London: John Reynolds, n.d.).

19. Kenny Meadows, *The Heads of the People,* 2 vols. (London: Robert Tyas, 1840–41).

20. See Martina Lauster, *Sketches of the Nineteenth Century: European Journalism and Its "Physiologies," 1830–1850* (Basingstoke, UK: Palgrave Macmillan, 2007), 269–78.

21. A more detailed account of the publication of Seymour's work can be found in Brian Maidment, "A Draft List of Published Book and Periodical Contributions by Robert Seymour," digital annex to vol. 38 of *Victorians Institute Journal* (2011), NINES (*Nineteenth-Century Electronic Scholarship Online*), www.nines.org/exhibits/Robert_Seymour. This account is, however, incomplete and misleading in several ways, although it does provide a fairly detailed narrative of Seymour's complex work.

22. Wallis's obituary was published on the back cover of the part issue of *Seymour's Sketches—Angling* (London: Thomas Fry, 1836).

23. Many prints bearing the superscription "Sketches by Seymour," but in a larger format than the original *Sketches,* appeared in 1839, bearing the inscription "Published for Mrs. Seymour, June 6th 1839 by William Spooner, No. 377 Strand."

24. For a range of Seymour's sporting prints, see David Beazley, *Images of Angling* (Haslemere, UK: Creel Press, 2010).

25. Robert Seymour, *Sketches by Seymour,* 5 vols. (London: G. S. Tregear, 1834–36?), 4:30.

26. Robert Seymour and "Crowquill" [Albert Forrester], *Seymour's Humorous Sketches* (London: Henry Bohn, 1843), chap. 13, unnumbered pages.

27. Robert Seymour and R. B. Peake, *An Evening's Amusement; or, The Adventures of a Cockney Sportsman* (London: privately printed, 1846), 54.

28. See John M. Picker, *Victorian Soundscapes* (Oxford: Oxford University Press, 2003), 3–11.

29. Seymour and Peake, *An Evening's Amusement,* 53–54.

TWO

Adapting *Alice in Wonderland*

Cultural Legacies in Contemporary Graphic Novels

MONIKA PIETRZAK-FRANGER

Lewis Carroll's *Alice in Wonderland* has been travelling across media, genres, languages, and cultures. The degree of its transferability and adaptability is indicative of both its global appeal and its culture-specific anchoring. While its thematic preoccupations and transcultural significance can be regarded in terms of cultural hegemony, the text's adaptations also participate in a fruitful discussion of the status quo of Carroll's text as part of a European heritage. Taking into consideration recent non-English adaptations of *Alice,* I discuss the extent to which they offer a space for a rethinking of this European culture and its legacies.

Contemporary critics have noted an unprecedented global expansion of the Alice industry. In "Anti-Essentialist Versions of Aggregate Alice: A Grin without a Cat," a review of recent developments in adaptation studies, Eckart Voigts-Virchow argues that the new tendencies in "transmedia polytexting" of Alice show that Lewis Carroll's work has functioned as an aggregate text: a text endowed with a degree of citability and iterability that lies at the core of contemporary neo-Baroque culture, characterized by the birth of "multimodal transmedia storytelling franchise[s]."[1] The "'natural' affinity of the Alice books' obsession with shapes, bodies and change," Voigts-Virchow contends further, makes it an ideal text for "cross-media transposition" and transmedia storytelling that use the book's "absence prèsente" to generate ever more narratives pivoting around Alice (66). Indeed, he insists that Alice has become a postmodern brand that is "in desperate need of recontextualization" and on which many capitalize (76). Referencing Kali Israel's assertion that "Alice is a name for wanting stories to have, stories to keep, and stories to continue,"[2] Voigts-Virchow sees Alice as "a cipher for [sexual and narrative] desire" (76). Likewise, in her article "Tie-Intertextuality, or, Intertextuality as Incorporation in the Tie-in Merchandise to Disney's *Alice in Wonderland* (2010)," Kamilla Elliott has shown that Alice has evolved into a trademark whose capitalist strength lies in the "Almost effect" of all the tie-ins.[3] The Alices that are produced for (sub)cultural consumption are always almost, but not quite, like Carroll's Alice. The Alice industry's strength derives precisely from this development as it generates an insatiable yearning for Alice that is always present but never quite satisfied by her never-ending reproductions and shape-shifting reiterations.

Processes of global reproduction and translatability have received growing attention from neo-Victorianists who, having delineated the major tendencies in contemporary rethinking of the Victorian era and its problems, are now turning toward the transnational and transmedial character of these preoccupations. These new developments contrast the alarming tendency of neo-Victorian studies to reproduce Victorian colonization mechanisms that Elizabeth Ho sketches in *Neo-Victorianism and the Memory of Empire*.[4] Ho resists the pervasive propensity toward "Anglocentricity" and "implied imperialism" that Ann Heilmann and Mark Llewellyn likewise caution against in their recent article, "The Victorians Now."[5] Pointing out that contemporary literary and critical works are liable to erase "cultural specificity" and homogenize heritage, they call for a more skeptical stance toward "universalism and globalism" and for an intensified focus on "internationally diverse re-memorialisations" of the Victorian era.[6] The 2013 neo-Victorian conference in Liverpool brought together more voices appealing for an interrogation of the "unconscious" imperialism of neo-Victorian studies. In her article resulting from that conference, "Other Neo-Victorians: Neo-Victorianism, Translation and Global Literature," Antonija Primorac "questions the assumptions that the production and cross-cultural dissemination of neo-Victorianism is inevitably an Anglophone affair."[7] Discussing the playful rewriting of

Sherlock Holmes in Mima Simić's Croatian *The Adventures of Gloria Scott* and its adaptations, Primorac attempts to "unsettle received notions about the production of neo-Victorianism as a phenomenon linguistically, geographically, and ideologically delimited by the maps of the British Empire."[8] She urges the necessity of including non-English rewritings of Victorian literature and culture and highlights the importance of critics and translators in expanding the field beyond the linguistic imperialism that has been intrinsic to it.[9]

This chapter attempts to bring together these tendencies in contemporary adaptation and neo-Victorian studies by reconsidering various local rereadings of Alice's wonderland, especially the way local geographies and temporalities have been reimagined in select European graphic novels based on Carroll's Alice. With particular focus on one Swiss and two Polish graphic novels—*Alice in Sussex* (2013) by Nicolas Mahler, *Alicja* ([Alice] 2006) by Jerzy Szyłak and Mateusz Skutnik, and *Alicja po Drugiej Stronie Lustra* ([Alice through the looking glass] 2008) by Jerzy Szyłak and Jarosław Gach—I explore how the graphic wonderlands offer a space for a rethinking of the global-local continuum with reference to European cultural legacies and their (non)hegemonic status.[10] That is why I set these novels in a broader context of several of the English-language graphic Alice adaptations that have received the most critical attention: Alan Moore and Melinda Gebbie's *Lost Girls* (2006), Bryan Talbot's *Alice in Sunderland* (2007), and Raven Gregory, Daniel Leister, and Nei Ruffino's *Return to Wonderland* (2009–11).[11]

Alice's Imperialist Penchant and Contemporary Wonderlands

Recent English-language adaptations of *Alice in Wonderland,* like much contemporary scholarship on Carroll's text, often criticize the imperialist subtext of the novel. For example, critic Daniel Bivona highlights Alice's colonialist attempts to function within the oneiric world of the wonderland. In the subterranean space, in which the rules of the Victorian social codes and the "conventional canon of precedence" find little application, Alice goes through an identity crisis that sets her off on a quest for knowledge.[12] Her attempts to comprehend the subterranean world and the rules that govern it verge on "semiotic imperialism," as she insists on interpreting the events in accordance with her own culturally inherited values (150). Alice's received notions of order, rules, and classifications preempt her comprehension of the subterranean world on its own terms as she turns her "failure" to understand into "a 'successful' act of imperial appropriation through the imposition of a discourse that, in circular fashion, 'produces' the sought-for object of knowledge" (165). For Bivona, the "solipsistic recentering" in which Alice engages is a reminder that "there is a bit of the imperial Alice in all of us who engage in the twin activities of both 'comprehending' and 'repeating'" (171). Contemporary graphic refashionings of Alice's wonderland evoke the complexities of intercultural comprehension that Bivona sees as central to Carroll's narrative. Late twentieth- and early twenty-first-century wonderlands offer spaces in which the major problems of our era can be rethought within a cultural matrix that shows a close intertwining of global and local histories.

The twentieth century marked the birth of an adult Alice in texts addressing new (dystopian) realities that invoke the legacies of cultural imperialism. In "'But I'm Grown Up Now': Alice in the Twenty-First Century," Catherine Siemann spots this tendency in contemporary multimedia adaptations of the text, as she examines Tim Burton's 2011 film alongside the video game *American McGee's Alice: Madness Returns* (2011) and Raven Gregory's graphic novel trilogy *Return to Wonderland* (2009–11).[13] Contrasted with Carroll's wonderland, these recent fantasies of subterranean worlds are clearly menacing, often representing a dystopian twenty-first century that is saturated with violence and crime. Cataloguing the threats evoked in Gregory's novels, Siemann notes that "suicide, murder, cannibalism, sadomasochism, rape, the kidnapping and exploitation of the innocent, and nearly any other horror trope imaginable" are inherent to this nightmarish wonderland (190). Despite its overindulgence in the various "trappings of graphic sexuality and ultraviolence," Siemann argues, the message of the trilogy "is not ultimately very different than those of the other iterations: the world (sex) can be dangerous, parents cannot always protect you, and only your own strength and resourcefulness will take you through Wonderland" (191). "[T]itillating and judgmental," this twenty-first-century iteration of wonderland allows for an evocation and exploitation of empowerment fantasies, in which a "Xena-esque" heroine combats evil while simultaneously parading as a fetish for male (visual) gratification (191). Yet despite their horror, these new versions of wonderland are both psychoanalytic and moralistic and thereby "oddly familiar and oddly Victorian" (191).

Apart from taking up issues of morality and (sexual) identity in the contemporary world, recent graphic adaptations of *Alice in Wonderland* address the question of history, including its nature, locale, and function. In *Lost Girls,* Alan Moore and Melinda Gebbie explore life stories of three grown-up women who remain trapped in their girlhood for generations of readers: Alice from Carroll's *Alice in Wonderland;* Dorothy from Lyman Frank Baum's *The Wonderful Wizard of Oz* (1900); and Wendy from J. M. Barrie's *Peter Pan* (1904). The three women's erotic adventures in Hotel Himmelgarten in Austria at the brink of the Second World War provide background for an investigation of the connections between sexuality and fantasy and their relation to individual and collective histories. For Jason B. Jones, Moore and Gebbie's graphic novel is a celebration of "voluntarism . . . of the imagination that transcends all limitations."[14] Similarly, Annalisa Di Liddo argues that on its canvas, individual life histories and memories become a never-ending "source of erotic bliss," which is also a basis for the women's empowerment.[15] However, in the ultimate failure of the sexual fantasy, followed by the brutal invasion of war imagery, the book juxtaposes "the eternal quality of the sexual encounter and the gloomy small-mindedness of human violence."[16] As Di Liddo conjectures, drawing connections between *Lost Girls* and Angela Carter's work, Moore and Gebbie become here "moral pornographer[s]" who see in erotica a "secret garden" of transhistorical rejuvenation.[17] Indeed, for Andrés Romero-Jórdan, the book is a denouncement of historically specific, early twentieth-century attitudes toward sexuality and its oppressive influence on many generations of women.[18] *Lost Girls* spotlights a destruction of (local) personal and collective liberties by the global politics of fascism.[19]

The intertwining of the global and the local and the interlacing of fact and fiction also lie at the core of Bryan Talbot's *Alice in Sunderland.* The graphic novel is a narrative and graphic compendium that links the local past of Sunderland with the mythical fabric that surrounds Lewis Carroll and *Alice in Wonderland.* In a double framing (a theater performance within a dream about a theater performance), the book foregrounds the theatricality of history and its intrinsic entwining with fiction. As Mária Kiššová aptly argues, it creates a complex "mytho-geo-graphical landscape," in which the stories surrounding the area are entangled with the history of the Empire Theatre, as, simultaneously, the micro-past of Sunderland becomes representative of Britain's history.[20] In her view, this hypertext questions the alleged ontological certainties in a manner characteristic of postmodernism.[21] It highlights the role of chance both in history and in historiographic projects, thus undermining the authority of grand narratives.

While there is no denying Bivona's contention that the activities of "repetition" and "interpretation," at least in Carroll's original Wonderland, are marred by imperialist impulses, contemporary English-language graphic novels question this imperialism as they indulge in iterations and interpretations that see the possibility of (political and generic) liberation in repetition(s) with a difference. Repetition with a difference is intrinsic to capitalism and to the art of storytelling, both of which underlie the construction of contemporary subjectivities. In fact, as Julie Sanders contends, this type of reiteration with variation is "less about echoes, repetitions, or re-phrasings . . . than about the identification of shared codes and possibilities."[22] In other words, the practice of adaptation itself may be helpful in a critical rethinking of the connection between the hegemonic and subversive discourses and representations. Alice's afterlife as a symbol also allows for a rethinking of the "semiotic imperialist" impulse that Bivona sees in Carroll's protagonist. If Carroll's *Alice* is both a "cipher" for an insatiable desire for stories and a "culture-text" that "embodies the changing realities of the times as it is recreated by each generation to articulate its cultural identity," as Paul Davis argues,[23] it certainly comments on its own spreadability and impact. The English and American adaptations of Alice explore the variation and difference that accompany the reproductions of her figure, thereby spotlighting the problems concomitant with the processes of individual and collective identity formations. Addressing these issues in an intertextual and intermedial matrix, the adaptations collapse fact and fiction, thereby highlighting the constructed and palimpsestuous nature of identities that are as much affected by global trends as they are rooted in local geographies.

Yet what happens when the "cipher" Alice and "culture-text" *Alice in Wonderland* change their cultural anchoring? In her topical *Theory of Adaptation,* Linda Hutcheon addresses the question of the context in the production and reception of adaptations. She considers "nations," "media," and "time" as highly relevant aspects in shaping the adaptation process.[24] Attention to the processes of transculturation has been foundational to translation studies. Contemporary efforts to bring these two disciplines together show that the traditional novel-to-film debate that has long animated adaptation studies has been expanding to include issues that go beyond the questions of transmedial transfer and include "intercultural encounter and accommodation."[25] As Hutcheon rightly notes, "indigenization" is irrevocably linked with the trappings of power but also with questions of agency.[26] Following Hutcheon's insights, in the pages that follow I consider these questions about the text's particular localizations and the cultural legacies these invoke: What are the quests of the Polish Alicja and the German/Swiss Alice? Do those Alices address a joint European heritage, or do they question it?

Alicja's Struggles: Rape, Violence, and Forgetting

Like its American counterparts, Jerzy Szyłak's underworld in *Alicja* (Mateusz Skutnik, 2006) and its sequel, *Alicja po Drugiej Stronie Lustra* (Jarosław Gach, 2008), are full of sexual and political violence. The two graphic novels authored by the literature and media scholar Szyłak and illustrated by two different artists take the reader to the subterranean world in a postapocalyptic future of the year 3241. In the futuristic Armpolis overground, police academy student Alice patrols the city in a zeppelin. During one of her missions, she falls down a hole into a death camp for mutants and deviants, and there she is continuously under threat of being sexually violated by the Hatter, his tea party companions, and innumerable mutants or their wardens (see fig. 2.1).

Summoned by the Red Queen, Alice witnesses the political and militant betrayal of the monarch and a slaughter of the Queen's followers. The cathedral in which the court has found refuge turns into a bloody battlefield where the Queen and her supporters are annihilated with the use of machine guns and tanks. Alice flees the battle only to be rescued from sexual assault by Ches, a somewhat double-faced incarnation of the Cheshire Cat. As it transpires in the sequel, *Alicja po Drugiej Stronie Lustra,* Ches and the Caterpillar were the ones who betrayed the Red Queen, and who now take care of her twin sister, the White Queen. The White Queen has been sentenced

FIG. 2.1   Alice in the threatening wonderland. Jerzy Szyłak and Mateusz Skutnik, *Alicja* (Warsaw: Timof i cisi wspólnicy, 2006), 15. Reproduced with permission.

to hibernation out of fear of her unparalleled psychic and physical powers and as a punishment for her lack of cooperation. The Queen, who even in this state has not lost her unmatched abilities, discloses to Alice her messianic function: in the Queen's oreinic visions, Alice liberates the occupied citizens of the underworld.

In the characteristic intertextuality and intermediality of the genre, the novel combines narratives of global appeal with culture-specific references to the Polish national past and its legacies. Apart from its references to European literary classics (such as Dante's *Divine Comedy,* Jonathan Swift's *Gulliver's Travels,* Shakespeare's *Hamlet,* J.R.R. Tolkien's *The Lord of the Rings*), children's literature (A.A. Milne's *Winnie-the-Pooh*), and television (Zdeněk Miler's *Krtek*), popular culture (*The Matrix Trilogy*), and dystopian fantasies (Aldous Huxley's *Brave New World*), it also references iconic visual and narrative elements of popular graphic novels (such as Andrevon/Pichard's 1979 dystopian vision of the technological tyranny in *Ceux-là*). In the narrative of *Alicja* and *Alicja po Drugiej Stronie Lustra,* these and other literary and media referents function primarily as cyphers and mnemonic triggers in Szyłak's poetics. They offer ways of approaching the Polish national past that is here understood in terms of memory. Recent neo-Victorian criticism, such as Ho's, proposes to view memory as a productive approach to the postmodern preoccupation with historical grand narratives and especially with the experience of postcolonialism.[27] Whereas Poland's tempestuous political past was marked by numerous instances of occupation, partition, and temporal colonization, it cannot be regarded as a colonized space in the traditional sense of the term. Nor can it be categorized as a primarily marginal space that speaks to the center through a reinvention of its Victorian past. Nonetheless, regarding the graphic novel from the perspective offered by Ho—that is, with reference both to the tensions addressed by neo-Victorianism and to postcolonialism—helps to foreground the ways in which *Alice in Wonderland,* as an instance of Western canonical literature, functions as a scaffold for the rethinking of the Polish past and its significance for the future of that nation.

References to Polish national history populate the various spatial levels of *Alicja* and *Alicja po Drugiej Stronie Lustra,* be it the postapocalyptic surface, the dystopian subterranean spaces, or the high echelons of the skies introduced at the end of the second graphic novel. Yet the allusions to the Polish past and cultural legacies take center stage in the wonderland. Although Alice's supervisor looks somewhat like the last Communist leader and the head of state from 1985 to 1990, Wojciech Jaruzelski, and the futuristic urban spaces of Armpolis include relics from the Polish architectural landscape, it is indeed in the subterranean world that the echoes of Polish past reverberate with the most poignancy. Most prominently, the visual idiom and narrative

FIG. 2.2   The camp for mutants and deviants in the subterranean world. Jerzy Szyłak and Mateusz Skutnik, *Alicja* (Warsaw: Timof i cisi wspólnicy, 2006), 24. Reproduced with permission.

development evoke the specter of the Holocaust. The watchtower and the fence that encircles the death camp for mutants and deviants bring the uncanny echoes of the visual legacy of the Second World War (see fig. 2.2). The cathedral in which the Red Queen resides with her followers, while remotely referencing the architecture of Stanisław Kostka Church in Warsaw, certainly spotlights the uneasy marriage of politics and religion that has been part and parcel of Polish history and which culminated in the persecution of Catholics by the Security Service (SB) of the Ministry of Internal Affairs in the People's Republic of Poland (1952–89). The uprising planned by the Red Queen suggests the developments in the final decades of the socialist Poland, associated with the anti-Communist movements such as that inspired by the Polish trade union federation Solidarity. The confessions of Ches and Caterpillar, in turn, resonate with echoes from the 1980s: both allegedly betray the Queen in exchange for the promise of central heating—an assertion that sounds plausible within the sociocultural mythology of the era.[28]

The graphic novel also alludes to the myths that have informed the process of Polish identity formation for centuries. Swedish Protestant invasions in the seventeenth century laid the foundation for the growing power of the church in the (self-)definition of the Polish nation. In the wake of the attacks, and with the privileged classes gaining in political power, images of Poland as a defender of Western values against the so-called heathen cultures of the Turks and Tatars became popular. The late eighteenth century brought numerous partitions, in the course of which Poland was gradually effaced from the geopolitical map of Europe. Such developments have been influential in establishing an ethos of martyrdom that has informed Polish self-fashioning for centuries.[29]

For those aware of these sociopolitical developments, Szyłak's novel takes up the issue of Polish foundation myths and their political effects as it also addresses the troubled relationship that the country has with its past. In its intertextual reference to Shakespeare's *Hamlet,* for example, the novel points to the uneasy situation of the Polish nation, which has been called "God's Playground."[30] Hamlet's idealism, but also his inability to make a decision, recalls the ways in which the Polish nation has been regarded by its own citizens for centuries. In the graphic novel, the theater performance that the Red Queen stages for the entertainment of her followers becomes an excruciating parody of this self-fashioning. As Hamlet recites his most famous soliloquy, Ophelia is being raped offstage (see fig. 2.3). Engaged in

FIG. 2.3   The performance of Shakespeare's *Hamlet* and Ophelia's rape. "'To die: to sleep; / No more; and by a sleep to say we end / The heart-ache.' 'The heart-ache?'" Jerzy Szyłak and Mateusz Skutnik, *Alicja* (Warsaw: Timof i cisi wspólnicy, 2006), 43. Reproduced with permission.

his monologue, Hamlet calmly observes the graphic scenes without making any attempts to help her. This sequence stands metonymically for the striking incapability of the Polish nation to take action and highlights the inadequacy of Shakespeare's play as a cultural referent that has served as a foundation for collective, national mythologies.

The same scene, however, also alludes to the national myth of Poland as the "Christ of the nations."[31] In contrast to Hamlet's apparent indifference to Ophelia's fate, Alicja does not hesitate to help others. She is capable of rescuing and willing to intervene on behalf of the Cheshire Cat, who has been imprisoned by the Red Queen. Her belated realization that she has been acting upon a misapprehension of Ches's character provides another link to Polish history and its uneasy positioning between the two great powers Germany and Russia. The graphic novel evinces the complexities of political decisions that the country has been making on the basis of its geographical and cultural alliances. In parallel, the rebirth of Alicja as the new heroine—the new Messiah—reinforces the persistent belief in ultimate liberation that has accompanied Polish attempts at self-definition. Importantly, this myth is retold through the lens of *The Matrix Trilogy*. The White Queen, like Morpheus, believes in Alicja's uniqueness and in her ability to make history. Clearly, in contrast to *Matrix,* both the seer and the hero are women. As much as she resembles the teenage Alice of the American *Return to Wonderland,* Alicja, like *Matrix*'s messianic Neo, carries a much heavier burden on her shoulders. Her struggle is not limited to overcoming the personal dangers of violence and sexual predation that saturate Gregory's wonderland; it extends to freeing the oppressed. Her agenda is sociopolitical in character and evokes the persistent belief in Polish martyrdom that has accompanied the nation irrespective of the current political system and the constellation of European and international powers. The analeptic and proleptic narrative modes, supported by the distinct visual styles in which Alicja's adventures are recounted, also suggest the circularity of history and deny the possibility of an ultimate resolution.

In this wonderland, Alicja's quest changes from personal to political as she abandons the thought of returning to Armpolis and instead decides to liberate the oppressed of the underworld. The wonderland itself becomes a bloody and violent restaging of the nation's history as it reiterates the uneasy interdependence of state and religion that has been integral to Polish national identity. The relegation of these problems to the subterranean world is indicative of the wish to bury the past and prevent it from resurfacing. At the same time, however, the graphic novel critiques this attitude. The spatial layering of the comic world brings with itself the danger of collapse as the deviants and the mutants threaten to break out and invade the futuristic spaces of Armpolis. *Alicja* and *Alicja po Drugiej Stronie Lustra* offer another appeal to learn from the past and simultaneously indicate that the struggle has not yet ended. They warn that burying our national past makes us forget the mistakes we might learn from. Alicja's blunders—especially her inability to recognize the true nature of Ches and the Caterpillar—can be read as proof of this liability that is instilled in the new generations of people who have lost their national consciousness as they indulge in the privileges of the globalized Armpolis. On a more general level, this is a narrative about the future of the nation, for whom its own past is as (sur)real as Alice's subterranean travel.

Whatever the novels' interpretations, clearly it is not Alicja who colonizes the subterranean world. Rather, the reverse is true: as a grotesque incarnation of the national past, Szyłak's wonderland colonizes Alicja's imagination and influences her actions. While she may perceive the traumas of the past from the perspective given to her through the global scripts diffused by such media events as *The Matrix Trilogy,* she cannot free herself from the shackles of those traumas. Not even in the futuristic postapocalyptic (surrealist) underworld can Poland's turbulent past be forgotten. If Alice is a cipher for the desire for more stories, then the Polish Alicja certainly evokes a yearning for more of the same story, even as this story may prove destructive to the process of collective identity formation.

Dada in Sussex: In Search of (Non)Sense and Imagination

The desire for stories and the related quest for knowledge is, likewise, the theme of *Alice in Sussex.* In the opening of Mahler's graphic narrative, an iconic, although blue rather than white, Rabbit appears in front of a no-less-iconic Alice, who is engaged in reading H. C. Artmann's 1969 *Frankenstein in Sussex,*[32] and promises to show her the first illustrated edition of the book, which he stores in the underground house (see fig. 2.4). Yet as they arrive at the Rabbit's house, the book appears to be missing, and Alice and the Rabbit embark on a

FIG. 2.4   "'What are we reading here?' 'Frankenstein in Sussex.' 'Oh dear, oh dear.'" Nicolas Mahler, *Alice in Sussex* (Berlin: Suhrkamp Verlag, 2013), 14. Reproduced with permission.

quest to find it. During their subterranean travel, they meet not only the creatures from Carroll's wonderland, including the Mock Turtle and the Caterpillar, but also Frankenstein's Creature from Artmann's book that Alice was reading. The Creature forces Alice to work for him. She is, however, soon liberated from the servitude by Frau Holle, a beautiful incarnation of the mythical deity that the Brothers Grimm refashioned in "Mother Hulda."[33] After watching the Creature and its treatment of Alice on television together with Mary Wollstonecraft Shelley, Frau Holle rescues the girl in a U-boat. Alice awakens as their expedition draws to an end only to recount her adventures to her sister, who in turn closes her eyes in pursuit of this magical world.

Alice in Sussex is fashioned on a complex referential frame as it freely redraws Carroll's narrative through Artmann's *Frankenstein in Sussex,* which merges the adventures of Shelley's Frankenstein's Creature and Carroll's Alice. Mahler's narrative—initially published in the German *FAZ* (*Frankfurt General Newspaper*) as a comic strip in black and white in installments and republished as a single volume in color—graphically and narratively adapts Artmann's iconotext. While the story's narrative structure remains largely unchanged, Mahler's iconotext has a distinctive visual style that shows no resemblance to the illustrations in *Frankenstein in Sussex*. Artmann's novel—first published together with *Fleiß und Indistrie* by Suhrkamp (1969) and re-published later with illustrations by Hans Arnold—has been regarded as a critique of moralistic-realistic narratives of the 1960s and a meta-commentary on the role of aesthetics in literary texts.[34] Because both Artmann's and Carroll's hypotexts and Mahler's adaptation evince a high degree of intertextuality and intermediality, we can think about them in terms of rhizomatic centers that activate many other narratives and visual referents. At first glance, however, Mahler's work appears as a polished upper layer of a palimpsest that superimposes a new aesthetic on the preexistent texts. His *ligne-claire* technique based on a three-color palette (black, white, and blue) seemingly erases the sexual subtext of Carroll's and Artmann's texts so that Mahler's wonderland appears to be a much less threatening place even as it hosts often-aggressive characters. In Artmann's novel, sexual allusions find a graphic realization in Arnold's explicit drawings, in one of which, for example, a diminutive and vulnerable, while clearly sexualized, Alice sits in the lap of the much-larger and threatening Frankenstein, apparently astride his erect phallus as she reaches for the keyboard of a grotesque pipe organ decorated with various demonic, skeletal, and totemic figures. Frankenstein's torso is covered in organic mat-ter—vegetation or fur—through which naked mouse-women climb. The iconotextual minimalism of Mahler's novel, however, annuls these sexual undertones (see fig. 2.5). In Mahler's version, the sinister Frankenstein stands at the edge of the panel, while Alice sits by her-self at the organ; gone are both Frankenstein's organic coverings and the organ's gothic decorations. In its ontological complexity, arising from the combination of mythical, popular-cultural, and real charac-ters, Mahler's wonderland offers a playground for Alice's intellectual development; however, just as this space has shed the air of sexual danger in Artmann's novel, it likewise dispenses with blatant didacti-cism, proposing, rather, an imaginary journey through the intellectual landscape of world philosophy and literature as a counterpoint to the boredom of the everyday. The plethora of intertextual echoes rever-berating between the gutters of the novel is a veritable encomium to imagination at play.

Since he repeatedly fails to find the illustrated version of *Fran-kenstein in Sussex,* the Rabbit instead offers to Alice a welter of texts with conflicting ideologies and introduces her to the pan-national

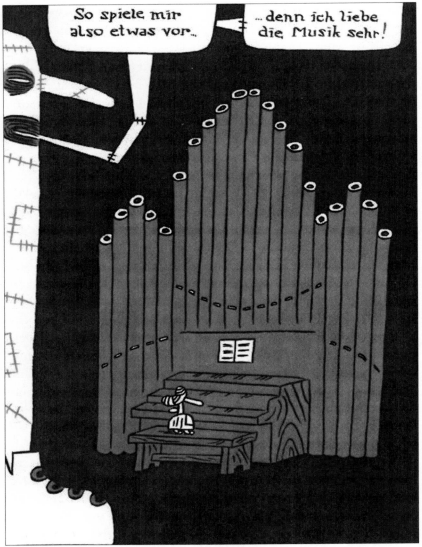

FIG. 2.5   "Why don't you play something for me . . . because I love music a lot!" Nicolas Mahler, *Alice in Sussex* (Berlin: Suhrkamp Verlag, 2013), 109. Reproduced with permission.

landscape of world intellectual legacy. Unlike the Polish Alicja, this German-speaking Alice is given a choice of readings but is never forced to select any particular one of them. The Rabbit first recommends the "wonderfully depressing" *The Trouble with Being Born* (*Vom*

Nachteil Geboren zu Sein, 1973) by Romanian philosopher and essayist
Emil M. Cioran.[35] Drenched in pessimism, nihilism, and skepticism,
the book addresses alienation, the illusory nature of reality, the tyranny of history, and the understanding of reason in terms of malady.
But Cioran's work also contains a spark of hope that many critics have
recognized in his urge to write despite his pessimism.[36] The German
translation of Prentice Mulfor's collection of essays, *Your Forces and
How to Use Them (Der Unfug des Lebens und Der Unfug des Sterbens),*
which the Rabbit introduces next, offers a counter-philosophy of
faith in the beneficial effects of thinking proposed by the American
New Thought movement.[37] The trust in the divinity of selfhood, in
the healing properties of reason, and in the multilayered, multisensorial
character of reality is an acute contrast to Cioran's teachings. Like them,
however, these precepts belong to the intellectual reservoir from which
a reader might choose in order to cultivate his/her imagination.

In addition to the philosophical canon, which also includes Friedrich Nietzsche and Gottfried Wilhelm Leibniz, Alice is introduced
to citations from literary works that include Herman Melville's *Moby-
Dick* (1851), Leo Tolstoy's *The Death of Ivan Ilyich* (1886), and Voltaire's
Candide (1759), along with publications little known in, let alone beyond, the German-speaking world, such as Gaby Schönthan's *Angenehme Müdigkeit* (1996) and Rudolf Schürzer's *Schwankende Gestalten*
(1926).[38] Whereas Tolstoy's novella addresses an array of sociopolitical
themes that include "the consequences of living without meaning,
that is, without a true and abiding connection to one's life"[39] and
Candide fails to offer a philosophical program other than a pragmatic
attitude to life, Schönthan's chick lit meanders through the life of a
theater actress and her love relationships. In a very unobtrusive way,
this assortment of literary and philosophical legacies can be regarded
as a lifestyle guide that lacks the determinism of recent publications
promoting the ecologies of self-cleansing (dietary and spiritual) at
the price of ignoring one's intellectual needs. Simultaneously, *Alice
in Sussex* praises cosmopolitanism and the concomitant respect for
cultural diversity. While the Polish graphic novels highlight the torpor
and stagnation resulting from the appropriation of world literature
for the perpetuation of national myths, Mahler's book explores the
attractions of cosmopolitanism as a vibrant and respectful matrix of
intercultural connectedness.

The array of philosophies collected in Mahler's wonderland provides a rich and productive intellectual landscape that hails imagination and philosophical travel as counterpoints to reality. This encomium to fantasy is further supported by the Mock Turtle, who extols the advantages of his "first-class" education, which goes far beyond Alice's study of French and music and encompasses two hours of "Unreliable Narration," four hours of "Performativity of Illness and Gender," eight hours of "Literalization of Childhood and Young-Adulthood in a Transcultural Context," sixteen hours of "Empirical Data Collection and Analysis," and, among others, sixty-four hours of "Television Aesthetics."[40] Although Mahler's Alice responds to this curricular litany with a skepticism not unlike that which Carroll's Alice maintains throughout her adventures ("I have never heard anything nearly as absurd"[41]), this accumulation of classes, which in fact were part of a 2012/13 winter term curriculum at the University of Vienna,[42] can be interpreted both as a surreptitious praise of imagination and as a critique of contemporary humanities. Carrollian puns "Reeling and Writhing," "Ambition, Distraction, Uglification, and Derision" that mock the school subjects of Victorian times have been here replaced with topics commonly covered by contemporary humanities courses.[43] Such topics—allow me to speculate—which would have been dismissed by any Victorian academic as absurdities, have become the touchstones of twenty-first-century humanist scholarship (even as they continue to perplex the proponents of other academic disciplines and the adherents of disciplinary specificity).

In Mahler's novel, the subterranean home is an oasis of imagination grounded in diverse intellectual and literary legacies. Its inhabitants not only combine an array of philosophical attitudes from diverse nationalities and traditions but also address the question of storytelling and literary production. The Cheshire Cat accuses Mouse Ismael of a lack of command over the art of poetry as he urges the namesake of Melville's character to "make it short."[44] The Rabbit, as he flees the Red Queen's trial, also reflects on the possibility of being decapitated for plagiarism: "An imprudent quotation makes one a head shorter."[45]

These references to the intricacies of narration and literary production also echo the hypotext of Artmann's *Frankenstein in Sussex*. Published in the late 1960s, the text was initially unfavorably received and was criticized for its montage-like character that allegedly contained no substance.[46] In his recent reinterpretation of the work's intertextuality, Marc-Oliver Schuster, however, argues that this negative response to Artmann's novel was due to the critical climate of the time, in which the playful lightness of the book and its parodic style, devoid of any ideological criticism, were seen as lacking any "pragmatic ethos" and thus clearly at odds with "literature proper."[47] Artmann's intertextual game in *Frankenstein,* argues Schuster, was a "defense of imaginative help-for-self-help" and "a poetic reaction against the politicization of German literature and literary criticism at the end of the 1960s."[48] Paradoxically, then, *Frankenstein in Sussex* praises the "liberal aesthetics of autonomy" in its continuous reference to other texts.[49]

In its minimalist style and narrative flow, and in its emphasis on pithiness, Mahler's adaptation continues this game by accumulating a plethora of meanings through constant links to the Western canon, local literary output, and the state of contemporary humanities. More than a playful game of associations, the comic is a praise of imagination, whose source it sees in the interaction of global and local intellectual traditions, which, variously combined, can provide a valuable perspective from which to interpret the everyday. The highly iconic character of Mahler's style invites readers to identify with Alice and to search among literary and cultural legacies for the frames of self-reference and for the stories through which to narrate our pasts and perceive our futures.

Relocating Alice

Alice's cipher-like existence fosters a never-ending production of stories. Whereas the Polish *Alicja* uses Carroll's text as a platform for a trauma-laden retelling of national myths, Mahler's *Alice* is a praise of creativity and imagination in a cosmopolitan intellectual wonderland. Both are chambers of echoes. The difference between them lies in the focus on what is being retold and on the form of this account. With a certain tragic vehemence and fatalism, Szyłak's books return to the concept of Poland as a Messiah of the Nations and use the framework of Carroll's *Alice* books to highlight the crucial role of this myth to the fashioning of national identities. As the Polish national past is evoked in the subterranean landscapes of Armpolis, the myth resurfaces yet again and threatens to devour any narrative that is incompatible with the familiar story of sacrifice and resurrection. Alice's text is here not a colonizing presence but rather another vehicle (mis)used to proliferate the same old stories, which threaten to result in intellectual stagnation.

In contrast, the minimalist, ordered style of Mahler's *Alice* offers a playful interpretation of the chaos of stories and literary echoes that dominate, Dada-like, the world of the subterranean house. Their resonances offer an excess that is at the same time a praise of creativity and imagination. As Alice meanders among the canonical and less canonical works, she enlivens the playfulness and imaginary potency of Carroll's nonsensical world. In fact, the subterranean house becomes here a type of a library or an imaginary archive. In times when library visits have been increasingly replaced by online access, this fanciful meandering reminds the reader of the (physical and intellectual) pleasures of browsing. At a double remove from Carroll's text, *Alice in Sussex* is an archive of stories for the twenty-first century, which highlights the palimpsestuous pleasures of cosmopolitanism and hails its imaginary potential. Relocated within the old-European and the new-European centers, Alice proves the significance of Carroll's text to our imagination.

Notes

1. Eckart Voigts-Virchow, "Anti-Essentialist Versions of Aggregate Alice: A Grin without a Cat," in *Translation and Adaptation in Theatre and Film,* ed. Katja Krebs (New York: Routledge, 2014), 70. Hereafter cited in text.

2. Kali Israel, "Asking Alice: Victorian and other Alices in Contemporary Culture," in *Victorian Afterlife: Postmodern Culture Rewrites the Nineteenth Century,* ed. John Kucich and Dianne F. Sadoff (Minneapolis: University of Minnesota Press, 2006), 258.

3. Kamilla Elliott, "Tie-Intertextuality, or, Intertextuality as Incorporation in the Tie-in Merchandise to Disney's *Alice in Wonderland* (2010)," *Adaptation* 7, no. 2 (2014): 208.

4. Elizabeth Ho, *Neo-Victorianism and the Memory of Empire* (New York: Continuum, 2012).

5. Mark Llewellyn and Ann Heilmann, "The Victorians Now: Global Reflections on Neo-Victorianism." *Critical Quarterly* 55, no. 1 (2013): 26.

6. Ibid., 37, 29, 30.

7. Antonija Primorac, "Other Neo-Victorians: Neo-Victorianism, Translation and Global Literature," in "Neo-Victorianism and Globalisation: Transnational Dissemination of Nineteenth-Century Cultural Texts," edited by Antonija Primorac and Monika Pietrzak-Franger, special issue *Neo-Victorian Studies* 8, no. 1 (2015): 48.

8. Ibid., 48.

9. The issues of globalization and neo-Victorianism are the focus of the special issue of *Neo-Victorian Studies* titled "Neo-Victorianism and Globalisation: Transnational Dissemination of Nineteenth-Century Cultural Texts," edited by Antonija Primorac and Monika Pietrzak-Franger (vol. 8, no. 1 [2015]: 1–206).

10. Nicolas Mahler, *Alice in Sussex* (Berlin: Suhrkamp Verlag, 2013); Jerzy Szyłak and Mateusz Skutnik *Alicja* (Warsaw: Timof i cisi wspólnicy, 2006); Jerzy Szyłak and Jarosław Gach, *Alicja po Drugiej Stronie Lustra* (Warsaw: Timof i cisi wspólnicy, 2008). Hereafter these works are cited in the text.

11. Alan Moore and Melinda Gebbie, *Lost Girls* (Atlanta, GA: Top Shelf Productions, 2006); Bryan Talbot, *Alice in Sunderland: An Entertainment* (Milwaukie, OR: Dark Horse Comics, 2007); Raven Gregory, Daniel Leister, and Nei Ruffino, *Return to Wonderland* (Fort Washington, PA: Zenescope Entertainment, 2009–11).

12. Daniel Bivona, "Alice the Child-Imperialist and the Games of Wonderland," *Nineteenth-Century Literature* 41, no. 2 (1986), 160. Hereafter cited in text.

13. Catherine Siemann, "'But I'm Grown Up Now': *Alice* in the Twenty-First Century," *Neo-Victorian Studies* 5, no. 2 (2012): 175–201. Hereafter cited in text.

14. Jason B. Jones, "Betrayed by Time: Steampunk & the Neo-Victorian in Alan Moore's *Lost Girls* and *The League of Extraordinary Gentlemen,*" *Neo-Victorian Studies* 3, no. 1 (2010): 112.

15. Annalisa Di Liddo, *Alan Moore: Comics as Performance, Fiction as Scalpel* (Jackson: University of Mississippi Press, 2009), 102, 155.

16. Ibid., 152.

17. Ibid., 156, 161. The concept of "moral pornography" is discussed at length in Angela Carter, *The Sadeian Woman and the Ideology of Pornography* (New York: Pantheon Books, 1978).

18. Andrés Romero-Jórdan, "A Hammer to Shape Reality: Alan Moore's Graphic Novels and the Avant-gardes," *Studies in Comics* 2, no. 1 (2011): 47.

19. Ibid., 48.

20. Mária Kiššová, "The Twenty-First Century Wonderland and What a Reader Finds There: Mytho-Geo-Graphical Landscape of Brian [sic] Talbot's *Alice in Sunderland,*" *Çankaya University Journal of Humanities and Social Sciences* 9, no. 1 (May 2012): 66.

21. Ibid., 70, 61.

22. Julie Sanders, *Adaptation and Appropriation* (London: Routledge, 2006), 154.

23. Paul Davis, *The Lives and Times of Ebenezer Scrooge* (New Haven, CT: Yale University Press, 1990), 15.

24. Linda Hutcheon, *A Theory of Adaptation*, 2nd ed., with contributions from Siobhan O'Flynn (London: Routledge, 2013), 144.

25. On this see, e.g., Katja Krebs, ed., *Translation and Adaptation in Theatre and Film* (New York: Routledge, 2014).

26. Hutcheon, *Theory of Adaptation*, 150.

27. Ho, *Neo-Victorianism*, 15. For more discussion of the neo-Victorian emphasis on memory, see Kate Mitchell, *History and Cultural Memory in Neo-Victorian Fiction: Victorian Afterimages* (Basingstoke, UK: Palgrave Macmillan, 2010); Mitchell views neo-Victorian fictions as "memory texts" that "communicate memory—that which is already known through a variety of media about the Victorian era, for example—and offer themselves as memory" (32).

28. Szyłak, *Alicja po Drugiej Stronie Lustra*, 16. Hereafter cited in text. For this and all remaining quotations from Polish- and German-language works, I have provided English translations in the text with the original language in the notes. All translations are my own.

29. On Polish nationalist mythology, see Genviève Zubrzycki, "Polish Mythology and the Traps of Messianic Martyrology," in *National Myths: Constructed Pasts, Contested Presents*, ed. Gérard Buchard (New York: Routledge, 2013), 110–32.

30. Norman Davies, *God's Playground: A History of Poland* (New York: Columbia University Press, 1982).

31. Zubrzycki, "Polish Mythology," 110–32.

32. H. C. Artmann, *Frankenstein in Sussex*, illus. Hans Arnold (Munich: Lenz, 1974).

33. Jacob and Wilhelm Grimm, "Mother Hulda," in *Household Stories from the Brothers Grimm Translated from the German by Lucy Crane* (London: Macmillan, 1882), 128–31.

34. Marc-Oliver Schuster, "Einleitung," in *Aufbau wozu: Neues zu H. C. Artmann*, ed. Marc-Oliver Schuster (Würzburg: Königshausen und Neumann, 2010), 13.

35. "*Wunderbar* deprimierend!" (Mahler, *Alice in Sussex*, 31, 48). E. M. Cioran, *Vom Nachteil Geboren zu Sein* (Frankfurt: Suhrkamp, 1979).

36. Harriet Köhler, "Das Buch meines Lebens: Harriet Köhler über E. M. Ciorans 'Vom Nachteil, geboren zu sein,'" *Der Spiegel* 10 (3 March 2008), www.spiegel.de/spiegel/print/d-56047457.html.

37. Mahler, *Alice in Sussex*, 52. Prentice Mulford, *Your Forces and How to Use Them* (New York: F. J. Needham, 1888–92); Mulford, *Der*

Unfug des Lebens und Der Unfug des Sterbens (Stuttgart: Stuttgarter Hausbücherei, 1955).

38. Mahler, *Alice in Sussex*, 52, 61–62, 71, 76, 79, 84, 85, 87, 93, 104, 128. Herman Melville, *Moby-Dick; or, The Whale* (New York: Penguin Books, 2013); Leo Tolstoy, *The Death of Ivan Ilyich* (New York: Bantam Books, 1985); Voltaire [François-Marie Arouet], *Candide* (New York: Bantam Books, 1959); Gaby Schönthan, *Angenehme Müdigkeit* (Hamburg: Marion von Schröder, 1965), Rudolf Schürzer, *Schwankende Gestalten* (Vienna: Burgverlag, 1926).

39. Marc Freeman, "Death, Narrative Integrity, and the Radical Challenge of Self-Understanding: A Reading of Tolstoy's 'Death of Ivan Ilyich,'" *Aging and Society* 17, no. 4 (2000): 373–98.

40. "Also, wir hatten 2 Stunden Unzuverlässiges Erzählen . . . 4 Stunden Performativität von Krankheit unf Geschlecht . . . 8 Stunden Literarisierung von Kindheit und Jugend im transkulturellen Kontext . . . 16 Stunden empirische Datenerhebung und–auswertung . . . [. . .] 64 Stunden Fernsehästhetik . . ." (Mahler, *Alice in Sussex,* 83).

41. "So etwas Wirres hab ich mein Lebtag noch nicht gehört" (ibid., 83).

42. "Bild 4 («Geist, Gehirn und Gesellschaft») Vorlesungsverzeichnis der Universität Wien, Wintersemester 2012/2013" (ibid., 140).

43. Lewis Carroll, *Alice's Adventures in Wonderland* (London: Macmillan, 1866), 143.

44. "Blicke der Wahrheit ins Gesicht, Maus: Die Kunst der Verdichtung Beherrscht Du nicht." "Fasse Dich kurz!" (ibid., 64, 65).

45. "*Ein* unüberlegtes Zitat, und schon ist man einen Kopf kürzer!" (ibid., 78).

46. See Jörg Drews, "Die neuesten Kunststücke des H. C. Artmann," in *Über H. C. Artmann,* ed. Gerald Bisinger (Frankfurt: Suhrkamp, 1972), 83–86.

47. Marc-Oliver Schuster, "'bei allem, was weiß ist': Intertextuelle Komplexität und implizite Ästhetik in H. C. Artmanns *Frankenstein in Sussex,*" in *Aufbau wozu. Neues zu H. C. Artmann,* ed. Marc-Oliver Schuster (Würzburg: Königshausen und Neumann, 2010), 206.

48. "Von hier aus liest sich *FiS* wegen des ironischen Einsatzes kämpferischen Rettungshandelns und wegen des Plädoyers für imaginative Hilfe-zur-Selbsthilfe zusätzlich als poetische Reaktion gegen die Politiesierung der bundesdeutschen Literatur und Kritik gegen Ende der 1960er" (ibid., 217).

49. Schuster, "Einleitung," 13.

II.

Graphic Epistemologies

THREE

Picturing the "Cosmic Egg"

The Divine Economy of a Hollow Earth

PETER W. SINNEMA

> By treating the earth as hollow, we have the solution of
> all the great mysteries . . . the supernatural giving way to
> the natural, as it always does with understanding, and relief
> comes to mind and body.
>
> —William Reed, *The Phantom of the Poles* (1906)

In this chapter I discuss verbal and visual strategies employed to represent radically alternative, cosmological paradigms. In particular, the cartoon-like ways in which arcane theories about the earth's inner structure were pictorially rendered provide unique insight into the nature of certain "problems in the anatomy of scientific belief," to borrow Thomas Kuhn's phrasing—problems that give rise to the central question motivating my investigations here: "How can a conceptual scheme that one generation admiringly describes as subtle, flexible, and complex become for a later generation merely obscure, ambiguous, and cumbersome?"[1] My specific focus is on once-feasible but ultimately discredited systems that experimented with, challenged, or abandoned altogether the heliocentric foundations of the Copernican universe, remaking the earth so that humankind might inhabit its rightful place—quite literally—*in* it. I explore how the heterodoxy of hollow-earth belief was conceived and championed at the interstice between fanciful imagery and abstruse language (or mere "autoch-thonous nonsense")[2] by examining three moments in the history of hollow-earth thought. I locate the origin of that thought in Enlight-enment England and trace its transatlantic migration to nineteenth-century America, in the process clarifying unconventional hypotheses to make sense of the enigmatic illustrations that accompany them. Pictures attest to the viability of the hollow-earth hypothesis by bringing the hidden into sight. Hollow-earth images play a strategic role in the "cultural history of an idea that was wrong and changed nothing—but which . . . nevertheless had an ongoing appeal."[3]

The first moment occurs with the use of a massive optical in-strument on the shores of the Gulf of Mexico by American eccentric Cyrus Reed Teed (1839–1908) to verify his theory about a "cellu-lar" geocosmos. Provocatively restyling himself "Koresh," Teed argued that the earth's surface was a "macrocosmic and composite shell or rind" enclosing the myriad "solar, lunar, and stellar manifestations" that we take to be celestial bodies.[4] His outlandish theory found its key provocation in a deep-seated apprehension about the possibil-ity of infinite space. A logical consequence of Copernican thought, spatial infinitude had dire implications for a maverick theist such as Teed, who "longed to return the cosmos to the small, tidy, womb-like character he found implied by Holy Scripture."[5] With that contrac-tion, he also hoped to relieve the profound disquiet that accompanied the conception of a limitless and inscrutable universe. "The Koreshan Cosmogony," Teed reassured his disciples, puts the originary "cause within the comprehension of the human mind. It demonstrates the possibility of the attainment of man to his supreme inheritance, the ultimate dominion of the universe, thus restoring him to the acme of exaltation,—the throne of the Eternal, whence he had his ori-gin" (Teed and Morrow, 11–12). Teed's real triumph was not so much a demonstration of the Copernican system's fallaciousness as it was the restoration of modern man to his place among the angels, only slightly below a newly comprehensible God.

Teed's idea was one incubation of a scientific idea originally ar-ticulated in seventeenth-century England, the scene of my second moment. Specifically, the seeds of American hollow-earth thought were sown in the fertile soil of early Enlightenment London. In an attempt to resolve the question of magnetic variation, Edmond Halley

(1656–1742) proposed to the Royal Society in 1691 that the earth's "External Parts . . . may well be reckoned as the Shell, and the Internal as a *Nucleus* or inner Globe included within."[6] Halley acknowledged that his hypothesis must appear both "Extravagant" and "Romantick" (564). But with his model of a multisphered globe, he offered a rational answer to the enduring conundrum of magnetic deviation, in the process giving the world its "first scientific theory of the hollow earth."[7] Grounding his proposal in Newtonian physics and conceiving of his subterranean orbs as livable, Halley attached a monochrome drawing of his brave new world to the printed version of his lecture, representing a radical but evidently long-cherished idea. When he posed for Michael Dahl for his final official portrait at the age of eighty, Halley held in his right hand a reproduction of this same enigmatic diagram, suggesting that the hollow-earth theory remained his "proudest achievement."[8]

Dahl's portrait, wherein the sitter serves as a pretext for the diagram's re-presentation, anticipates the palimpsest-like properties of a picture accompanying the third moment I examine: the 1820 publication of Captain Adam Seaborn's scientific romance, *Symzonia: A Voyage of Discovery,* an important fictional adaptation of hollow-earth thinking. In this, "the first American work of utopian fiction," the pseudonymous Seaborn "availed himself of all the lights and facilities afforded by the sublime theory of an internal world, published by Captain John Cleve [*sic*] Symmes."[9] In fact, aside from a few communiqués and lecture notes of the 1820s, former soldier and Indian trader John Cleves Symmes (1779–1829) never published a full account of his hollow-earth theories. Instead, after disseminating his infamous "Circular" in 1818 pledging his life "in support of this truth"—that "the earth is hollow, and habitable within; containing a number of solid concentrick spheres, one within the other, and that it is open at the poles 12 or 16 degrees"—Symmes devoted his energies to the public lecture circuit, relentlessly promoting his belief in massive polar openings, the much-derided "Symmes's Holes" that would provide access to a well-stocked and capacious inner world.[10] But in recounting a distinctly Symmesian nautical journey to a subterranean land inhabited by a race of pearly-skinned Internals, *Symzonia* has rightly been called a "key link" between Symmes's theories and the many hollow-earth novels that exploded onto the American literary scene in the 1880s and '90s.[11] Like Halley's "Account," Seaborn's adventure narrative was supplemented with a sectional view of the hollow earth, overlaid with "scientific" rubrics and equations. This cryptic picture allowed readers to imagine, however sketchily, the contours of a spectacularly other world: an inner paradise of natural and technological wonders inhabited by a race so "intelligent and refined" that it must remain largely "beyond the conception of external mortals" (Seaborn, 115). The illustration challenged the mundane testimony of readers' eyes with compelling evidence of a terrestrial globe shaped according to alien cosmological assumptions, chief among them the "notion of an 'abundant Providence,' the idea that creation must be as copious as possible because that would logically be part of the Creator's plan."[12]

By inquiring into the representational complications revealed by illustrations of esoteric geophysical theory, I address from a new angle a question posed recently by Kate Flint in her discussion of "the relationship between empirical, quantifiable data, and 'the mind's eye.'"[13] The need to produce visual models of the basic premises of the hollow-earth theory—to inscribe an image of the cosmic egg in the mind's eye—is part of modernity's appropriation of visual culture, its relentless compulsion to make visible the concealed and obscure. "How may a non-specialist audience," Flint asks in her critical survey of the Victorian *culte des images,* "be made to see those forces and operations within nature which remain invisible to the naked eye of observation?"[14] How, in the present context, might pictures be used to vindicate and popularize untestable theories?

⊶◆⊷

Just after 8:00 on the morning of 18 March 1897, a group of amateur geodesists, attended by an investigating committee and corps of staff assistants, gathered on Naples Beach, Florida, to monitor the operations of a large T-shaped, mahogany-and-steel measuring apparatus (see fig. 3.1). The respectably dressed Koreshan Geodesic Survey took its name from the remarkable man who had established the commune of New Jerusalem on the nearby Estero River three years earlier: Cyrus Teed, author of the System of Universology ("science applied to all the concerns of practical life") and sine qua non of renegade cosmological thought (Teed and Morrow, 11). The unwieldy

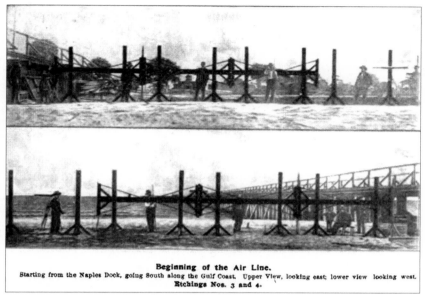

FIG. 3.1   Cyrus Reed Teed and Ulysses Grant Morrow, "Beginning of the Air Line," *The Cellular Cosmogony, or the Earth a Concave Sphere* (Chicago: Guiding Star, 1898), 92.

instrument the Koreshans leveled in the shallows of the Gulf of Mexico had been fabricated by the Pullman Palace Car Company of Illinois on the designs of Teed's collaborator and apologist, Ulysses Grant Morrow (1864–1950), self-described "head of the Expedition" and "director of Hypsometric Operations" (Teed and Morrow, 112). Resting their contraption on underwater pads, the surveyors ensured that its line of sight was fixed precisely 128 inches above the gulf's surface. The "Rectilineator," as Teed and Morrow later recounted in their opus, *The Cellular Cosmogony, or the Earth a Concave Sphere* (1898), was constructed to demonstrate with scientific certainty the great truth Teed had received in his "Illumination" of 1869, when God took the form of a beautiful woman to impart to him the secret of the universe: its organic, cellular "integralism." The trial at Naples Beach was to verify that the earth has the form of a concave sphere—that our globe is an enormous electromagnetic cell, a "great cosmic egg," the *inside* of which serves not only as our human habitation but also as the container of the entire universe (18). Reduced to measurable scale and brought into the field of vision, such an inner universe would secure humanity's rightful place at the center of things.

Happily, the Rectilineator's sight line "hit" the water just over four miles from shore, proving that the earth's surface curves up at a rate of eight inches per mile.[15] Teed and Morrow boasted at length about the experiment's success, triumphing in their disclosure of "evidences of the earth's concavity . . . conclusive and absolute" (77). We live, they declared with new conviction, on the "*inner* surface of a great cell about 8,000 miles in diameter" (130). Emphasizing that their long-held hollow-earth beliefs had been corroborated empirically by the Rectilineator, the authors credited a rigorous application of "optical science" with debunking the "gigantic fallacy and farce of the benighted Copernicus," whose "atheistic" universe was illimitable and hence, distressingly, incomprehensible (12). "The Koreshan Cosmogony," in reassuring contrast, "reduces the universe to proportionate limits, and its cause within the comprehension of the human mind" (7).

The Rectilineator objectified vision to shrink the universe. As a mechanical device independent of the subjects whose perception (and consequent understanding) it enhanced, it generated an apodictic view that corrected the many optical illusions produced by the unaided eye. Whereas unassisted observation, imperfect and distorting, deludes us into believing that we tenant the surface of a convex planet, the air- or recti-line—an ingenious invention "afforded through the application of the principles of accurate geodetic survey"—shows us otherwise: "The earth's form, the determination of which has baffled the skill and vexed the ingenuity of the scientific world, is at last demonstrated to be *cellular,* with its habitable surface concave!" (131, 130). The Rectilineator's successful operation suggested that the cosmos must be apprehended internally, or through the mind's eye, if it was to be properly understood, free from "the illusion of the sense of vision" (41).

Indeed, only a full appreciation of the revolutionary implications of the rectiline would allow the imagination to render with graphic fidelity a true picture of our hollow earth, such as the one adorning the *Cosmogony*'s rather baroque cover (see fig. 3.2). Here, the earth's shell is cracked open like a cartoon egg, partially separated to reveal a yolk (or "stellar center") that houses the "sun and stars" and "also the reflections called the planets and the moon" (13). This innovative schema of a bounded world-universe floating in a limitless ether of nothingness is a replete system, intelligible and ultimately reassuring. It represents a colossal but intellectually graspable extension of

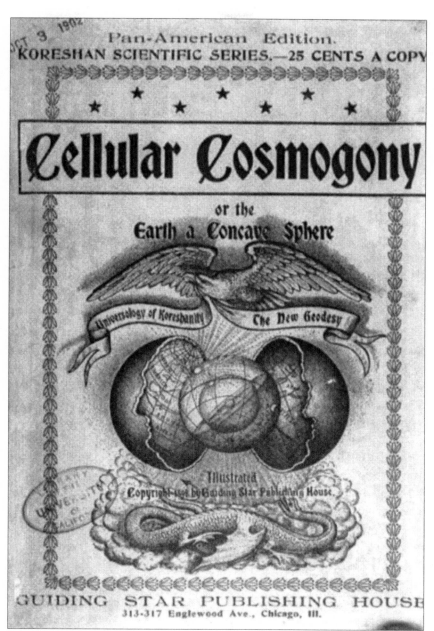

Pan-American Edition.

KORESHAN SCIENTIFIC SERIES.—25 CENTS A COPY

Cellular Cosmogony

or the
Earth a Concave Sphere

Universology of Koreshanity — *The New Geodesy*

Illustrated

Copyright 1898 by Guiding Star Publishing House.

GUIDING STAR PUBLISHING HOUSE
313-317 Englewood Ave., Chicago, Ill.

FIG. 3.2   Cover of Cyrus Reed Teed and Ulysses Grant Morrow, *The Cellular Cosmogony, or the Earth a Concave Sphere* (Chicago: Guiding Star, 1898).

the conservative, inward-looking community of New Jerusalem itself, which enjoyed economic and social independence fostered by such local industries as a bakery, sawmill, and boat-building yard.

Some two centuries before Teed published his curious representation of a cracked earth-egg, Halley had appended his similarly eye-catching diagram to his "Account of the Cause of the Change of the Variation of the Magnetical Needle; With an Hypothesis of the Structure of the Internal Parts of the Earth"—the print version of his 1691 lecture published in the *Philosophical Transactions* the following year (see fig. 3.3).[16] In the "Account," Halley addressed the intractable problem of the slow changes recorded by the compass, a mystery that had significant repercussions for mariners of the Restoration period vexed by their incapacity to measure longitudinal position. Halley's response to the magnetic needle's unpredictability was to propose to his colleagues at the Royal Society that "the whole magnetical system" that constitutes our earth "is by one or perhaps more Motions translated" (567). He challenged his fellow savants to imagine a "moving thing" internal to the earth, in which a set of subsidiary poles are rooted. This "thing" we must "suppose . . . to turn about the Centre of the Globe, having its Centre of Gravity fixt and immoveable in the same common Centre of the Earth" (567). In other words, the earth might profitably be imagined as a globe-within-a-globe, both moving together in the same diurnal rotation but at slightly different velocities with the help of a hydraulic substance separating the spheres. "'Tis plain," Halley summarized, "that the fixt Poles are the Poles of this External Shell or *Cortex* of the *Earth,* and the other two Poles of a Magnetical *Nucleus* included and moveable within the other. . . . In order to explain the change of the Variations, we have [therefore] adventured to make the Earth hollow and to place another Globe within it" (572). But what purpose or use could this "Globe within" have? For what or whom was it designed? "In Halley's day," Duane Griffin observes, "the question of utility was a significant issue that could not be ignored."[17] As the corporeal expression of divine intelligence, the earth testifies in every detail of its structure to the expedience of providential thrift: the Creator would not frame a planetary habitation that wastes space.

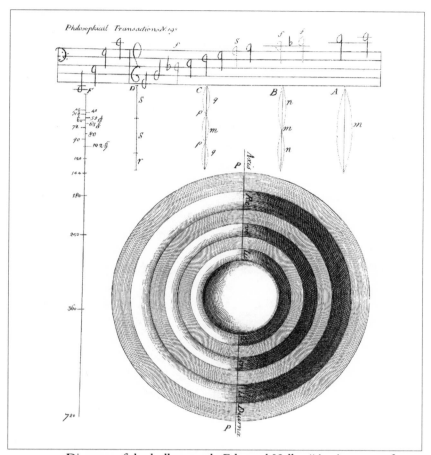

FIG. 3.3   Diagram of the hollow earth. Edmond Halley, "An Account of the Cause of the Change of the Variation of the Magnetical Needle; With an Hypothesis of the Structure of the Internal Parts of the Earth: As It Was Proposed to the Royal Society in One of Their Late Meetings," *Philosophical Transactions* 16 (1692): 579.

In contemplating the numinous instrumentality of inner space, Halley cited a calculation about lunar relative density from Isaac Newton's *Principia Mathematica* (1687)—a world-changing work that saw the light of day only thanks to Halley's various interventions, which included dogged encouragement of its author and personal financing of its printing at the Royal Society's behest:[18] "Another Argument favouring this Hypothesis is drawn from a Proposition of . . . Mr. *Newton*, where he determines the force wherewith the *Moon* moves the *Sea* in producing the *Tides*. . . . Now if the Moon be more solid than the Earth as 9 to 5, why may we not reasonably suppose the Moon, being a small Body and a Secondary Planet, to be solid Earth, Water, and Stone, and this Globe to consist of the same Materials, only four ninths thereof to be Cavity, within and between the internal Spheres" (574–75). Halley's application of the illustrious Newton's computation to his hypothesis about the earth's structure functioned as a powerful endorsement of the earth's cavernous anatomy.[19] The earth's lesser mass, demonstrated convincingly in Newton's discussion of tidal movements, can be explained by its hollow interior.

Halley returns late in the "Account" to the question of utility, an inquiry that leads him to the remarkable proposition that the hollow earth may be capable of supporting life and that its structure may be as complex as that shown in figure 3.3. Such a fantastic suggestion can be entertained if the fluid or ether that separates the inner globe (or, now, globes) from the outer is endowed with a capacity to produce its own vivifying light: "the Medium itself may be always luminous after the manner of our Ignes fatui" (577). Or perhaps an inner sun, a "peculiar luminary," sheds its light at the very core of the earth. Our ignorance on these matters, Halley argues, as on many questions of divine creation, does not preclude the possibility of their existence: "Why . . . should we think it strange that the prodigious Mass of Matter, whereof this Globe does consist, should be capable of some other improvement than barely to serve to support its Surface? Why may not we rather suppose that the exceeding small quantity of solid Matter in respect of the fluid Ether, is so disposed by the Almighty Wisdom as to yield as great a Surface for the use of living Creatures as can consist with the conveniency and security of the whole?" (576). Halley's explanatory hypothesis doubles as an imperial mandate justified by providential economy. He invites his audience to imaginatively colonize the earth's capacious interior, that "great surface" contrived to accommodate a surplus of "living Creatures." This mandate was to be enthusiastically converted by later novelists into the chief modus operandi of hollow-earth explorers. Seaborn, for example, pauses long enough on the "verge" of the subterranean kingdom of Symzonia to marvel at the fact that he is about to "open an intercourse with a new world and with an unknown people; to unfold to the vain mortals of the external world new causes for admiration at the infinite diversity and excellence of the works of an inscrutable Deity" (96).[20]

Halley closes his "Account" with a concise explanation of the illustrated "Scheme" itself,

> wherein the Earth is represented by the outward
> Circle, and the three inward Circles are made nearly
> proportionable to the Magnitudes of the Planets *Venus,*
> *Mars* and *Mercury.* . . . The Concave of each Arch, which
> is shaded differently from the rest, I suppose to be made
> up of Magnetical Matter; and the whole to turn about
> the same common Axis *p. p.* only with this difference,
> that the Outer Sphere still moves somewhat faster than
> the Inner. . . . Thus I have shewed a possibility of a much
> more ample Creation, than has hitherto been imagined. (576)

Halley's diagram "shews" with facility what his figurative language must labor to depict. His picture of a "more ample creation" is an indispensable accessory to the speculative diction of circles, arches, and spheres: it presents a visually coherent solution to the puzzle of magnetic variation, taking its place as a viable contender in the "warfare among explanatory systems [that] had great impact upon approaches to the Earth" in the latter part of the seventeenth century.[21] (The freethinking Halley also probably felt compelled to allude to God's infinite grace in creating a multisphered earth at a moment when his application for the vacant Savilian Chair of Astronomy at Oxford was being strongly contested.[22] His radical amplification of living space is in part an inspired gesture of conciliation.)

Halley never abandoned the hollow-earth idea, nor this particular representation of it. When in 1736 he sat for his legacy portrait at the brush of Michael Dahl, the venerable polymath held in his right hand—the hand typically used for important oratorical gestures—a surprisingly accurate reproduction of the 1692 diagram (see fig. 3.4). Dahl's is one of two Halley portraits in the Royal Society's picture collection that serve as reminders of Halley's many contributions to the institution in its pursuit of "Natural Knowledge": as an elected fellow from 1678 (reelected in 1700) until his appointment as clerk in 1686, in which office he also edited the *Philosophical Transactions* for six years, and as the society's secretary from 1713–21.[23]

FIG. 3.4   Michael Dahl, portrait of Edmond Halley, ca. 1736. Oil on canvas,
126.7 cm × 102 cm. © The Royal Society. Reproduced with permission.

Visitors to the society's gallery whose knowledge of Halley goes
no further than his fame as a predictor of comets will find Dahl's
portrait rather perplexing. On the one hand, "Dr E Halley, Aged 80"
signals the conventions of a branch of luminary portraiture originating in the early sixteenth century that specialized in representing

members of the fraternity of mathematicians and astronomers. Its chief iconographic features, "the representation of the person at half-length in a physical space, and the activity of the hands [typically] at a worktable with instruments of measurement and writing[,] . . . serve a kind of collective commemorative function."[24] Such portraits emphasized dignity of comportment and the analogical function of both background and gesture in expressing the essence of the individual character: the "symbolic iconography of the genre," in which painters portrayed "a self who was conscious of the presence of others and whose character showed in outward appearance, dress and manners . . . the idealised subjectivity of the gentleman."[25] Halley's consciousness "of the presence of others" is registered in a penetrating gaze that addresses the viewer's gaze directly. His still-erect frame, foregrounded against opaque drapes pulled aside to reveal bookshelves laden with substantial tomes, elicits the gravitas of the educated burgher class, whose prosperous members held Dahl in high esteem and whose patronage made him for a time the busiest and richest portraitist in England. His painting adheres with seeming fidelity to portrait convention, demonstrating the artist's invention within the fairly limited terms of portraiture's common practice as a systematic art that elevates and ennobles the subject.

The deeper import of the sitter's attitude, on the other hand, is to draw the viewer's attention to the boldly illuminated feature in the lower half of the canvas. To the uninitiated, the sharply limned, perspectively anomalous black-and-white diagram is a mystery that confutes the portrait's conventionality. Its series of concentric spheres are rendered perfectly round, allowing for an unrestricted anterior scrutiny of such details as the transecting line, the letters along its axis, and the not-quite-legible caption, even while their position on a piece of paper depicted in two-point perspective would suggest that they should be elliptical to accord with the angled plane on which they are inscribed. Dahl flouts the rules of perspective, while Halley tips the paper forward, inviting close study. His reposed left hand points loosely toward the shaded sphere at its center, acting as an additional index of its importance. Halley's attitude underscores the enigma at the heart of the painting. To grasp the diagram's meaning is to grasp what it is that this eminent man of science was intent on advertising for posterity at a ripe old age: his ongoing affection for a hypothesis about the earth's structure that he had first articulated some forty-five years earlier.[26]

＊

Halley's hollow-earth model is, to borrow Flint's language, "an example *par excellence* of imaginative figuration and scientific inquiry operating in inseparable co-operation with one another," a hybrid product of the search for "an adequate vocabulary, an expressive set of visual images through which to convey . . . particular explanations for the operations of the unseen."[27] Halley's "imaginative figuration" inspired other hollow-earth philosophers to embark on a similar quest for appropriate verbal and graphic expression. A line of intellectual descent can be drawn from Halley's diagram to the frontispiece of *Symzonia,* which satirizes imperial ambition by fashioning an alternative inner world structurally and visually analogous to the one proposed in Halley's "Account" (see fig. 3.5).[28]

This subterranean realm, both "a virtual imaginary space" and an "alternate present," represents an alluring antidote to the exhausted civilization Seaborn flees in the novel's opening scene.[29] Under the pretense of an extended sealing expedition, the jaundiced sea captain abandons "the humanity and kindness of the world" to pilot his revolutionary steam vessel the *Explorer* from New York to the southern polar regions, where he navigates "a passage to a new and untried world"—the antithesis of modern America, with "its wealth monopolized, its wonders of curiosity explored, its every thing investigated and understood!" (Seaborn, 13). Symzonia is also, fleetingly, the object of Seaborn's imperialist daydreams. On surveying the shores of the new world from his ship's deck, he fantasizes that he is "about to secure to [his] name a conspicuous and imperishable place on the tablets of history, and a niche of the first order in the temple of Fame"; even the great Columbus's voyage, Seaborn muses, "was but an excursion on a fish pond . . . compared with mine" (96–97). But the *Explorer's* crew is allowed to sojourn only briefly among the advanced Symzonians, and Seaborn's grandiose language is revealed to be a satirical "jape at the genre of writing produced by imperial ventures."[30] Disgusted by the Americans' "gross sensuality, intemperate passions, and beastly habits," the morally and politically superior Internals eject

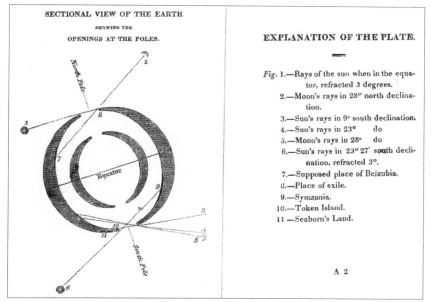

SECTIONAL VIEW OF THE EARTH.
SHOWING THE
OPENINGS AT THE POLES.

EXPLANATION OF THE PLATE.

Fig. 1.—Rays of the sun when in the equator, refracted 3 degrees.
2.—Moon's rays in 28° north declination.
3.—Sun's rays in 9° south declination.
4.—Sun's rays in 23°   do
5.—Moon's rays in 28°   do
6.—Sun's rays in 23° 27′ south declination, refracted 3°.
7.—Supposed place of Belzubia.
8.—Place of exile.
9.—Symzonia.
10.—Token Island.
11 —Seaborn's Land.

A 2

FIG. 3.5   John Cleeves Symmes, "Sectional View of the Earth" (frontispiece), from Captain Adam Seaborn, *Symzonia: A Voyage of Discovery* (New York: J. Seymour, 1820).

them with the stern warning "not to approach the coasts of Symzonia in expectation of being allowed any intercourse or traffic, whilst they remained besotted in vice and iniquity" (Seaborn, 134, 209). After a series of misadventures on his return to America across the South Seas—"troubles, mortifications, and miseries" that include the loss of his Symzonian curiosities and manuscripts—Seaborn arrives again in New York, determined to model his chastened self on "the pious resignation, the humility, the contentment, the peacefulness and happiness of the Symzonians" (242, 243–44). He records his adventures with the hope that the narrative's sales will finance "another visit to Symzonia, and an aerial excursion thence to the inner spheres" (248).

These inner spheres are denoted synecdochically by the interior crescents of figure 3.5. The double-page frontispiece is in turn an emblematic rather than a precise representation of the uneven body of pronouncements that constitute Symmes's theory, which took varying formulations, from five spheres to a Teed-like, single-husked hollow earth.[31] There is, however, no direct evidence of Halley's influence on *Symzonia*. Nor do we know whether the "Capt. Symmes" whose "sublime theory" inspired Seaborn was familiar with Halley's writings.[32] The ideological provenance of *Symzonia*'s "Sectional View of the Earth" in Halley's annotated diagram, however, is obvious. Symmes's devoted follower James McBride made the attribution explicit in his treatise *Symmes's Theory of Concentric Spheres* (1826), the earliest, and most reliable, "methodical arrangement" of his mentor's ideas.[33] McBride praises the "celebrated Dr. Halley" for having "advanced a novel hypothesis" that Symmes brought to its splendid conclusion with his ground-breaking "idea of Polar Openings." These so-called Symmes's Holes allowed for "communication from the outer surface to [the] interior regions" (McBride, 131–32). Their discovery and penetration, McBride argued, would supplant Halley's conjectural postulations with material proof of the inner earth's hollow structure and livability. Whereas Halley postulated an indwelling, sun-like substance as the animating principle for his closed system, Symmes described a dynamic and harmonious interplay between superterranean and subterranean climates. The sun's rays act reciprocally with an inner element—"light, subtile, [and] elastic"—to energize an underworld sure to "abound with animals" (McBride, 37). Symmes's Holes enjoy a structural advantage over Halley's enclosed spheres: confirmation of their existence would literally open up the possibility of reciprocal effect—of physical interaction and communication—between surface and center.

Symzonia's frontispiece must therefore be interpreted through the double lens of the fictional narrative it prefaces and the cosmological theory it illustrates. First, it is in part a readers' guide to the novel's topography, a cartographic supplement to Seaborn's written accounts as he and his crew traverse unfamiliar landscapes. Territories adjoining the verges between inner and outer worlds—those Seaborn discovers and appropriates symbolically through the act of naming (Token Island, Seaborn's Land, and Symzonia itself) and those he learns of but never visits (Belzubia, and the "Place of exile," where morally lapsed Internals are sent so their "gross appetites might be scourged out of them")—are bulleted in the "Explanation," identified as significant features of this imaginary terrain (Seaborn, 177–78). Second, with its clearly demarcated polar openings pierced by invigorating solar and lunar rays, the picture also stands as a prototype for myriad "classic" hollow-earth schemes of the nineteenth and twentieth centuries. These embraced as cosmological doctrine a universe composed of planetary bodies shaped like "hollow concentric spheres . . . more or less open at their poles" (McBride, 28). The "view" is thus also the ur-map to hollow-earth fiction and theory in Symmes's wake, a motley patrimony that nevertheless attained a certain unity through frequent allusion to the concept of divine economy.

This point is demonstrated with cursory reference to an example from each genre. William Bradshaw's imperial fantasy, *The Goddess of Atvatabar* (1892), represents a histrionically violent take on the Symmesian journey. In search of the North Pole, Commander Lexington White mistakenly pilots his steel-plated steamer into "the mouth of an enormous cavern."[34] This Symmes's Hole leads White to the democratic realm of Bilbimtesirol, whose denizens have harnessed the power of "magnicity" to develop telegraphs, phonographs, electric lights, and flying machines. But these technological marvels prove useless against White's superior weaponry. He subjugates the Bulbimtesirolians, leaving behind "piles of dead and wounded bodies" in his ruthless pursuit of the kingdom's throne (282). Only late in the narrative does White point readers to a map of the conquered "Interior World" that fronts *Atvatabar* (see fig. 3.6), another cartoon that traces the outlines of "many more continents . . . yet unknown to [him], to explore which will be [his] ambition" after he settles his political affairs (316). The thematic similarities between Bradshaw's

FIG. 3.6 William R. Bradshaw, "Map of the Interior World" (frontispiece), from *The Goddess of Atvatabar, Being the History of the Discovery of the Interior World and Conquest of Atvatabar* (New York: J. F. Douthitt, 1892).

and Seaborn's novels—cutting-edge sea vessels, polar quests, triumphalist narrators—are compounded by their roughly analogous maps.
Reached through a polar "vestibule," illuminated by its own "rosy
orbit of light," Bilbimtesirol's "oceans, continents, mountain ranges,
lakes, cities . . . spread like an immense map on the concave vault of
the earth overhead" (37, 44, 52). It is the quintessential Symmesian
world: "widely open at [its] poles," as McBride describes it, "lighted
and warmed according to those general laws which communicate
light and heat to every part of the universe" (28, 35). Its graphic figuration lends context to Hester Blum's observation that, "strikingly,
nearly all hollow-earth fictions set the North and/or South Poles as
the entry points for the inner world."[35]

William Reed's cagey vindication of the hollow-earth idea (and
imagery) likewise testifies to the stamina of Symmes's theory. *The
Phantom of the Poles* (1906) includes a delightful evocation of the
hollow earth traversed and penetrated by miniature barques through
vast polar openings (see fig. 3.7).[36] "This earth is not only hollow, or
double," Reed proclaims, "but suitable in its interior to sustain man
with as little discomfort . . . as on its exterior" (18). If Halley's hollow globe resolves the puzzle of magnetic variation, and Teed's mini-
cosmos reveals the very "mysteries of Deity" (Teed and Morrow, 28),
the ameliorative potential of Reed's double earth is no less impressive. "Vast territories of arable land" under the earth's surface, "made
accessible to mankind with one-fourth the outlay of treasure, time
and life that it cost to build the subway in New York City," represent new frontiers for exploration and the promise of renewal for the
human condition (Reed, 275–76). Reed's salutary conclusion, cited
in the chapter-opening epigraph, echoes the sanguine expectations
of Teed's reduced and comprehensible universe. It offers nothing less
ambitious than a hollow-earth credo for the modern era: Symmes's
Holes are portals to the primal scene of nature's "great mysteries,"
whose resolution will relieve the anxieties of "mind and body."

Seaborn's own "voyage of discovery" is motivated by a similar
desire to locate in nature's physical arrangement evidence of deeper
purpose and meaning (13). "I had undertaken this perilous voyage,"
he explains to his internal inquisitors shortly after first contact, "only
to ascertain whether the body of this huge globe were an useless
waste of sand and stones, contrary to the economy usually displayed

FIG. 3.7 William Reed, "Globe Showing Section of the Earth's Interior," from *The Phantom of the Poles* (New York: W. S. Rockey, 1906), 27.

GLOBE SHOWING SECTION OF THE EARTH'S INTERIOR

The earth is hollow. The poles so long sought are but phantoms. There are openings at the northern and southern extremities. In the interior are vast continents, oceans, mountains and rivers. Vegetable and animal life are evident in this new world, and it is probably peopled by races yet unknown to the dwellers upon the earth's exterior.

THE AUTHOR.

in the works of Providence, or, according to the sublime conceptions of one of our Wise men, a series of concentric spheres, like a nest of boxes, inhabitable within and without, on every side, so as to accommodate the greatest possible number of intelligent beings" (143). Seaborn's veiled allusion to Symmes, magus of transcendent discernment, might have contradicted the impression gained from one of the maverick's "halting lectures" in Ohio or Pennsylvania, through which he "doggedly spread the gospel of a new world underfoot."[37] An unprepossessing demeanor tended to rouse ambivalent enthusiasm for the "round-headed hero . . . with his . . . contracted brow, his nasal voice, and [his] hesitating manner."[38] Seaborn's lionizing of dusty heroism, however, piggybacks on an equally deferential commitment to the law of divine economy. Like Halley's "Account," *Symzonia* espouses utility of design as a central tenet. The assumption that nature displays a persistent frugality of composition operates as the base logic of hollow-earth reasoning, and hence as an essential key to unlocking the full meaning of the theory's pictorial representations.

The economy precept was expressed in the first of Newton's "Rules of Right Reasoning in Natural Philosophy," a series of imperatives that preface book 3 of the third edition of the *Principia* (1726)—a work that would have languished in manuscript form, as already noted, without Halley's considerable help. Newton's "Rule 1" states that "no more causes of natural things should be admitted than are both true and sufficient to explain their phenomena. As the philosophers say: Nature does nothing in vain, and more causes are in vain when fewer suffice. For nature is simple and does not indulge in the luxury of superfluous causes."[39] Hollow-earth theory from the time of Newton and Halley frequently invoked the imperatives of simplicity and utility as rudimentary starting points for all inquiry into terrestrial structure.

McBride's précis of Symmes's theory—an indispensable narrative supplement to *Symzonia*'s frontispiece—illustrates this point nicely. "According to Symmes's Theory," McBride recounts,

> The earth, as well as all the celestial orbicular bodies
> existing in the universe, visible and invisible . . . are all
> constituted . . . of a collection of spheres, more or less
> solid, concentric with each other, and more or less
> open at their poles; each sphere being separated from its
> adjoining compeers by space replete with aerial fluids. . . .
> [E]very portion of infinite space, except what is occupied
> by spheres, is filled with an aerial elastic fluid, more
> subtile than common atmospheric air; and constituted of
> innumerable small concentric spheres, too minute to be
> visible to the organ of sight. (25)

Symmes's "collection of spheres, more or less solid" represents a physically unified and coherent model of the universe. It provides a tenaciously comparative way of thinking about the hollow earth and its galactic habitat—a cosmology that accounts for the universal, concave structure of orbicular matter from the evanescent and molecular ("aerial elastic" fluids) to the astronomic and celestial (the visible planets and stars). There is an implicit connection between analogy and divine economy in this summary. If, along with McBride, we take it "for granted, that there is a God, and that he is the first cause of all things," then we must also share with him "the opinion, that a construction of all the orbs in creation, on a plan corresponding with Symmes's theory, would display the highest possible degree of perfection, wisdom, and goodness—the most perfect system of creative economy" (56). One suspects that Halley would have been delighted with Symmes's amplification of his theory and its ingenuous reasoning by utility: "If a hollow globe would answer the ends of supporting organic life as well as a solid one—why not be hollow?" (McBride, 54).

McBride's version of Symmes's "perfect system" augmented Halley's three original "Subterraneous Orbs" with an additional two, all furnished with massive diametrical openings. "Composed of at least five hollow concentric spheres, with spaces between each, an atmosphere surrounding each; and habitable as well upon the concave as the convex surface," Symmes's hollow earth could house a nearly unbounded human population (McBride, 28). Its capacity to sustain multitudinous life resides in the fact that "the rays of the sun ... would pass the lower part of the verge and fall on the opposite concave surface, [and] be reflected back in all directions, and most probably light the whole interior of the sphere" (116).

It was to a fervid defense of this theory of sunlight's subsurface transmission—"the most common objection" to Symmes's theory, just as it was for Halley's—that Symmes's son Americus applied his rhetorical ingenuity more than fifty years after his father's death.[40] "The rays of light come parallel from the sun to the earth," Americus explained in a volume that plagiarized the title and much of the content of McBride's book, "and, if [the sun] were no larger than the earth, they would fall at least twelve degrees upon the concave interior surface, as they passed over the lower part of the verge both north and south. But the earth in her annual revolution, owing to the inclination of the poles to the plane of her orbit, alternately permits the incident rays to fall much more than twelve degrees upon the interior surface. . . . [T]hose rays . . . would produce abundant light and heat throughout the whole interior."[41] Symmes's hollow earth, then, enjoys an atmosphere tempered and animated by our sun. What is more, clouds formed in the skies of the outer world float in through the polar openings, providing the interior with rain and snow. But there is also an internally generated fuel that reinforces these migrant winds and completes Symmes's atmospheric model for our wonderful hollow planet, called into existence, to borrow McBride's inimitable phrasing, by "the Almighty Fiat . . . for the support and maintenance of living creatures, innumerable, and endless in the variety of their organization, their colours, their passions, and their pursuits" (126). "The disciples of Symmes," McBride explains, "believe that each sphere has a cavity, or mid-plane space near the center of the matter composing it. . . . The gas escaping from these spaces is, no doubt, the cause of earthquakes; and supply the numerous volcanoes. . . . This aerial fluid with which the mid-plane spaces are filled, may possibly be adapted to the support of animal life; and the interior surfaces of the spheres formed by them, may abound . . . with organs only adapted to the medium which they are destined to inhabit" (37). Symmes's habitable inner earth is thus climatically modulated by internal and external sources of energy. The dashed lines in *Symzonia*'s sectional view are a literal realization of Symmes's theories of light reflection and dispersion. The land of Symzonia, "covered with verdure, [and] chequered with groves of trees and shrubbery," seems to be especially favored by its location at point 9 (Seaborn, 99). It benefits from what Seaborn calls "the mild oblique rays of the morning sun," whose trajectory is demarcated by the line drawn from the stylized star (6).

McBride devoted the final chapters of his book to an appeal for financial backing of an expedition to explore the polar regions and discover Symmes's Holes. Such an undertaking, he believed, would "bespeak a spirit of liberality, and a desire to promote scientific enterprize" highly commendable to American backers (137). Sadly, McBride's solicitation was about as successful as Symmes's petitions of the early 1820s, a long series of appeals to Congress and state assemblies for expeditionary financing, rejected outright or indefinitely postponed. No polar expedition was ever connected with McBride's name, and his *Symmes's Theory of Concentric Spheres* remains the only memorial to his otherwise obscure personal history. Symmes, however, was not only buried with full military honors in May 1829, but also his remains at the old bury-ing ground in Hamilton, Ohio, were covered with a still-standing monument, erected by Americus, inscribed to the memory of "Captain John C. Symmes," the New Jersey–born "philosopher . . . [who] contended that the earth is hollow and habitable within." This unpretentious plinth-and-column structure surmounted by a hollow globe carved in freestone is yet another material gratifica-tion, in Flint's words, of the "desire to excavate the subterranean, to bring to the surface that which lies hidden and dormant."[42] The monument remains a singular pasquinade to cosmological dissent, even while it takes its place in a voluminous repertoire of hollow-earth imagery that, from the time of Halley's "Account," sought to reveal our inner world.

With the uncluttered economy—the symbolic condensation—of delineative black-and-white diagrams, the illustrations accompanying Halley's, Teed's, and Seaborn's texts produced simple graphic models of convoluted geophysical theories. These pictures are capable of in-spiring the comprehension, if not the ready assent, of even the most incredulous audience.[43] In this way, each of the hollow-earth illustra-tions examined here does the ideological work of the cartoon as Scott McCloud has memorably described it. Each functions as a representa-tional abstraction or "vacuum into which our identity and awareness are pulled, an empty shell [happy pun in the present context!] that we inhabit which enables us to travel in another realm."[44]

Notes

1. Thomas S. Kuhn, *The Copernican Revolution: Planetary Astronomy in the Development of Western Thought* (Cambridge, MA: Harvard University Press, 1957), 39, 76.

2. L. Sprague de Camp and Willy Ley, *Lands Beyond* (New York: Rinehart, 1952), 309.

3. Peter Standish, *Hollow Earth: The Long and Curious History of Imagin-ing Strange Lands, Fantastical Creatures, Advanced Civilizations, and Marvelous Machines Below the Earth's Surface* (Cambridge, MA: Da Capo, 2006), 13.

4. Cyrus Reed Teed and Ulysses Grant Morrow, *The Cellular Cos-mogony, or the Earth a Concave Sphere* (Chicago: Guiding Star, 1898), 49. Hereafter cited in text.

5. Martin Gardner, *Fads and Fallacies in the Name of Science* (New York: Dover, 1957), 23.

6. Edmond Halley, "An Account of the Cause of the Change of the Variation of the Magnetical Needle; With an Hypothesis of the Structure of the Internal Parts of the Earth: As It Was Proposed to the Royal Society in One of Their Late Meetings," *Philosophical Transactions* 16 (1692): 568. Hereafter cited in text.

7. Standish, *Hollow Earth,* 12. I have argued elsewhere that Halley's 1691 lecture, "Account of the Cause of the Change of the Variation of the Magnetical Needle," is the originating moment of hollow-earth theory conceived scientifically as opposed to mythologically. Peter W. Sinnema, "10 April 1818: John Cleves Symmes's 'No. 1 Circular,'" *BRANCH: Britain, Representation, and Nineteenth-Century History,* ed. Dino Franco Felluga. Extension of Romanticism and Victorianism on the Net, www.branchcollective.org/ (accessed 13 June 2012).

8. David Kubrin, "'Such an Impertinently Litigious Lady': Hooke's 'Great Pretending' vs. Newton's *Principia* and Newton's and Halley's Theory of Comets," in *Standing on the Shoulders of Giants: A Longer View of Newton and Halley,* ed. Norman J. W. Thrower (Berkeley, CA: University of California Press, 1990), 71.

9. Duane Griffin, "Hollow and Habitable Within: Symmes's Theory of Earth's Internal Structure and Polar Geography," *Physical Geography* 25, no. 5 (2004): 393; Captain Adam Seaborn, *Symzonia: A Voyage of Discovery* (1820; repr., New York: Arno, 1975), vi (hereafter cited in text). "Seaborn" is clearly a pseudonym—a "nicely allegorical Divine Human sobriquet," as Victoria Nelson calls it in *The Secret Life of Puppets* (Cambridge, MA: Harvard University Press, 2001), 149. The author's identity remains controversial. J. O. Bailey and David Seed argue that Symmes himself wrote the novel. See respectively: J. O. Bailey, "Introduction," in *Symzonia: A Voyage of Discovery,* by Captain Adam Seaborn (1820; repr., Gainesville, FL: Scholars' Facsimiles and Reprints, 1965), n.p.; David Seed, "Breaking the Bounds: The Rhetoric of Limits in the Works of Edgar Allan Poe, His Contemporaries and Adaptors," in *Anticipations: Essays on Early Science Fiction and Its Precursors,* ed. David Seed (Syracuse: Syracuse University Press, 1995), 77. For an alternative opinion, see Hans-Joachim Lang and Benjamin Lease, "The Authorship of *Symzonia:* The Case for Nathaniel Ames," *New England Quarterly* 48, no. 2 (1975): 241–52.

10. John C. Symmes, "No. 1 Circular" (1818), in *Hollow Earth Theory,* Oliver's Bookshelf, http://olivercowdery.com/texts/1818symm.htm#item1 (accessed 10 May 2007). Ohio historian Henry Howe commented in 1900 that "the papers in the decade between 1820 and 1830 were more or less full of Symmes's Hole. If one suddenly disappeared, the reply

often was, and with a grin: 'Oh, he's gone, I expect, down into Symmes's Hole.'" Quoted in Lester Chaplow, "Tales of a Hollow Earth: Tracing the Legacy of John Cleves Symmes in Antarctic Exploration and Fiction" (master's thesis, University of Canterbury, New Zealand, 2011), 34.

11. Chaplow, "Tales," 57. See also Hester Blum's observation that "hollow-earth fiction traces its genealogy at least to the early modern period, and earlier if we include the underworlds of classical epics; its zenith, however, coincided with the polar expeditions launched in the mid-nineteenth to early twentieth centuries." Blum, "John Cleves Symmes and the Planetary Reach of Polar Exploration," *American Literature* 84, no. 2 (2012): 259. Some better-known hollow-earth titles of the decades mentioned are Mary E. Bradley Lane, *Mizora: A World of Women* (1880–81; New York: G. W. Dillingham, 1890); Mrs. J. Wood, *Pantaletta: A Romance of Sheheland* (New York: American News, 1882); William R. Bradshaw, *The Goddess of Atvatabar, Being the History of the Discovery of the Interior World and Conquest of Atvatabar* (New York: J. F. Douthitt, 1892); Will N. Harben, *The Land of the Changing Sun* (New York: Merriam, 1894); John Uri Lloyd, *Etidorpha* (Cincinnati: Robert Clarke, 1895); Jack Adams [Alcanoan O. Grigsby and Mary P. Lowe], *Nequa, or the Problem of the Ages* (Topeka, KS: Equity Publishing, 1900); and Charles Willing Beale, *The Secret of the Earth* (New York: F. Tennyson Neely, 1899).

12. Standish, *Hollow Earth,* 32.

13. Kate Flint, *The Victorians and the Visual Imagination* (Cambridge: Cambridge University Press, 2000), 33

14. Ibid., 117.

15. For a detailed description of the Rectilineator experiment and an explanation of the errors in mechanics and calculus that produced the results Teed anticipated, see Donald E. Simanek, "Turning the Universe Inside-Out: Ulysses Grant Morrow's Naples Experiment," *Myths and Mysteries of Science: Removing the Mystery,* maintained by Donald E. Simanek, www.lhup.edu/~dsimanek/hollow/morrow.htm. (accessed 4 May 2013).

16. The upper stave, along with the vertical lines descending from its foot, are part of a paper-saving illustration to Francis Roberts's essay on trumpet notes in the same issue of *Philosophical Transactions,* pages 559–63.

17. Duane Griffin, "What Curiosity in the Structure: The Hollow Earth in Science," unpublished manuscript, Bucknell University Department of Geography, www.facstaff.bucknell.edu/dgriffin/Research /Griffin-HE_in_Science.pdf, 7.

18. Halley has reasonably been called "midwife to Newton's brainchild" by I. Bernard Cohen, "A Brief History of the *Principia*," in *The*

Principia: Mathematical Principles of Natural Philosophy, by Isaac Newton, trans. I. Bernard Cohen and Anne Whitman (Berkeley: University of California Press, 1999), 21.

19. Thanks in no small part to Halley's advocacy and material help, by the 1690s Newton enjoyed a position at the "summit of the British intellectual world." Richard S. Westfall and Gerald Funk, "Newton, Halley, and the System of Patronage," in *Standing on the Shoulders of Giants: A Longer View of Newton and Halley,* ed. Norman J. W. Thrower (Berkeley: University of California Press, 1990), 5.

20. As Blum presciently observes, "*Symzonia* presumes—even stipulates—an imperial drive," although not toward "traffic and imperial competition between nation-states but [toward] the extranational zones of material and imaginative resources . . . the indeterminate, transitional space between the external and internal worlds." Blum, "John Cleves Symmes," 245–46.

21. Roy Porter, *The Making of Geology: Earth Science in Britain, 1660–1815* (Cambridge: Cambridge University Press, 1977), 33.

22. Accused by some of being a skeptic for his unorthodox views on the matter of terrestrial history at a time when "the belief in the eternity of the world was seen as genuinely heretical," Halley's suitability for the Savilian Chair of Astronomy—which eventually went to the Scottish mathematician David Gregory—was suspect. Simon Schaffer, "Halley's Atheism and the End of the World," *Notes and Records of the Royal Society* 32, no. 1 (1977): 18.

23. The second, by Thomas Murray, is of a much younger Halley, again holding a diagram, in this case in his left or appurtenant hand. Its simple combination of parabolic and straight lines relates to Halley's paper on cubic and quartic equations published in the *Transactions* of 1687, dating the portrait to that year.

24. Angela Mayer-Deutsch, "'Quasi-Optical Palingenesis': The Circulation of Portraits and the Image of Kircher," in *Athanasius Kircher: The Last Man Who Knew Everything,* edited by Paula Findlen (London: Routledge, 2004), 108.

25. Manuel Portela, "A Portrait of the Author as an Author," reprint of essay in *Novas Histórias Literárias/New Literary Histories,* ed. Isabel Caldeira (Coimbra, Portugal: Minerva, 2004), *Manuelportelaweb* www1.ci.uc.pt /pessoal/mportela/arslonga/MPENSAIOS/a_portrait_of_the_author .htm#[N], n.p.

26. Patricia Fara suggests that the diagram's inclusion was Halley's attempt "to display the foolishness of his youth, or else advertise his magnetic success to counter his mediocre reputation as Astronomer Royal." Fara,

"Hidden Depths: Halley, Hell and Other People," *Studies in History and Philosophy of Science* 38, no. 3 (2007): 581. For a view more in line with my own, see Standish, *Hollow Earth:* "Of the hundreds of projects he'd involved himself in, with accolades given for his work in dozens of areas, [Halley] remained fond and proud enough of his hollow earth theory to have it memorialized in what he must have suspected would be the last official portrait done of him" (36).

27. Flint, *Victorians*, 138, 119.

28. Like Blum, Gretchen Murphy is persuasive in her reading of *Symzonia* as a "parody of spread-eagle nationalism, intemperate and ambitious." Murphy, "*Symzonia, Typee,* and the Dream of U.S. Global Isolation," *ESQ* 49, no. 4 (2003): 262.

29. Istvan Csicsery-Ronay Jr., *The Seven Beauties of Science Fiction* (Middletown, CT: Wesleyan University Press, 2008), 5.

30. Blum, "John Cleves Symmes," 261.

31. "Whilst Symmes initially proposed that there were five concentric hollow spheres, his later writings concentrated on a single hollow earth." Chaplow, "Tales," 18.

32. While in his twenties, Symmes could have stumbled upon the hollow-earth idea while perusing works on cosmology and geography in the private library of his distinguished uncle, the Judge J. C. Symmes of Symmes Purchase fame. "[T]he books of [Symmes's] uncle's library would most likely have laid a significant foundation of general knowledge on which he would later develop his theory of a hollow earth." Ibid., 22.

33. As James McBride notes, these had formerly been aired only in "detached Newspaper essays, published at different and distant times." McBride, *Symmes's Theory of Concentrix Spheres, Demonstrating that the Earth Is Hollow, Habitable Within, and Widely Open about the Poles* (Cincinnati: Morgan, Lodge and Fisher, 1826), viii. Hereafter cited in text.

34. Bradshaw, *Goddess of Atvatabar,* 37. Hereafter cited in text.

35. Blum, "John Cleves Symmes," 259.

36. William Reed, *The Phantom of the Poles* (New York: W. S. Rockey, 1906), 44. Hereafter cited in text.

37. Irving Wallace, *The Square Pegs: Some Characters Who Dared to Be Different* (London: Hutchinson, 1958), 212.

38. "Symmes and His Theory," *Harper's New Monthly Magazine* 65 (October 1882): 744.

39. Isaac Newton, *The Principia: Mathematical Principles of Natural Philosophy,* trans. I. Bernard Cohen and Anne Whitman (Berkeley: University of California Press, 1999), 794.

40. Americus Symmes, *The Symmes Theory of Concentric Spheres, Demonstrating That the Earth Is Hollow, Habitable Within, and Widely Open about the Poles* (Louisville, KY: Bradley and Gilbert, 1885), 65.

41. Ibid.

42. Flint, *Victorians,* 139.

43. Halley challenged potential detractors to "inform themselves of the Matter of Fact and then try if they can find out a more simple Hypothesis, [or] at least a less absurd" one than that represented in his schema. Halley, "Account," 577.

44. Scott McCloud, *Understanding Comics: The Invisible Art* (New York: HarperCollins, 1993), 36.

FOUR

Mixed Media

Olivia Plender's *A Stellar Key to the Summerland* and the Afterlife of Spiritualist Visual Culture

CHRISTINE FERGUSON

W hen Modern Spiritualism spread across the United States and then crossed the Atlantic in the early 1850s, it initiated not only a radical heterodox and political movement but also a rich visual culture in which proof of spiritual survival was explained and evidenced through an elaborate system of cosmological maps and illustrations, emblems, photographs and phrenological medium portraits, spectacular demonstrations, and spirit drawings whose goal was to make the inquirer see anew.[1] One of the most significant and intricate of the early movement's illustrated books, *A Stellar Key to the Summer Land* (1867), by American Harmonial philosopher Andrew Jackson Davis, forges its argument for the Spiritualist hypothesis through a mixed-media synthesis of image and text in which the mundane and supernatural worlds are placed on the same visual plane. In her striking 2007 hand-drawn comic of almost identical name, *A Stellar Key to the Summerland,* research-based British artist Olivia Plender recovers the forgotten iconography and visual ephemera of nineteenth-century transatlantic Spiritualism—including mastheads from Spiritualist newspapers, medium portraits, proselytizing posters, and diagrams of séance equipment—to track, probe, and then ultimately undo the movement's seeming complicity with the subsequent cultures of New Age libertarianism and neoliberal capitalism. Framing her text as a New Age self-help book dictated by the departed spirit of Andrew Jackson Davis, Plender explores the ways in which Spiritualism's reformist and socialist agenda was mediated and tempered by the spectacular forms of modern capitalism, its pictures of the hitherto unseen world of spirit framed to sell pitiless schemes of colonial violence and libertarian self-reliance. At the same time, however, her detailed reiterations and adaptations of the movement's most iconic images reveal their continued ability to surpass the instrumentalist purposes to which they have often been put to use in the commodity culture of the New Age. This chapter examines *A Stellar Key to the Summerland*'s compelling meditation on the ideological ambivalence of the twinned exoteric image cultures in which it participates: that of the nineteenth-century Spiritualist movement and that of contemporary popular comics.

Modern Spiritualism and the Visual Culture of Liberation

In its inexpensive comics format, Plender's book pays homage both to the democratic and populist tenor of Spiritualist belief and to the movement's prioritization of the visual as a medium for social equality.[2] In the séance room, uneducated and seemingly artistically untrained mediums could be supernaturally endowed with the gifts of painting and drawing, their compositions then reproduced and circulated through the transatlantic Spiritualist press rather than the closed academy system.[3] Further, the belief of some Spiritualists that the other world was the ur-site for all aesthetic production and inspiration worked to dispel the myth of the solitary (and typically male) genius figure,[4] replacing it with a vision of the social in which all humans were potentially equal through their shared capacity to act as a channel for artistic abilities they could manifest without ever personally and permanently possessing—and hence without ever trademarking or selling their products. We can see both of these paradigms in the first issue of the short-lived American Spiritualist art journal *Gallery of Spirit Art*. An article by J. Winchester on drawing mediums Pet and Wella Anderson declares that "in all the phenomena attending the advent of spiritualism, from the tiny raps to the full form materialization, none can claim a more important place than that of SPIRIT ART."[5] The value of the Andersons' productions, the article continues, lay not simply in their beautiful finished form—although Winchester insisted, somewhat unconvincingly, that they "compare favorably with those of the best artists of this, or any former age"—but also in the democratic implications of their mode of production.[6] If the allegedly unschooled Wella Anderson could produce assured portraits of Confucius or the ancient Atlantean Orondo with no seeming preparation and at a rapid-fire pace, then so could anyone; art need no longer be an exclusive practice of or product for the rich and well educated but had become a populist enterprise open to all citizens of the cosmos, whether living or dead.

W. J. Colville's spirit-channeled "Ode to Spirit Art," also published in the seminal issue of *Gallery of Spirit Art,* accepts and further extends Winchester's conviction in the popular, egalitarian, and even anticapitalist potential of Spiritualism's new modes of aesthetic production. Attributing the inspiration for all earth-produced art to those who live "Beyond the world of matter / Above the realm of clay,"[7] Colville then lauds the higher spheres for their liberation from the crass financial concerns and material limitations that characterize the contemporary art market.

> In Heaven there's nothing borrowed,
> And nothing bought or sold,
> For in a world of beauty
> That soul is dark and cold,
> Who has not once developed
> The inward spirit
> Which brings the form and colour
> Of spirit forms most nigh.[8]

Exhibiting an awkward syntax adopted to fit Colville's rhyme scheme, the poem suggests that while it is not impossible to be an antiaestheticist in the afterlife—there are souls that remain "dark" and "cold"—most spirits have developed an ability to appreciate and manipulate artistic form as they manifest in the séance room and across the cosmos. In the spirit realm, art is free, democratic, ubiquitous, and universally beautiful because the numinous demos, now free from their earthly shells, can truly make and see art for this first time.

These brief examples from the massive and as yet still largely underexplored corpus of Spiritualist art writing suggest that the visual cultural turn only recently inaugurated in contemporary art history was well under way in the nineteenth-century heterodox movement,[9] manifest in its attention to what Ian Heywood and Barry Sandywell have described as "the generative conditions, assumptions, and implicit methods at work in visual analysis."[10] Nineteenth-century believers, quite simply, did not accept the visual field as given; they were fascinated by the conditions that allowed certain objects to be seen or to be invisible, by the cultural, spiritual, and economic forces that shape our encounter with the image.

These preoccupations run through Davis's *Stellar Key to the Summer Land,* a treatise devoted to documenting life in the upper spheres and, more importantly, to expounding a clairvoyant theory of vision that would convince even the most hard-line of empiricists by appealing to their rationalist ontology. The book's careful attention to the processes by which the unseen transforms into the seen and vice versa must surely have formed part of its appeal to Plender, whose own mixed-media work has repeatedly interrogated the visual reification of social movements and countercultural ideologies. Davis billed the work as an attempt to "furnish scientific and philosophical evidences of the existence of an inhabitable sphere or zone among the suns and planets of space" for those "who seek a solid, rational foundation on which to rest their hopes of a substantial existence after death."[11] Given this target audience, *A Stellar Key* largely favors black-and-white technical diagrams and astronomical illustrations over fanciful spirit-produced drawings of disembodied citizens; these images are intended to demonstrate Spiritualism's truths without being products of a mediumship that nonconverted readers have yet to credit. Indeed, Davis is at pains through the first half of the work to conceal the supernatural provenance of his schema, working through induction until his reader is (presumably) convinced enough by his preliminary speculations on matter to accept his authority as a seer. "If I were to present exclusively my own interior perceptions, and leave unnoticed all the important corroborations of physical science," he declared, "the world would discard the whole as 'speculation'" (94).[12]

As Davis's *Stellar Key* continues, however, such distinctions between interior and exterior sight, and between hard matter and ethereal spirit, are ultimately revealed as spurious. We are presented instead with an ambitious and astronomically sublime vision of the universe in which all substances are ultimately transmutable, one that anticipates in its account of the mutability of the physical and spiritual worlds the fin-de-siècle revival of alchemy recently documented by Mark Morrison.[13] The summer land—or, rather, summer *lands,* for Davis, like his key predecessor Emanuel Swedenborg, held that there were seven of these spheres[14]—was no subjective concept or hazy internal feeling but an actual "inhabitable zone, or circular belt of refined matter in the heavens" (Davis, *Stellar Key,* 18). During Davis's time, scientific telescopes detected it only as light, but the clairvoyant eye, one that more and more humans would learn to develop, recognized it as a populated territory inhabited by spirits who migrated there at death. There the dead were not so much born anew but, in Davis's alchemically suggestive terms, "resmelt[ed]" into a higher form, as they would be again in all the subsequent zones they passed through on their way to ultimate union with the Divine (142). Fascinatingly, if somewhat grotesquely, Davis proposed that the summer land's landscape, built environment, and citizens were all composed of the same substance: the discarded base elements of human flesh and bone: "According to my most careful examinations of the physical structure of the Summer Land, the fertile soils, and the lovely groves and vines and flowers which infinitely diversify the landscape, are *constituted of particles that once were in human bodies!*" (115; emphasis in the original). While this detail might seem no more than one of Davis's trademark eccentric flourishes, it is central to the book's humanist ecology. The human body is not wasted but recycled upward into a series of higher and higher forms as it ascends through the spheres, changing but never entirely losing its material form as it progresses from one scopic realm (that of the earth) to another (that of the summer land). Vision, matter, and human personality are alike refined in this meliorist cosmological process, resulting, according to *A Stellar Key* at least,[15] in an effortless postlife utopia whose inhabitants engaged in constant study, formed missionary and reform societies to help the newly dead, and repented for past sins while forgiving their transgressors.[16] Of all the accounts of the summer land that Davis produced throughout his lengthy career as a clairvoyant seer, this version was one of the most idyllic and reassuringly progressive. As such, it provides a perfect foil for Olivia Plender's disenchanted exploration of Spiritualism's legacy, one enacted through the phantasmagoria of the movement's rich visual traditions.

Disenchanting the Summerland:
Olivia Plender and the Occultural Turn

Published in 2007, Plender's *A Stellar Key to the Summerland* was re-
leased as part of a suite of performances and installations based on
the Modern Spiritualist movement; its other components included a
walking tour of Spiritualist landmarks in London and a museological
installation named after the nineteenth-century Spiritualist newspaper *The Medium and Daybreak*.[17] This sustained multimedia project arc
participates in what Tessel Bauduin and Nina Kokkinen have recently
described as the "occultural turn" in contemporary art, one characterized by a fascination with the materials, affective power, and countercultural potential of eclipsed forms of mystical, spiritualist, or occult
belief.[18] Other British artists working in this vein include Suzanne
MacWilliam, whose 2009 Venice Biennale installation *Remote Viewing*
paid tribute to the technological sublime of psychical research; Ben
Judd, whose video and performance work draws on the histories of
Swedenborgianism, New Thought, and New World syncretic pagan-
ism; and Suzanne Treister, who adopts the graphic styles of alchemical
texts, kabbalistic charts, and the tarot to meditate on the occulted
nature of state and other forms of coercive power.[19] Plender's choice
of the comics medium to address this territory is immediately a
provocative one, the form offering in its accessibility, popular cultural
status, and comparatively low price an antidote to the closed distribution networks and secrecy associated with occult organizations, if not
with the more exoteric Spiritualist movement.

A Stellar Key to the Summerland was not Plender's first foray into
the comics medium,[20] and she has spoken on several occasions about
the form's ongoing allure for her as an artist interested in probing
both the history of social movements and the politics of the art world.
"[G]enerally speaking," she states in the catalogue to the 2007 *Cult
Fiction* touring group exhibition, "comics have the potential to reach
a mass audience whereas artists distribute their work through a fairly
elitist network of galleries and museums."[21] But Plender's engagement
with populist forms is by no means naïve or uncritical. Indeed, much
of her mixed-media output over the past decade has been devoted to
interrogating the unspoken hierarchies, limitations, and value judgments latent in democratizing cultural experiments and ideologies.[22]
One early hint that a similar spirit of critique runs through her *Stellar*

Key lies in its suggestive formal similarity to, if not direct inspiration by, the graphic style of the world's most prolific and controversial religious comic artist, Jack Chick,[23] whose hate-fuelled but free and mass-distributed Armageddonist comics remind us that accessibility is no unmixed boon or necessary correlative to social equality. Another hint lies in her subtle truncation of Davis's title from *A Stellar Key to the Summer Land* to *A Stellar Key to the Summerland,* an act of compounding that suggestively transforms the original site designation into what sounds like a brand name or corporate logo.

In all other respects but this, Plender's title is identical to Davis's, a replication that might lead us to expect in the comic a closely referential adaptation of its nineteenth-century source. Instead, we find a creative appropriation that replaces Davis's narrative about the unity of matter and spirit with an account of Modern Spiritualism's birth, dissemination, and mergence with the tenets and identity politics of the New Age. What both the nineteenth- and the twenty-first-century text share, however, is a deep awareness of the evidential and ideological power of the visual image. As we have seen, Davis's text insists that the other world quite literally *matters* enough to be seen, even if, at the time of his writing, it was discernable only through the mystical technology of clairvoyance; this argument in his *Stellar Key* is supported by numerous illustrations that map the mundane and the numinous onto overlapping territory. Yet it is worth remembering that the faith Davis evinces in the power of drawn images to explain Harmonial principles here—diagrams, maps, charts, engravings, and illustrations—stood in inverse relation to his simultaneous distrust, and later complete rejection, of phenomenal spiritual demonstrations, one that, according to R. Laurence Moore, considerably sidelined him from the movement when materialization séances came into vogue in the 1870s.[24] Séance room spectacles of disembodied hands or linen-swathed spirits, Davis felt, could only hurt the movement by providing opportunity for fraud and deception. Better to abolish the demonstrative side of Spiritualism altogether, he argued in an 1882 manifesto published in the American *Religio-Philosophical Journal,* than to stake the movement's credibility on false images and phenomena designed to part the gullible from their money.[25]

Plender's comic retains this suspicion, or rather ambivalence, about the manipulative power of the image without attributing it to Davis, who acts as her comic's narrator and initial protagonist. Indeed, the Davis of the 2007 *Stellar Key* is no ethical or self-scrutinizing truth seeker but rather a callous New Age entrepreneur returned from the Summerland to vaunt the self-help potential, profitability, and limitless market force of the movement that he helped to inaugurate. He addresses us directly in the introductory speech that follows the title page image of a drawn curtain, one suggestive both of a theatrical drape and of the acts of unveiling and exposure to which nineteenth-century spirit cabinet mediums were frequently subject. What follows, this composition suggests, will be both revelation and performance. Davis first congratulates readers on their decision to purchase this "new revolutionary fitness book for the soul" before extolling the movement's achieved and future contributions to neoliberal ideology in seven of the celestial spheres:[26]

> Since the social revolution of nineteen hundred and sixty-eight (that did so much to popularize many of the ideas herein contained), one part of my particular message that wealth results from inner harmony has been adopted by the New Age counter-culture to create an expanding prosperity-focused wing. Though Spiritualism in its original form is now only practiced in the Northern-most reaches of Britain, where many regret the loss of its radical aspects in favour of economic liberalism, it is clear then alighting upon the question of what the origins of good health and unlimited worldly success in business truly are, the rational mind *naturally* arrives at SELF-ACTUALIZATION as the cause. Other beliefs and causes formerly considered as rational notions, such as poverty or lack of educational opportunity, can be cast aside as so much superstition. Rest assured my friends, that success has no limits! . . . [O]ther aspects of the Modern Spiritualist Movement can be set aside for the sake of dissemination of this one idea of the ascendancy of the individual. (2; emphasis in original)

This speech provocatively positions Davis as both the movement's authentic originary voice and also as a brash, destructive modernizer who has gleefully abandoned the egalitarian and socialist aspects of the movement to which only a few nostalgic radicals still cling. Yet this new phase of Spiritualism's development is positioned here less as a betrayal than as a fulfilment of its initial radical tendencies through their apotheosis in that most revolutionary and iconoclastic of economic systems: contemporary capitalism. This metamorphosis is further emphasized across the portrait and expository panels in the first half of the comic that are styled to resemble nineteenth-century show bills and advertising placards (see figs. 4.1 and 4.2).

FIG. 4.1   Olivia Plender, "Andrew Jackson Davis, the Poughkeepsie Seer," from *A Stellar Key to the Summerland* (London: Book Works, 2007), 29. Reproduced with permission.

The spirits are in
CONSTANT CORRESPONDENCE
with the material realm and with their assistance
WE CAN CHANGE THE WORLD WE LIVE IN;
abolish slavery of all kinds,
including the pestilential institution of marriage
— WHICH MAKES FEMALES —
THE SLAVES OF THEIR HUSBANDS.
LET US MEET ON TERMS OF EQUALITY
according to the co-operative principles
of Charles Fourier and Robert Owen,
IN ORDER TO LIVE IN HARMONY
THROUGH THE PRACTICE OF FREE LOVE

FIG. 4.2   Olivia Plender, Victorian-style placard from *A Stellar Key to the Summerland* (London: Book Works, 2007), 31. Reproduced with permission.

Davis's opening paean to the absorption and neutralization of Spiritualism's egalitarian vein by the twin forces of free-market capitalism and liberal individualism is given a further sinister gloss through its tacit endorsement of colonial genocide. Discussing his presidential namesake, he explains, "Andrew Jackson . . . rid America of its Natives with his Indian Removal Act, thereby sending the majority to live in the spirit realm in the 1830s. . . . Though their loss is much to be regretted, it can be said that they are now able, from the other side, to teach their ancient wisdom to the citizens of our New Age, wherever they may live in the world, through the use of the spiritual telegraph" (1). Here, in a fantasy scenario by no means uncommon in nineteenth-century American Spiritualist writing,[27] the white medium imagines a meliorist rationale for racial extinction, one accepted by Native American spirits themselves, whose righteous anger and acts of self-defense have been neutralized through their violent translation into an otherworldly sphere where territory and resources are boundless. The queasy racist complicity suggested by this passage is further emphasized in a subsequent panel that, quite literally, frames the famous Fox sister mediums with scenes of encounter and brutal contact between European settlers and American indigenous people (see fig. 4.3). Titled "Advent of Spiritualism," the panel features a

FIG. 4.3   Olivia Plender, "Advent of Spiritualism," from *A Stellar Key to the Summerland* (London: Book Works, 2007), 41. Reproduced with permission.

central portrait of the three sisters and their parents; surrounding it are twelve smaller frames featuring episodes of settler incursion, indigenous displacement, and intraethnic violence from the hundred-year history of Hydesville, New York, leading up to the 1848 onset of the Fox rappings. Spiritualism's progressive otherworldly foreground, the composition suggests, is inseparable from this bloody background.

The procolonial, aggressively individualist, and sometimes tangibly racist tendencies emphasized in these passages certainly do exist in parts of Davis's original Harmonial philosophy and in transatlantic Spiritualist discourse more broadly, as Robert Cox, Bridget Bennett, Molly McGarry, and others have pointed out.[28] But in Davis's lifetime they were counterweighted by a principled commitment to the universal enfranchisement of all humans, particularly women and African Americans. These latter aspects of Davis's thought are muted in Plender's *Stellar Key*,[29] replaced with a parodic vision of the Spiritualist afterlife as a catalyst for contemporary American capitalism, one visualized in a two-page spread with a pastoral "Spirit Realm" populated not only with nineteenth-century white settlers and—situated significantly in the background—Native Americans but also with Colonel Sanders and Ronald Reagan in the far right corner (see fig. 4.4). As our eyes move horizontally across the page, eighteenth-century figures give way to nineteenth- and twentieth-century ones, their positioning suggesting a historical telos that finds its necessary realization in Reaganomics. As ridiculous as this numinous panorama is clearly intended to be, it at least lacks the featureless sterility of the kitsch neo-Classical upper spheres through which Davis had been led earlier in the text by his spirit guide, Emanuel Swedenborg (see fig. 4.5). Largely devoid of

FIG. 4.4   Olivia Plender, "The Spirit Realm," from *A Stellar Key to the Summerland* (London: Book Works, 2007), 36–37. Reproduced with permission.

FIG. 4.5   Olivia Plender, "The Upper Spheres," from *A Stellar Key to the Summerland* (London: Book Works, 2007), 18. Reproduced with permission.

people and animation, these vast empty spaces seem ripe for the kind of economic expansion and commodification that Plender's Davis identifies in the introduction as the central ambition of Spiritualism in its New Age incarnation: "[T]here are still six remaining spheres to be conquered, each containing market places and inhabitants waiting to be relieved of their coin" (2). Nothing could be further removed from W. J. Colville's socialist aesthetic afterlife than this harrowing vision of the Summerland as an eternal market where the dead live on only to buy, sell, and consume.

As the comic proceeds, however, its focus on Spiritualism's mercenary legacy begins to give way to other, more ambivalent images of the movement. Despite initially extolling the new faith's potential for commercial exploitation, the comic recounts the early history of the Fox sisters without supporting, and indeed, only briefly referencing, their controversial late-life admission to having been charlatans. Only twelve and fifteen, respectively, when they first heard unearthly raps in their Hydesville farmhouse, Kate and Maggie Fox fell into poverty and alcoholism in adulthood and publicly renounced the mediumistic abilities that had shot them to fame at such young ages. For convinced Spiritualists, this was no truthful confession at all but rather a desperate act of two vulnerable women financially coerced into false recantation; for nonbelievers, the confession represented a vindication of rationalism, even if it did not have the disenchanting effects on believers they would have liked.[30] When Plender comes to draw the young sisters (see fig. 4.6), nowhere does she show the girls illicitly cracking their toes in the dark, as they would later claim to have done to make the raps; instead, she concentrates on their initial terror, whether feigned or real, as the disembodied noises ring out across their room. By withholding textual comment on these eerie, largely uncaptioned scenes, the comic refuses to align itself explicitly with either Spiritualist or rationalist ontology. The panels sit uneasily between two worldviews, one in which supernatural "seemings," as Henry Maudsley described Spiritualist phenomena,[31] were only ever the products of sleight of hand or trick of eye, and another in which they were too indisputably real to require any comment.

Plender encourages this ontological disorientation not only through the images she creates for the comic but also in her manipulation of the original nineteenth-century Spiritualist illustrations that she incorporates within it. Despite its critiques of early Spiritualism's political ideology, *A Stellar Key to the Summerland* remains thoroughly in thrall to the movement's popular iconography, which it refuses to imagine solely as crass commercialist propaganda. We can

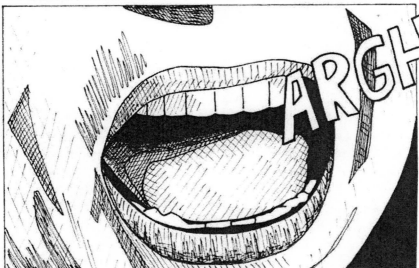

FIG. 4.6 "Clap, clap": the young Kate and Maggie Fox. Olivia Plender, from *A Stellar Key to the Summerland* (London: Book Works, 2007), 51. Reproduced with permission.

see this respect in the care with which the comic reproduces some of transatlantic Spiritualism's most arresting and recognizable visual motifs and images, including illustrations from Davis's books—"the Summer Land Zone within the Milky Way" from his *Stellar Key* and

"A Death Scene" from *The Magic Staff* (1857)—alongside ones from Robert Hare's *Experimental Investigations of the Spirit Manifestations* (1856), the London Spiritualist newspaper *The Medium and Daybreak* (1869–95), Arthur Conan Doyle's *History of Spiritualism* (1926), and Emma Hardinge Britten's *Modern American Spiritualism* (1870).[32] The Britten appropriation provides a particularly compelling example of Plender's alternately faithful and irreverent approach to her comic's nineteenth-century visual precedents (see fig. 4.7). She reproduces the illustrated title page from Britten's text, which features a bearded male head with light emanating from its forehead hovering over one of the great pyramids (see fig. 4.8). At first glance, this figure might appear to be Jesus, but a subtitle in the 1870 original—one omitted from Plender's reproduction—tells us differently: this is Oress, an "ancient angel" born of an advanced race of humans who lived on earth millennia before the birth of the biblical Adam.[33] As with all of the historical Spiritualist images incorporated into *A Stellar Key to the Summerland,* the image lacks the tonal density and elegance of line of the original, as if the same process that turned the ambitious utopianism of the early movement into neoliberal propaganda has also blunted its aesthetic features. Yet the new drawing is, if anything, less rather than more ideologically coherent than its source; stripped of its textual anchors, it stands unmoored on the page without any verbal clues to its meaning. Captivating, obscure, and difficult for the noninitiate to interpret in its synthesis of Western and Near Eastern spiritual iconography, this image seems to exist well beyond the frame of the market-driven and wealth-producing new spiritualities whose advertising and proselytizing paraphernalia clutter the inside covers of the comic (see fig. 4.9).

A further and final dislocation from Davis's numinous entrepreneurialism occurs in the comic's last section, which transports us from nineteenth-century America to England in the nineteenth, twentieth, and twenty-first centuries. Spirit and temporary narrative guide Swedenborg lifts up a two-page covering drape to reveal scenes from the Industrial Revolution in Keighley (see fig. 4.10). From this follows a brief history of northern British Spiritualism in the Edwardian period and then a drawn record of a visit to a 2004 service at the Barrow-in-Furness Spiritualist Church. The panels guide us through a series of densely packed terrace houses to the humble premises of the

FIG. 4.7 Title page from Emma Hardinge Britten, *Modern American Spiritualism: A Twenty Years Record of the Communion between Earth and the World of the Spirits* (New York: privately published, 1870).

FIG. 4.8 Reworking of Emma Hardinge Britten's title page. Olivia Plender, from *A Stellar Key to the Summerland* (London: Book Works, 2007), 25. Reproduced with permission.

FIG. 4.9   New Age and religious/spiritual advertising on the inside cover of
Olivia Plender, *A Stellar Key to the Summerland* (London: Book Works, 2007).
Reproduced with permission.

Psychological Hall, where a small group of the faithful and the curious gather to sing hymns and seek contact with their beloved dead.
The service is led by two mediums: one being the more usual, speaking variety, and the other, an artist medium named Gladys who draws

FIG. 4.10 Scenes from the Industrial Revolution. Olivia Plender, from *A Stellar Key to the Summerland* (London: Book Works, 2007), 92–93. Reproduced with permission.

in direct images what her male counterpart can only describe in words. Gentle and good-humored, the self-declared "double act" fields questions from the audience while reproducing in its collaborative structure Plender's image-textual approach to Spiritualist phenomena.

Significantly, the messages the pair channel are a world away from the triumphalist promises of Davis's individualist philosophy, consisting instead of banal greetings, vague pieces of encouragement, and only limited and prosaic advice on self-actualization. A widow, for example, is presented with "a lovely picture" of her dead husband Charlie, "sitting in a deckchair on the lawn drinking tea" (111), an image then wordlessly reproduced for readers in an upper right panel to create the illusion of our direct insight into the other world (see fig. 4.11). Later, Gladys tells an audience member that her departed mother says, "[Y]ou should do something about those curtains . . . the green ones in your living room. She can't stand them. She says that you looked at some new ones the other week and you should go for those and all" (117; see fig. 4.12). However trivial, inconsequential, or disturbingly claustrophobic these messages might seem—surely no one wants their dead mother as a constant domestic voyeur or disembodied shopping

FIG. 4.11 Charlie in a deck chair. Olivia Plender, from *A Stellar Key to the Summerland* (London: Book Works, 2007), 111. Reproduced with permission.

FIG. 4.12 Voices from beyond. Olivia Plender, from *A Stellar Key to the Summerland* (London: Book Works, 2007), 117. Reproduced with permission.

companion—they demonstrate none of the narcissistic individual-ism or rampant wealth-based aspirationalism earlier trumpeted as the reigning legacy of the movement. Gazing shyly at each other in the hall's darkening gloom, these congregants seek in Spiritualism com-forts for their aches and pains and advice on minor house purchases or career decisions; the "pictures" they receive remain personal and sentimental rather than propagandistic or commercial.

The Barrow-in-Furness scenes thus represent at once a massive di-minishment of and a welcome release from the loftier and more com-prehensive political vision earlier attributed to the nineteenth-century Spiritualist movement and contemporary new religious belief alike. In its place, Plender substitutes closeup drawings of the modest ar-tifacts that adorn the hall: a tablecloth and a wall plaque that bear the "Light, Nature, Truth" motto of the Spiritualists' National Union (see fig. 4.13) and a wall decoration featuring lines from Henry Wad-sworth Longfellow's "Resignation" (1849): "There is no Death, What seems so is transition."[34] These uncaptioned closeup panels lead us to the comic's final image, a full-length unframed drawing of what appears to be the inside—or, as the image's disorienting choice of perspective allows, possibly outside—of a nineteenth-century spirit medium's partially veiled cabinet (see fig. 4.14).[35] An empty chair sits in the foreground, in front of a partial gap in the curtains, opening to reveal a space of impenetrable blackness. The ambiguous spatial arrangement allows us to read this shadowy rift as either the mysteri-ous, and here ultimately unknowable, space of spectral manifestation, presuming that we are on the outside of the cabinet looking in, or, if the perspective is reversed and the chair is for an absent medium, as a portal into a darkened audience space where séance attendees eagerly await a supernatural display, unaware that the performer is absent.

This remarkable closing image represents a powerful culmination of the comic's alternately disenchanted and enthralled encounter with the visual culture, and cultural visions, of nineteenth-century Spiritualism. The panel shifts our attention from the movement's aftermath to the visual and performance conditions that precipitated its emergence as a social and political force. Readers are positioned uncertainly between the space of performance and spectatorship, waiting for a demonstra-tion that is yet to come or viewing a stage from which the medium performer has fled. What is the object and import of our historical gaze

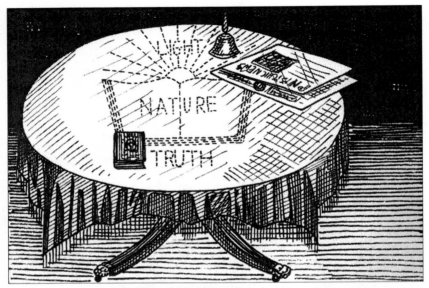

(above) FIG. 4.13 Olivia Plender, "Light, Nature, Truth," from *A Stellar Key to the Summerland* (London: Book Works, 2007), 118. Reproduced with permission.

(right) FIG. 4.14 Olivia Plender, "Spiritualism's Closing Curtain," from *A Stellar Key to the Summerland* (London: Book Works, 2007), 120. Reproduced with permission.

here? Do we witness an anachronistic space of illusion, irrationality, and deception whose dangerous populist appeal still lingers? Or do we see intimations of the inchoate realm of Spiritualism's as yet unrealized social, political, and ethical potential? No textual anchor guides our way; the panel lingers simply on an uncaptioned and unframed moment when the numinous image—real or faked, of this world or the next— has not yet come into, or no longer exists in, a state of being where it can be commodified and consumed. *A Stellar Key to the Summerland* concludes by embracing the pre- or nonvisual, the not yet, or what is no longer capable of being seen, as an alternative to the capitalist reification of Spiritualism's other visions, both political and artistic.

This closing rejection of revelation also has important implications for neo-Victorianism as a contemporary cultural mode. Neo-Victorian texts have become increasingly associated with the remediative tasks of historical recovery, exposure, and correction, tasked with the retrieval of subversive identities and voices left out of the period's official discourses.[36] Yet as others and I have pointed out elsewhere,[37] the neo-Victorian investment in the hermeneutics of suspicion creates its own suppressive orthodoxy, replete with a set of limiting clichés that pit the period as hostile witness under interrogation from more liberated and knowing critic-experts. By refusing us the suppressed "truth" about Spiritualism—indeed, by slowly withdrawing all verbal referents as the comic reaches its elusive drawn curtain finale—Plender suggests that such acts of revelation are no less the products of textual construction and manipulation than the orthodoxies they repetitively expose. There is simply nothing to be seen, a blank nullity where we might have been led to expect an always-present if hitherto concealed secret. To retreat into affectless silence in front of Spiritualism's half-drawn curtain is to pay tribute to the irreducible unreadability, evasiveness, and fundamental grotesquerie of the movement's complex project of visual enlightenment.

Notes

Acknowledgments: Thanks to Olivia Plender and Book Works for their kind permission to reproduce images from *A Stellar Key to the Summerland*.

1. For more on the role of phrenology in Spiritualist art and visual culture, see Charles Colbert's *Haunted Visions: Spiritualism and American Art* (Philadelphia: University of Pennsylvania Press, 2011).

CHRISTINE FERGUSON

2. Spiritualism is distinguished from more hierarchical contemporary occult movements by its insistence that the spirit world was accessible to everyone; it had no formalized system of initiates and adepts.

3. In addition to the *Gallery of Spirit Art,* the London-based Spiritualist paper *The Medium and Daybreak* is also particularly notable for its efforts to reproduce and disseminate new works of spirit art and phrenologically based medium portraits.

4. See, e.g., Mrs. E. B. Duffey's *Heaven Revised,* which suggests that there is "no such thing as originality among mortals" and that "Earth is only the reflex of the spirit world." Duffey, *Heaven Revised: A Narrative of Personal Experiences after the Change Called Death* (Manchester, UK: Two Worlds, 1909), 50.

5. J. Winchester, "Spirit Art," *Gallery of Spirit Art: An Illustrated Quarterly Magazine Dedicated to Spirit Photography, Spirit Painting, the Photographing of Materialized Forms and Every Form of Spirit Art* 1, no. 1 (August 1882): 3.

6. Ibid., 4. See this work for a fuller account of the Andersons' working methods and their resemblance to those of virtuosic Glasgow painting medium and author David Duguid.

7. W. J. Colville, "Ode to Spirit Art," *Gallery of Spirit Art: An Illustrated Quarterly Magazine Dedicated to Spirit Photography, Spirit Painting, the Photographing of Materialized Forms and Every Form of Spirit Art* 1, no. 1 (August 1882): 14. An endnote indicates that the young Anglo-American medium Colville met Wella Anderson at a reception held by the Brooklyn Spiritualist Association in 1882; his poem, although originally produced for the *Psychometric Circular* in 1880, is here presented as a tribute to Anderson.

8. Colville, "Ode to Spirit Art," 14.

9. This is not say that Spiritualist art has been completely ignored in recent years; indeed, we have witnessed a resurgence of interest in spirit photography, evident in works such as Tom Gunning, "Phantom Images and Modern Manifestations: Spirit Photography, Magic Theater, Trick Films, and Photography's Uncanny," in *Fugitive Images: From Photography to Video,* ed. Patrice Petro, 42–71 (Bloomington: Indiana University Press, 1995); Clément Chéroux, ed., *The Perfect Medium: Photography and the Occult* (New Haven, CT: Yale University Press, 2005); Louis Kaplan, *The Strange Case of William Mumler, Spirit Photographer* (Minneapolis: University of Minnesota Press, 2008); Jennifer Cadwallader, "Spirit Photography and the Victorian Culture of Mourning," *Modern Language Studies* 37, no. 2 (2008): 8–31; and Sarah Willburn, "Viewing History and Fantasy through Victorian Spirit Photography," in *The Ashgate Research Companion to Nineteenth-Century Spiritualism and the Occult,* ed. Tatiana

Kontou and Sarah Willburn (Farnham, UK: Ashgate, 2012), 359–81. Sometimes this emphasis on spirit photography seems to have come at the expense of attention to Spiritualism's substantial painting, sculpture, and graphic traditions, although recent works have begun to correct this imbalance. See, e.g., Colbert, *Haunted Visions;* Rachel Oberter, "Esoteric Art Confronting the Public Eye: The Abstract Spirit Drawings of Georgina Houghton," *Victorian Studies* 48, no. 2 (2005): 221–32; and Oberter, "'The Sublimation of Matter into Spirit': Anna Mary Howitt's Automatic Drawings," in *The Ashgate Research Companion to Nineteenth-Century Spiritualism and the Occult,* ed. Tatiana Kontou and Sarah Willburn (Farnham, UK: Ashgate, 2012), 333–58.

10. Ian Heywood and Barry Sandywell, "Introduction: Critical Approaches to the Study of Visual Culture," in *The Handbook of Visual Culture,* ed. Ian Heywood and Barry Sandywell (London: Berg, 2010), 5.

11. Andrew Jackson Davis, *A Stellar Key to the Summer Land,* 5th rev. ed. (Boston: Colby and Rich, 1867), n.p. Hereafter cited in text.

12. This rhetorical strategy generated consternation among participants in transatlantic Spiritualism's public sphere who saw in it a kind of narrow pandering to the very materialist prejudices that Spiritualism was attempting to evade. "[T]he kingdom of God cometh not with observation," remarked English Christian Spiritualist Thomas Shorter in a review of Davis's earlier work *Death and the Afterlife* (1865), "and is not reached by travel in or beyond the interstellar spaces. It is *within us,* or it is nowhere." Shorter, "Death and the Afterlife," *The Spiritual Magazine* 5, no. 11 (September 1870): 420.

13. See Mark Morrison, *Modern Alchemy: Occultism and the Emergence of Atomic Theory* (Oxford: Oxford University Press, 2007).

14. "The Spiritual Spheres have recently been termed Summer Lands, and there are, counting man's earthly existence the first sphere of human life, in all six spheres in the ascending flight towards the Deity, who fills the seventh sphere, and is infinitely greater than millions of such univercoelums as man can conceive." Davis, *Stellar Key,* 6.

15. Although Davis in this work concentrates exclusively on the progressive features and potential of postlife existence, he did not believe that all residents of the spheres were paragons. Elsewhere, he wrote about the existence of malevolent and degenerate spirits in the summer lands; see, for example, *The Diakka* (1873), which focuses on those beings who "tak[e] insane delight in juggling, tricks, in personating opposite characters; to whom prayers and profane utterances are of equi-value." These he held responsible for the dismaying frequency of fraudulent mediumship. In *A Stellar Key,* however, Davis largely ignores these

regressive and dangerous residents of the higher spheres to focus on a primarily meliorist account of afterlife existence. Andrew Jackson Davis, *The Diakka and Their Earthly Victims, Being an Explanation of Much That Is False and Repulsive in Spiritualism* (New York: A. J. Davis, 1873), 10–11.

16. Chapters 15 ("The Spiritual Zones among the Stars"), 16 ("Travelling and Society in the Summer Land"), and 17 ("The Summer Land as Seen by Clairvoyance") in Davis's *Stellar Key* discuss these attributes of spirit society at length.

17. For more on the nature and range of Plender's approach to modern Spiritualism throughout this project, see Robert Stasinski, "Olivia Plender: I'll Give You Television," *Flash Art* 42, no. 267 (2009): 52–54.

18. See Tessel Bauduin, "Occulture and Modern Art," *Aries: Journal for the Study of Western Esotericism* 13 (2013): 1–5; and Nina Kokkinen, "Occulture as an Analytical Tool in the Study of Art," *Aries: Journal for the Study of Western Esotericism* 13 (2013): 7–36. Dan Smith also discusses this direction in contemporary mixed-media art in "New Maps of Heaven," *Art Monthly* 338 (July–August 2010): 11–14.

19. Examples of these artists' work can be found in their exhibition catalogues and websites; see Suzanne MacWilliam, *Remote Viewing* (London: Black Dog Publishing, 2008); Suzanne Treister, *Hexen 2.0* (Black Dog Publishing, 2012); and videos of and essays on Judd's performances at the website http://benjudd.com.

20. See also Olivia Plender's 2002–6 breakthrough piece, *The Masterpiece,* a graphic narrative that evokes and parodies the myth of the male Romantic genius in its sordid tale of a Swinging Sixties–era painter being alternately courted and menaced by a group of Satanists in a Dennis Wheatley-esque English country house.

21. Olivia Plender, *Cult Fiction* (London: Southbank Centre, 2007), 91. The accessibility and affordability of the comics form is also touted— not without some unintentional irony—in the headnote to Plender's *The Masterpiece* on the Saatchi Gallery website, a venue perhaps more commonly associated with £8,000,000 pickled sharks than with its championship of low-cost popular art forms. Nonetheless, the site explains that "Plender uses the format of the comic book as an alternative mode of distribution for art, capitalizing on its inexpensive accessibility as means to challenge cultural ideals." Saatchi Gallery, *The Masterpiece,* pt. 4, *A Weekend in the Country,* by Olivia Plender, www.saatchigallery.com/artists/olivia_plender.htm (last updated 2016).

22. See Plender's 2006 Tate Triennial piece *Monitor* and her recent installation *Rise Early, Be Industrious* (2012), which draws on the 1970s arts curriculum of the Open University.

23. For examples of the Chick aesthetic, readers are encouraged to visit *Chick Tract Publications,* www.chick.com/catalog/tractlist.asp (accessed 13 July 2013).

24. R. Laurence Moore, *In Search of White Crows: Spiritualism, Parapsychology, and American Culture* (Oxford: Oxford University Press, 1977), 10.

25. Close transatlantic links between the British and American Spiritualist press meant that Davis's manifesto was picked up and reported quickly in the United Kingdom, where at least one leading British journal, the *Psychological Review,* lauded his campaign to abolish phenomenal séances in dark rooms. See "The Law of Deterioration as Applied to Spiritual Phenomena," *Psychological Review* (June 1882): 339–43.

26. Olivia Plender, *A Stellar Key to the Summerland* (London: Book Works, 2007), 1. Hereafter cited in text.

27. Versions of this "Happy Dead Indian" or "Happy Dead Slave" scenario abound in nineteenth-century séance records; readers may wish to consult Mrs. J. H. Conant's *Flashes of Light from the Spirit-Land* (Boston: William White, 1872) and her columns for the Boston-based *Banner of Light* Spiritualist newspaper. Davis's *Answers to Ever-Recurring Questions: A Sequel to the Penetralia* (New York: A. J. Davis, 1862) includes an inspired discussion of the inevitable and predestined extinction of Native Americans because of their status as a mere "transition branch" of the human race (359). For further reading on the treatment of race in the American movement, see note 28.

28. See Robert Cox, *Body and Soul: A Sympathetic History of American Spiritualism* (Charlottesville: University of Virginia Press, 2003); Bridget Bennett, *Transatlantic Spiritualism and Nineteenth-Century American Literature* (Basingstoke, UK: Palgrave Macmillan, 2007); Molly McGarry, *Ghosts of Futures Past: Spiritualism and the Cultural Politics of Nineteenth-Century America* (Berkeley: University of California Press, 2008); and Christine Ferguson, *Determined Spirits: Eugenics, Heredity, and Racial Regeneration in Anglo-American Spiritualist Writing, 1848–1930* (Edinburgh: Edinburgh University Press, 2012).

29. A brief exception lies in the poster panel on page 31, which features a closeup drawing of Davis's face next to a description of his commitment to "abolish slavery of all kinds, including the pestilential institution of marriage." Plender, *Stellar Key,* 31.

30. For more on their notorious confession and the glee with which it was received in the anti-Spiritualist community, see Reuben Briggs Davenport, *The Death-Blow to Spiritualism: Being the True Story of the Fox Sisters, as Revealed by the Authority of Margaret Fox Kane and Catherine Fox Jencken* (New York: G. W. Dillingham, 1888).

31. Henry Maudsley, *Natural Causes and Supernatural Seemings* (London: Kegan, Paul, Trench, 1886).

32. The *Medium and Daybreak* launched on 8 April 1870 and featured the iconic masthead that Plender reproduces from 15 September 1873 to its close on 10 May 1895.

33. Britten, *Modern American Spiritualism,* 309. British artist and Spiritualist Henry Bielfeld, who also created the second masthead for *The Medium and Daybreak* (which ran from 1872 to 1874), designed the illustration for Britten. For more on Bielfeld's work as an artist for the Spiritualist cause, see Paul J. Gaunt, "Henry Bielfeld (1802–1892)," *PsyPioneer Journal* 6, no. 7 (2010): 171–78.

34. Henry Wadsworth Longfellow, "Resignation," line 17, available at *Literature Online,* http://lion.chadwyck.co.uk.

35. The chair and curtain scene might represent two common nineteenth-century séance room arrangements; either the chair is for the medium, in which case we are situated inside the spirit cabinet, or it might, alternatively, be for her chaperone or assistant, in which case we are situated outside the cabinet looking into a black space where the medium sits unseen.

36. See Ann Heilmann and Mark Llewellyn, *Neo-Victorianism: The Victorians in the Twenty-First Century, 1999–2009* (Basingstoke, UK: Palgrave Macmillan, 2010).

37. See Christine Ferguson, "Neo-Victorian Presence: Tom Phillips and the Non-hermeneutic Past," *Australasian Journal of Victorian Studies* 18, no. 3 (2013): 22–57; Anna Maria Jones, *Problem Novels: Victorian Fiction Theorizes the Sensational Self* (Columbus: Ohio State University Press, 2007); and Marie-Luise Kohlke and Christian Gutleben, eds., *Neo-Victorian Tropes of Trauma: The Politics of Bearing After-Witness to Nineteenth-Century Suffering* (Amsterdam: Rodopi, 2010).

III.

Refigured Ideologies

FIVE

A New Order

Reading through Pasts in Will Eisner's
Neo-Victorian Graphic Novel, *Fagin the Jew*

HEIDI KAUFMAN

In the opening frames of Will Eisner's neo-Victorian graphic novel *Fagin the Jew* (2003) the infamous Fagin summons his creator, Charles Dickens, to his prison cell on the evening before his execution.[1] Despite the reader's familiarity with Dickens's novel, the caption on the page insists that the story is completely new. "I am Fagin the Jew of Oliver Twist," the narrator declares. "This is my story, one that has remained untold and overlooked in the book by Charles Dickens."[2] Drawing from fragments of memory, stories heard and collected, and knowledge gleaned from the pages of *Oliver Twist,* Moses Fagin explains how he has been "wrongfully portrayed!" and will be "doomed to wear for eternity that warped and evil image!" (112). Fagin's aim in recounting his history is not to revive the popular parish boy's progress, nor does he intend to recover an idealized Victorian world through a twentieth-century lens. On the contrary, Fagin's objective is to redress a critical silence and a dangerous injustice on the pages of Dickens's novel.

Importantly, and somewhat curiously, Eisner insists in the foreword that his graphic novel "is *not* an adaptation of *Oliver Twist!* It is the story of Fagin the Jew" (n.p.; emphasis added). He adds that while his earlier work on the popular comics series *The Spirit* regrettably drew heavily from racist stereotypes, in subsequent years he attempted to fill out the story in ways that would (he hoped) diminish or counter his earlier offenses. Despite these efforts, Eisner confesses, he realized he was still "feeding a racial prejudice" (n.p.). Eventually he abandoned the project, but his interest in racism and stereotyping remained throughout his career. Eisner explains, "Upon examining the illustrations of the original editions of *Oliver Twist,* I found an unquestionable example of visual defamation in classic literature. The memory of their awful use by the Nazis in World War II, one hundred years later, added evidence to the persistence of evil stereotyping. Combating it became an obsessive pursuit, and I realized that I had no choice but to undertake a truer portrait of Fagin by telling his life story in the only way I could" (n.p.). Eisner's emphasis on the way we read Dickens now, following the Holocaust, is a helpful place to begin thinking about the rising popularity and recognition of neo-Victorian novels in the past thirty years and the growth of scholarly research on this important subject.[3] Ann Heilmann and Mark Llewellyn note that the designation "'neo-Victorian' is *more than* historical fiction set in the nineteenth century. To be part of the neo-Victorianism[,] . . . texts (literary, filmic, audio/visual) must in some respect be *self-consciously engaged with the act of (re)interpretation, (re)discovery and (re)vision concerning the Victorians.*"[4] Louisa Hadley adds, in reference to the recent popularity of neo-Victorian fiction, that "the return to the Victorian era is prompted by an awareness of its difference from our own period. Such accounts are often motivated by a *nostalgic impulse* which positions the Victorian era as a 'golden age' from which the present has dropped off."[5] Similarly, Cora Kaplan maintains, "However much the Victorian world, refracted through its imaginative writing, acts as a foil for arguments about culture and politics today, it is *the rediscovered joys* of Victorian literature that draws [*sic*] modern novelists back to the nineteenth century."[6] Yet if neo-Victorian literature tends toward a nostalgic yearning for the "rediscovered joys of Victorian literature," how then do we understand Eisner's neo-Victorian novel with its emphasis on Victorian anti-Semitism?

Logically, such critical methodologies emphasize the correspondence between the Victorian past and our present, or they underscore the overlapping nature of adaptations and their subjects.[7] Eisner's introductory remarks suggest, however, that neo-Victorian texts are situated not only *around* us and them but also in relation to histories that stand *between* us and them. Eisner's interest in considering the Holocaust in his novel about Fagin reminds us that neo-Victorian novels have the power to imagine the past as an accumulation of histories rather than as a historical relationship linking contemporary readers and Victorians. Accordingly, Eisner's graphic narrative follows less of a leapfrog path (from there to here) than a furrow through imagined and shifting historical channels. Eisner might have thought of other genocides, other examples of what he terms "visual defamation" or "evil stereotyping." Still, this one named history in his foreword anchors *Fagin the Jew* in a particular historical event and shows, in the process, why that event affects our engagement with a Victorian text that precedes it.

Working against the image of Fagin as the evil, pitchfork-wielding Jew that George Cruikshank made famous (see fig. 5.1), Eisner creates Fagin anew, as a product of an anti-Semitic culture and as an orphan struggling to survive in London's criminal underworld. Eisner's choice to recover Fagin's history and voice in the medium of the graphic novel simultaneously raises questions about the blending of comics and neo-Victorian fiction. According to Hilary Chute, one common feature of the medium of comics or graphic narrative is both an interest in the recovery of history and an awareness of the fragmentary incompleteness of memory. Chute explains that the medium frequently displays "an awareness of the limits of representation" that is "integrated into comics through its framed, self-conscious, bimodal form; yet it is precisely in its insistent, affective, urgent visualizing of historical circumstance that comics aspires to ethical engagement."[8] As the following discussion makes clear, Eisner uses the comics form to illustrate the challenge and importance of humanizing Fagin. In creating Fagin's past—albeit in a form that strategically resists closure—Eisner enables this infamous character to emerge as more than just an ugly stereotype, but as a multifaceted character, one whose complex history and perspective also enrich the better-known tale of Oliver Twist's progress. I am interested in considering *Fagin the Jew*'s foregrounding of the illusory and fractured construction of history and memory from a variety of historical moments. Julian Wolfreys notes that neo-Victorian writing reminds us to listen to the recovered voices of the Other that are often omitted from Victorian literature. As he puts it, "[O]ur ethical responsibility is registered as being open

FIG. 5.1   George Cruikshank, "Oliver Introduced to the Respectable Old Gentleman," from Charles Dickens, *Oliver Twist,* 3 vols. (London: Richard Bentley, 1838), vol. 1: facing page 132. Image courtesy of Cadbury Research Library: Special Collections, University of Birmingham.

to the other's coming, which creates the possibility that the other might arrive or return so as to speak in its own voice, however 'channelled' [*sic*] that voice or its transcription might be."[9] And in listening to Fagin's voice channeled through Eisner's art, readers encounter the palimpsestuous nature of the comics medium—its folds and fractures certainly, but also its recovery of the multiple and distinguishable histories and voices of young Oliver and Fagin woven through and against one another.

In constructing Fagin's story through word-image correspondence, Eisner exposes the way racial stereotyping flattens characters by wrestling with the possibilities of historical recovery and literary (re)invention. In addition to emphasizing the disturbing and powerful legacy of anti-Semitic stereotypes in *Oliver Twist,* Eisner imagines a way of reading these texts in a new order—that is, the form and content of this graphic novel present the Victorian period in forward *and* backward sequence.[10] Ultimately, *Fagin the Jew* reminds us that if we cannot change the literary past and its legacy, at the very least we can change the way we read representations of one past in light of several others.

———◆———

W ill Eisner and Charles Dickens have much in common, including their leading roles as innovators of literary forms. In 1836–37, Dickens revolutionized the novel with the serialization of *Pickwick Papers.* The *Quarterly Review* claimed that this act was "one of the most remarkable literary phenomena of recent times."[11] As numerous scholars and readers have since noted, sequenced publishing enabled a fuller readership, a less costly product, and a riveting story that had to sell and, by extension, had to keep readers interested. Dickens replicated the form of *Pickwick* in *The Adventures of Oliver Twist; or, The Parish Boy's Progress,* published in monthly installments from 1837 to 1839 in *Bentley's Miscellany.*[12] In this work, Dickens included vivid illustrations created by the well-known artist George Cruikshank. Among other things, the use of word and image collaboration helped readers visualize and recall characters from one monthly installment to the next.

Dickens and Eisner drew from overlapping literary and artistic trajectories. Both authors created a blending of social criticism and progress narrative, as some have argued, responding to the tradition of William Hogarth's well-known sequential engravings, including *The Harlot's Progress* (1732) and *The Rake's Progress* (1735).[13] Brian Maidment notes that in these works Hogarth "constructed several layers of verbal presence that, while not overlaying or obtruding onto the image, nonetheless frame it with words" (see chapter 1, this volume). In contrast, the narrative of *Oliver Twist* uses illustration as a framing device for the narrative. Despite these important differences, when Dickens began composing *Oliver Twist* he was drawing as much from the rich tradition of novels depicting character development as he was from Hogarth's illustrations satirizing the potential for individual progress.

Eisner has been credited with helping to develop the medium of comics. Born in 1917 of Jewish immigrants—a mother from Romania and a father from Austria—Eisner was raised in Brooklyn, New York. As a child he studied art, sold newspapers, and later worked in print shops, all of which helped foster his interest in the comics medium. Finally in 1936, he published his first comic in *Wow!* Not until 1939, however, did Eisner's career as a comics artist begin to take off. Jeremy Dauber explains that in that year "Eisner was asked by Busy Arnold, the owner of Quality Comics Group, to join the group to produce a sixteen-page supplement to be nationally syndicated in the Sunday editions of major newspapers, a project that had never been done before. . . . The supplement . . . contained three four-color features developed by Eisner, with *The Spirit*—a central character in the history of the comic book—as its lead feature."[14] Eisner's transition from the shorter work of comic books to longer graphic novels evolved over the course of many years. In fact, he claimed early in his career, "I had been long convinced that I was involved with a medium that had real 'literary potential.'"[15] Although Eisner abandoned *The Spirit* after twelve years, he remained closely connected with the medium. In time, he began his groundbreaking work *A Contract with God and Other Stories* (1978), a text in which Eisner explored lives of New Yorkers. The longer length and sophisticated image/text interactions allowed Eisner to handle with tremendous adeptness the nuances of character interiority, memory, and emotion. Eisner later published comics focused on history and literature, in addition to producing two scholarly books: *Comics and Sequential Art* (1985) and *Graphic Storytelling* (1996).[16]

Fagin the Jew, written much later in Eisner's career, depicts the life of a young boy, Moses Fagin, educated by a father well versed in the tricks of street thievery. When young Fagin's father is murdered in a vicious act of anti-Semitism and his mother perishes from illness and hunger, a wealthy Jewish man, Mr. Eleazer Salomon, takes Fagin into his home and helps him find work. Subsequently, at the age of seventeen, Salomon hires Fagin to clean up a building slated to be used as a school to educate the East End Jewish poor. Here, Fagin meets and falls in love with Rebecca Lopez, the daughter of another philan-thropist involved in the school-renovation initiative. When Rebecca's father discovers the lovers in a romantic embrace, he banishes Fagin from the school. With little education, no family or social network, and no professional training, Fagin becomes the prey of street crimi-nals. In time, the authorities catch Fagin selling stolen goods—which he did not realize were stolen—and sentence him to hard labor in a penal colony. Fagin returns to London ten years later, as he puts it, "aged beyond my years. Broken in body, in fragile health, I was in appearance a shuffling greybeard, the result of the horrors of penal life and imprisonment" (43). He adds, "However, I still had my wits about me. Sharper than ever were my skills, which were honed in the penal colonies" (43). Eisner suggests that while crime may be learned on the streets, its antidote—punishment in a penal colony—has the effect of increasing crime on the very streets where it began.

The remainder of the novel weaves together Oliver's well-known history with Fagin's ruminations on his life of crime. Fagin is clearly different from other criminals in his circle. For example, when Bill Sikes robs Salomon's house, Fagin returns the stolen property to the family. In such moments, Eisner imagines Fagin as a thief with a powerful conscience. Eisner's point is not to excuse Fagin's behavior. Rather, in charting Fagin's history and demise, Eisner shows the pro-cess by which characters and people become criminal. On this point Eisner is not original: Dickens similarly explored the complicated so-cial problems that led to the rise of crime in early nineteenth-century London. Criminal behavior, both authors suggest, is the product of depraved social conditions and individual acts of desperation. While Eisner takes this narrative one step further to consider London's nineteenth-century Jewish world, like Dickens he traces the unset-tling progress of children toward a life of crime. Given no other op-tion, Eisner's Fagin plays by rules he did not create, and teaches Oliver those very rules in order to give him an advantage in negotiations of street culture. In a turn on Dickens's well-known rendering of Fagin's interest in desensitizing children to criminal acts, Eisner imagines criminal education as essential to survival.

Despite their shared interest in London crime, Dickens's and Eis-ner's novels are products of entirely different media forms. Dickens's serialized text and Cruikshank's engravings were synchronized, certainly, but as artists, Dickens and Cruikshank worked independently.[17] Dickens rooted his narrative in words, paragraphs, chapters, and monthly parts; with images and captions; and with an omniscient narrator who speaks alternately with a tone of satire, sympathy, and exposition. Eisner uses a medium no more or less complex, but his draws from an entirely different range of conventions that mediate and produce the novel's subject matter. In his scholarly work, based on his teaching at the School of Visual Arts in New York, Eisner claims, "Reading in a purely textual sense was mugged on its way to the twenty-first century by the electronic and digital media, which influenced and changed how we read."[18] Admittedly, multiple forms of media shaped Victorian reading strategies. Eisner's claim is nevertheless important because of the rise of new media over the course of the twentieth century. Hence, according to Eisner, "The reading process in comics is an extension of text. In text alone the process of reading involves word-to-image conversion. Comics accelerates that by providing the image. When properly executed, it goes beyond conversion and speed and becomes a seamless whole. In every sense, this misnamed form of reading is entitled to be regarded as literature because the images are employed as a language" (xvii). Others have argued in contrast that one of the defining features of the medium is its attention to its fractures. Hilary Chute notes, for example, that graphic narrative proceeds by a "manifest handling of its own artifice, its attention to its seams. Its formal grammar rejects transparency and renders textualization conspicuous, inscribing the context in its graphic presentation."[19] Readers of graphic novels may interpret a cohesive language, but one of the abiding aesthetic concerns of the medium, according to Chute and others, is the problem of the breaks on the page, which often stand for the ideological or conceptual breaks in narrative. Thus, while many forms of storytelling seek to bind or blend fractures in an effort to make the story seem whole, comics artists frequently use the medium's form, which deploys visual fractures, to play with or amplify traces of narrative gaps.

Graphic novels may respond to illustrated Victorian novels; however, they do not deploy image/word correspondence in quite the same way. Scott McCloud describes the unique structure of comics using visual/sound metaphors. As he puts it, one of the defining features of the comics medium is that its "panels fracture both time and space, offering a jagged, staccato rhythm of unconnected moments."[20] Chute adds that not only does the comics medium adeptly showcase fractures of time and space but comics, as she puts it, "register[s] temporality spatially": "Comics moves forward in time through the space of the page, through its progressive counterpoint of presence and absence: packed panels (also called frames) alternating with gutters (empty space). [Comics] doesn't blend the visual and the verbal—or use one simply to illustrate the other—but is rather prone to present the two nonsynchronously; a reader of comics not only fills in the gaps between panels but also works with the often disjunctive back-and-forth of *reading* and *looking* for meaning."[21] The juxtaposition of image with blank spaces in *Fagin the Jew* elucidates the challenge of creating a cohesive story with an absolute, complete blending of parts. Eisner's use of fractures and spaces to chart time draws attention to the narrative's contractedness, its seams and gaps, its jagged voices alternately frozen or broken by frames and gutters, and the staging of the narrator's historical recovery of Fagin's life. Similarly, Eisner echoes this visual process in his choice of subject. Dickens created Fagin without a history. Therefore, Eisner must first recover a missing story Dickens *did not* write (the history of Fagin) before he can show the impact of that story on the one Dickens *did* write (the history of Oliver Twist).

Eisner draws from the formal conventions of his medium to widen and accentuate gaps within Dickens's narrative. His artistic choices effectively collapse and expand time. As a neo-Victorian text, *Fagin the Jew* works to recover through invention a past filtered through intermediating histories. Yet Eisner also uses the comics form to recover or invent Fagin's past. For example, by using sepia tones and blurred frame edges, Eisner creates a sense of fading photographs. The existence of gutters may seem to separate events or to evoke pauses in time, but Eisner softens the edges of his frames with gentle, memory-like fadeouts. Moreover, Eisner uses closeup and panned-out images, or scenes broken into a chain of angled shots as the eye moves in a circular pattern to capture its subject. Such visual strategies echo and reflect on both the Victorian novel that prompted it and the significance of Dickens's submersion of Fagin's past. On the surface Eisner's story would seem to replay a familiar social problem: the Anglicized orphan is saved while the Jewish child perishes. The following reading suggests, however, that Eisner's final twist in the plot offers instead an original ending that builds from *Oliver Twist*'s historical gaps and absent perspectives, which the neo-Victorian graphic novel is uniquely poised to recover because of its form and narrative lens.

———————

Above I argue that in his creation of Fagin's life, Eisner's novel looks through, and in turn is influenced by, the histories that stand between us and the Victorians. The path to the Victorian past is central to Eisner's artistic lens. Yet it is also a paradigm for the creation of Fagin's character. In his memoir Fagin weaves together an identity that draws from various events throughout his life. As a neo-Victorian text, *Fagin the Jew* does not merely create a character but reshapes a character well known to readers, if not through the pages of Dickens's novel then from the stage or film adaptations of *Oliver Twist*. In this way, *Fagin the Jew* presents a compelling study of how one author enters and revises a discourse that is both already in place and susceptible to fluctuations with each generation of writers, illustrators, producers, and audiences.

Using the conventions the comics medium makes possible, Eisner emphasizes both the complexity of Fagin's character and the problem of combating a stereotype. To begin with, Eisner creates a frame narrative whereby Fagin and Dickens engage in a discussion about *Oliver Twist*'s anti-Semitic stereotypes in the opening and closing sequences of the novel. Thus, Fagin has called his creator to his cell because he is disturbed by Dickens's portrayal of Jewish identity in *Oliver Twist*. Midway through Fagin's narration, readers alternate between the story we know well (Oliver Twist's history) and the one new to us (Moses Fagin's history). Finally, following the end frame, Eisner includes an epilogue that draws from a series of flashbacks to recover/reimagine Fagin's past from multiple perspectives, including those unknown to Fagin. Readers thus move backward and forward through time: we read an old novel from the perspective of a new one; we revisit Fagin's story following his death; and we re-see Fagin's narrative in light of the story that Adele Brownlow, Oliver's wife and the granddaughter of Fagin's love interest, tells in the novel's epilogue. The result is a palimpsestuous text in which several narratives told out of sequence and through the graphic novel's fragmented structure corroborate to remake Fagin's character and revise Dickens's novel.

I proceed, then, by building from Sarah Dillon's helpful observation that palimpsests "were created by a process of layering whereby the existing text was erased, using various chemical methods, and the new text was written over the old one." "Although the first writing on the vellum seemed to have been eradicated after treatment," Dillon continues, "it was often imperfectly erased. Its ghostly trace then reappeared in the following centuries as the iron in the remaining ink reacted with the oxygen in the air, producing a reddish-brown oxide."[22] Dillon stresses that the earlier shapes do not remain static but change over time in response to new physical contexts—air, light, chemicals with which they become mixed—as well as ideological content from later historical moments. Thus, as a neo–Victorian novel *Fagin the Jew* leans on, shadows, or evokes the ghosts of *Oliver Twist*. In turn, the ever-changing litany of histories that stand between these two novels alters the way we read both. The resulting structure is palimpsestuous not just because it contains separable elements from different historical moments but also because of the way each historical moment continually plays upon and alters our understanding of the rest. Eisner achieves this effect both in his use of the fractured qualities of comics storytelling and in the sequencing of his narrative. Through this process Eisner invites readers to consider the potentially dangerous power of words and images to simplify, demonize, or otherwise falsely construct human character as anything less than complex.

Writing in 1996, Eisner claimed in *Graphic Storytelling and Visual Narrative* that stereotype "has a bad reputation not only because it implies banality but [also] because of its use as a weapon of propaganda or racism." The stereotype, he adds, "is a fact of life in the comics medium" because "[comic] book art deals with recognizable reproductions of human conduct" and depends on "the reader's stored memory of experience to visualize an idea or process quickly" (11). The real problem with stereotypes, he suggests, is that they are put to inappropriate uses by creators and audiences. Eisner adds that comics artists invoking stereotypes must have "a familiarity with the audience and recognition that each society has its own ingrained set of accepted stereotypes" (13).[23] According to this view, stereotypes are not essentially bad. Eisner implies that forms of character reduction and simplification can be used intentionally to draw out a narrative's complexity or ideological aims. When misused, however, stereotyping achieves the reverse by playing into misplaced or dangerous cultural constructions that overdetermine—rather than open up—a text's meaning.

Dickens's portrayal of Fagin draws from early nineteenth-century stereotypes of Jewish criminals. Frank Felsenstein points out, "In common with many earlier representations of the diabolized Jew-figure, [Dickens's] Fagin is depicted throughout the novel in terms that render him less than human, both brutish and repulsive."[24] Yet beyond just demonizing and dehumanizing, Dickens's narration and Cruikshank's iconography work together to render Fagin a member of the Sephardim, the group of Jewish immigrants who began fleeing Spain and Portugal in 1492 with the start of the Inquisition during the reign of Ferdinand and Isabella. In 1656 descendants of this group gained formal admission to England. Eisner's choice to transform Fagin from a Sephardic to an Ashkenazi Jewish figure profoundly alters the meaning of his criminal behavior. In the afterword to his novel, Eisner explains,

> Until about 1700, the Sephardim were the dominant
> Jewish population in England, but the "lower class"
> who arrived during the eighteenth century were mostly
> Ashkenazim. They came from Germany and Middle
> Europe, where they had lived in small villages until driven
> out by intolerance, repression, and pogroms. Rural life
> and peasant culture had rendered them less educated and
> cruder in their ways. As a result, when they arrived in
> London they had difficulty assimilating. . . . Impoverished
> and illiterate, they took up marginal occupations in the
> grimier quarters of London. It is reasonable to assume
> that Fagin came from such origins. (n.p.)

Sephardim and Ashkenazim had distinct social and economic identities throughout much of the nineteenth century and accordingly became part of different ideological and aesthetic trajectories in Victorian print and visual culture.[25] Eisner notes that Cruikshank's illustrations of Fagin "were based on the appearance of the Sephardim, whose features . . . were sharper with dark hair and complexions" (n.p.). Yet redrawn as a member of the Ashkenazi group in Eisner's text—as a struggling immigrant lacking educational opportunities—Fagin stands as a victim of the very same social and economic problems with which Dickens's Oliver struggled. Thus while Cruikshank's illustrations construct Fagin, as Felsenstein notes, as a Sephardic-looking devil, with dark skin and foreign-looking features, in Eisner's construction Fagin does not look all that different from Oliver. In fact, in two frames (see fig. 5.2 and fig. 5.3), Fagin and Oliver wear the same clothes, and their comments echo one another. In these moments Eisner uses stereotypes strategically. By replacing one Jewish stereotype with another, Eisner transforms Fagin from a foreigner and villain into a victim of missed opportunities and deep-rooted Victorian social problems.

In the first sequence of Eisner's novel, Fagin introduces his younger self as a stereotype of the Ashkenazi Jewish peddler. Readers witness Fagin's father teaching him how to steal on the street. His father claims that "these are times that ask for certain skills of survival"—an explanation the young boy accepts (9). Fagin's inauspicious beginning as a

FIG. 5.2   Fagin (*far left*):"Ten pounds . . . not a farthing more!" Will Eisner, *Fagin the Jew* (Milwaukie, OR: Dark Horse Comics, 2013), 32. Reproduced with permission. *Fagin the Jew* © 2003 Will Eisner Studios, Inc.

FIG. 5.3   Oliver (*far left*):"We work so hard."Will Eisner, *Fagin the Jew* (Milwaukie, OR: Dark Horse Comics, 2013), 58. Reproduced with permission. *Fagin the Jew* © 2003 Will Eisner Studios, Inc.

criminal-in-training would seem to suggest that the stereotypes are true—Jewish criminals are prolific, and London crime is the result of the presence of dangerous foreigners. Todd Endelman notes that an "upswing in Jewish criminal activity . . . began in the late 1760s and early 1770s [and] continued to rise over the next five decades."[26] As with crime among other groups or individuals, Jewish crime in the early nineteenth century was linked to poverty, limited access to educational opportunities, and immigrant struggles to acculturate. Endelman adds, "The majority of English Jews, including the very poorest, were probably no more dishonest or no more virtuous than their English counterparts. But to minds accustomed to thinking in a stereotypical fashion about Jews . . . it seemed that criminality within the Jewish community was coterminous with the entire Jewish community."[27]

Fagin's history begins with a visit to a fight by the popular and successful Sephardic pugilist Daniel Mendoza (1764–1836). This is a "very important day for Jews," Fagin's father explains to his son: "Today, Daniel Mendoza, our great Jewish Boxer, will fight Joe Ward the gentile!" (11). Following the successful fight, Fagin's father enters a bar to collect his winnings. He tells his young son to wait outside, explaining, "[T]his is not a place for you!" (14). Readers see Fagin's father ask for his money, which he won by betting on Mendoza; we witness the ensuing anti-Semitic comments; and we watch as Fagin's father is beaten to death and tossed onto the street. Fagin witnesses none of this, and yet, as the narrator speaking many years later, he manages to convey the events that led to his father's death. Readers are left wondering, how can he know what took place in the pub when he stood outside? We recall Chute's earlier point that "comics doesn't blend the visual and the verbal—or use one simply to illustrate the other—but is rather prone to present the two nonsynchronously."[28] Thus, while Fagin tells his story with words, the visual images convey a separate narrative. When the young Fagin pleads for help from a couple passing by his bleeding father, the man replies, "Careful, it's a Jewish street trick! Don't stop!" (15). Unlike the reader, who can see the events that take place in the bar, Fagin does not witness the scene of his father's assault. Therefore, he narrates with a limited perspective. The man's anti-Jewish comments, however, stand in for the beating Fagin misses.

Eisner's arrangement of word and image illuminates a tension in the murder scene and signals what Frank L. Cioffi characterizes as a form of pause used by cartoonists. He explains, "An image will conjure up something in the reader, something rather immediate and specific. . . . The words accompanying the image, however, take a slightly longer time for the reader to process. Between image comprehension and word comprehension ensues a slight pause, such as the pause in a movie theater where a subtitled film is being shown and the audience must read the subtitles before understanding what has been said."[29] The movements from bar scene to street, from absent voices to dismissive comment, create gaps or pauses in the middle of the story sequence. In addition to our delay in processing the series of events, this gap mirrors Fagin's act of reconstructing events he never witnessed. Why has his father been beaten to death? Readers, like the young Fagin, must account for the transition from scenes of violence in the bar to the passing couple's expression of apathy and suspiciousness, with the pleading Fagin in the middle. We must also make sense of the transition from the earlier depiction of Fagin's father justifying his act of cheating a man out of a coin by teaching his son that crime is a fact of life—literally, in this case, a matter of survival. Fractures in these early moments in the narrative anticipate larger breaks in subsequent scenes, thereby laying the groundwork for Eisner's fuller exploration of the shaping of character.

Following the death of his mother and his banishment from the school for Jewish poor, the helpless Fagin becomes the prey of street criminals. When Oliver finally makes his way to London, he follows in Fagin's footsteps. Thus the well-known story of Oliver becomes familiar not just because of *Oliver Twist* but also because it echoes the story Eisner has created about Fagin. In effect, then, Eisner continually moves readers backward and forward through time—that is, from our knowledge of Oliver in *Oliver Twist* to our new understanding of Fagin in *Fagin the Jew* and back to Oliver in *Fagin the Jew*. In this way he presents a story that precedes Oliver's history and that Oliver's history, in turn, repeats. In addition to aligning the plight of the two boys, Eisner's neo-Victorian lens replays time, reorganizing our understanding of both orphan children in light of that revised sequence of events.

More than just reworking the chronology, Eisner deploys corresponding visual tactics that further underscore the complexity of Fagin's character. In Fagin's final conversation with Dickens, which takes place in the closing frame of Fagin's narrative, Eisner evokes one of the most famous images from *Oliver Twist:* Fagin awaiting his execution in the jail cell (see fig. 5.4). Here, in Fagin's final hour, Eisner's illustrations circle around Fagin, freezing each angle and perspective along the way (see fig. 5.5). First we see Fagin in the shadow; next we see Fagin from behind; then we see him up close; panned out; and finally from the side. Dickens's face remains hidden, which helps to keep this scene focused on Fagin's plea. While Dickens claims that the image of the criminal Jew is "a truth that needs to be told," Fagin shoots back defiantly, "Truth?? . . . Is referring to a man only by his race the truth? . . . Or is 'Jew' as a word for criminal true?" (112). Fagin's point is that Dickens should see beyond stereotypes, considering instead the history and contexts that lead characters into a life of crime. This is a point Dickens makes in his depiction of Brownlow's desire to see Oliver not as a criminal but as a child who has been wronged by society. Presenting Fagin from a range of angles, moving the lens around his body, alternately panning in and out, functions as a visualization of Fagin's complicated place in a culture that both villainizes Jews and criminalizes the poor. In the variety of perspectives that present Fagin's body in this final hour, the action stands still. Imagined in this way, the page's visual rhetoric makes the same point as Fagin: to understand people we must see them from multiple angles. The fragments and gaps, gutters, and shifting narrative gaze recall both the need to see a fuller picture and the impossibility of ever doing so completely. Thus, Eisner's images help to raise one of the central dangers of stereotypes: if, after all, portraying character requires so many angles and so much attention to fissures in a person's history, how can audiences ever accept a flat stereotype as "the truth"?

In a final plot twist, the epilogue to *Fagin the Jew* opens with Oliver Twist Brownlow telling his own life story. After announcing his marriage to Adele, the granddaughter of Fagin's former love interest, Rebecca Lopez, Oliver asks his wife to complete the narrative. Adele Lopez Brownlow begins her account by recalling events that took place before her birth—events that readers have already encountered in Fagin's narrative. In his memoir Fagin explains that he returned Salomon's stolen goods. Yet Fagin never knew that Rebecca Lopez was in the house at the time. In Fagin's narrative, readers witness a desperate—but honest—Fagin looking deflated in the rain after dropping off *(right)* FIG. 5.4 George Cruikshank, "Fagin in the Condemned Cell," from Charles Dickens, *Oliver Twist*, 3 vols. (London: Richard Bentley, 1838), vol. 3: facing page 296. Image courtesy of Cadbury Research Library: Special Collections, University of Birmingham.

(below) FIG. 5.5 Fagin confronts Dickens. Will Eisner, *Fagin the Jew* (Milwaukie, OR: Dark Horse Comics, 2013), 112–13. Reproduced with permission. *Fagin the Jew* © 2003 Will Eisner Studios, Inc.

the loot. In contrast, Adele's narrative captures a conversation between her grandmother (Rebecca) and Adele's unnamed mother. According to this new version of the story, Rebecca senses that Fagin has returned the goods, because, as she puts it, "No beggar returns loot and does not accept a reward!! It could only be Fagin! I know it!" (121). Rebecca Lopez subsequently elaborates on Salomon's despair upon Fagin's departure. In an effort to find the boy he had come to think of as a son, Salomon has a portrait made of Fagin, which he places in his gold watch. Once again echoing Brownlow's interest in finding Oliver, Salomon shares the picture with strangers, hoping to be reunited with the boy who "disappeared into the slums of London!" (120).

The two fragments depicting Fagin's visit to the Salomon household are linked by a third. Upon his return to London following transportation, Fagin pickpockets a man who notices instantly that he has been robbed. When the man calls out, Fagin drops the watch in the street and pretends to have discovered it, a street trick probably common among those making a living from crime. In this exchange, a woman walking with the man turns out to be Rebecca. She recognizes Fagin but hesitates to speak to him. In hindsight, with the knowledge we gain from Adele's story, we are led to wonder if this watch was the very same one encasing Fagin's picture. Did Fagin come *that* close to discovery and the chance to live an honest life? Yet Eisner's choice to link different events in Fagin's life with a watch—a symbol of time—extends his point about both the challenge of fully recovering events from the past and the comics medium's proclivity for representing time as fractured when visualized on the page. Thus, a single event (the loot-return scene) is presented by two moments in time and is subsequently recontextualized by a third event (Rebecca's act of recognizing Fagin on the street). Rebecca's moment of silence—or refusal to recognize Fagin on the occasion of the watch's disappearance—foreshadows her later pronouncement to her unnamed daughter to pass down Salomon's watch, containing a picture of Fagin. Juxtaposing scenes in this way enables Eisner to comment on lost and imagined stories of Fagin through his sequencing of the plot. What readers encounter in the middle sections of the novel changes our understanding of what follows, just as what we learn in the final pages of the novel leads us back to a new interpretation of the novel's beginning. *Fagin the Jew* is therefore not just a story of two moments in time (then and now) but also of the histories that continually reframe our understanding of the Victorians and our own shifting cultural moment.

Adele's recounting of her grandmother's past concludes with a sequence in which Eisner does not use standard gutter space between the panels but superimposes three windows against the brick wall of a house (see fig. 5.6). The leftmost window could at first be read as belonging to the house, though upon closer inspection we see that its edges do not follow the angle of the wall. The middle and far windows hover more obviously outside the visual structure.[30] The positioning of the windows helps to position readers standing outside the house in precisely the place where Fagin stood after returning to look back on his old home. The wall functions as a kind of historical boundary while also—because the windows float in the air—demonstrating how stories move from one generation to the next. This kind of sequence raises questions about the lineage of the story. Rebecca tells her daughter, "Here, my dear! . . . I give this watch to you! . . . Keep it! In this way Moses Fagin will, symbolically at least, belong to a family!" (121). On the very next page Adele explains, "My mother died as I was born. As the first and only child, of course, I received the locket. . . . But I knew nothing of Fagin until I married Oliver" (122). Oliver has the final word on Fagin: "Alas. . . . The only testimony to his life is a book and a presumed heirloom!" (122). It is unclear if the book Oliver mentions is the one written by Dickens or Eisner while mention of a "presumed heirloom" (as opposed to a real one) recalls the fictionality of both novels. We cannot help but wonder, if Adele's mother died in childbirth, how does she know her grandmother's story? It seems that as stories and objects are passed down they are anchored by their narrators, whose perspectives shape what listeners and readers understand to be true, presumed, told, witnessed, and ultimately fractured.

The choice to thread the symbol of the watch through the various generations of storytellers helps to raise the question of time and perspective. Yet the watch—echoing the locket that linked Oliver Twist to his mother—also signals the impossibility of recovering the past fully. Time moves forward, after all, even as characters look back. Whereas the pieces of history may point to the fictionality of both novels, the emphasis in Eisner's text rests on questions of interpretation and a continuous process of revising the past.

FIG. 5.6   Fagin remembered. Will Eisner, *Fagin the Jew* (Milwaukie, OR: Dark Horse Comics, 2013), 121. Reproduced with permission. *Fagin the Jew* © 2003 Will Eisner Studios, Inc.

Eisner creates a complicated narrative architecture with an opening and closing frame, an interior memoir that details events the narrator could never have known, and an epilogue whose narrator shares a mysteriously unrecorded history of Fagin. The novel is further circumscribed by Eisner's foreword and afterword. Narrative discontinuities throughout the text turn the plot inside out to show seams of memory and historical displacement, of wall and window frames, and events in the lives of two little boys who fall tragically into a life of crime. In the process, Eisner creates a palimpsestuous structure out of a language rooted in word and image correspondence and of boys orphaned and abandoned to the criminal underworld of London. A deep division separates their outcomes, such that one boy is saved and the other perishes. Eisner in this process not only humanizes Fagin by granting him a history that explains why he perishes but also invents a history out of the graphic novel's unique storytelling language. Unlike so many other neo-Victorian texts that draw on a nostalgic longing for a past we can never fully reach, Eisner offers instead a meditation on how we might reread Victorian novels today through the histories that stand between us and them and shape our understanding and engagement with earlier texts.

Eisner's challenge is not unlike that of Walter Benjamin's angel, hoping to stay and awaken the dead, to make whole what has been broken, to fix what has been lost, to return to a moment in time when the stereotype of the evil Jew was an unfortunate consequence rather than a justification for genocide.[31] Yet readers of the graphic novel know that this concession plays no part in overwriting the damage of Fagin; it does nothing to thwart the progression toward death camps and gas chambers. *Fagin the Jew* nevertheless engages powerfully with Dickens and Cruikshank by recovering Fagin's voice and by revising Oliver's progress. This is not the same thing as reading anachronistically; nor is it necessarily a symbol of desire or reverence for an idealized Victorian past. As I have tried to suggest, Eisner's novel signals some of the ways in which events accumulate, and hence our turn to the past prompts us to process that level of accumulation in some way. As a neo-Victorian graphic novel, *Fagin the Jew*'s form and aesthetic innovations move readers repeatedly backward and forward so that we can read and reread the past out of sequence, in a new order. In registering the uncomfortable burdens of history, we engage in forms of intellectual remediation; and in shifting from one genre or medium to another—from illustrated novel to graphic novel—we witness and experience Eisner's process of artistic remediation. Thus, old stories are made new by the narrative's acts of folding back, of interruption and amplification, and of interventions that reach toward a form of closure to "classics" we come to know through time.

Notes

1. I use the terms *graphic novel, graphic narrative,* and *comics* interchangeably throughout this chapter. *Fagin the Jew* is a work of fiction, and therefore *graphic novel* may seem like the best label to describe it. Because Eisner's fictional narrative engages with conventions more often found in graphic memoirs, however, it might make more sense to refer to *Fagin the Jew* as a *graphic narrative,* a term Hilary Chute has developed in *Graphic Women: Life Narrative and Contemporary Comics* (New York: Columbia University Press, 2010). In his foreword, Eisner claims that he "began to produce graphic novels with themes of Jewish ethnicity and the prejudice Jews still face" (n.p.), suggesting that *graphic novel* is Eisner's preferred classification for *Fagin the Jew.* Will Eisner, *Fagin the Jew,* 2nd ed. (Milwaukie, OR: Dark Horse Comics, 2013), n.p.

2. Eisner, *Fagin the Jew,* 5. Hereafter cited in text.

3. In *Neo-Victorian Fiction and Historical Narrative: The Victorians and Us* (Basingstoke, UK: Palgrave Macmillan, 2010), Louisa Hadley notes that the popularity of the neo-Victorian novel represents a significant turn in the history of the contemporary British novel. Hadley points to the success of A. S. Byatt's *Possession: A Romance* (1990) as a "crucial nodal point" in neo-Victorian fiction: "Winning both prestigious literary prizes, such as the Man Booker Prize and the *Irish Times*–Aer Lingus International Fiction Prize, and a place on the bestsellers' lists, *Possession* catapulted neo-Victorian fiction into the mainstream." Hadley, *Neo-Victorian Fiction,* 2.

4. Ann Heilmann and Mark Llewellyn, *Neo-Victorianism: The Victorians in the Twenty-First Century, 1999–2009* (Basingstoke, UK: Palgrave Macmillan, 2010), 4. Emphasis in the original.

5. Hadley, *Neo-Victorian Fiction,* 8. Emphasis added.

6. Cora Kaplan, *Victoriana: Histories, Fictions, Criticism* (New York: Columbia University Press, 2007), 106. Emphasis added.

7. Scholars of adaptation theory, such as Linda Hutcheon, have been especially attentive to the palimpsestuous nature of historical accumulation or overlaps in relational texts. Although Eisner claims that his novel is not an adaptation, its narrative and ideological architecture function palimpsestuously because of the histories with which his novel engages and the way he structures his narrative in relation to *Oliver Twist.*

8. Hillary Chute, "Comics as Literature? Reading Graphic Narrative," *PMLA* 123, no. 2 (2008): 457.

9. Julian Wolfreys, "Notes Towards a Poethics of Spectrality: The Examples of Neo-Victorian Textuality," in *Reading Historical Fiction: The Revenant and Remembered Past,* ed. Kate Mitchell and Nicola Parsons (Basingstoke, UK: Palgrave Macmillan, 2013), 156.

10. Sarah Dillon adds that "'Palimpsestuous' does not name something as, or as making, a palimpsest. Rather, it describes the complex (textual) relationality embodied in the palimpsest. Where 'palimpsestic' refers to the process of layering that produces a palimpsest, 'palimpsestuous' describes the structure with which one is presented as a result of that process, and the subsequent reappearance of the underlying script." Dillon, "Reinscribing De Quincey's Palimpsest: The Significance of the Palimpsest in Contemporary Literary and Cultural Studies," *Textual Practice* 19, no. 3 (2005): 245.

11. Quoted in Stephen Gill, introduction to *Oliver Twist,* by Charles Dickens, edited by Kathleen Tillotson (Oxford: Oxford University Press, 1999), vii.

12. *Oliver Twist* was published in overlapping editions. The serialized edition appeared from 1837 to 1839. A second edition appeared in a three-volume format in 1838. Although these early editions contained some differences with regard to their illustrations, those discussed in this chapter were identical in both editions. Images reproduced here are from the triple-decker volume because of the superior image quality.

13. For a detailed discussion of the narrative implications of Hogarth's work, see chapter 1, this volume.

14. Jeremy Dauber, "Comic Books, Tragic Stories: Will Eisner's American Jewish History," in *The Jewish Graphic Novel: Critical Approaches,* ed. Samantha Baskind and Ranen Omer-Sherman (New Brunswick, NJ: Rutgers University Press, 2008), 23–24.

15. Quoted in ibid., 24.

16. *Comics and Sequential Art* (Poorhouse Press, 1985) was republished in a revised, expanded edition in 1990 with the same title. *Graphic Storytelling* (Will Eisner Studios, Inc., 1996) was republished with a new title, *Graphic Storytelling and Visual Narrative: Principles and Practices from the Legendary Cartoonist* (Will Eisner Studios, Inc., 2008). Both were republished as Norton paperbacks in 2008.

17. For excellent discussions of the Dickens-Cruikshank collaboration, see Robert L. Patten's *George Cruikshank's Life, Times, and Art,* vol. 2, *1835–1878* (New Brunswick, NJ: Rutgers University Press, 1996), esp. chap. 27; and Catherine J. Golden, "Cruikshank's Illustrative Wrinkle in *Oliver Twist*'s Misrepresentation of Class," in *Book Illustrated: Text, Image, and Culture, 1770–1930,* ed. Catherine J. Golden (New Castle, DE: Oak Knoll Press, 2000). 117–46.

18. Will Eisner, *Graphic Storytelling and Visual Narrative: Principles and Practices from the Legendary Cartoonist* (1996; repr., New York: W. W. Norton, 2008), xvi. Hereafter cited in text.

19. Chute, "Comics as Literature?," 457.

20. Scott McCloud, *Understanding Comics: The Invisible Art* (New York: HarperCollins, 1993), 67.

21. Chute, "Comics as Literature?," 452. Emphasis in the original.

22. Dillon, "Reinscribing De Quincey's Palimpsest," 244.

23. For an important discussion of stereotypes and Jewish representation in English culture, see Frank Felsenstein, *Anti-Semitic Stereotypes: A Paradigm of Otherness in English Popular Culture, 1660–1830* (Baltimore, MD: Johns Hopkins University Press, 1995), esp. chaps. 1 and 2; and Sander Gilman, *The Jew's Body* (New York: Routledge, 1991). On caricature and race, see Martha Banta, *Barbaric Intercourse: Caricature and the Culture of Conduct, 1841–1936* (Chicago: University of Chicago Press, 2003), esp. chap. 2.

24. Felsenstein, *Anti-Semitic Stereotypes,* 241.

25. See, e.g., Frank Felsenstein and Sharon Liberman Mintz, *The Jew as Other: A Century of English Caricature, 1730–1830; An Exhibition, April 6–July 31, 1995, The Library of the Jewish Theological Seminary of America* (New York: Library of the Jewish Theological Seminary of America, 1995); Sharon Liberman Mintz, Havva Charm, and Elka Deitsch, *Image and Impression: Rare Prints from the Collection of the Library of the Jewish Theological Seminary of America* (New York: Library of the Jewish Theological Seminary of America, 2002); Felsenstein, *Anti-Semitic Stereotypes;* and Todd M. Endelman, *The Jews of Georgian England, 1714–1830: Tradition and Change in a Liberal Society* (Philadelphia: Jewish Publication Society of America, 1979).

26. Endelman, *Jews of Georgian England,* 203.

27. Ibid., 213.

28. Chute, "Comics as Literature?," 452.

29. Frank L. Cioffi, "Disturbing Comics: The Disjunction of Word and Image in the Comics of Andrzej Mleczko, Ben Katchor, R. Crumb, and Art Spiegelman," in *The Language of Comics: Word and Image,* ed. Robin Varnum and Christina T. Gibbons (Jackson: University Press of Mississippi, 2001), 98.

30. I am indebted to Diana Schutz, Will Eisner's editor at Dark Horse Comics, for her careful reading of this chapter and for noting that none of the windows on this page are aligned with the angle of the building.

31. In "Thesis on the Philosophy of History," Walter Benjamin describes what he calls "the angel of history": "His face is turned

toward the past. Where we perceive a chain of events, he sees one single catastrophe which keeps piling wreckage upon wreckage and hurls it in front of his feet. The angel would like to stay, awaken the dead, and make whole what has been smashed. But a storm is blowing from Paradise; it has got caught in his wings with such violence that the angel can no longer close them. The storm irresistibly propels him into the future to which his back is turned, while the pile of debris before him grows skyward. This storm is what we call progress." Benjamin, "Thesis on the Philosophy of History," in *Illuminations: Essays and Reflections,* ed. Hannah Arendt, trans. Harry Zohn (New York: Harcourt Brace Jovanovich, 1968), 257–58.

SIX

The Undying Joke about the Dying Girl

Charles Dickens to Roman Dirge

JESSICA STRALEY

About the heartrending passing of the heroine of Charles Dickens's *The Old Curiosity Shop* (1841), Oscar Wilde famously quipped, "one must have a heart of stone to read the death of Little Nell without laughing."[1] While many nineteenth-century British readers mourned the death of Dickens's noble Nell, modern readers tend to side with Wilde and snicker at the novel's maudlin sentimentality. Little Nell has come to symbolize the vast numbers of fictional Victorian characters who, as Garrett Stewart sardonically notes, "die more often, more slowly, and more vocally . . . than ever before or since."[2] In particular, young women, children, and childlike innocents such as Dickens's heroine die off in droves, and not simply between the pages of the Victorian novel: nineteenth-century artists' canvases and photographers' prints likewise captured and fetishized the beautiful dying woman and the serenely dead child. The sheer ubiquity of these images partially accounts for how renderings of such unspeakably sad events could, by century's end, lend themselves to humor. But it hardly explains why, in the twentieth and twenty-first centuries, writers and visual artists like Edward Gorey and, more recently, Roman Dirge have revived the dead and dying Victorian girl for their audience's amusement. When we laugh at this figure, what exactly are we laughing at?

The first answer is that we are laughing at a cliché, or rather a profusion of textual and visual clichés. For Victorians, death was both script and spectacle. According to the script, the dying person was expected to call together her loved ones, to offer heartfelt goodbyes, and to utter a dying wish that perfectly encapsulated her life, spiritual prospects, and legacy on earth; according to the requirements of spectacle, this was to occur in a modestly arranged deathbed, surrounded by friends and family in the latest mourning fashions, and should be followed by a grand funeral procession decked with all the right accouterments.[3] The cataloguing and exhibition of conventions within Victorians' final moments and funeral services announced death's importance as both the end of material existence and the portal to the hereafter, just as the appropriately garbed mourners voicing platitudes demonstrated that they understood the solemnity of the occasion. The aesthetic performance of death, then, superimposed the preconceived emblems and utterances of death onto the memory of the recently deceased. When not commemorating the passing of a particular person, writers, painters, and photographers were able to choose death's ideal victim and found two subjects that maximized the dramatic effect: the beautiful woman and the innocent child. These figures became predictable fixtures in representations of death. The sentimentalized death of a Victorian *girl,* then, is a gift-wrapped bundle of banalities for a satirist like Wilde.

The excessive textual and visual iconography surrounding Victorian death, crystallized in the image of the dying girl (female *and* child, beautiful *and* innocent), defined nineteenth-century representations and opened the door to twentieth- and twenty-first-century parodies. Examples of this phenomenon can be seen in two well known Victorian death portraits—Henry Peach Robinson's 1858 photograph *Fading Away* and Dickens's *The Old Curiosity Shop*—that operate as palimpsests, layering sets of conventions both narratively and graphically.[4] Robinson's image satisfies the expectations of Victorian death, but its manipulation of the beautiful woman and the photographic process exposes its presentation of death as an artificial compendium of contradictory customs and practices. Dickens's description and George Cattermole's accompanying illustration of Little Nell's death add to the visual iconography of the beautiful woman the sentimentalized narrative of the death of the innocent child, and in so doing, I argue, they extend metaphors about death's "meaning" in even more paradoxical directions. Gorey's illustrated tales of children's violent ends, *The Hapless Child* (1961) and *The Gashlycrumb Tinies* (1963), and Dirge's graphic comic book series, *Lenore: Cute Little Dead Girl* (1998–2007 and 2009–),revive the dead metaphor of the dead girl. More starkly than the nineteenth-century texts and images that they mock, these twentieth- and twenty-first-century graphic parodies show that Victorian death was not simply a compilation of clichés but also an infinite regression of empty metaphors. Death, femininity, and childhood bear hefty symbolic weight but no singular meaning; the combination of these concepts produces an endless round of deferred and ultimately unresolvable signification. Thus, rather than adding new layers to the already palimpsestuous Victorian portrait of death, Gorey's and Dirge's representations seek to strip death down to the essential, and essentially meaningless, skeletal symbols that we have inherited from the nineteenth century. By unmasking the very problem of representation inherent in Victorian death, these parodies offer a second cause for laughter: we laugh, despite ourselves, at the limitations of our aesthetic practices and perhaps of our own imaginations.

Robinson's Young Consumptive

Victorians were not the first to memorialize the dead through funereal rituals and aesthetic representations. However, the nineteenth century uniquely transformed death into an elaborate performance: the century saw the invention of the modern cemetery, the elaboration of the funeral into an extravagant and expensive visual spectacle, and the codification of mourning attire and etiquette.[5] Scholars explain Victorian attitudes toward death as the result of the timely confluence of three traditions: the Gothic fixation on the mysterious and the melancholic, the Romantic veneration of nostalgia and decay, and the Evangelical view of death as a lesson for the living.[6] In addition to these cultural inheritances, the Victorian relationship with death was also enabled by an invention new and peculiar to the nineteenth century: the camera. Though this chapter primarily focuses on illustration, the visual dimensions of Victorian death were developed by and through the photograph: a medium whose ostensible veracity and actual manipulability were perfectly suited to capture the ambivalent blend of truth and artificiality that constituted Victorian death.

Photographs depicting the dead as if asleep, propped up among living relatives in family portraits or painted so that their eyes appear eerily open, now circulate in contemporary media as evidence of the Victorians' morbid obsession with death.[7] In reality, photography offered a reasonable and expedient means of preserving a loved one, especially a lost child whose likeness had never before been taken. Thus, in the nineteenth century, photographers readily advertised that they were "prepared to take pictures of a deceased person on one hour's notice."[8] But the popularity and practicality of postmortem photography do not resolve the inherent paradox of the enterprise. Examining photographs from nineteenth-century America, Jay Ruby argues that "the motivation for the image contains a fundamentally contradictory desire—to retain the dead, to capture some of the essence of being now gone, to deny death."[9] Postmortem photography thus both memorializes and obscures death; it attempts to present the dead as if they are alive, to erase the very distinction that demands the image in the first place. The editor of the *Photographic and Fine Art Journal* gestured toward this conflict when he wrote in 1855, "How sublime the thought that man, by a simple process, can constrain the light of heaven and fix the fleeting shadow of life, even as it lingers upon the pallid features of death."[10] Constrained rigidity and fleeting movement, heavenly light and earthly shadow, life and death—the postmortem photograph presents an incongruous phenomenon even at its most sincere.

The contradiction implicit in the ubiquitous nineteenth-century postmortem photograph is amplified in one of the most famous Victorian photographic images of death: Henry Peach Robinson's *Fading Away*, a deathbed scene exhibited at the Crystal Palace in 1858 (see fig. 6.1). Like the funeral, the Victorian deathbed had become a ritualized scene, and Robinson's photograph contains all the elements that viewers were coming to expect from the show. Jannie Uhre Mogensen argues that *Fading Away*'s presentation of death as a "restorer of innocence" makes it the quintessential exhibition of the "good death" as understood by Victorians.[11] According to Pat Jalland's essential study *Death and the Victorian Family*, this "good death" came out of the Evangelical insistence that death function as a lesson to the living. To demonstrate that, for Christians, death is a welcome release of the soul into heavenly bliss, the "good death" required certain staid features: it must happen at home, slowly enough to allow for goodbyes, atonement, and amends, and it must be attended by mourners who hear

FIG. 6.1   Henry Peach Robinson, *Fading Away* (1858). Albumen print photograph. Image courtesy of the Royal Photographic Society Collection / National Media Museum, UK.

and fulfill a last dying wish and can attest to the beauty, peacefulness, and resolve of their dying loved one.[12] In Robinson's photograph, the dying girl's smooth face, gently closed eyes, and relaxed body indicate that she has borne the throes of death with fortitude and that she is materially and spiritually prepared to join the divine. The open window in the photograph's center offers an unimpeded route for her soul to enter an embracing eternity. Mogensen argues that for the young woman's body to bear so much representational meaning, not simply the window but "her horizontal figure always lies manipulably 'open' before the spectator" (2). Her death is not her own; she is a spectacle to be witnessed, a lesson to be learned, and a collection of metaphors about the meaning of life as it is culturally consumed.

As an open book in need of a reader, the dying woman is only part of the symbolism in Robinson's photograph. While she fades to white just right of the center, the darker, living figures are more visually prominent. Viewers have speculated that the three people are sister, mother, and fiancé or mother, grandmother, and father, but their precise relation is irrelevant (Mogensen, 5). What matters is that they make the required tableau. In "Death-Bed Scenes in Victorian Fiction," Margarete Holubetz writes that in the typical scene, "the sufferer thus slowly takes leave of his family, embraces them and kisses them goodbye. . . . He may give some last orders or express some death-bed wish usually held sacred by the bereaved."[13] As befitting the occasion, then, in Robinson's photograph, the younger visitor lovingly gazes down on the dying young woman while the older woman rests at her feet ready perhaps to hear her dying words or to fulfill a last wish. The man staring out the window with his back to the women is more mysterious; perhaps his presence can be traced to the Gothic or Romantic death conventions that Victorians enacted alongside Evangelical traditions. Mogensen suggests that "his placement in the centre of the composition along with his fatalistic solidarity with the dark, cloudy sky outside give the reader the impression that this narrative is as much about his tragedy" as about her death (5). Given that he may be fiancé or father, what that tragedy might be remains ambiguous, but the fact that he attends the deathbed suggests that he may receive the lesson that "the good death" has to offer those left behind.

For that lesson to be conveyed in its most powerful form, the subject must be a woman, and she must be beautiful. Robinson's image and its title, indicative of slow death, "Fading Away," suggest that the young subject has fallen victim to that very Victorian illness: consumption (Mogensen, 7–8). According to Jalland, consumption featured frequently in nineteenth-century representations of death because among its effects was the brightening of the complexion that increased the subject's attractiveness in her last moments.[14] The enhancement delivered a moral message: the beauty of the dying girl was an assurance of her entrance into heaven and thus a testimony to her virtue. Elisabeth Bronfen suggests that there is more to this spectacle. Seeking to explain Edgar Allan Poe's assertion in "The Philosophy of Composition" (1846) that "the death of a beautiful woman is, unquestionably, the most poetical topic in the world," Bronfen argues that Poe's pleasure comes from the recognition that the beautiful dead woman is both contradiction and "rhetorical redundancy" and ultimately a representational impossibility.[15] On the one hand, woman is associated "with life-bringing and nourishing nature" and opposed to death (60); on the other hand, woman's identification with nature links her to "unruly disorder, uncivilized wilderness, famines and tempests that threatened generation" and brought death (66). Beauty is likewise, Bronfen writes, "only superficially death's antithesis": contrasting the "disintegration, fragmentation and insufficiency" of death but similarly adverse to the deficiencies and vicissitudes of life (62). Metaphorical vehicles without stable corresponding tenors, all three elements—"beautiful," "woman," and "death"—gesture toward a meaning that lies beyond expression and is, thus, unresolved. Rendered by an aesthetic medium employed for its transparent capture of lived reality, the postmortem or immediately premortem photograph limns the margins of representational possibility. The image straddles the line not only between life and death but also between perfection and disintegration, presence and absence, fullness of meaning and meaninglessness.

Fading Away, however, reveals further discordant notes. Unlike postmortem photographers who presented the dead as if they were alive, Robinson sought to present the fully alive as if on the verge of death. His figures are models, and the deathbed scene is a synthetic manufacture. The photographer described the subject at the center of *Fading Away* as "a fine healthy girl of about 14," posed for his aesthetic rendering "to see how near death she could be made to look."[16] According to Jennifer Green-Lewis, this fiction sparked public criticism of the image, whose subject matter was so somber and whose medium was so trusted.[17] But the posed actors are just the start of the photograph's deviation from reality. *Fading Away* is a photomontage of five stills layered on top of one another; none of the four figures were ever assembled together. Robinson was a founding practitioner of "pictorialist photography"—or "combination printing" or "Pre-Raphaelite photography," as it was also called—in which dramatic effects are produced by doctored images and double exposures.[18] Because its touching deathbed scene only ever existed as retouched and highly mediated art, Robinson's amalgamation of various negatives into one rhetorically satisfying whole reveals how fully aestheticized— or more cynically, how cloying and false—death was becoming in nineteenth-century representations. *Fading Away,* then, is the perfect picture of Victorian death: beautiful, sentimental, and contrived.

Dickens's Virtuous Girl

Robinson's photograph was widely seen and sold over the next decade, becoming the most prominent visual representation of the beautiful dying woman, but it nowhere equaled in the public imagination the devastation felt at the fictional death of Charles Dickens's woman-child, Little Nell. Presented in *The Old Curiosity Shop* through both narrative and illustration almost two decades before Robinson's photograph, Nell's final goodbye drew from and, indeed, helped to solidify the literary and artistic conventions of the Victorian deathbed. In fact, here Dickens amasses just about every platitude about death, femininity, and beauty circulating in the middle of the century and adds to this collection of terms another metaphorical nexus: the child, or at least childlike, heroine. Judith Plotz finds herself amenable to Wilde's critique of Little Nell's death, sensing that "there's altogether too much pleasure, too much gusto in Dickens' depiction of Nell's death."[19] Surely, there is just too much of everything in Dickens's presentation, so much so that we can perhaps not help but laugh along with Wilde at the surfeit of symbolism. Embellished by so many metaphors aimed at meaning so much, the death of the beautiful girl and perfect child becomes too overburdened to be taken seriously, and the very confusion created by competing textual and visual claims to metaphysical significance becomes comical.

Little Nell's death contains all the narrative ingredients of the Evangelical "good death." Though her death results from a long journey, she dies slowly in her own bed, surrounded by those who love her. She bears her hardship with fortitude, for "she had never murmured or complained."[20] Her friends dutifully deck her deathbed with winter berries and green leaves, fulfilling her dying wish that she be near "something that has loved the light, and had the sky above it always" (540). Dying leisurely enough to resolve earthly matters, Nell has time to send her love to her friend Kit, and she begs that the others gathering around her "would kiss her once again" (541). As befits the survivors of a girl who has suffered a "good death," the mourners grieve as they ought: "Many a young hand dropped its little wreath, many a stifled sob was heard. Some—and they were not a few—knelt down. All were sincere and truthful in their sorrow" (544). In "Laughing at the Death of Little Nell," Marcia Muelder Eaton calls Dickens out for such "trite phrases, cliches, inflated vocabulary, [and] stock metaphors," which she argues circumvent sincere emotion and protect us from the horrors of contemplating real death.[21] At least here, we laugh not at the death of a child but at the literary practices that compel us to mourn in predictable ways.

Not simply formulaic, Dickens's description is internally inconsistent and yanks readers dizzily through contradictory postures toward death.[22] Readers are asked to lament with Nell's grandfather, who suffers inconsolable grief at her loss, and simultaneously to rejoice along with the schoolmaster, for whom Nell's passing is a merciful reward; the schoolmaster rhetorically exclaims, "[I]f one deliberate wish expressed in solemn terms above this bed could call her back to life, which of us would utter it!" (540). Like the opposing effects of her death upon the mourners, Nell's virtue also finds incongruous expressions. In accordance with the script of the "good death" that demands a clear-headed, rational, and moral subject, Nell is lucid until the end—except when her mind wanders "once" to heed the "beautiful music which she said was in the air" (541). For Dickens, however, this temporary delirium is not a detraction from Nell's morality as she approaches death, but rather its supreme expression; the narrator augments her reverie with the conjecture that "God knows. [The beautiful music] may have been" real enough. The Evangelical "good death" here clashes with the Romantic beautiful one, and both are at odds with the description's intermittent materialism. Compared with her pet bird—"a poor slight thing the pressure of a finger would have crushed . . . stirring nimbly in its cage" while "the strong heart of its child-mistress was mute and motionless for ever"—Nell is briefly an animal body whose death is an ultimate end to corporeal life (540). But with the "peace and perfect happiness" of the next line, she quickly, if incompatibly, returns to being a slumbering, immaterial soul awaiting heavenly reanimation.

In case Dickens's description of Nell's death does not accrete enough meanings or generate enough of a muddle, George Cattermole's illustration of Little Nell on her deathbed supplements the text with a further encyclopedia of visual signifiers (see fig. 6.2). Like Robinson's young consumptive, Nell lies peacefully in her bed. Though she is pictured alone, the absence of mourners leaves a space that Cattermole fills with meaningful accouterments; some appear in the narrative, like the winter berries and green leaves of her dying wish, while his illustration freshly adds others, such as the Bible under her lightly resting hand and the open window that was becoming a staple in the death scene. Patrick J. McCarthy contends that Cattermole's illustration layers Catholic imagery onto Dickens's narrative as well: "She is pictured before an icon of the child Jesus in the arms of the Virgin Mary, and then [is] assumed bodily to heaven like Mary

FIG. 6.2   Little Nell's deathbed. George Cattermole for Charles Dickens, *The Old Curiosity Shop* (London: Chapman and Hall, 1841), 210. Image courtesy of the Rare Books Division, The New York Public Library, Astor, Lenox and Tilden Foundations.

herself."[23] The Catholic iconography of the heavily ornate headboard also visually competes with the adjacent open window: one part of the illustration implies that Nell's body will be physically conveyed in Mary's arms while the other suggests that her airy spirit will be lightly borne by the winds. Readers are invited to feel, all at once, buoyancy and solidity, relief and anguish, justice and injury, beauty and horror, transcendence and decay. If every interpretation of Nell's death is accompanied by its opposite, both sentimentality and ridicule seem peculiarly appropriate responses to the occasion.

Our reaction to Nell's death becomes more convoluted by Dickens's construction of her as not only a young woman but also a child. The dead child, like the dying beautiful woman, was both a Victorian fixation and a nexus of metaphorical contradictions. In "Literary

Ways of Killing a Child," Judith Plotz traces "an obsessive nineteenth-century drive" to revel in the incongruity of the dead child: the juxtaposition between the child, active and uninhibited, on the one hand, and the corpse, "dead or doomed and boxed in, contained, fixed, preserved, stilled, revered, and revisited," on the other.[24] Cattermole's illustration overlays the conventions of the beautiful woman's death (the peaceful visage, the open window, and the accessible and pliant body) with the added cues of confinement (the heavy bedstead, the flatness of Nell's body, and the shadows enclosing the bed on three sides) that Plotz identifies as associated with the child's death. The paradox presented by the illustration of the child's death—the expectation of childish activity versus the stillness of the corpse, the playful exuberance associated with childhood versus the confinement of the deathbed—is, however, the lesser of the representational ambiguities that *The Old Curiosity Shop* suggests in the passing of Little Nell.

What is offered as a contradiction in the illustration (the dead, stilled child) is, indeed, presented as identity in the accompanying narrative. Nell's death is, to repeat Bronfen's words, a rhetorical redundancy: to be a child is to be already dead. Buffeted by external circumstances and unable to fight back, the vulnerable child and the defenseless corpse share the same story. John Kucich maintains that even while she is alive, Nell's "existence is inseparable from the idea of its loss," and Garrett Stewart likewise calls her "a wraith so long virtually fleshless and otherworldly" that her "death loses its drama."[25] Having never really been alive, Nell hardly changes in death. For Dickens, this is more a blessing than a curse. To die is to become a child again, to return to the state of innocence before life's suffering. The narrator of *The Old Curiosity Shop* thus gratefully dwells on the peacefulness visible on Nell's dying face and asks, "Where were the traces of her early cares, her sufferings, and fatigues?" (540). In the very next paragraph, he insists that Nell looks exactly as she always did as a child: "And still her former self lay there, unaltered in this change. Yes. The old fireside had smiled upon that same sweet face; it had passed like a dream through haunts of misery and care. . . . So shall we know the angels in their majesty, after death" (540). Her death—the cataclysmic event on which the readers' emotional response to the novel depends—is simply a return to an unblemished childhood. The visual iconography of death undoes the narrative consequences of life.

This representational fracture, making paradoxical even the rapport between image and narrative, is the unique result of the coincident contrast and consistency of the dead child.

The dying beautiful woman gives us one grouping of unresolvable metaphors, and onto this network, Dickens lays another web of contradictions about the dead child. While the dying woman was a staple of nineteenth-century visual representations, the congruence of death and childhood was a favorite of the novel. Not only are Victorian narratives full of dead children, as scholars like Plotz have pointed out, but they also often represent death as a return to childhood: Emily Brontë's Catherine Linton, Elizabeth Gaskell's Alice Wilson, and William Makepeace Thackeray's Colonel Newcome, for instance, flash back to their earliest years while on their deathbeds.[26] Victorian authors turned the biblical dictum "Except ye be converted, and become as little children, ye shall not enter into the kingdom of heaven" into an aesthetics of literary representation.[27] On the one hand, Dickens's overwrought symbolism presents death as a palimpsest of the divergent rhetorics (Romantic, Evangelical, Catholic) that irreconcilably combined into the nineteenth century's "good death." On the other hand, Nell gives us the purest expression of the Victorian's minimalist equation between childhood and death. Death erases life back into childhood; childhood excludes life to mirror death. Rooting Victorian attitudes to death in Romanticism, Plotz claims that "the nineteenth-century way of killing a child is to restore, indeed increase, presence."[28] But I would argue that the dead child is also an absence of signification. Childhood and death are associated states, and thus the child's death is a nonevent. The perversity lay not in the death of the child but in the elaborate textual clichés and visual iconography with which Dickens decorates this void: the death of the already dead.

Gorey's Unfortunate Tinies

When Edward Gorey revives the dead child in the 1960s, he recognizes the tension between the abundance of signifiers and the absence of meaning that characterize the death of the Victorian girl.[29] Gorey's books are generally series of black-and-white panels with short captions that compose either a continuous story, like *The Hapless Child,* or a catalog of related events, like his abecedarium *The Gashlycrumb*

Tinies. Both works show that childhood and death, bookends to an intervening narrative of life, mirror each other with their reflected absences. Rather than adding to the signification of death that the Victorians had already piled on, Gorey pares down both text and image to the essential components of childhood and death. The very brevity and compression of his captions, for instance, reflect the mutual stasis of childhood and death; by refusing to become complete or explanatory narratives, the captions undo themselves even as they begin. Gorey's illustrations too are truncated versions of their Victorian predecessors; they suggest the familiar stock images but withhold them, forcing us to recognize their prevalence and inauthenticity by their very omission. Employing both text and image in this expression of emptiness, Gorey makes us laugh, first at the triteness of the formula and then at ourselves for expecting, and maybe even desiring, that hackneyed concoction.

The Hapless Child is Gorey's reworking of narratives like Dickens's *The Adventures of Oliver Twist* (1837–39) and Frances Hodgson Burnett's *Sara Crewe; or, What Happened at Miss Minchin's* (1887–88), in which long-suffering, virtuous orphans are finally, miraculously rescued by loving families.[30] In contrast to these Victorian tales, Gorey's *Hapless Child* conveys all the patterns of lost and redeemed childhood but none of the narrative satisfactions. The first panel of the story presents Charlotte Sophia, a young girl with "well-to-do" parents and a home decorated in heavy Victorian furniture and overbearing fabrics (see fig. 6.3). Charlotte's "father, a colonel in the army, was ordered to Africa" and "reported killed in a native uprising," and very soon after, "her mother fell into a decline that proved fatal."[31] Newly orphaned like many of her literary predecessors, Charlotte is sent to a boarding school where she is treated badly and escapes only to be mugged, kidnapped, and forced into oppressive labor making artificial flowers. The combination of cruelty and bad lighting make her go blind, and when she tries to escape again, she is struck by a car and left to die in the street. In a familiar Victorian twist, her father—presumed dead but actually alive—returns to England and is driving along the very street into which she runs, and then he unwittingly runs her down. Stopping the car, he rushes to his daughter's side, and though faithful readers of Victorian texts might expect the customary moment of tearful recognition when the dying girl gets to become

There was once a little girl named Charlotte Sophia.

FIG. 6.3   Charlotte Sophia, the heroine of Edward Gorey's *The Hapless Child* (1961; reprint San Francisco, CA: Pomegranate Communications, Inc., 1989), n.p. Reprinted by permission of Donadio & Olson, Inc. Copyright 1961 Edward Gorey.

again the unblemished child she once was, Gorey's last panel shows a man holding a body that remains a stranger to him (see fig. 6.4): "[S]he was so changed," the caption reads, "he did not recognize her." By withholding the recognition scene, Gorey exposes the absurdity of conceiving death as the "restorer of innocence," which Mogensen sees in portraits like Robinson's.

Visually, Gorey conveys the absurdity of the familiar narrative clichés through his manipulation of the graphic form. Though neither *The Hapless Child* nor *The Gashlycrumb Tinies* could be classified as a comic book or a graphic novel, Gorey's works share some of the grammar of these genres; in particular, each panel presents itself as the inevitable result of the previous panel's action and the inalterable cause of the next panel's event, spatially rendering a cause-and-effect

She was so changed, he did not recognize her.

FIG. 6.4   Charlotte Sophia's unfortunate demise. Edward Gorey, *The Hapless Child* (1961; reprint San Francisco, CA: Pomegranate Communications, Inc., 1989), n.p. Reprinted by permission of Donadio & Olson, Inc. Copyright 1961 Edward Gorey.

sequence. Hillary Chute characterizes comics' panels as "punctual, framed moments alternating with the blank space of the gutter onto which we must project causality."[32] When Gorey's side-by-side panels say that his heroine's father was killed in Africa and, immediately after, her mother fell fatally ill, the silent space between the two images—known as the "gutter"—impels readers to forge a causal, indeed compulsory, connection between the images. Charlotte Sophia's subsequent downfall follows like an inescapable fate, linking our introduction to her in the first panel with her death in the last. In the two-panel sequence that conveys her death, the first shows her running frantically into the street, and the next presents her lifeless body and the back wheels of the car pulling out of the frame to the right.

Gorey's heroine dies literally and figuratively in the gutter: face down in the street after being struck by the car and between panels. Scott McCloud calls characters' deaths that occur in the gutter the "special crime" of the readers because it is we, not Gorey, who visualize the car actually striking poor Charlotte Sophia.[33]

Filling in the narrative gap of the gutter, the readers may be responsible for killing off Charlotte Sophia, but like a good Victorian girl, she is already dead. Gorey renders his heroine's inevitable demise not merely through the Victorian narrative conventions that he borrows and parodies but through purely pictorial means. In each illustration of *The Hapless Child* lurks a little black figure, faint at first, who develops into a bat by the last panel and into a two-headed demon on the back cover. Coaxing us to search for it is one of Gorey's visual games, but the omen also tells us that, like Nell, Charlotte Sophia is destined for an early death from the first frame.[34] Even beyond this figure, Gorey's illustrations exploit the problem of the already dead Victorian child. In the first panel, Charlotte appears a white-faced, white-haired, and altogether bleached-out paper doll at odds with the dark, textured furniture, curtains, and wallpaper of her home. To be the picture of perfect unsullied childhood innocence, it seems, is to be a ghost. In contrast, though pathetically bedraggled and limp in the last panel, the dying little girl looks more a part of the living world that she inhabits. *The Hapless Child* presents the equation between childhood and death as an unsolvable paradox. Charlotte's unwashed and unredeemed dirtiness in death halts her father's ability to recognize her and thus to transport her back into childhood, but it was her unblemished childhood that predicted and produced her inevitable death. *The Hapless Child* thus presents a double lack: never surpassing childhood, Charlotte never gets a life, but failing to return to her childhood, she also does not achieve the good Victorian death. The joke is on us, for our complicity in Charlotte Sophia's death through which she is neither redeemed nor indeed altered—for a tragedy that was both inevitable and superfluous.

Gorey's send-up of dead children continues two years later in *The Gashlycrumb Tinies; or, After the Outing,* which satirizes both the cautionary tale of children's literature and the "good death" of Evangelicalism. For each letter of the alphabet, a child whose name begins with that letter meets a speedy and violent death: "A is for AMY who fell down the stairs. / B is for BASIL assaulted by bears," and so on.[35] Delivered in rhymed couplets and accompanied by black-and-white ink illustrations, Gorey's alphabet derives its humor from the multiple discordant notes it strikes: the singsong of its rhythm against the gruesomeness of its content, and the action described by the text against the picture (usually) portraying the moment just before the catastrophe occurs. The comedic effect is also produced by the anticipated but omitted narrative and visual signs of Victorian death. In juxtaposition with the languorous "good death" that allows the sufferer to settle her earthly business, to display her fortitude, and to prepare herself for eternity, Gorey's "tinies" die suddenly and unexpectedly. The peaceful and beautiful young woman lying in her carefully adorned bed is replaced by the clueless child drowning in a lake, battered on the street, or squashed under a train. Even more pointedly mocking Victorian art are those children killed by the overly ornate and fussy elements of their own homes: "G is for GEORGE smothered under a rug," for instance. Instead of being surrounded by loved ones to comfort them in their last moments and to gain death's moral lessons, these children all die alone, and their final solitary moments have no apparent didactic value.

Each of the twenty-six children is introduced only in order to die immediately in the course of a single panel and caption, as if the Victorian child can have no other narrative than death: in other words, no narrative at all. Unlike recent graphic texts, like Will Eisner's *Fagin the Jew* that Heidi Kaufman discusses in the previous chapter, *The Gashlycrumb Tinies* does not seek to overlay a Victorian text with newly invented backstories capable of recuperating a maligned character. Gorey offers not a palimpsest but rather a paring down of Robinson's and Dickens's accumulations of textual and visual iconography to the solitary dyad: child and death. Both Gorey's parodies of Victoriana and his manipulation of twentieth-century comics engender this reductio ad absurdum. Indeed, according to Eisner's analysis of his genre, the language of comics relies on reduction and repetition: "In its most economical state, comics employ a series of repetitive images and recognizable symbols. When these are used again and again to convey similar ideas, they become a language—a literary form, if you will."[36] It is surely no coincidence that Eisner's first illustration of this principle is the pictorial death of a character from his *Spirit* stories.

As with Charlotte Sophia's death, which takes advantage of the gutter to implicate the readers in her murder, our ability to recognize the emblems of death in a single illustration reveals the conventionality of its images and symbols.

The Gashlycrumb Tinies is at its most Victorian in the deaths that suggest excruciating slowness though, like the others, contained within a single sentence: "C is for CLARA who wasted away" and "N is for NEVILLE who died of ennui." It is in Clara's death that Gorey plays most obviously with the visual emblems of the Victorian deathbed (see fig. 6.5). For most of Gorey's readers, Clara's blackened eyes recall Charlotte Sophia's blind visage as well as the comic iconography of *X*'s over eyes signifying death. But for those familiar with the Victorian textual and visual death conventions, Clara appears in a recognizable pose, reclining in her bed with the hint of a window in the upper left corner of the panel. A. Robin Hoffman argues that "the inclusion of Clara's nonviolent death, particularly so close to the

C is for CLARA who wasted away

FIG. 6.5 The Victorian "good death" reinterpreted. Edward Gorey, *The Gashlycrumb Tinies* (1963; reprint Boston: Harcourt Brace & Company, 1991), n.p. Reprinted by permission of Donadio & Olson, Inc. Copyright 1963 Edward Gorey.

beginning of the book, merely serves to heighten the contrast between the other children's violent ends and the nonviolent Victorian precedents."[37] However, I would suggest that Clara's death, far from being an outlier, crystallizes Gorey's satire of the dead Victorian child that runs throughout *The Gashlycrumb Tinies*. Clara's posture in her deathbed recalls the final moments of both Robinson's consumptive and Dickens's Little Nell, but recognizing these allusions only makes the sparseness of her surroundings and the absence of other familiar death motifs more striking. In contrast to the deathbeds of her Victorian predecessors, there are no mourners to learn from her death, no final kisses to conclude her temporal existence, no meaningful trifles to commemorate her life, no beauty to manifest death's peaceful embrace, and no ample text to mitigate those absences. Even the window peeking into the frame appears shut; no open portal assists her soul's flight to heaven.

Invoking the Victorian cues that it strikingly withholds, Clara's demise and the rest of the deaths in Gorey's alphabet make us laugh at what is missing. Mark T. Rusch draws our attention to the most notable omission in Gorey's illustrations: the parents. He argues that the evidence of the children's material wealth juxtaposed with the deficiency of any parental supervision or care makes *The Gashlycrumb Tinies* a darkly humorous social satire.[38] But the absences in Gorey's illustrations, compared with the Victorian portraits of children's deaths that they parody, go much further than negligent guardians. *The Gashlycrumb Tinies,* in particular, reveals the superfluity of Victorian death conventions, as well as their confused attempts at signification. If the abundantly overlain signs that surround Little Nell's death point in all different directions (grief, relief, temporality, eternity, embodiment, transcendence), then the sparseness in Gorey's depictions prevents death from obtaining any metaphorical meaning or didactic value. Perhaps we laugh because the illustrations refuse the expected literary and aesthetic vehicles required for any other reaction. But more sinisterly, by paring down death's decorative features in *The Gashlycrumb Tinies* and omitting the recognition scene from *The Hapless Child,* Gorey removes any distraction from the two most important metaphorical vehicles: childhood and death. These two figures stare emptily at each other, showing us that we do not make one mean anything simply by linking it with the other. Over and over again, Gorey's portraits expose the dead metaphor of the dead child.

Dirge's Cute Little Undead Girl

The dead child—and the dead metaphor—received new life half a century later in Roman Dirge's comic series *Lenore: Cute Little Dead Girl,* published roughly yearly by Slave Labor Graphics from 1998 to 2007 and then revived by Titan Books in 2009. The name of this diminutive vampire is inspired by Poe's 1843 poem that forms an epigraph to Dirge's first issue. In Poe's "Lenore," the speaker meditates over the inauthenticity of nineteenth-century death customs and painfully recognizes the redundancy of the dead maiden, who is "doubly dead in that she died so young."[39] For Dirge's "cute little dead girl" of the same name, being doubly dead is the same as being undead; having died a century ago, this Lenore is a vampire who kills a seemingly endless series of people and animals, acting out of cluelessness rather than malice; while babysitting, for instance, she puts a bag of birdseed in the stroller and unwittingly invites a flock of birds to peck the baby to death. Merging the vampire with the innocent child, Dirge creates his bizarrely endearing heroine, now the subject of twenty comic book issues (and counting) as well as twenty-six flash animated shorts.[40] In the backstory given in later issues, readers discover that Lenore's connection to the nineteenth century is not merely allusive: she is a Victorian girl brought back to life. But whereas Robinson's photograph and Dickens's textual and visual portrait pile on death's clichés and Gorey's captioned illustrations empty the Victorian death scene of all its superfluous symbolism, Dirge's graphic series reanimates and reexamines some of the more troubling metaphors associated with girls' deathbeds.

In an episode fittingly entitled "Lenore in 'The Raven'" (1998) from Dirge's second issue, Lenore gobbles down the ominous bird rapping on her windowsill before he can tell his tale of horror, but her vampiric doll, Ragamuffin, offers to tell her another story about herself when "it was a different time and you were a different person" (see fig. 6.6).[41] For the first time, the series takes the readers back to the end of the nineteenth century, when Lenore lived briefly as "a super-duper girl" before succumbing to an early death.[42] The image of the healthy Lenore and the use of "super-duper" seem drawn more from the 1950s than the 1890s, but her deathbed scene inverts the familiar Victorian conventions. Like Victorian heroines dying the "good death," Lenore dies slowly in her bed. Her coughing death is reminiscent of Robinson's consumptive, but instead of the peace and beauty of that reclining figure, Lenore's ghastly face and blackened eyes viewed straight on give death a grubbiness never admitted in Victorian portraits. She enjoys no loving visitors at her bedside, only a sleeping cat who in the next frame stares at her dead body with a quizzical "meow?" devoid of any sympathy and incognizant of any moral lesson to be gained from her death. No open window awaits the flight of her soul, and no image of the Virgin Mary promises heavenly transport; instead her headboard's primary decoration is the variously spelled "coff cough coff" that emanates from her putrid lungs. In the absence of death's usual Victorian embellishments, this image of the dying Lenore might remind us of Gorey's Clara; death and the child seem fitting and sufficient bedfellows.

When its heroine awakens as a vampire in this early issue, *Lenore* indulges the late twentieth-century trope more familiar to Dirge's contemporary audience (the vampire as alienated teenager), but when Dirge wrote a second volume in 2009, he dug deeper into his dead girl's Victorian origins. The opening story, "Lenore in 'The Macabre Malevolence of Mortimer Fledge,'" promises that "revealed at last" is "the shocking secret of her REBIRTH."[43] "100 Years Ago," according to

FIG. 6.6   Lenore's Victorian backstory. Roman Dirge, "Lenore in 'The Raven,'" *Lenore* 1, no. 2 (1998), in *Roman Dirge's Lenore: Noogies, Collecting "Lenore," Issues 1–4* (San Jose, CA: Slave Labor Graphics, 1999), 5. Reproduced with permission. © Roman Dirge.

the banner introducing the inset tale, two Victorian-looking gentlemen in black coats and top hats bring the body of a recently deceased "10 year old girl. Pneumonia victim" to Nevermore Mortuary Services to be readied for burial. Insisting on a "good embalming"—"quick, simple, and by the book"—the mortician, Mortimer Fledge, has the girl placed on his operating table, saws her open, and weighs her organs. But when he inserts the embalming tube, Lenore fills up like a balloon, suddenly comes to life, explodes from the excess liquid, and shoots a stream of fluid into Fledge's mouth. While she quickly collects her extricated organs—what she calls "my stuffs"—and departs the laboratory, the remaining strip follows Fledge, whose monomaniacal obsession with Lenore's reanimation causes him to lose his wife, his business, and his home. This flashback explains why in the present day, Fledge, preserved like Lenore, seeks to track her down and to destroy her. The Victorian laboratory, like the series' investment in nineteenth-century staples like vampires, taxidermy, tea parties, Edgar Allan Poe, and Harry Houdini, joins with gross-out humor and a twenty-first-century sensibility; Ragamuffin kills Fledge, for instance, in homage to James Cameron's *Aliens* (1986). *Lenore's* humor is its mishmash of disemboweled and recollected cultural "stuffs."

Despite Dirge's eclectic influences, the cover illustration for "The Macabre Malevolence of Mortimer Fledge" makes a sharp satire on specifically Victorian death (see fig. 6.7). The bulgy-eyed surprise of both Lenore and Fledge has a long history in cartoons, but other elements of Dirge's cover manifest and manipulate the visual clichés of the "good death." The properly prepared bed is replaced by a cold and unadorned operating table. Instead of the spiritual illumination conveyed by the Christian iconography of Nell's headboard, an examination lamp sheds a clinical light on the girl. A glass cabinet filled with countless canisters of embalming fluid usurps the position of the open window. The medical rather than domestic setting strips death of its supposed comforts, its suggestion of eternal peace, and the return "home" that, for the Victorians, linked death and childhood. Lenore's stunned body on the table shifts the focus from spirituality to corporeality, and the encased embalming fluid filling the space of the open window suggests her eternal entrapment in a mortal body that even this endless supply of solution cannot stop from rotting. As the only witness to her reanimation, Fledge proves a strange version

FIG. 6.7   Lenore's resurrection (cover). Roman Dirge, "The Macabre
Malevolence of Mortimer Fledge," *Roman Dirge's Lenore* 2, no. 1 (London:
Titan Publishing Group, 2009). Reproduced with permission. © Roman Dirge.

of Dickens's schoolmaster who remarks on the blasphemy of wishing Nell restored to life; Fledge's faith in the biochemical laws of death and decomposition, not his desire for moral justness, is what Lenore's re-birth destroys. Swapping out Victorian symbols, Dirge deftly erases the sentimental and morally efficacious "good death" and offers instead the purely comical, off-color, and delightfully gross "bad rebirth."

When Lenore awakens, combusts, and ejaculates into Fledge's gap-ing mouth, the humor needs no nineteenth-century precedents, but this moment is the series' most critical, if unconscious, satire on the Vic-torian uses of the dead girl's body. The consummate Victorian portrait of the consumptive, Robinson's *Fading Away,* presents the dead girl's body as "manipulably 'open,'" in Mogensen's words, and ready to im-part its lesson about moral virtue and the "good death." But Mogensen contends that this openness is never wholly innocent: "Death scenes, visual or literary, with young girls depicted in their nighties, performing shows of moans, howls, and final gasps that reach near orgasmic heights, denote a passionate physicality beyond actual description, and com-pletely outside the Victorian dogma of self-control" (11). *Fading Away* illustrates her point because, as she points out, only in the composite (manipulated) photograph does the woman's body exemplify the moral virtue of female passivity; the original still of the woman alone conveys a different message. Titled *She Never Told Her Love,* the image of the young woman without her superimposed well-wishers presented death from lovesickness. Here, Mogensen argues, the girl's "motionless body" is not an image of righteous submission but "a house of sexual repres-sion," similar to that image of sexualized womanhood that terrified the Victorians: the female vampire (10). For Mogensen, Robinson's palimp-sestuous photograph meant to convey spiritual innocence is haunted by this prior image of corporeal transgression peeking through. Thus, at the center of one of the nineteenth century's paradigmatic examples of the "good death" is the specter of the "bad rebirth," of female re-sistance to Victorian stereotypes, and of the visual iconography of the death scene turning against itself to express its opposite. Reanimated by Dirge's satirical pen, which transforms the visual clues of Victorian iconography, Lenore refuses to be "opened up" and disemboweled for male profit and is thus transformed into an oddly empowered vampire.

Lenore's body becomes both the incarnation and the antithesis of the neo-Victorian text. In "The Macabre Malevolence of Mortimer

Fledge," Dirge gives us the backstory that in other neo-Victorian texts like A. S. Byatt's *Possession* (1990), Sarah Blake's *Grange House* (2000), and Eisner's *Fagin the Jew* return to the past to recover lost origins, heal old hurts, and rectify prior prejudices.[44] Dirge's second volume of *Lenore* thus participates in the very Victorian and neo-Victorian narrative conventions denied by Gorey's *Hapless Child* and *The Gashlycrumb Tinies*. Despite being caught in this narrative of recovery, however, Lenore's body rejects it: she pukes out the embalming fluid meant to preserve her as the staid image of unaltered feminine death. Twentieth-century neo-Victorianism, according to Cora Kaplan, demonstrates that "the Victorian age is at once ghostly and tangible, an origin and an anachronism."[45] The ghostliness of the Victorian age—like the specter of Robinson's overlaid images—is reinforced in the metaphor of the palimpsest that this volume adroitly uses to illustrate the neo-Victorian. However, as a vampire rather than a ghost, Lenore offers a slightly different way of imagining the reanimation of Victorian tropes and visuals: what we unearth from the tomb of the nineteenth century receives new life from us, but it may not facilely bend to our will. Lenore is the Victorian dead girl who refuses to stay dead and wreaks havoc on the modern world into which she has been reluctantly disinterred.

In his foreword to *Roman Dirge's Lenore: Cooties* (2010), the third volume of the series, Neil Gaiman praises Dirge for "know[ing] that, after a while, the inevitability of a joke becomes the funniest thing about it."[46] However, Gaiman's pithy assertion does not explain how a joke becomes inevitable or what that inevitability tells us about our own narrative and cultural expectations. The prevalence of the dead girl arises out of the nineteenth-century confluence of death and femininity, on the one hand, and death and childhood, on the other, as embedded identities and contradictions that—each mirroring the other's hollowness as meaningful signifier—offer an endless regression of empty metaphors reflecting only other empty metaphors. The resulting excess of absence, the redundancy of lack, cannot be melancholic (for there is literally nothing to mourn) and turns humorous instead. Robinson's photograph illustrates the inauthenticity of death's iconography. Dickens's novel reveals how metaphorically overburdened the fictionalized death of a child had become even by the 1840s. Gorey's books expose the meaninglessness of the dead child by vacating that very vacuity and refusing to complete the circularity of the Victorian trope. Dirge's graphic series, rather than emptying out the visual and textual clichés, turns them upside down and forces us to see that the sentimentalized dead girl was always already her opposite: the vampire whose body resists all attempts to make her lie still. For the Victorians, the dead girl could hardly be tragic because good girls were already dead; for us, the dead girl can be comic because bad girls (the best girls) never really die.

Notes

1. Though this quotation is repeated frequently without citation, its original source is Ada Leverson, *Letters to the Sphinx from Oscar Wilde* (London: Duckworth, 1930); quoted in Joseph Pearce, *The Unmasking of Oscar Wilde* (San Francisco, CA: Ignatius Press, 2004), 45.

2. Garrett Stewart, *Death Sentences: Styles of Dying in British Fiction* (Cambridge, MA: Harvard University Press, 1984), 8.

3. See, especially, Pat Jalland, *Death and the Victorian Family* (Oxford: Oxford University Press, 1999); and Mary Elizabeth Hotz, *Literary Remains: Representations of Death and Burial in Victorian England* (Albany: State University of New York Press, 2009).

4. See Anna Maria Jones and Rebecca N. Mitchell's introduction to the present volume for a fuller discussion of the palimpsest, its prevalence in Victorian and neo-Victorian literary and artistic production, and its usefulness as a controlling metaphor for the neo-Victorian.

5. See John Morley, *Death, Heaven, and the Victorians* (Pittsburgh: University of Pittsburgh Press, 1971); John Kucich, "Death Worship among the Victorians: *The Old Curiosity Shop*," *PMLA* 95, no. 1 (January 1980): 58–72; and James Stevens Curl, *The Victorian Celebration of Death* (Thrupp, UK: Sutton Publishing, 2000).

6. See Jennifer Green-Lewis, *Framing the Victorians: Photography and the Culture of Realism* (Ithaca, NY: Cornell University Press, 1996); Judith Plotz, "Literary Ways of Killing a Child," in *Aspects and Issues in the History of Children's Literature,* ed. Maria Nikolajeva (Westport, CT: Greenwood Press, 1995), 1–26; and Jalland, *Death.* Green-Lewis focuses on the Gothic tradition, Plotz the Romantic, and Jalland the Evangelical.

7. See, e.g., Lisa Vollrath, "I See Dead People: Victorian Post-Mortem Photography," *Bad Influence: From the Studio of Lisa Vollrath* (October 2006): 12–14. There are also numerous collections of Victorian postmortem photographs online, on sites like Pinterest, Buzzfeed, and io9, among others, advertising the bizarreness of their subject matter and the historical era that created it.

8. Jay Ruby, *Secure the Shadow: Death and Photography in America* (Cambridge, MA: MIT Press, 1995), 52.

9. Ibid., 29.

10. "Personal and Art Intelligence," *Photographic and Fine Art Journal* 7 (July 1855): 224; quoted in Ruby, *Secure the Shadow,* 66.

11. Jannie Uhre Mogensen, "Fading into Innocence: Death, Sexuality and Moral Restoration in Henry Peach Robinson's *Fading Away,*" *Victorian Review* 32, no. 1 (2006): 1. Hereafter cited in text.

12. Jalland, *Death,* 26–36.

13. Margarete Holubetz, "Death-Bed Scenes in Victorian Fiction," *English Studies* 67, no. 1 (1986): 18. Hereafter cited in text.

14. Jalland, *Death,* 40.

15. Edgar Allan Poe, "The Philosophy of Composition," *Graham's American Monthly Magazine of Literature and Art,* no. 244 (April 1846); quoted in Elisabeth Bronfen, *Over Her Dead Body: Death, Femininity and the Aesthetic* (Manchester: Manchester University Press, 1992), 59; and Bronfen, 63. Bronfen hereafter cited in text..

16. H[enry] P[each] Robinson, *The Elements of a Pictorial Photograph* (Bradford, UK: Percy Lund, 1896), 102; for a discussion of this quotation, see Green-Lewis, *Framing the Victorians,* 54.

17. Green-Lewis, *Framing the Victorians,* 54.

18. See Robinson's description of his work in H[enry] P[each] Robinson, *Pictorial Effect in Photography: Being Hints on Composition and Chiaroscuro for Photographers* (London: Piper and Carter, 1869).

19. Plotz, "Literary Ways," 3.

20. Charles Dickens, *The Old Curiosity Shop,* ed. Norman Page (1841; London: Penguin, 2000), 541. Hereafter cited in text.

21. Marcia Muelder Eaton, "Laughing at the Death of Little Nell: Sentimental Art and Sentimental People," *American Philosophical Quarterly* 26, no. 4 (October 1989): 275.

22. Margarete Holubetz contends that Dickens "mingles the concept of justice on earth with the idea of heavenly reward, the suggestion that life is finite with the belief in personal immortality, the anguish at an irreplaceable loss with the consoling usefulness of such death, and he asks the reader to partake in the grief of the bereaved, yet to be comforted by assurances of Nell's eternal bliss." Holubetz, "Death-Bed Scenes," 26–27.

23. Patrick J. McCarthy, "The Curious Road to Death's Nell," *Dickens Studies Annual* 20 (1991): 31.

24. Plotz, "Literary Ways," 2.

25. Kucich, "Death Worship," 63; Stewart, *Death Sentences,* 184.

26. See Emily Brontë, *Wuthering Heights,* ed. Pauline Nestor (1847; London: Penguin Books, 2003); Elizabeth Gaskell, *Mary Barton,* ed. Jennifer Foster (1848; Toronto: Broadview Press, 2000); and William Makepeace Thackeray, *The Newcomes,* ed. David Pascoe (1855; London: Penguin Books, 1996).

27. Matthew 18:3, in *The Official King James Bible Online,* www. kingjamesbibleonline.org/book.php?book=Matthew&chapter=18 &verse=2.

28. Plotz, "Literary Ways," 7.

29. For discussions of Gorey's parodic use of Victorian iconography, see Mark T. Rusch, "The Deranged Episode: Ironic Dissimulation in the Domestic Scenes of Edward Gorey's Short Stories," *International Journal of Comic Art* 6, no. 2 (Fall 2004): 445–55; and Victor Kennedy, "Mystery! Unraveling Edward Gorey's Tangled Web of Visual Metaphor," *Metaphor and Symbolic Activity* 8, no. 3 (1993): 181–93.

30. Charles Dickens, *Oliver Twist,* 1837–39, ed. Kathleen Tillotson (Oxford: Oxford University Press, 1999); and Frances Hodgson Burnett, *Sara Crewe; or, What Happened at Miss Minchin's,* 1887–88 (New York: Charles Scribner's Sons, 1888).

31. Edward Gorey, *The Hapless Child* (1961; repr., San Francisco, CA: Pomegranate Communications, Inc., 1989), n.p.

32. Hillary Chute, "Comics as Literature? Reading Graphic Narrative," *PMLA* 123, no. 2 (2008): 460.

33. Scott McCloud, *Understanding Comics: The Invisible Art* (New York: HarperCollins, 1993), 68.

34. For more on these bad omens, see Kennedy, "Mystery!" 185–87.

35. Edward Gorey, *The Gashlycrumb Tinies; or, After the Outing* (1963; repr., Boston: Harcourt Brace & Company, 1991), n.p.

36. Will Eisner, *Comics and Sequential Art: Principles and Practices from the Legendary Cartoonist,* 1985 (New York: W. W. Norton, 2008), 2.

37. A. Robin Hoffman, "G Is for Gorey Who Kills Children," *Studies in Weird Fiction* 27 (Spring 2005): 25.

38. Rusch, "Deranged Episode," 447–51.

39. Roman Dirge, *Lenore* 1, no. 1 (February 1998); reprinted in *Roman Dirge's Lenore: Noogies, Collecting "Lenore," Issues 1–4* (San Jose, CA: Slave Labor Graphics, 1999), 5. Poe's "Lenore" was published in *The Pioneer* (1843); Dirge cites the date of an earlier version titled "The Pæan" (1831).

40. The flash animated shorts were created and written by Roman Dirge, produced by Adelaide Productions, and distributed by Sony Entertainment in 2002.

41. Roman Dirge, "Lenore in 'The Raven'" in *Lenore* 1, no. 2 (June 1998); reprinted in *Roman Dirge's Lenore: Noogies,* 32.

42. Ibid., 5.

43. Roman Dirge, "Lenore in 'The Macabre Malevolence of Mortimer Fledge,'" *Roman Dirge's Lenore* 2, no. 1 (London: Titan Publishing Group, 2009), n.p.

44. Ann Heilmann and Mark Llewellyn offer an excellent discussion of neo-Victorian novels, including Byatt's and Blake's, that are invested in the "re(dis)covery of a personal and/or collective history and the reconstruction of fragmented, fabricated, or repressed memories" in *Neo-Victorianism: The Victorians in the Twenty-First Century, 1999–2009* (Basingstoke, UK: Palgrave Macmillan, 2010), 34.

45. Cora Kaplan, *Victoriana: Histories, Fictions, Criticisms* (New York: Columbia University Press, 2007), 5.

46. Neil Gaiman, introduction to *Roman Dirge's Lenore: Cooties,* by Roman Dirge (London: Titan Publishing Group, 2010), 6.

IV.

Temporal Images

SEVEN

Prefiguring Future Pasts

Imagined Histories in Victorian Poetic-Graphic Texts, 1860–1910

LINDA K. HUGHES

This chapter revisits Victorian illustrated poems through the lens of neo-Victorian graphic texts and twentieth- and twenty-first-century comic books. For this purpose, I designate illustrated poems in Victorian periodicals as "poetic-graphic texts." Rather than approaching illustrations as interpretations of texts,[1] I underscore the inseparability of word and image in hybrid texts, a perspective essential to graphic fiction and comics and their theorization.[2] Poetic-graphic texts, in fact, link text and image more firmly than does the more familiar Victorian illustrated serial fiction. Whereas in shilling part formats, two illustrations at the front are offset by a succession of unbroken text-only pages, poetic-graphic texts often appear on a single page and rarely exceed five pages.[3] Thus, text always has an intimate proximity to image. Moreover, because poetry is compressed and surrounded by white space, words themselves acquire iconicity in poetic-graphic texts, as in comics and graphic novels.[4] Another key feature of comics and graphic novels applies to poetic-graphic texts as well: the coming together of past, present, and future on the page.[5] And like comics and graphic novels, poetic-graphic texts in periodicals are readily aligned with popular culture and seriality.

The sheer number of poetic-graphic texts in periodicals also indicates their significance. An initial search of just one database, Pro-Quest's British Periodicals, returned 20,151 hits for the paired search

LINDA K. HUGHES

terms *poem* and *illustrations* from 1860, when the "golden age" of periodical illustration was bolstered by new illustrated family magazines, through the end of the Edwardian period in 1910. Many hits represent satiric comic poems, editorials, or jokes more than complex hybrid visual-verbal texts. When photographs, mere headpiece or tailpiece designs, or unrelated poems and images juxtaposed on pages are eliminated from the hits, a significant number of poetic-graphic texts remain. Within them, one group has special relevance to neo-Victorianism. As Paul Goldman and Simon Cooke observe of "golden age" illustration in books and magazines from 1855 to 1875, its most common subjects were domesticity and medievalism.[6] The medieval revival in literature and art had been ongoing at least since 1765, when Thomas Percy's *Reliques of Ancient English Poetry* appeared, and encompassed high and popular culture, since medieval legends still clung to topography (as at Glastonbury) and Gothic churches were familiar sights. After the French Revolution's destruction of an ancien régime, medievalism also acquired new British associations with unbroken tradition and national identity—hence the significance of Gothic style for the new Parliament buildings after the fire of 1834 destroyed St. Stephens's.[7] By midcentury, Alfred, Lord Tennyson's "The Lady of Shalott" had inspired Pre-Raphaelite illustration in the 1857 Moxon edition of his poems; and his *Idylls of the King* quickened the vogue for medievalism in poetry after 1859.

The "golden age" illustrations noted by Goldman and Cooke were of course not medieval but *neo*-medieval, highly self-conscious because they necessarily shuttled among known historical details, legends, and an imagined, re-created past that, when disseminated by new technologies of high-speed printing and reproduction, also announced their own modernity.[8] Neo-medievalism became a mobile graphic and verbal idiom that could serve divergent aesthetic, social, and political ends while captivating wide audiences. Victorian poetic-graphic texts in a neo-medieval register thus form a prehistory of neo-Victorian graphic texts, since both look back to a past they revise and recirculate in a modern idiom; many also anticipate features of modern comics. In what follows, I sample important precedents from a single database while also attending to specifically Victorian constructs in their negotiation of gender and medieval iconography. To establish a frame of reference, I briefly discuss contested masculinities in three examples from the 1860s. These clarify the degree to which representations of a fantasized past illuminated middle-class masculine ideals versus solecisms while nonetheless allowing for freer exploration of gender roles than was possible in a realist idiom. These examples also reveal nascent visual techniques that would become more fully developed in modern comics and graphic novels. More-striking anticipations of modern comics and graphic novels occurred in poetic-graphic representations of women in the 1860s, perhaps not surprisingly, since neo-medieval fantasy permitted artists and poets to register some implications of contemporary changes in women's education and women's increasingly activist roles in society, as well as to experiment visually. In turning from 1860s "golden age" texts to later decades, I trace anticipations of neo-Victorianism itself, whether in terms of inventive visuality, interrogatory critique, or mobilization of conservative nostalgia.

As an instance of Victorian conservative, even imperial, content paired with graphic techniques that adumbrate comics' temporal complexity, I begin with "King Sigurd, the Crusader" (*Good Words*, 1862).[9] The 1860s poetic-graphic texts I located mention the Crusades more often than King Arthur, perhaps because Crusaders' religious warrant for appropriating lands abroad suited audiences after Britain began direct rule of India following the 1857 rebellion. The text of "King Sigurd, the Crusader" celebrates the valor, patriotism, and erotic fidelity of its title character, who vows not to marry until he has won acclaim in the Crusades. En route he meets the "Paynim foe" and "Corsairs of brown Barbary," and he then is victorious in Palestine, firmly resisting the beautiful maidens of Jerusalem because "The maids of all the world beside / Are not like those at home" (248, lines 119–20). The king's steady gaze and the strong verticals of Sigurd and his beloved Hinda in Edward Burne-Jones's illustration, in contrast to the attendant women's sorrow, forecast Sigurd's victories abroad and his moral steadfastness (see fig. 7.1). The design depicts the king's departure but incorporates a past, present, and implied future because it doubles as an image of Sigurd's return, when his fidelity to God, country, and his beloved, like his chivalric prowess, are confirmed and the sorrowing maidens become the bride's wedding attendants.

In "Faint Heart Never Won Fair Ladye" (*Once a Week*, 1863),[10] nothing could be further from normative masculinity than the visual

"See, over them, Jerusalem,
   And far, and farther o'er,
Where maid and wife, as dear as life,
   Are waiting on the shore !

" Let truth betide the Sea-king's bride,
   Whose breast is like the foam ;
The maids of all the world beside
   Are not like those at home."

He raised his crown from off his head,
   But turn'd he not his eye ;
As beauteous as a beauteous maid,
   As stately pass'd he by.

" These men are men," said Baldwin, then,
   " Are kings from head to heel,
To death, to life, to love and strife,
   As true as ice-brook steel ;

" And blest the clime o'er all the earth,
   The land where'er it be,
The mothers all who gave them birth,
   These Norsemen of the sea !

And long and well, as minstrels tell,
   They fought the Paynim foe,
And Acre's rock-built ramparts fell,
   Before the Norsemen's blow.

FIG. 7.1   "King Sigurd, the Crusader," text by William Forsyth, illustration by Edward Burne-Jones, engraving by Dalziel, *Good Words* 3 (December 1862): 248. Image courtesy of Cadbury Research Library: Special Collections, University of Birmingham.

image that dominates the second page (see fig. 7.2). It shows a dan-
dified, mustachioed courtier in an elaborately embroidered tunic, a
yo-yo ("bandelore" to Victorians) dangling from his right arm, his left
hand raised in meditative introspection to his lips, while his lyre and
hoops lie off to the side—an intriguing anticipation of Bunthorne,
the comical, high-Aesthetic poet in Gilbert and Sullivan's satirical
1881 operetta *Patience,* from the gaudy flowers on the suitor's tunic to
his effeminate stance and coiffure. His "toys" suggest the playthings of
adolescence rather than achievements of manhood, and the woman
he courts stands with her back to him, a baffled or rueful expression
on her face. The text, a dialogue, opens with the lady declaring that
if her suitor will not fight when "rebels fill the gate," she will (97,
line 2). But gender norms are quickly reinstated once he speaks—"It
needs not I should courage learn / From any ladye fair" (98, lines
27–28)—and the poem ends with their own future past, when their
children and grandchildren recall his valor and her wifely support. If
the text teaches what belongs to masculinity, the image introduces an
alternative and calls norms into question, since the effeminate dandy
and the valorous warrior on the field inhabit the same person. Insofar
as this poetic-graphic text fissures masculine identity and interrogates
simultaneously a past and current gender ideology, "'Faint Heart'"
anticipates the back-and-forth of time frames and multivalent significance of much neo-Victorianism.[11]

"Ballad of the Page and the King's Daughter," inspired by a German ballad of Emanuel Geibel's, provides yet another perspective on
1860s masculinities by introducing issues of class and male tyranny.[12]
In the poem, the king, objecting to the lowly status of the handsome
page with whom his daughter has fallen in love, kills the page and
throws his body into sea, where it is found by mermen, who fashion
a harp from the "gleaming body white as snow" (657, line 115). On
the day the princess dutifully prepares to marry a prince selected by
her father, her blanched cheeks indicating her feelings, the court musicians halt when the mermen's haunting harp music is heard in the
hall. The melody "pierce[s]" the king's heart (658, line 185), induces
the prince to make a hasty exit, and, because it imparts a sense of the
page's presence, kills the princess. If this text is fairly conventional,
the arresting visual design, which creates an unconventional vantage
point in the picture frame (see fig. 7.3), is more proleptic. Viewers

" And in its stead the waving plume
  Shall crest my woman's brow,
The armour gall my woman's limbs;—
  What ! art thou recreant *now* ? "

" Oh ! be not wroth, sweet ladye mine,
  For by my sword I swear,
It needs not I should courage learn
  From any ladye fair."

" Now say'st thou well, and forth shalt
    thou
  At once mine own true knight;
Myself will buckle on thy spurs
  As thine own valour bright !"

Forth, forth he went, and round his arms
  On that all-glorious day
His prowess wreathed a coronet
  No Time shall pluck away.

And still his children's children tell
  Their valiant grandsire's fame ;
And still his children's children bless
  The Ladye Edith's name,

Who, zealous for the " English Rose,"
  Herself arrayed her lord,
And gave to Valour's deeds of might
  Young Beauty's best reward.
                    ASTLEY H. BALDWIN.

FIG. 7.2 "Faint Heart Never Won Fair Ladye," text by Astley H. Baldwin,
illustration by M. J. Lawless, engraver unidentified, *Once a Week,* 18 July 1863, 98.

"Before thy castle gates, Sir King,
   We hear the merman's lay,
When to his harp we hear him sing
   Our music we must stay."

And hark! from out the sea there flow,
   Into the festal hall,
Through the clear night, sweet sounds and low
   Which on their ears soft fall.

The sound into the bride's soul steals,
   As if in that same hour
Her dead love's presence it reveals
   By some strange magic power.

She knows not why, but from her eyes
   Fast fall the tear-drops down;
Upon her breast the rose-bud dies,
   Low lies her myrtle crown.

To the King's proud soul it pierced through,
   He cursed it in his heart;
The Prince to seek his charger flew,
   And hurried to depart.

With broken heart the Bride lies dead,
   For Grief hath power to kill;
And when the morning breaketh red,
   The Merman's Harp is still.   E. C.

FIG. 7.3   "Ballad of the Page and the King's Daughter (Translated from Giebel [sic])," text by E[llen] C[ook], illustration by Edward J. Poynter, engraving by Joseph Swain, *Once a Week,* 6 June 1863, 658.

are positioned just above the princess, looking down on her as she sinks to the floor surrounded by attendants, while a sartorially elegant server, his back and buttocks facing the viewers, extends a glass of wine. The design, moreover, indicates several planes of action, almost several panels, at once: the musicians at the back of the frame, whose interrupted performance alerts the king to trouble; the king (appropriately cut down to size) in the left middle ground, shouting while being ignored; and the hubbub in the foreground, where a beautiful attendant at the center reaches for the glass of wine to revive the princess, who is already dead or dying. The artist's evident delight in the welter of textures and shapes of medieval fashion and fabrics, and his design's knowing perspectival inventiveness, anticipate neo-Victorian graphic texts that likewise borrow and visually riff upon Victorian material culture, as in Bryan Talbot's *Alice in Sunderland,* which reinvents a Morrisian-style Kelmscott book (see fig. I.9), or the cover of the first number of *The League of Extraordinary Gentlemen.*[13]

If the suffering princess of "Ballad of the Page" or the faithful waiting figure of Hinda in "King Sigurd" enforce conventional femininity, other poetic-graphic texts of the 1860s adapt medieval women for feminist afterlives or as action heroes and villainesses that anticipate those of neo-Victorian novels and comics. Late in the nineteenth century, Jeanne d'Arc became a familiar icon of militant suffragists, but already in November 1867, the same year that J. S. Mill first submitted a bill for women's franchise in Parliament, "Joan of Arc" in *Cornhill Magazine* demonstrated the liberatory possibilities of reimagining a past. Preceded by an epigraph from Friedrich Schiller's *Die Jungfrau von Orleans* (1801), in which Joan vows to undergo the sternest penance for having elevated herself above others,[14] an italicized verse prologue makes explicit the work's fantasia on history: *"with two lines of German in my head,"* the poet *"shaped her after-life in moody rhyme,"* in which, rather than being burned at the stake, Joan *"fled, / And lived in silent honour, nobly wed."*[15] The next page pictures the "nobly wed" Joan, pensive, eyes downcast, slightly frowning, garbed in a conical hat and veil, with her long skirts flowing from a cinched waist, and wearing a necklace with a large cross. The image doubly signifies through an initial impression born of stereotypes and a revised meaning when the image is paired with the text.[16] At first seeming to have effected the transformation of Joan from overweening woman warrior to conventional domestic wife, the image comes to signify imprisonment and frustrated rage instead: it is no coincidence that her hands occupy the same position as would the bound hands of a woman burned at the stake.[17] Joan longs for the call of the trumpet, even the "chain" and "stake," rather than her bondage: "O God! is there worse pain in hell than this,— / To taste and loathe the quietness of bliss" (585, lines 77–78). It is not fame she misses but "famous deeds to do! / Why am I kept idle?" (588, lines 181–82). The text ends when her husband, overhearing her, exclaims upon the insatiable triad of "God, and any woman's heart, and hell"; she responds ironically, half smiling and lifting her head for a kiss: "'I go to give our maids fresh work,' she said, / 'They are insatiable of spinning wool'" (588, lines 204–5). The penance announced in Schiller's lines, in this reimagined past, is conventional marriage—an implied critique of wives' usual confinement to the home. In using the past to comment on the present, in assuming women's fitness for heroic action, and above all in self-consciously creating a fictional afterlife, "Joan of Arc" anticipates neo-Victorianism.

Gender politics are subordinate to ambiguity and complex visuality in "Rosamond, Queen of the Lombards." Frederick Sandys's striking drawing *Rosamond, Queen of the Lombards* (1861) is familiar to scholars of Pre-Raphaelite art and visitors to the FitzWilliam and Delaware Art Museums, its title alluding to a medieval historical legend: "According to tradition, Alboin [king of the Lombards] was assassinated by order of his wife Rosamund," whom he married following the death of his first wife, "after he had forced [Rosamund] to follow the Lombard custom of drinking from the skull of her slain father." Viewed apart from the text, Sandys's design might seem to underscore the daughter and unwilling sexual victim, since a contemplative Rosamond embraces her father's skull while kneeling before a crucifix illuminated by a lamp; a rosary depends from a stand holding the skull, which rests on a prie-dieu decorated with religious carvings (including what appears to be a crowned Virgin Mary). But Sandys's image acquires altered meanings when read as part of the poetic-graphic text in *Once a Week* (see fig. 7.4).[18] Not only does "Rosamond, Queen of the Lombards" generate multiple, incoherent female identities that render femininity a hermeneutic problem rather than fixed essence, but it also anticipates elements of graphic fiction in its handling of visual spaces.[19]

II.

She sate those bearded lords among,
    Scorning the Lombard swine,
While they, with burly battle song,
Drained down, with clamours loud and long,
    The dark Falernian wine.

III.

The king in wrath hath started up:
    Grim grew his face and red,
"By the bleeding Rood! but thou shalt sup
The good wine from thy master's cup,
    Made of thy father's head."

IV.

The king's red face grew pale with re,
    He smote upon the board:
"Pour up the wine which flames like fire,
And drink damnation to thy sire,
    And glory to thy lord!

V.

"Thy sire is rotting in his grave,
    Thy sire, my beaten hound,
And thou art but my leman-slave,
The whitest-bosomed toy I have,
    My lady Rosamond!"

VI.

She raised the scull-cup to her lips,
    Queenlike she gazed around,
Across her heart a shadow slips—
"Ah me! how sharp the memory grips
    Of wild Lord Cunimond!"

VII.

Smiling, she touched it, bubbling fresh,
    Like the broth of a wizard's charm.—
That night she caught him in her mesh,

And slew him, gorged with wine and flesh,
    With her ivory-moulded arm.

VIII.

So sharply to his false heart sped
    The knife of Rosamond:
With his wild eyes all blurred with red,
Within the dwellings of the dead,
    He met Lord Cunimond!

CJE.

FIG. 7.4   "Rosamond, Queen of the Lombards," text by C. J. E., illustration by Frederick Sandys, engraving by Swain, *Once a Week,* 30 November 1861, 631.

In the poetic-graphic text, Rosamond herself does the killing after her captor, in addition to forcing her to drink from her father's skull, taunts her with being his sexual slave:

> V.
>
> "Thy sire is rotting in his grave,
>   *Thy* sire, *my* beaten hound,
> And thou art but my leman-slave,
> The whitest-bosomed toy I have,
>   My lady Rosamond!"
>
> VI.
>
> She raised the scull-cup to her lips,
>   Queenlike she gazed around,
> Across her heart a shadow slips—
> "Ah me! how sharp the memory grips
>   Of wild Lord Cunimond!"
>
> VII.
>
> Smiling, she touched it, bubbling fresh,
>   Like the broth of a wizard's charm.—
> That night she caught him in her mesh,
> And slew him, gorged with wine and flesh,
>   With her ivory-moulded arm.
>
>   (631, lines 21–35; emphasis in the original)

Stanza 5 is unusual in its sexual explicitness, as is the poem in making Rosamond both a fierce warrior (rather than a mere plotter) and a sexual victim. Combined with Sandys's representation of a Pre-Raphaelite "stunner" whose abundant curling hair and richly detailed surroundings recall Dante Gabriel Rossetti's "St. Cecilia" (an image for Tennyson's "The Palace of Art" in the 1857 Moxon edition), the poetic-graphic text looks ahead to the lethal but sexy comic book villainesses whose martial and physical powers threaten men even as their nubile bodies lure them on.[20] Yet in murdering her captor, Rosamond also recalls the biblical heroine Judith, who, after being commanded to enter the bed of Holofernes, decapitates him to save her city. Avenging her father's cruel murder and the dishonoring of his body, Rosamond enacts an approved role as dutiful daughter. But whereas Judith commits murder before she is sexually violated and thus remains a pure woman, the *Once a Week* Rosamond is sexually experienced, hence a fallen woman. Indeed, the text aligns the "white-bosomed toy" with the "ivory-moulded arm" that drives a knife into her captor's heart while in bed with him.

Possibly Sandys visualizes Rosamond just before she retires, as she embraces her father's remains in a space designated for prayer and steels herself to enter the drunken king's bed. But joined to the text, the image as readily represents Rosamond fresh from the murder. A dagger rests under a brazier, and even on the prie-dieu, sharp scissors—another potential murder weapon—are visible immediately below the skull. As with Burne-Jones's King Sigurd, Sandys's design can thus represent both a before and an after. And these multiple potential temporalities are complemented by a handling of space that approximates separate panels of action: the wall hanging that serves as a backdrop to the crucifix separates divine from profane details to the left, where the king, drunk or dead, slouches on the bed, his wine cup and footstool overturned. Rosamond's magnificent hair complicates these divisions because it begins in sacred and then billows into profane space, perhaps registering her complex identity. Like neo-Victorian works, then, this poetic-graphic text appropriates a past while opening up an array of female subjectivities and experiences that challenge any single view of womanhood. Possibly a new Victorian development enabled the ambiguity of "Rosamond, Queen of the Lombards," for it appeared around the same time that Lady Audley, another beautiful woman associated with Pre-Raphaelite art who is willing to kill to achieve her purposes, was enthralling audiences.[21]

Two poetic-graphic texts of 1866–67 eschew the intriguing ambiguity of "Rosamond" but prefigure heroic twentieth-century female action figures.[22] In "The Bride of Rozelle: A Jersey Legend" and "The Huntress of Armorica: A Tale of St. Michael's Mount," attractive women rescue the men they love through feats of physical daring.[23] A "legend" or "tale," allowing for the counterfactual and implying a distant past, enables such plots. The text of "The Bride of Rozelle" tells of a new bride whose husband, hunting a dragon while accompanied only by his friend, is reported dead when the friend returns; she complies with her husband's reported last wishes, sealed with his ring, that she wed the survivor. But as soon as she completes the ceremony, she announces to her people that she will seek her husband, requiring their obedience to their new prince with the caveat that if her pet bird returns it is a sign that her lord still lives and that his friend is a traitor. Wending her way alone through the labyrinthine, monster-haunted forest where the men lately hunted, she finds her wounded husband, releases her bird, and causes swift justice back home. The poem itself intervenes in conventional womanhood and earlier versions of the legend, as a footnote indicates, since the story usually ends with the woman's marriage to the successor or her first husband's return by supernatural means. Here, the bride's intrepid action is the engine of justice. But the accompanying illustration is equally crucial, for it shows her, in full-length gown and veil, athletically grasping a bough to swing across a stream and aid her husband, who passively rests against a tree. The illustrator's choice to capture the bride mid-action, as "[s]he seized a bough, and slung herself to land," rather than after she lands "on her knees at those dear feet," reinforces her power (663, lines 96 and 98).

"The Huntress of Armorica" is even more proleptic. The text opens frankly celebrating a woman's physical prowess and derring-do:

> Tower lordly as thou wilt, rise bold to heaven
> Thou heaved-up pyramid of Careg Luz,[24]
> No match art thou for woman in her will!
> Strike with the terrors of thy granite bulk
> The bondman gazing on thy spar-lit heights,
> Thou dauntest not the Huntress of the Hills!
> She who hath scaled wild peaks to hunt the wolf
> In wide Armorica . . .
>
> (706, lines 1–8)

Like "Joan of Arc," the poem also celebrates women's rights just when votes for women were being discussed as part of the Second Reform Bill. Eian, niece to King Cathon, has been detained for refusing to marry her cousin, the king's heir. Summoned to the king's presence, she defies him again, the king explicitly censuring her as "Unmannered and unwomanly" for daring to stand before him "as [if] thou equal wert" (706, lines 45, 47). He threatens that if she continues to resist his will, Malo, the imprisoned man she loves, will be placed in a boat and pent in a sea cave until he starves. At this point she demands her "liberty," only to be told,

"That is for man."
"For woman too.—Oh! miserable man,
That on the vigour and the might Heaven gave
For his self-use, himself will put the curb!—
Give me my liberty.—Or take my life."

(707, lines 79–83)

The king swiftly dispatches Malo to the hollow cave with henchmen. But because she hunts, Eian knows of an outlet on the other side. She becomes an action heroine indeed when she emerges atop the mount "armed, / Body and soul," leaping "from crag to crag" (707, lines 116-18),

. . . a shield behind her slung
By two light paddles crossed, like pirate flag
Bearing its skull and fleshless bones aloft . . .

(707, lines 123–25)

Upon spying the boat holding her lover, who is bound hand and foot, she takes a daring leap into it, unlooses his hands, uses her shield to deflect arrows from the king's men as Malo rows, then "bade him bear the shield aloft, / And in her stronger hands the paddles seized" (707, lines 162–63). Eventually they make their way to Armorica (present-day Brittany), and she nurses her lover back to health, afterward meeting him on the hills to carry the "spoils" of *his* hunting, and later still teaching her children how to scale the slopes with "firm free foot" (708, lines 194, 196).

Once more the illustrator might have selected the concluding, more conventional moment for his design. Instead, the image (see fig. 7.5) presents Eian on the heights of St. Michael's Mount as she completes her daring leap, the shield and paddles slung behind her, her hair streaming, her arms bare, and her skirt billowing up to her knees to reveal her sandal-clad feet. More than any other poetic-graphic text I located, "The Huntress of Armorica" looks ahead to comics iconography: Eian is, for all purposes, a Victorian Wonder Woman. And the image was accorded greater prominence because, as an "extra" illustration in a Christmas-season issue, it took the form of a full-page plate tipped in rather than placed on a page with surrounding text. Significantly, St. Michael's Mount was associated with

THE HUNTRESS OF ARMORICA.—BY PAUL GRAY.

FIG. 7.5   "The Huntress of Armorica," text by Eleanora L. Hervey, illustration by Paul Gray, engraving by Swain, *Once a Week,* 29 December 1866, facing 707.

Arthurian legend (708). "The Huntress of Armorica" reinscribes this famous landmark with female rather than male heroism. And because in the case of Tennyson's *Idylls,* past legend was being coopted as a commentary and guide for the present, perhaps this poetic-graphic text also had a contemporary application, particularly to debates in the late 1860s over women who fox hunted and rode fast horses.[25] The poetic-graphic texts devoted to Joan of Arc, the Queen of the Lombards, the Bride of Rozelle, and Eian the huntress challenged the exclusive suitability of domestic roles for women and, together with the other 1860s works noted above, demonstrate the self-conscious use and adaptability of neo-medievalism, which could shore up conservative masculinity and imperialism or question masculine authority and the efficacy of middle-class female domesticity while embroidering or reinventing the past.

The number of neo-medieval poetic-graphic texts in the Pro-Quest database steeply declines after 1869 (from more than forty to some thirteen in the 1870s), suggesting that a media vogue had largely run its course after Tennyson's 1869 *Idylls.*[26] The 1870s work most proleptic of neo-Victorianism comes, surprisingly, from *Quiver,* devoted to Sunday reading, in which "A New Elaine" (see fig. 7.6) adapts and repurposes Tennyson's neo-medieval characters as modern characters in revised narratives.[27] The illustration depicts four women and a man in up-to-date dress, lounging on an Isle of Wight hillside overlooking the sea. The text invokes a past reading of the "idyl of Elaine" (561, line 2), when among the reading group was Nelly, "a lily maid indeed . . . / to another 'falsely true'" (562, lines 10–12). But though Nelly's story had then inspired sorrow, this post-Tennysonian Elaine has a different ending:

> Come back, and read in Nelly's eyes,
> The promise of a brighter life;
> The past may still be sad, and yet
> I think God helps us to forget.
>
> (562, lines 21–24)

This adaptation of Tennyson serves the conservative end of teaching religious consolation, but it is *avant la lettre* (*et l'image*) in self-consciously looking back to an earlier scene of reading and representation and re-playing it in a modern idiom, the two together forming a palimpsest.

(Drawn by M. Kerns.)

A NEW ELAINE.

D O you remember how you read
　　The pensive idyl of Elaine?
　The summer skies were overhead,

And like a gleaming sapphire plain,
　The quiet sea lay warm and bright
　Around our flowery Isle of Wight.

FIG. 7.6　"A New Elaine," text by Sarah Doudney, illustration by M. Kerns, engraver unidentified, *Quiver* 11 (January 1876): 561. Image courtesy of Cadbury Research Library: Special Collections, University of Birmingham.

In the 1880s, aside from a continuing spate of humorous cartoons, the most relevant poetic-graphic texts likewise suggest the emergence of nascent neo-Victorianism, especially two that involve palimpsestuous spaces in which the old is also starkly modern and the "now" takes shape as (and out of) the past. Text and image are always inseparable in poetic-graphic texts, but they are unusually interdependent in "King Goll" (*Leisure Hour*, September 1887), the first periodical poem of W. B. Yeats.[28] For the image is by Yeats's father, Jack Yeats, who depicts his son as the Irish King Goll, his long hair entangled in the harp strings, which he destroys in his frenzied singing. The poet thus provides the words and also looks out at us from the image, his hands on the harp. Insofar as the harp tropes poetry itself, Yeats dominates the entire poetic-graphic work, asserting total identification with his text. Yet in another respect, Yeats is performing a filial role, submitting to representation mediated by his father—an intriguing metacommentary on the affiliation and contested subordinations and dominations of word and image discussed by Lorraine Kooistra and others.[29] Yeats's text seems highly self-aware of all this, since it obliquely comments on the "marriage" of diverse media (harp music and human voice), while his parenthetical refrain not only introduces an uncanny note but also registers multiple voices and perspectives: "Of some unhuman misery / Our married voices wildly trolled— / (They will not hush, the leaves that round me flutter—the beech leaves old)" (636, lines 58–60).

The Yeats poetic-graphic text with its tacit generational contest allots roughly equal space to text and image. In "A Tennysonian Study" (*London Society*, July 1885),[30] the image dominates text by the Victorian poet laureate so that in spatial terms he already seems superseded (see fig. 7.7). Yet the image also realizes what Tennyson had imagined in *The Princess*, his neo-medieval poem of 1847.[31] At the bottom of the page of "A Tennysonian Study," six lines express Lilia's fantasy of being "some great princess" who built "Far off from men a college like a man's, / [Where] I would teach them all that men are taught" (lines 2, 3–4); in six other lines, a masculine narrator subordinates women to roles as objects of the gaze, saying how "Pretty were the sight / If our old halls could change their sex" and show "sweet girl-graduates in their golden hair" (lines 7–8, 10). The textual excerpts effectively restage the battle of the sexes and call attention to historical fantasy and projection in Tennyson's poem, in which Victorian contemporaries

A TENNYSONIAN STUDY.
BY FRANK GODART.

. . . . "' O I wish
That I were some great princess, I would build
Far off from men a college like a man's,
And I would teach them all that men are taught;
We are twice as quick!' And here she shook aside
The hand that play'd the patron with her curls.

And one said smiling, ' Pretty were the sight
If our old halls could change their sex, and flaunt
With prudes for proctors, dowagers for deans,
And sweet girl-graduates in their golden hair.
I think they should not wear our rusty gowns,
But wove as rich as Emperor-moths.'' . . . .

THE PRINCESS; *A Medley.*

FIG. 7.7   "A Tennysonian Study," text by Alfred Lord Tennyson, design and engraving by Frank Godart, *London Society* 48, no. 283 (July 1885): v.

look back to an imagined past in order to look forward to an altered footing between the sexes while glancing anxiously at the present. Artist Frank Godart in turn reaches back to a mid-Victorian poem to illustrate Lilia's desire yet crafts an image that enacts its distinctive modernity, since by 1885 women university students wandered amid neo-medieval buildings designed by Alfred Waterhouse at Girton College. Tennyson is displaced by the Tennysonian, for only the title indirectly acknowledges his authorship, whereas the artist–engraver enjoys a double signature and his image dominates the page. Like many neo-Victorian graphic texts, "A Tennysonian Study" glances toward and briefly dips into a Victorian text but mainly circulates arch-modernity through newly revised Victorianism.[32]

Neo-medievalism remained an important reference point at century's end in the Holy Grail tapestries of Edward Burne-Jones and Aubrey Beardsley's illustrations for the J. M. Dent serial issue of Sir Thomas Malory's *Le Morte d'Arthur* (1893–94).[33] But the idiom exerted little force in poetic-graphic texts at the turn of the century. "From a Ruined Tower" and "A Ballad of a Shield" deploy neo-medievalism only to interrogate its barbarous violence, while the use of neo-medieval imagery in "One Day" and "Among the Tombs" might as well have been modern for all the relevance the images bring to the texts.[34] However, a canonical Victorian poet and an artist identified with decadence together created a poetic-graphic text that can be said to mark the birth of neo-Victorianism as we know it: "An Echo from Willowwood" (see fig. 7.8), with text by Christina Rossetti and designs by Charles Ricketts. For this hybrid text explicitly quotes and replays in a different register the visual and verbal works of D. G. Rossetti.[35] The text is doubly belated, since its title announces an after-sound or echo, while the poet's last name identifies the surviving sister of Dante Gabriel Rossetti, whose line forms the sonnet's epigraph and a legend on the visual border between Ricketts's two images ("O ye, all ye that walk in willowwood"). In the "Willowwood" sonnets, also first published in a periodical, a bereaved lover sits beside a spring with Love personified; and as Love strums a lute and sweeps the water with his wing, the face of the lost beloved rises to the surface, the lover's lips meeting hers in a long kiss that lasts only so long as Love sings.[36] In the sister's "Echo," the woman is no longer a ghostly phantom rising to the water's surface but an equal sharer of gazing, longing, and loss: "Two gazed into a pool, he gazed and she, . . . / Each eyed the other's aspect, she and he, / Each felt one hungering heart leap up and sink" (lines 1, 5–6). Everywhere true to the tone, theme, and formal choices of the "Willowwood" sonnets, the "Echo[ing]" text also revises the former in making the woman an active agent and participant, a decidedly modern note in 1890.

Ricketts's design also looks back to, yet revises, his precursor's art. The upper half of the diptych is clearly indebted to D. G. Rossetti, as Lorraine Kooistra notes, in its "crowded" visual scene, neo-medieval trappings, and frame that pays homage to D. G. Rossetti's own visual designs for books.[37] The shells on the bereaved man's cape also recall decorative devices on the frames of Rossetti's paintings, while the

FIG. 7.8   "An Echo from Willowwood," text by Christina G. Rossetti, illustration by Charles Ricketts, *Magazine of Art* (January 1890): 385.

empty boat perhaps alludes to his Moxon illustration for "The Lady of Shalott," in which Lancelot leans over the dead woman and her boat.[38] In contrast, Ricketts's image in the lower half of the diptych, beautifully attuned to the swirling water that joins the lovers' faces in Christina Rossetti's text, shifts to an art nouveau style while also graphically marking (as Kooistra notes) the sonnet's division between octave and sestet.[39] In paying such homage to D. G. Rossetti and his verbal-visual idioms, then sweeping away from them in both text and design, thus marking the temporal distance of this 1890 work from them, the poetic-graphic text "An Echo from Willowwood" estab-lishes the very groundwork of later neo-Victorianism: adapting Victorianism to circulate modernity and difference.

"An Echo from Willowwood" marks a turning point in Victorian neo-medievalism, from a prehistory to the inception of neo-Victorianism. But some graphic texts of the early twentieth century appropriate Victorian neo-medievalism to promote conservative agendas, just as neo-Victorianism in the 1980s included the recuperation of Victorian "hard work" and "thrift" by Prime Minister Margaret Thatcher to shore up her policies.[40] The Boer War (1899–1902), costly and achieving at best ambiguous results, is the likely source of belated chivalric medievalism used to extoll the virtues of God, country, and sacrifice. In "The Strife Song" (1900), a panel above the text depicts a white knight attacking a black knight with additional foes massed beyond and smoke rising in the distance; the refrain of the poem's six stanzas celebrates the "heart that may not yield," whether facing a hunt, a pilgrimage, "tides of battle," a "lonely quest . . . / Through bleak lands and regions drear," "craven traitors," or shipwreck.[41] Both the dark versus white knights and "bleak lands . . . drear" are consistent with the anxieties of a distant war in South Africa. "Proud Princess" (1910),[42] conversely, initially sug-gests mid-Victorian feminism as well as 1860s neo-medieval visuality in its headpiece representing the princess in splendid isolation (see fig. 7.9), just as the text at first represents a woman impervious to marriage:

> Against her jewelled throne she leant,
> More pale than driven snow,
> And suitors came and suitors went,
> But Proud Princess said "No!"
>
> (1046, lines 9–12)

All changes when, instead of offering her agency as a coruler or proposing for the strategic advantage of adjoining kingdoms, the last suitor declares, "I want—a wife!" (1047, line 37). The princess's cheek glows, her eyes soften, and she smiles as he continues: "A simple woman she must be / My heart of hearts her home, / My laughing children round her knee" (1047, lines 45–47). In the work's final image

PROUD PRINCESS

BY LYDIA BUSCH.

ILLUSTRATED BY HERBERT COLE.

PROUD Princess sat day by day
Upon her throne of gold,
And watched the hours drag away
With tired eyes and cold.
The perfumed courtiers bent and bowed
Around her without cease,
All lonely in that glittering crowd
Her heart cried out for peace.
Against her jewelled throne she leant,
More pale than driven snow,
And suitors came and suitors went,
But Proud Princess said " No ! "

" Proud Princess !   I want a queen ! "
Said a gallant prince one day,
" To rule my court with stately mien."
(She sighed and turned away.)
" A thousand slaves for your delight
Shall dance in every town."
(Her jewelled fingers, slim and white,
Plucked at her silken gown.)
" Great wealth have I and gems untold,
And men to come and go ! "
Her tired eyes grew hard and cold,
And Proud Princess said " No !

1046

FIG. 7.9   "Proud Princess" (headpiece), text by Lydia Busch, illustration by
Herbert Cole, *Pall Mall Magazine* (December 1910): 1046.

(see fig. 7.10), the suitor may be on bended knee, but the princess has risen from her throne and is delivering herself into his arms, and the text announces the sequel:

> He leapt to his feet like an arrow darts,
>   As she swayed in her silken dress,
> Then he clasped her to his heart of hearts,
>   For Proud Princess said "Yes!"
>
> (1048, lines 57–60)

Possibly this graphic text had been accepted months earlier, but it was published less than two weeks after Black Friday (18 November 1910), when three hundred suffragists demonstrating against Prime Minister Herbert Henry Asquith, who had prevented a partial suffrage bill from coming to a vote, rushed the House of Commons and violence ensued.[43] The self-subordination of a woman of power in "Proud Princess" to normative mid-Victorian domesticity gains greater legibility if read as a recuperation of neo-medievalism to insist on conservative gender roles and social policies.

As this selective survey of neo-medieval poetic graphic texts from 1860 to 1910 indicates, the relation among Victorian poetic-graphic texts, contemporary neo-Victorianism, and twentieth- and twenty-first-century comic book art is certainly palimpsestuous. Though creators of comic book super-heroines are unlikely to have known or to have been directly inspired by "The Huntress of Armorica," and though few (if any) scholars of neo-Victorianism have cited "An Echo from Willowwood" as a nodal point in the field's emergence, this partial exploration of the immense archive of Victorian illustrated poems in periodicals from 1860 to 1910 reveals antecedents for a wide range of neo-Victorian practices and comic book conventions. In addition to embodying temporal complexity in self-conscious imaginings of the past that imbricate the past and modern preoccupations, these neo-medieval texts, like neo-Victorian works, also offer complex representations of gender and sexuality. Bringing awareness of neo-Victorian work to the study of Victorian poetic-graphic texts in turn offers the opportunity to reread older productions as hybrid texts. In them, inseparable images and words create complex meanings and also alert us to the disputed grounds or social fissures underlying this Victorian body of work, as well as the conservative ends to which they could be put—a prefiguring of future pasts indeed.

"Then he clasped her to his heart of hearts,
For Proud Princess said 'Yes!'"

Proud Princess stepped slowly down
  From her jewelled throne of gold,
She heeded not her father's frown
  Nor yet her henchmen bold—
She held his eyes with a long, long look
  As he dropped on his bended knee,
And his heart lay there as an open book
  For the Proud Princess to see.
He leapt to his feet like an arrow darts,
  As she swayed in her silken dress
Then he clasped her to his heart of hearts,
  For Proud Princess said " Yes ! "

FIG. 7.10 "Proud Princess," text by Lydia Busch, illustration by Herbert Cole,
Pall Mall Magazine (December 1910): 1048.

Notes

I wish to thank Mary McCulley for research assistance for this chapter; my thanks also to Joanna Schmidt, Beth Newman, and Ashley Miller.

1. See the influential example of Lorraine Janzen Kooistra, *The Artist as Critic: Bitextuality in Fin-de-Siècle Illustrated Books* (Aldershot, UK: Scolar Press, 1995).

2. See Will Eisner, *Comics and Sequential Art* (New York: W. W. Norton, 2008), 127–29; Julia Round, "Visual Perspective and Narrative Voice in Comics: Redefining Literary Terminology," *International Journal of Comic Art* 9, no. 2 (Fall 2007): 316–29. To underscore the inseparability of word and image in Victorian poetic-graphic works, I cite them by title, generally identifying poets, illustrators, and engravers (when known) only in notes.

3. Monthly magazine serial parts of fiction rarely included more than two full-page illustrations and a few vignettes out of some twenty to thirty pages in all. In weekly serials, always shorter, text and image came closer together, though the proportion of word to image was still starkly asymmetrical.

4. John Hollander, *Vision and Resonance: Two Senses of Poetic Form* (New York: Oxford University Press, 1975), 3; Eisner, *Comics and Sequential Art,* 2–4.

5. See Scott McCloud, *Understanding Comics: The Invisible Art* (New York: HarperCollins, 1993), 95–96, 100.

6. Paul Goldman and Simon Cooke, eds., *Reading Victorian Illustration, 1855–1875: Spoils of the Lumber Room* (Farnham, UK: Ashgate, 2012), 1–2.

7. See, e.g., Mark Girouard, *The Return to Camelot: Chivalry and the English Gentleman* (New Haven, CT: Yale University Press, 1981); Debra Mancoff, *The Arthurian Revival in Victorian Art* (New York: Garland, 1990); Roger Simpson, *Camelot Regained: The Arthurian Revival and Tennyson, 1800–1849* (Cambridge, UK: D. S. Brewer, 1990).

8. Compare Simon Joyce, *The Victorians in the Rearview Mirror* (Athens: Ohio University Press, 2007), 4.

9. "King Sigurd, the Crusader," text by William Forsyth, illustration by Edward Burne-Jones, engraving by Dalziel, *Good Words* 3 (December 1862): 247–49. Hereafter cited in text. Burne-Jones's design is reproduced in Paul Goldman, *Victorian Illustration: The Pre-Raphaelite, the Idyllic School and the High Victorians* (Aldershot, UK: Scolar Press, 1996), plate 1.51, 45.

10. "Faint Heart Never Won Fair Ladye," text by Astley H. Baldwin, illustration by M. J. Lawless, engraver unidentified, *Once a Week,* 18 July 1863, 97–98. Hereafter cited in text.

11. Marie-Luise Kohlke, "Introduction: Speculations in and on the Neo-Victorian Encounter," *Neo-Victorian Studies* 1, no. 1 (2008): 13.

12. "Ballad of the Page and the King's Daughter (Translated from Giebel [*sic*])," text by E[llen] C[ook], illustration by Edward J. Poynter, engraving by Joseph Swain, *Once a Week,* 6 June 1863, 656–58.

13. Bryan Talbot, *Alice in Sunderland* (Milwaukie, OR: Dark Horse Comics, 2007), 232–49; Alan Moore and Kevin O'Neill, *The League of Extraordinary Gentlemen,* vol. 1 (La Jolla, CA: American's Best Comics, 2000), cover.

14. William Peter translated these lines in which Joan speaks to her sister Margot as follows: "[I will] with severest penance expiate / The crime of having set myself above you." *The Maid of Orleans,* from the German *Die Jungfrau von Orleans* (1801), by Friedrich Schiller. *The Maid of Orleans, and Other Poems* (Oxford: John Owen, 1843), 164.

15. "Joan of Arc," text by G. A. Simcox, illustration by George Du Maurier, engraving by Swain, *Cornhill Magazine* 16 (November 1867): 584. Du Maurier's full-page illustration was tipped in after page 584. Simcox, an Oxford don, was brother to feminist activist Edith Simcox. Hereafter cited in text.

16. For the speed of intake of images, the function of stereotypic images, and the possibility of surprise in comics and graphic novels, see Will Eisner, *Graphic Storytelling and Visual Narrative: Principles and Practices from the Legendary Cartoonist* (1996; repr., New York: W. W. Norton, 2008), 9–11, 52.

17. My thanks to Ashley Miller for pointing out this detail.

18. "Rosamond, Queen of the Lombards," text by C. J. E., illustration by Frederick Sandys, engraving by Swain, *Once a Week,* 30 November 1861, 630–31. Hereafter cited in text.

19. For a discussion of the issue of time and space as it is treated in comics theory, see the introduction to this volume.

20. "St. Cecilia," illustration by D. G. Rossetti to "The Palace of Art," in Alfred Tennyson, *Poems* (London: Edward Moxon, 1857), 113. For instances of female villainesses, see Karl G. Larew, "Planet Women: The Image of Women in Planet Comics, 1940–1953," *Historian* 59, no. 3 (1997): 591–612. Poison Ivy, in the Batman series, is another example (my thanks to Mary McCulley for pointing her out).

21. Mary Elizabeth Braddon, *Lady Audley's Secret* (London: Tinsley, 1862).

22. For a discussion of heroic women in 1940s comics, such as Gale Allen (drawn by Fran Hopper), a futuristic military leader who often saves her boyfriend, see Larew, "Planet Women."

23. "The Bride of Rozelle: A Jersey Legend," text by Eleanora L. Hervey, illustration by Arthur Boyd Houghton, engraving by the Swain School, *Once a Week,* 8 June 1867, 662–64 (hereafter cited in text); "The Huntress of Armorica: A Tale of St. Michael's Mount," text by Eleanora L. Hervey, illustration by Paul Gray, engraving by Swain, *Once a Week,* 29 December 1866, 706–8 (hereafter cited in text). Both poems were reprinted in Eleanora L. Hervey, *Our Legends and Lives: A Gift for All Seasons* (London: Trübner, 1869). Hervey also authored an earlier neo-medieval prose work, *The Feasts of Camelot, with the Tales That Were Told There* (London: Bell and Daldy, 1863).

24. I.e., St. Michael's Mount in Cornwall.

25. See, e.g., "Hunting Ladies," *Saturday Review,* 6 May 1865, 533–34; and appendix A of the Broadview edition of the sensation novel *Aurora Floyd,* by Mary Elizabeth Braddon, ed. Richard Nemesvari and Lisa Surridge (Peterborough, ON: Broadview, 1998), 551–59.

26. Poetic-graphic texts in *Belgravia* during and after Mary Elizabeth Braddon's editorship are notable for ironizing knighthood and emptying out neo-medieval ideals. "Sir Dinadan's Death" kills off the lovable jokester of Malory's Round Table at the hands of Sir Mordred, who stabs him and then carries away the beloved woman whom Sir Dinadan has met in the woods. Rape is clearly indicated as the sequel: the image is titled with this line from the text—"God help her in that stound!"—and shows Dinadan dead in the foreground and Mordred, his back to viewers, carrying off the woman screaming in agony and grief. See "Sir Dinadan's Death," text by unidentified poet, illustration by E. Wagner, engraver unknown, *Belgravia* 37 (February 1879): 75–78.

27. "A New Elaine," text by Sarah Doudney, illustration by M. Kerns, engraver unidentified, *Quiver* 11 (January 1876): 561–62, lines 10–12. Hereafter cited in text.

28. "King Goll," text by W. B. Yeats, illustration by Jack Yeats, *Leisure Hour* (September 1887): 636–37 (hereafter cited in text). This work is briefly discussed in Ronald Schuchard, *The Last Minstrels: Yeats and the Revival of the Bardic Arts* (Oxford: Oxford University Press, 2008), 2; and Matthew Campbell, "Thomas Moore, Daniel Maclise and the New Mythology: The Origin of the Harp," in *The Voice of the People: Writing the European Folk Revival, 1740–1914,* ed. Matthew Campbell and Michael Perraudin (London: Anthem Press, 2012), 84. Jack Yeats's *Leisure Hour* drawing is reproduced in Campbell, "Thomas Moore," 83. The *Leisure Hour* text is preceded by a note explaining the legend, as in "The Huntress of Armorica" discussed above.

29. I refer to Lorraine Kooistra's theory of the competition and gendering of word and image in illustrated literary texts. See Kooistra, *The Artist as Critic*, 5 and *passim*.

30. "A Tennysonian Study," text by Alfred Lord Tennyson, design and engraving by Frank Godart, *London Society* 48, no. 283 (July 1885): v, lines 3–4, 7–8.

31. Daniel Maclise had provided neo-medieval illustrations for the 1866 gift book edition of *The Princess;* for analysis and several reproductions, see Kooistra, *Poetry, Pictures, and Popular Publishing: The Illustrated Gift Book and Victorian Visual Culture, 1855–1875* (Athens: Ohio University Press, 2011), 193–206.

32. Sir Thomas Malory, *The birth, life, and acts of King Arthur, of his noble knights of the Round Table, their marvelous enquests and adventures, the achieving of the San Greal, and in the end, Le morte Darthur with the dolorous death and departing out of this world of them all*, illus. Aubrey Beardsley (London: J. M. Dent, 1893–94).

33. For a recent neo-Victorian image that nods toward Tennyson while circulating postmodernity, see Mélanie Delon's steampunk Lady of Shalott, *Trapped* (2009), www.melaniedelon.com/gallery.html.

34. "From a Ruined Tower," text by Lewis Morris, illustrations by E. F. Skinner, Swantype engraving, *Pall Mall Magazine* 7 (November 1895): 321–25; "A Ballad of a Shield," text by Cosmo Monkhouse, illustration by Charles Ricketts, *Magazine of Art* (January 1892): 421–22. Ricketts was trained in wood engraving but abandoned it to focus on original designs; by the 1890s most illustration was photographically reproduced. See J. G. P. Delaney, *Charles Ricketts: A Biography* (Oxford: Clarendon Press, 1990), 27–29. "One Day," text by Ella Wheeler Wilcox, illustrations by Herbert Cole, Swantype engraving, *Pall Mall Magazine* 19 (September 1899): 1–3; "Among the Tombs," text by Henry Newbolt, illustrations by Patten Wilson, *Pall Mall Magazine* 19 (September 1899): 68–69.

35. "An Echo from Willowwood," text by Christina G. Rossetti, illustrations by Charles Ricketts, *Magazine of Art* (January 1890): 385. Hereafter cited in text.

36. Dante Gabriel Rossetti, "Of Life, Love, and Death: Sixteen Sonnets," *Fortnightly Review* 5 (March 1869): 266–67.

37. Lorraine Janzen Kooistra, *Christina Rossetti and Illustration: A Publishing History* (Athens: Ohio University Press, 2002), 53–54.

38. "The Lady of Shalott," illustration by D. G. Rossetti, in Tennyson, *Poems*, 75.

39. Kooistra, *Christina Rossetti*, 53–54.

40. Joyce, *Victorians,* 111–22; see also Louisa Hadley, *Neo-Victorian Fiction and Historical Narrative: The Victorians and Us* (Basingstoke, UK: Palgrave Macmillan, 2010), 8–10.

41. "The Strife Song," text by John Kindred, illustration by Gilbert James, Swantype engraving, *Pall Mall Magazine* 21 (August 1900): 482–83, lines 8, 16–17, 24–26, 32–33, 40, 48.

42. "Proud Princess," text by Lydia Busch, illustration by Herbert Cole, *Pall Mall Magazine* (December 1910): 1046–48. Hereafter cited in text.

43. Sophia A. van Wingerden, *The Woman's Suffrage Movement in Britain, 1866–1929* (London: Macmillan, 1999), 123.

EIGHT

Before and After

Punch, Steampunk, and Victorian Graphic Narrativity

REBECCA N. MITCHELL

When asked by an interviewer to define "what exactly is steampunk," Paul Di Filippo—termed the "Steampunk Godfather" in a special issue of *Neo-Victorian Studies* dedicated to the genre—did not exactly provide a definition. He began instead by noting a distinction: "I adore steampunk fiction. I'm not so much into the material aspects of the genre: clothes or artefacts."[1] Privileging of fiction is not uncommon in steampunk scholarship or in neo-Victorian studies more broadly. Yet representations of clothes and artifacts are among the most recognizable indicators of steampunk in one genre of fiction: the graphic text, in which the visual milieu is inseparable from theme, plot, or other literary conventions. Even as the intersection of the textual and the visual or material remains underexplored, scholars are increasingly attuned to the extraliterary manifestations of steampunk, treating it, for example, as a subculture or as a mode of creative production.[2] Many studies foreground the ambivalence of the aesthetic that, by definition, embraces anachronism and a past that includes ideologies and reanimates technologies long since outdated.[3] Because of steampunk's willingness to engage that past, scholars have traced the ways that steampunk objects or practices lay bare or, to use a word often invoked in the discussion of the movement, negotiate the social tensions of the Victorian era as well as the corresponding tensions of the contemporary moment of production. Brigid Cherry and Maria Mellins argue that steampunk undertakes "complex negotiations of modernity and identity," "articulates complex discourses concerning gender and class," and illustrates "the ways in which 'punk' has become a highly contested and problematic label, for a set of lifestyle and identity factors which appropriate a quasi-nostalgic look to an imagined (and idealized) past."[4] Margaret Rose argues that steampunk texts "do not undermine the idea of the reality of the past but instead explore the intersections and limitations of the various textual ways in which we access it."[5] And Christine Ferguson suggests that steampunks must mediate the politics of a practice that "simultaneously requires and de-realizes a verifiable Victorian past," so that they may "visually quote the Victorian period without seeming to slavishly repeat and emulate its clichéd ideological significations."[6]

This line of inquiry owes much to Fredric Jameson's and Linda Hutcheon's articulations of the relationship of the postmodern to history; it is a theoretical foundation that cannot be ignored but also one that encourages a backward-looking critical approach to steampunk, asking what such postmodern phenomena can tell us about our received notions of the past.[7] Further, positioning a metatextual or meta-imagistic postmodern in contradistinction to what came before encourages a monolithic understanding of the Victorian past as being singular, stable, and unreflective. To be sure, this practice has been critiqued in literary studies for some time.[8] Yet many analyses of steampunk continue to rely on a static notion of the Victorian, perhaps because the nature of steampunk itself is still being debated by its practitioners: these debates tend to focus on defining which contemporary practices should count as steampunk, while the matter of which past practices, styles, or ideas should count as Victorian remains relatively untroubled.[9] Suggesting a productive movement away from this bind, Ferguson notes that steampunk subcultures complicate Jameson's "well-known diagnosis of postmodern cultural production."[10] She counters that steampunk practices are based "on questions of epistemology, on how we establish, frame, and fix the period visual tropes rendered up for appropriation."[11] This chapter asks similar questions in relation to the Victorian era: Did Victorian graphic artists "establish, frame, and fix" the visual tropes that we now appropriate, and if so, how? How do we know, or think we know, what a "verifiable Victorian past" looks like, so that we might "visually quote it"? When did these images—which steampunks must now negotiate—become "clichéd ideological significations"?

Literary antecedents to steampunk narratives have been traced to proto–science fiction, dystopian/utopian narratives, and early counterfactual stories,[12] in which social and natural histories are contested, if not outright rejected. Literary scholars have in recent years recognized that Victorian fiction depends heavily on optative, counterfactual, and proleptic modes, and on accounting for what might have been or what is yet to be.[13] What is less explored is the extent to which these modes are reflected in Victorian graphic productions. Some strategies for effecting visual temporal shifts were based in the reanimation of past aesthetic paradigms—such as, for example, the revivalist iconography that defined the neo-medieval,[14] Pre-Raphaelite, and Arts and Crafts movements—whose production methods and visual vocabulary stand in stark contrast to the conventional trappings of the day, from fashion and furniture to printing processes. Other visual strategies, though, shirk direct revivalism and are intended not to challenge the status quo but rather to document it.[15] Indeed, some of the very techniques that steampunk works use to subvert normative Victorian iconography or ideology were codified in the popular Victorian illustrated periodical.

To explore Victorian pictorial negotiations of their own history, I turn to one exemplary Victorian work heavily invested in representing, celebrating, and commenting on the passage of time: the Diamond Jubilee issue of *Punch,* which deploys several iconographic modes not only to codify the "Victorian" but also, and perhaps more importantly, to parse subperiods and submovements, making distinctions within the Victorian. In some images, historical personages from different time periods comingle; in another, a Victorian moment is reset in a different historical period;[16] and, in a visual trope repeatedly deployed to great effect, image pairs are used to create a before-and-after or then-and-now topos, offering a condensed form of graphic narrative that renders seismic social shifts in two simple frames. These varying image modes represent a range of strategies used in the late nineteenth century to consolidate the past as an identifiable group of signs.

In what follows, I take up cartoons in the 1897 Diamond Jubilee issue of *Punch* as examples of images that visually historicize nineteenth-century British culture, before considering the way some neo-Victorian texts employ the visual language codified by that practice. There is the risk here of falling into what Joseph Bristow terms a "cybernetic loop," an endless recursion in which analysis reveals that neo-Victorian works simply repeat a mode of creation or reflection long ago perfected by the Victorians themselves.[17] Being mindful of that risk, I focus expressly on the consolidation of visual markers of period (and their attending ideologies), as they are made readable through temporal contrast. I do not wish to suggest that these examples are necessarily representative of all Victorian iconography; rather, I hold up these iconographic modes to demonstrate that the Victorian historicization or periodization of images was a self-conscious, intentional project, the relative success of which can be seen in the steampunk adoption of the same visual vocabulary. This is evident in two steampunk comics set in the British fin de siècle, concurrent with the *Punch* issue: Grant Morrison and Steve Yeowell's *Sebastian O* (1993), an edgy three-issue series centering on a group of decadent Aesthetes,[18] and Alan Moore and Kevin O'Neill's *The League of Extraordinary Gentlemen* (1999–), which also takes 1890s London as a setting for the adventures of a team of corruption-fighting misfits drawn from various literary texts.

Picturing Time

That historical narrative can be depicted visually is practically uncontested, though accounts vary as to how exactly narrative or time is inscribed or suggested in pictures. Writing in 1988, Wendy Steiner noted that "the narrative of pictures is virtually a nontopic for art historians,"[19] having been established by Gotthold Ephraim Lessing's notion of the "pregnant moment," a scene depicted whose visual markers suggest the events that immediately preceded and followed.[20] Sacheverell Sitwell adopted a nearly identical formulation in his influential study *Narrative Pictures* (1936), wherein he describes "the painting of anecdote" as depicting "the chosen moment in some related incident, and looking more closely into its details we must see hints or suggestions of the before and after of the story."[21] Steiner troubles this model by suggesting that "the discreteness of temporal events is not enough to create the equivalent of literary narrativity."[22] Instead, she insists that visual narrative requires the repetition of figures with discernable difference:"We know that we are looking at narrative painting because we see the subject repeated, and because reality only repeats in time."[23] Since Steiner's intervention, others have tackled the issue of the narrative potential of the image, but fundamental questions—such as "Can a Single Still Picture Tell a Story?"—remain open for debate.[24] Whether in a single frame or in repeated images, with repetition comes the introduction of difference, and in the hiatus between the two comes the interpretive gesture.[25]

Because any two images with repeated characters or icons may open up similar possibilities for narrative certainty or—conversely— narrative polysemy, the interpretation of consecutive images is of especial concern to comics theorists. Thierry Groensteen raises the question of the narrative capability of the single image in his field-defining *System of Comics,* where he suggests that narrative depends on "the triad composed of the panel that is currently being read, the panel that precedes it, and the panel that immediately follows it."[26] Later, he refines his definition to focus on development, writing that the "defining quality of a narrative" "is that it necessarily includes a beginning and an end" and requires "an element of development of the action, of evolution of the initial state A to state B."[27] Moreover, Groensteen argues that within the context of a comic, "the hiatus between two consecutive images, in a sequential narrative, can be programmed so that all readers will necessarily reconstruct the virtual content of the narrative ellipsis in exactly the same way."[28] In Scott McCloud's telling, this predictably interpretable sequencing of images is what defines the comic form: comics are "juxtaposed pictorial and other images in deliberate sequence, intended to convey information and/or to produce an aesthetic response in the viewer."[29] The idea that "all readers" will understand visual or narrative ellipses in "exactly the same way" or that a graphic text can be written to "produce an aesthetic response in the viewer" depends on the supposition that the reading audience will be familiar with the conventions of the form.

British fin-de-siècle readers would indeed have been well versed in reading the conventions of graphic narrative forms. As late as 1904, a *Punch* cartoon adapted the first engraving from Hogarth's *Industry and Idleness* (1747)[30] as the basis for satire, suggesting that the graphic narrative sequence was still part of a shared cultural tradition and required no explanation.[31] Central to that moral lesson of Hogarth's pair of apprentices is the vast gulf between their different states—which grow further apart as the series progresses—thus communicating to the viewer the ultimate effects of good versus bad behavior, the ostensible result of a series of decisions. There are, though, (at least) two ways of moving through the sequence of images: one can track the idle apprentice's development (plates 1, 3, 5, 7, 9, and 11) and the industrious apprentice's development (plates 1, 2, 4, 6, 8, 10, 12) chronologically, or one can follow the precedent of the first plate and compare the pair at each stage of their development (plates 2 and 3, 4 and 5, 6 and 7, and so forth). Whereas the first approach emphasizes the passage of time between each of the images in either apprentice's life, the second approach emphasizes the temporal simultaneity of the complementary succeeding images in the series: the apprentices are industrious and idle, respectively though concurrently.

When taken together, the plates in the Hogarth series inscribe a narrative, but the first image depicts contrasting figures, and while the many visual symbols (and Hogarthian captions) might suggest much about the young men's backgrounds, personalities, and habits, they do not quite suggest the events preceding the scene. This kind of paired image—that of simultaneous contrast—was frequently exploited by *Punch* and other illustrated magazines through the dual-panel cartoon, and because the format derives meaning from contrast, it is not surprising that gender differences were a central theme. A throwaway gag from a January 1856 issue of *Punch* offers one example (see fig. 8.1): the dual-paneled frame juxtaposes the "Highland Officer in the Crimea, according to the Romantic Ideas of Sentimental Young Ladies," on the left with the same man, "according to the Actual Fact," on the right.[32] The passage of time is neither implied nor necessary to the cartoon's meaning, as the punch line requires only contrast. In this case, the caption tethers the punch line to gender difference, exposing the gulf between idealized expectations (the "romantic ideas" of "sentimental" girls) and the harsher realities of masculine experience.[33] In cases such as these, the pictorial "hiatus"—to use Groensteen's term—represents synchronous difference but not necessarily the passage of time between the images. Another form of split panel image, however, does expressly depend on the passage of time and on repetition with difference: the before-and-after image.

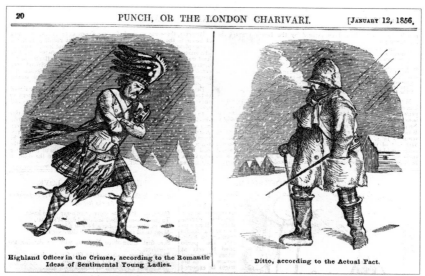

20   PUNCH, OR THE LONDON CHARIVARI.   [JANUARY 12, 1856.

FIG. 8.1   "Highland Officer in the Crimea," *Punch,* 12 January 1856, 20. Image courtesy of Cadbury Research Library: Special Collections, University of Birmingham.

The development of the before-and-after trope largely coincides with the history of photography. Both were quickly conscribed for promotional or prescriptive uses. In these pairs, the hiatus does, by definition, suggest not only the passage of time but also an intervening event: the transformative moment on which the "after" hinges. For a viewer to grasp the nature of that event, visual clues must be provided, and/or the audience must be relied on to respond with generally consistent interpretations. With good reason, much of the analysis of such images tends to focus on the ideological undercurrents that shape the viewer's interpolations of the hiatus event. As Seth Koven has ably described, in the 1870s, Dr. Thomas Barnardo used widely engraved and reprinted before-and-after photographs of London street waifs to raise funding for his homes for indigent children by showing the extraordinary change rendered by his intervention: the dirty, ragged street child is turned, as if by magic, into a clean, industrious worker (see fig. 8.2).[34] These pairings are, to use Lessing's term, pregnant with implied counterfactuals: were it not for Barnardo's presence, these girls or boys would have been left on the street, with little hope for change. Barnardo was neither the first nor the only to apply the inherent didacticism of the before-and-after

image to advertise ideology; it was "standard practice for charities at this time."[35] Other applications of the trope foregrounded the value of objects, and if ideological prejudices were engaged, so much the better. Advertisers were quick to recognize this potential, and the inscriptions of various ideologies are easily readable in Victorian ads.[36] Thomas Richards, for example, describes a before-during-after sequence of photographs showing an infant transforming from malnourished to healthy, used to advertise Mellin's food for infants: "[T]he three photographs progress from contraction to composure, from lower-class poverty to middle-class satisfaction."[37] Following Richards, Anne McClintock's analysis of Pears' Soap ads demonstrated that when coupled with suggestive imagery, nationalistic jingoism could be exploited to sell something as banal as soap, which could in turn reinforce that imperialist ideology.[38] Because the intervening events or changes taking place in the hiatus between the before and the after are merely implied, the collective unconscious can be con-scribed or manipulated to the image creator's end.

A Reign in Retrospect: *Punch*'s Diamond Jubilee

That collective unconscious is certainly shaped by shared experience, a fact put to excellent use by *Punch* in its celebratory issues. For the fiftieth anniversary of Victoria's coronation in 1887, *Punch* published a special three-volume series, *Mr. Punch's Victorian Era,* which reviewed the entire run of the weekly satirical magazine. The publication of *Punch* began in 1841, only four years after the start of Victoria's reign, making the magazine's ascendancy nearly synchronous with the mon-arch's rule. These volumes reviewed work already printed in *Punch,* reprinting cartoons along with helpful commentary to jog readers' memories, offering necessary context for the sociopolitical moments that the cartoons satirized. The effect was of a scrapbook of memo-ries. Subtitled *An Illustrated Chronicle of Fifty Years of the Reign of Her Majesty the Queen from the Contemporary Pages of "Punch,"* the collec-tion was clearly intended to provide an overview, charting the course between the past and the reader's present.[39] Whereas the 1887 volumes traced the chronological threads linking then and now, the Diamond Jubilee issue, dated 19 June 1897, took a different approach. This num-ber is notable because it is composed almost entirely of illustrations, with relatively little accompanying text, offering a veritable catalog of

modes to visualize history (or historicize images). Further, nearly each
of these modes complicates the accounts of narrativity in both Lessing's description of paintings and Groensteen's and McCloud's analyses of comic structure. Some of the images elide temporal distinctions
by depicting characters who are historically out of time, sharing the
same space and the same moment. In other images, the passage of
time is foregrounded explicitly and the differences between the start
of Victoria's reign and the then-present day are shown to be stark, and
not necessarily for narrative ends. Meaning in these images is based
in counterfactual synchronicity or drastic asynchronicity or is derived
from the codification of imagery aligned with various moments in
Victoria's reign: the *Punch* issue, in other words, functions as a key to
the meaning of date-specific imagery.

Setting the laudatory tone that would continue throughout, the
opening page features Victoria on the throne, in her present age, surrounded by the "Great Queens of History," including Catherine of
Russia, Isabella of Spain, Elizabeth I, Phillipa, Cleopatra, Sheba, Maria
Theresa of Austria, and Queen Anne. The accompanying poem describes the scene as the "strangest of all dreamland's scenes,"[40] and one
might be tempted to dismiss the vignette as just a "dreamland" gallery
of famous faces, with no intended connection to any real place or time.
In the issue's first full-page cartoon, though, the importance—and the
sheer duration—of the Jubilee period (1837–97) is foregrounded in
both image and caption. An allegorical figure for fashion oversees a
swirling parade of men and women in "Madame la Mode Reviews
a Few of Her Vagaries during the Last Sixty Years" (see fig. 8.3). Here,
the "vagaries" of fashion are readily readable (or would have been to
contemporary viewers), as the width of skirt and style of hair and bonnet and of whiskers and hat represent the major trends of the previous
six decades; yet the figures dance arm in arm, clearly sharing the same
moment on the page. Other images of blurred periodicity include
"Design for a Parliamentary Car for the Queen's Procession," featuring
"A Combined Assembly of Distinguished Members of Both Houses
during Her Majesty's Reign."[41] As in the case of Madame La Mode's
parade of fashion, the celebratory impact of the image derives from
the comingling of figures who would have otherwise never shared the
same page of *Punch*: the greater the temporal disparity in the figures
presented, the greater the impact of "Her Majesty's Reign." Another

MADAME LA' MODE REVIEWS A FEW OF HER VAGARIES DURING THE LAST SIXTY YEARS.

FIG. 8.3   "Madame La Mode Reviews a Few of Her Vagaries during the Last Sixty Years," *Punch,* 19 June 1897, 291. © Punch Ltd. Reproduced with permission.

iteration of this kind of ahistorical scene finds Mr. Punch overseeing a "reception of notable histrions" from Victoria's reign.[42] Again, the scene's visual impact is due to the crush of people, whose varied attire and appearance, amplified because some of the actors are in period costume, suggest the breadth and range of the queen's reach. A more democratic version of comingled past and present is featured in the final cartoon of the issue, the two-page "A Diamond Jubilee Dream of Victorian Derby Days," which depicts a crowd scene at the derby with a cross section of Victorians from across the century. If these images playfully disrupt historical veracity or the limits of realist depiction, they also suggest that the present is always informed by the past, its actors always in conversation with those who have gone before.

Another group of featured cartoons performs a very different function from the counterfactuals or comingled group depictions: the issue also contains a striking number of paired past-and-present images depicting contrasts between the time that Victoria ascended the throne and the then-present day. Rather than emphasizing continuity or range, these images insist upon articulating difference, often emphasizing change in easily readable terms. These paired images appear in various formats: in some, a single frame encloses two images; in others, separate panels are juxtaposed side by side; and other pairs are split, separated across pages. Employing varied formats and a notable lack of captions, the volume's editors and illustrators appear to have been confident that readers would have no trouble making meaning of the image pairs. Many of the split images address aspects of women's changing gender roles, some more overtly than others. On a page featuring a grid of four images (see fig. 8.4), the bottom pair depicts, as its caption suggests, the life of "The Journalist—Then" and "The Journalist—Now." The change privileged in the image and the caption is the journalist's move from "Fleet Prison" to "Fleet Street," from poverty and shame to relative comfort and respectability. A less obvious shift is the position of the journalist's family: in the background of the "Then" frame lurk the shadowy figures of a child and its mother, whose saintliness is suggested by the halo-like lines that surround her head. In the "Fleet Street" image, the family is no longer present, though the improvement of circumstance attending the journalist suggests that his wife and child's absence from the work site implies their greater comfort and security: they are at home.

While mother and child are relegated to the background in the "Journalist" cartoons, the top pair, captioned simply "1837" and "1897," takes the family as its subject. In the "1837" frame, a young family enjoys a walk in the countryside. A man, in a mustache and sideburns and with a top hat and walking stick, is depicted in profile; directly behind him is a woman (presumably his wife), attired in a

1837.

1897.

THE JOURNALIST—THEN.
THE FLEET PRISON.

THE JOURNALIST—NOW.
FLEET STREET.

FIG. 8.4 "1837/1897; Journalist—Then/Journalist—Now," *Punch*, 19 June 1897, 293. Image courtesy of Cadbury Research Library: Special Collections, University of Birmingham.

wide bonnet and an ornate dress with a shawl. She holds the hand of a young girl—in a light dress with a dark sash and carrying her own bonnet in her hand—and adjacent to the man is a young boy, with his back to the viewer, in a sailor suit, waving a flag at a horse-drawn carriage that has recently passed by. A winding country lane leads into the distance, toward a snug church, the steeple of which is plainly visible. It is a scene of familial pastoral.

The companion "1897" cartoon provides a suggestive contrast, and with no caption to indicate the artist's intended message, one must draw conclusions from the elements of the scene that have changed. The country idyll of 1837 has been entirely replaced. What was a country road is now a more urban scene, or at least a village scene, with what appear to be paved, fence-lined streets. The undulating, grass-covered ground of "1837" is expressed in multidirectional short hatchings; in "1897," the road beneath the bicycles is rendered in a series of unidirectional lines, suggesting movement and speed. In the "1897" image, the mustachioed man wears a Norfolk suit and boots, his top hat replaced by a high bowler and—in one of the most startling interventions—his walking stick replaced by a bicycle. Indeed, both the man and the woman are riding bicycles in "1897." In place of her highly detailed dress and shawl are a simple blouse and solid skirt. Her wasp-waisted silhouette marks a change from the 1837 moment, and the leg-of-mutton sleeves and high neckline keep her more covered than the deep décolleté of the earlier dress: it is the style of the New Woman, as demarcated in numerous *Punch* cartoons in the previous decade. She is, moreover, mobile, employing the same mode of transportation as the man and even wearing a collar and bow tie that decidedly borrow from masculine dress.

In another pointed contrast, the woman, whose gaze in "1837" is directed at her daughter, faces the viewer directly, even as the man is still shown in profile. Not only is the positioning more direct and more active, it calls attention to a major omission: in "1897" no children appear in the frame. The only other figure in the scene is a second young woman, also on a bicycle, riding in the opposite direction in the background, suggesting not only that mobile women were becoming more common but that their options for movement were also increasing. While in "1837" the wife does not face her husband, she is depicted in his shadow, slightly beneath his, and there is no suggestion that she will part from the route that he and their children are pursuing. In "1897," conversely, though both the man and the woman are still close to each other, she is now at the same level in the frame, and the fact that their bicycles are heading in opposite directions suggests that as time progresses, they will simply (and quickly, thanks to the speed of the bicycle) get farther and farther apart. In fact, in the absence of children, there is nothing to suggest that the man and woman pictured have any relation to each other whatsoever, apart from the "1897" image's propinquity to the "1837" image.[43]

Taken together, this pair does not merely illustrate gendered symbols; it helps ossify them. Readable signs include clothing and hairstyles, but the importance of contextual markers—both within the single frame and in relation to the paired image—becomes clear when we consider that "Madame La Mode" also displayed changing fashions. In the "1837/1897" cartoon, the shift of environment from rural to urban is significant, but the presence of the bicycle and the absence of a family are even more telling. By eliding any intermediary scenes, the staggering difference between the two moments is emphasized, and with it the enormity of changes that occurred in the seemingly interminable reign of the queen. These changes were punctuated by many events that would have been immediately familiar to *Punch's* readers in 1897: the Married Women's Property Acts of 1870 and 1882, the establishment of Newnham and Girton Colleges, the development of the bicycle, and the New Woman debates, to name only a few. Instantly readable differences in fashion and trappings thus become aligned not merely with the decade in which they were popular but also with the range of social changes that led to the "1897" frame. This is not to say that old values did not linger, but rather that these graphic consolidations helped to label traditional or conservative values *as* old. As noted, if the "1897" image were viewed on its own, it might not be understood as a critique of the expanding role of women in the social sphere and the changes wrought by that changing role in the home. Yet when set next to an image of an idyllic family from "sixty years hence," the resulting hiatus becomes freighted with meaning: the woman's clothing and bicycle have displaced the family, and difference has displaced the unity that had existed.

In light of this context of shifting roles, many of the other image pairs from the issue take on new valences of meaning; even in the pairs that do not feature women explicitly, the "after" frames suggest a world in which men are hemmed in or thwarted. In "Past and Present, A Sportsman's Diary," hunters on horseback and their dogs jump over wooden fences, taking "a splendid line" over stream and dale in 1837.

In the 1897 frame, the horses pull up short, faced with a barbed wire fence, and the caption informs the reader that "several hounds [were] killed on the railway."[44] One single-panel cartoon features an older man, a younger man, and a dog in a muzzle. "Just think of it, my boy," the elder man says. "In those days we had no electric light, no x rays, no cinematograph, no—." The younger man interjects, "Muzzling Order."[45] If the 1837 man can marvel at the technological innovations that benefit the younger generations, the younger man (and his dog) seems to long for a time when laws did not constrain.

The meaning accumulated by the cartoons in the issue suggests wistfulness for times that were simpler, slower, and unchallenged by upstart women or the lower classes. To reinforce the message of the images, a recurring series of three minidialogues or plays, each under the title "Extremes Meet; or, Some Victorian Contrasts," underscores the temporal and social dissonance pictured in the then-and-now cartoons. The second features a "Street boy, early Victorian" and "Street boy, late Victorian," both portrayed as ignorant and with heavy accents, but the late Victorian boy extolls his compulsory "heddication."[46] In the third play, a "Miss Flora" (early Victorian), Miss Bloomer (mid-Victorian), and Miss Latchkey (New Woman) compare notes on men's reactions to their clothing. Miss Latchkey insists, "I ignore man's very existence—except as a comrade and rival, to be met and crushed in the struggle for existence."[47] Such textual pieces buttress the visual suggestions of the issue's cartoons, making clear not only that the Latchkey kind of woman aims to "crush" men but that she represents an extreme deviation from other kinds of earlier Victorian women. Taken as a whole, the Diamond Jubilee issue demonstrates ways that nineteenth-century artists defined and deployed iconography to codify an array of ideas and ideals associated with passing times. And the artists and writers of *Punch* seem to be fully conscious of their role in the process: one telling pair of cartoons contrasts the clothing of the "Early Du Maurier Crinoline Period, 1860" with the "Charles Keene-esque Croquet Period, 1866," aligning dates with particular styles and with the cartoonists who captured those styles for the magazine.[48]

Neo-Victorian Applications

Suzanne Barber and Matt Hale have argued that steampunk depends on the simultaneous negotiation of "multiple temporalities" and multiple

nexus events to dictate their counterfactual plots.[49] For the chronological elision to be readable—for readers to recognize that characters
sharing a page or a frame derive from asynchronous sources—steampunk
graphic texts use a visual vocabulary that is chronologically marked.
Because twentieth- and twenty-first-century readers cannot be
counted on to grasp subtle differences in nineteenth-century clothing
or context, the distilled iconography of works such as *Punch* (those
"clichéd ideological significations") is used instead. Grant Morrison
and Steve Yeowell's protosteampunk comics series *Sebastian O,* issued
originally in three monthly installments in 1993, employs these visual
tropes effectively.[50] Replete with allusions to the literature and illustrations of the decadent 1890s, particularly the works of Oscar Wilde,
Sebastian O earns its steampunk bona fides by introducing anachronistic technologies into fin-de-siècle London, where the dandy–cum–
action hero Sebastian must thwart the plans of his nemesis Lord Laven-
der, who hopes to rule England. Such a coup d'état would be possible
because Queen Victoria has died, replaced by a computer-generated
video image, an ur–Big Brother.

Within this world, clothing and décor are visual signifiers that draw
on the ideological undercurrents that dictated the interpretation of the
Punch Jubilee cartoons. One couple's characterization depends almost
entirely on those signifiers: George Harker is introduced while shooting
game with a trusty setter, wearing a version of a hunting suit with knee
breeches and spats while holding a gun (see fig. 8.5). Joining George in
the hunting party is a woman, identified only as Phoebe, seated behind
on the grass. She holds a parasol and wears a bonnet and pink gown
with a massively full skirt, spread in all its glory on the ground. The
clothing communicates George's hypermasculinity (hunting suit) and
Phoebe's hyperfemininity (enormous crinoline), though the styles are not
chronologically coterminous.[51] Insisting on historical accuracy in steampunk is a nonstarter, but in this case it is not the historical inaccuracy
but rather the discordant pairing that is telling: the woman's exaggerated skirt and bonnet are appropriate to the mid-1850s, while Harker's
suit typifies a later era. Phoebe, in other words, would have been at
home in the "1837" *Punch* cartoon, not the "1897" one. *Sebastian O* includes at least one other female character who is dressed in typical 1890s
fashion—contemporary with the ostensible setting of the comic—in a
narrow skirt and cuirass bodice, suggesting that Phoebe's dress is not an

FIG. 8.5 Hunting party: Phoebe and George. Grant Morrison and Steve Yeowell, *Sebastian O,* no. 2 (New York City: Vertigo, 1993), 22. From "Sebastian O" #2 ™ and © Grant Morrison and Steve Yeowell. Courtesy of DC Comics. Available in *Sebastian O.*

accidental or unintentional anachronism. Her voluminous skirt appears markedly dated, even within the context of the story, and intentionally so. Phoebe is represented throughout her narrative arc as a supplicant, most frequently sitting at George's feet, eyes averted. In both clothing and action, then, Phoebe seems to be a throwback, reanimating the outmoded gender roles of the 1850s, a regression signaled by her dress and amplified by the temporal contrast between her attire and George's. At the fin de siècle, the hunting suit with knee breeches came to represent a traditional masculinity at least in part because it was invoked as the polar opposite of the attire of the caricatured, foppish Aesthete that George Du Maurier made famous in the pages of *Punch* and that features throughout *Sebastian O.*[52] Through this combination of the Angel in the House figure of the 1850s with the archetypally masculine British man of the 1890s, the resultant pair—George and Phoebe—appear overdetermined in their heteronormativity.

As it happens, a heteronormative reading turns out to be misplaced. In the third and final issue of *Sebastian O,* which opens with a vignette of George smoking a pipe in a wing chair in front of a roaring fire and Phoebe on the ground again in her billowing skirt, George is revealed to be a woman. The nature and extent of *Sebastian O*'s investment in transgressive politics are unclear, and George and Phoebe are ambivalent sexual radicals, at best. Aside from their gender, their relationship seems to conform to the most entrenched stereotypes of the high Victorian roles of husband and wife. A scene in which they explain their relationship to outsiders does not help clarify the comic's ideological intentions: when a group of policemen approach George and Phoebe's home, where Sebastian O is hiding, George dismisses them with a warning: "We suffer from tribadism, a disease of women, a nymphomania of the senses. . . . Despite the shame and horror of it, we cannot stop ourselves, officer. Your men are free to enter, but we cannot guarantee that they will not carry the contagion back to their wives and loved ones" (see fig. 8.6).[53] On the one hand, she cleverly plays into the policemen's homophobia to facilitate Sebastian's escape. On the other hand, by framing same-sex desire as a contagion, the comic references its early 1990s subtext of AIDS-fueled hysteria in a way that may be read as a self-conscious critique but may also be read as a problematic reanimation of Victorian stereotypes. In terms of *Sebastian O*'s plot, the revelation of George's

FIG. 8.6   Confrontation with police. Grant Morrison and Steve Yeowell, *Sebastian O,* no. 3 (New York City: Vertigo, 1993), 7. From "Sebastian O" #3 ™ and © Grant Morrison and Steve Yeowell. Courtesy of DC Comics. Available in *Sebastian O.*

subversive gender performance packs a greater punch because it had been shrouded in fashion that visually signified heteronormativity.

Similarly ambivalent—or ambiguous—motivations are evident in Alan Moore's *The League of Extraordinary Gentlemen,* which is often vaunted for its provocative mixing of figures from different literary worlds, set in different times.[54] This ostensibly postmodern mixing was in fact handily used by the Victorians. As significant as the chronological blending is Moore's revision of the well-known plots of some of the characters that the story appropriates from other novels. Mina Murray (of Stoker's *Dracula*), for example, leads the league after having divorced Jonathan Harker.[55] While the sartorial detail in *The League of Extraordinary Gentlemen* is limited when compared to that in *Sebastian O,* it still depends on the same visual vocabulary established in the fin de siècle. With a wasp-waisted silhouette, leg-of-mutton sleeves, a sensible flat-brimmed straw hat, and an ever-present neck scarf that echoes the ties and cravats of the men that surround her (see fig. 8.7), Mina's dress marks her as a New Woman, as does her smoking.

Markers of fashion combine with stylistic illustration choices to reinforce the dating of the story and, at times, to highlight the temporal dissonance of the characters. In one of the first images of the first volume of *The League of Extraordinary Gentlemen,* Mina's silhouette is graphically cast in black and yellow, recalling Aubrey Beardsley's striking covers for the *Yellow Book* (1894–97). Mina's style, though, is expressly not Aesthetic—others in the comic take that role, with Hawley Griffin adorning his invisible body in quilted-lapel smoking robes that denote Oscar Wilde's Sarony photographs or, again, Du Maurier's

FIG. 8.7   Mina as a New Woman. Alan Moore and Kevin O'Neill, *The League of Extraordinary Gentlemen,* vol. 1 (La Jolla, CA: America's Best Comics, 2000), 58. From *The League of Extraordinary Gentlemen, Volume 1* ™ and © Alan Moore and Kevin O'Neill. Courtesy of DC Comics.

Aesthetic parodies. Within the pages of the issues, Mina's New Woman attire matches her New Woman behavior: newly divorced, willing and able to lead men, and delighted to spurn social codes. Curiously, however, the covers of the first volume of *The League of Extraordinary Gentlemen* depict Mina in clothing (and in positions) that differs from her representation within. On the cover of the comic's first issue, Mina's face appears in a close-cropped portrait in the center of the page, with a caption noting "Lady 'With Past' Kept Peculiar Company"; in a small frame to the left, she appears bare-breasted, being assaulted, with the caption "An affront to womanhood in foreign parts." Thus, if her character in the comic resists gender norms, the cover seems to embrace them, emphasizing her sensational "past" and promising sexual assault within. While one could argue that the cluttered cover of the first issue is self-consciously critiquing hyperbolically sensationalist Victorian advertising, it is also depending on that same sensationalism to attract a readership to a new work. The second issue again mimics Victorian advertising by featuring the comic's main characters à la cigarette cards. Emphasizing the literary and temporal mash-up that was the comic's central innovation, each picture/card is dated, and the dates are conspicuously asynchronous: despite appearing in the comic together, Miss Mina Murray is captioned 1897 (the year that Stoker's *Dracula* was published), while Auguste Dupin is dated 1841 (the year the character appeared in Edgar Allan Poe's "The Murders in the Rue Morgue"), and other characters are dated according to the publication date of their original appearance. While Mina's picture is tagged "1897," her dress is not visible, and thus it is not visibly datable. The only woman on the cover, with her hair in a prim bun and with a conspicuously bare neck and décolletage, Mina shows no trace of the physical prowess or leadership that she possesses in the story. Not until the cover of the fifth issue (of six in the first volume), does she appear in the same late-'90s dress that she wears in the issue. And when the first volume was published in an omnibus trade edition (2000), the cover again emphasized Mina's conventional femininity by setting her against a backdrop featuring the male characters and a picture gallery of men's portraits, as well as by depicting her in a dress that hews closer to mid-Victorian than fin-de-siècle standards, including a dramatically full, crinolined skirt and fussy lace details (see fig. 8.8). Only her barely visible cigarette and facial expression suggest

FIG. 8.8   Mina in picture gallery. Alan Moore and Kevin O'Neill, cover of
trade publication of *The League of Extraordinary Gentlemen,* vol. 1 (La Jolla, CA:
America's Best Comics, 2000). From *The League of Extraordinary Gentlemen,
Volume 1* ™ and © Alan Moore and Kevin O'Neill. Courtesy of DC Comics.

her New Woman character. Even as these covers signal "Victorian" to readers, they demonstrate that the "vagaries" of "Madame la Mode" can be manipulated to communicate relative levels of convention or subversion. Whereas the more comfortably conforming images of Mina on the cover might appeal to readers who fetishize an early Victorian incarnation of femininity, those images can be displaced, or at least overwritten by the more transgressive signifiers within.

Even, then, as these steampunk comics depend on a diffuse set of images and styles to communicate a generic Victorian-ness, closer examination demonstrates that more specific markers of Victorian movements or trends are employed as a shorthand for character traits. Phoebe's massive crinoline represents a host of traits aligned with the domesticated woman of the mid-nineteenth century: docility, submission, and wifely duty. Mina's New Woman attire denotes her independence, unconventionality, and rejection of marriage. These stereotypes, I argue, were not twentieth-century inventions, the reductive condensation of complex nineteenth-century realities. Rather, they were the result of ongoing pictorial negotiations by Victorians, who sought ways to represent visually the passage of time and its attendant changes. Invested in representing the varying incarnations of the Victorian era, the Diamond Jubilee issue of *Punch* functions as a concordance of these types, distinguishing between "then" and "now," "past" and "present" in visual terms that were mapped—sometimes explicitly and sometimes implicitly—onto the social trends or sensibilities that were concomitant with the period's readable signifiers of clothing and style.

Notes

1. Lisa Yaszek, "Democratising the Past to Improve the Future: An Interview with Steampunk Godfather Paul Di Filippo," *Neo-Victorian Studies* 3, no. 1 (2010): 190. Yaszek writes, "Critically acclaimed science fiction author Paul Di Filippo is regularly recognised as a founding figure in the neo-Victorian aesthetic movement known as steampunk. His 1995 short story collection, *The Steampunk Trilogy,* has been credited with giving this movement its name" ("Democratising the Past," 189).

2. For examples of analyses of steampunk as literature, see Jay Clayton, *Dickens in Cyberspace: The Afterlife of the Nineteenth Century in Postmodern Culture* (New York: Oxford University Press, 2006); and

Margaret Rose, "Extraordinary Pasts: Steampunk as a Mode of Historical Representation," *Journal of the Fantastic in the Arts* 20, no. 3 (January 2009): 319–33. On steampunk as subculture, see Christine Ferguson, "Surface Tensions: Steampunk, Subculture, and the Ideology of Style," *Neo-Victorian Studies* 4, no. 2 (2011): 66–90; and Brigid Cherry and Maria Mellins, "Negotiating the Punk in Steampunk: Subculture, Fashion, and Performance Identity," *Punk & Post-Punk* 1, no. 1 (September 2011): 5–25. On steampunk as a mode of artistic production, see Karen Christians, "Steampunk: Future Past," *Metalsmith* 31, no. 3 (August 2011): 18–19; and Jake Von Slatt, *The Steampunk Workshop,* www.steampunkworkshop.com (accessed 4 March 2014).

3. This tendency is evident even in the titles of many studies: Christians's "Steampunk: Future Past," Heidi Weig's "'Rebuilding Yesterday to Ensure Our Tomorrow': An Overview of Steampunk Aesthetics and Literature" (*Inklings: Jahrbuch für Literatur und Ästhetik* 30 [2012]: 135–50), and Jason B. Jones's "Betrayed by Time: Steampunk & the Neo-Victorian in Alan Moore's *Lost Girls* and *The League of Extraordinary Gentlemen*" (*Neo-Victorian Studies* 3, no. 1 [2010]: 99–126), among others.

4. Cherry and Mellins, "Negotiating the Punk," 7.

5. Rose, "Extraordinary Pasts," 322.

6. Ferguson, "Surface Tensions," 72.

7. See Fredric Jameson, *Postmodernism; or, The Cultural Logic of Late Capitalism* (Durham, NC: Duke University Press, 1991); Linda Hutcheon, *A Poetics of Postmodernism* (New York: Routledge, 1988); and Hutcheon, *The Politics of Postmodernism* (New York: Routledge, 1989). For example, Rachel A. Bowser and Brian Croxall write, "Through its own instability, enacted via nonlinear temporality and blended surfaces steampunk reminds us of the instability and constructedness of our concepts of periodisation and historical distance." Bowser and Croxall, "Introduction: Industrial Evolution," in special issue, *Neo-Victorian Studies* 3, no. 1 (2010): 1–45.

8. One of the first, and still most important, texts to address this question is John Kucich and Dianne F. Sadoff's edited collection *Victorian Afterlife: Postmodern Culture Rewrites the Nineteenth Century* (Minneapolis: University of Minnesota Press, 2000). In a review of that collection, Simon Joyce elegantly articulates the competing theoretical approaches detailed in the collection: "[W]e either look skeptically at postmodernist claims to liberation, exposing the ways that any attempt at periodization or retroaction inevitably produces a warped and politically serviceable version of the past; or we take pleasure in the available opportunities

for intertextual connection that such a project opens up, as 'politically progressive, […] offering effective strategies for the fashioning of political positions, values, and subjectivities' (xxv). Heads you're with Fredric Jameson, tails with Michel Foucault." Joyce, review of *Victorian Afterlife: Postmodern Culture Rewrites the Nineteenth Century,* by John Kucich and Dianne F. Sadoff, eds., *Victorian Studies* 44, no. 3 (Spring 2002): 556.

9. See Jess Nevins, "It's Time to Rethink Steampunk," *io9,* posted 27 January 2012, http://io9.com/5879231/its-time-to-rethink-steampunk.

10. Ferguson also demonstrates that some of the problems of the "alternative historiography of New Historicism" can be revived in steampunk texts. Christine Ferguson, "Victoria-Arcana and the Misogynistic Poetics of Resistance in Iain Sinclair's *White Chappell Scarlet Tracings* and Alan Moore's *From Hell,*" *LIT: Literature, Interpretation, Theory* 20, nos. 1–2 (2009): 46.

11. Ferguson, "Surface Tensions," 81.

12. These categories are contested. In addition to works like Edwin A. Abbott's *Flatland: A Romance of Many Dimensions* (London: Seeley, 1884) and Walter Besant's *Inner House* (New York: Harper, 1888), steampunk forbears might include Benjamin Disraeli's *The Wondrous Tale of Alroy* (London: Saunders and Otley, 1833) or Nathaniel Hawthorne's "P's Correspondence" (*United States Magazine and Democratic Review* [April 1845]: 337–45). For a more comprehensive introduction to the genesis of the term and the genre, see Jess Nevins, "Introduction: The 19th-Century Roots of Steampunk," in *Steampunk,* ed. Ann VanderMeer and Joe R. Lansdale (San Francisco: Tachyon, 2008), 3–12.

13. For perspectives on the Victorians' relationship with what might have been and what might be, see, e.g., Andrew H. Miller, "'A Case of Metaphysics': Counterfactuals, Realism, *Great Expectations,*" *ELH* 79, no. 3 (2012): 773–96; Kelly J. Mays, "Looking Backward, Looking Forward: The Victorians in the Rearview Mirror of Future History," *Victorian Studies* 53, no. 3 (Spring 2011): 445–56; and Jesse Rosenthal, "The Large Novel and the Law of Large Numbers; or, Why George Eliot Hates Gambling," *ELH* 77, no. 3 (2010): 777–811.

14. See chapter 7, this volume.

15. Mary Elizabeth Leighton and Lisa Surridge's suggestion that illustrations of serialized fiction "may be proleptic (anticipating plot events to follow) or analeptic (referring to previous plot events) and may represent the personal or the grand historical narrative" is applicable to nonfictional narratives as well. Leighton and Surridge, "Making History: Text and Image in Harriet Martineau's Historiettes," in *Reading Victorian*

Literature, 1855–1875: Spoils of the Lumber Room, ed. Paul Goldman and Simon Cooke (Farnham, UK: Ashgate, 2012), 142.

16. In E[dward] T. Reed's "A Prehistoric Jubilee" (*Punch,* 19 June 1897, 311), the Jubilee procession is staged among dinosaurs and cavemen in a style that anticipates the 1960s animated television series *The Flintstones.*

17. Joseph Bristow, "Whether 'Victorian' Poetry: A Genre and Its Period," *Victorian Poetry* 42, no. 1 (2004): 82.

18. The three-issue series was published by Vertigo, an imprint of DC Comics designed for anyone "who enjoys alternative music, foreign and independent films, or other entertainment outside the mainstream." Art Young, "On the Ledge," in *Sebastian O,* by Grant Morrison and Steve Yeowell, no. 1 (May 1993): 28.

19. Wendy Steiner, *Pictures of Romance: Form against Context in Painting and Literature* (Chicago: University of Chicago Press, 1988), 8.

20. Gotthold Ephraim Lessing, *Laocoon: An Essay on the Limits of Painting and Poetry,* trans. E. C. Beasley (London: Longman, Brown, Green, and Longmans, 1853), 132.

21. Sacheverell Sitwell, *Narrative Pictures: A Survey of English Genre and Its Painters* (1936; repr., London: Batsford, 1969), 1.

22. Steiner, *Pictures of Romance,* 14.

23. Ibid., 18.

24. Klaus Speidel, "Can a Single Still Picture Tell a Story? Definitions of Narrative and the Alleged Problem of Time with Single Still Pictures," *Diegesis* 2, no. 1 (2013): 173–294. Speidel offers a helpful review of developments in visual narratology since Steiner's work.

25. One foundational Victorian example of such interpretation is John Ruskin's reaction to Augustus Egg's triptych *Past and Present,* first shown at the Royal Academy of 1858. In his review of the paintings, Ruskin first noted that "several mistakes have been made in the interpretation" of the triptych and then asserts that he will "give the true reading of it" before offering a summary of the narrative he envisions. Ruskin attests to the certainty both that a singular implied narrative is readable in images ("true reading") and that such image sequences are nevertheless open to misreading ("several mistakes" in "interpretation"). Ruskin, *Notes on Some of the Principal Pictures Exhibited in the Rooms of the Royal Academy,* vol. 5 (London: Smith, Elder, 1855), 26.

26. Thierry Groensteen, *The System of Comics,* trans. Bart Beaty and Nick Nguyen (Jackson: University Press of Mississippi, 2007), 111.

27. Thierry Groensteen, *Comics and Narration,* trans. Ann Miller (Jackson: University Press of Mississippi, 2013), 23.

28. Ibid., 29.

29. Scott McCloud, *Understanding Comics: The Invisible Art* (New York: HarperCollins, 1993), 9.

30. For Hogarth's image, see fig. 1.3 in the present volume.

31. "Practice and Precept," *Punch,* 2 November 1904, 302. For a discussion of Hogarth's impact on British graphic narratives, see chapter 1 in the present volume.

32. "Highland Officer in the Crimea," *Punch,* 12 January 1856, 20.

33. With a different caption, the same image pair could be read in a wholly different register. If, for example, instead of describing the kilted officer on the left as a product of the sentimental imagination of women, the label read "Highland Officer in the Crimea, as Imagined by Young Men before Enlisting," the cartoon could be understood as a much sharper critique of the miseries of war.

34. Koven demonstrates that the "before" shots, through their depiction of children with exposed flesh, often fetishized and sexualized the children's poverty. Seth Koven, *Slumming: Sexual and Social Politics in Victorian London* (Princeton: Princeton University Press, 2004). See also Lindsay Smith, "The Shoe-Black to the Crossing Sweeper: Victorian Street Arabs and Photography," in *The Politics of Focus: Women, Children and Nineteenth-Century Photography* (Manchester: Manchester University Press, 1998), 111–32.

35. Clare Rose, *Making, Selling, and Wearing Boys' Clothes in Late-Victorian England* (Farnham, UK: Ashgate, 2010), 45. John Hannavy writes that missionaries seized upon photography, and lantern slide shows were used as tools for education and to encourage evangelical zeal: "Publicity, support and fundraising for their missions in Europe were furthered by juxtaposed, staged photographs of naked and dirty, clothed and orderly 'natives' before and after conversion." Hannavy, *Encyclopedia of Nineteenth-Century Photography* (New York: Routledge, 2008), 117.

36. Advances in color lithography made mass production of color advertising cards fiscally viable, and a vast array of these cards used before-and-after images to suggest the improvements in health, wealth, and attractiveness that were made possible through the application or use of the product advertised. Ben Crane documents a host of American versions of the before-and-after trade cards, many of which involve trick folds or pullouts to effect the desired change. See Crane, *The Before and After Trade Card* (Schoharie, NY: Ephemera Society of America, 1995).

37. Thomas Richards, *The Commodity Culture of Victorian England: Advertising and Spectacle, 1851–1914* (Palo Alto, CA: Stanford University Press, 1991), 189.

38. Anne McClintock, *Imperial Leather: Race, Gender, and Sexuality in the Colonial Contest* (New York: Routledge, 1995), 222.

39. Text was added to give readers context for the cartoons, many of which were topical and political. In the preface to the third and final volume, editor E. J. Milliken writes that "the Chronicle has been compiled mainly with a view to linking and elucidating the illustrations." Milliken, preface to *Mr. Punch's Victorian Era: An Illustrated Chronicle of Fifty Years of the Reign of Her Majesty the Queen,* vol. 3 (London: Bradbury, Agnew, 1888), n.p.

40. "Great Queens of History," *Punch,* 19 June 1897, 289.

41. E[dward] T. Reed, "Design for a Parliamentary Car for the Queen's Procession," *Punch,* 19 June 1897, 294.

42. "Thalia and Melpomene, Assisted by Mr. Punch, Hold a Reception of Notable Histrions of the Past Sixty Years," *Punch,* 19 June 1897, 299.

43. The pairing thus challenges Wendy Steiner's requirement of repeated subjects to encourage narrative reading.

44. George Denholm Armour, "Past and Present, A Sportsman's Diary," *Punch,* 19 June 1897, 297.

45. "Just Think of It," *Punch,* 19 June 1897, 312. Muzzling orders for the containment of rabies could be issued under the Dogs Act of 1871, much to the consternation of many owners.

46. "Extremes Meet; or, Some Victorian Contrasts, II," *Punch,* 19 June 1897, 308.

47. "Extremes Meet; or, Some Victorian Contrasts, III," *Punch,* 19 June 1897, 310.

48. "Charles Keenesque Croquet Period" and Leonard Raven-Hill, "Early Du Maurier Crinoline Period," both in *Punch,* 19 June 1897, 312.

49. Suzanne Barber and Matt Hale, "Enacting the Never-Was: Upcycling the Past, Present, and Future in Steampunk," in *Steaming into a Victorian Future: A Steampunk Anthology,* ed. Julie Anne Taddeo and Cynthia Miller (Plymouth, UK: Scarecrow Press, 2013), 167.

50. See Joseph Good, "'God Save the Queen, for Someone Must!': *Sebastian O* and the Steampunk Aesthetic," *Neo-Victorian Studies* 3, no. 1 (2010): 208–15.

51. Shu-chuan Yan writes that "crinolines, beauty, and femininity were conflated in *Punch*." Yan, "'Politics and Petticoats': Fashioning the Nation in *Punch* Magazine, 1840s–1880s," *Fashion Theory* 15, no. 3 (September 2011): 353.

52. See the discussion of figure I.4 in the introduction to this volume.

53. Grant Morrison and Steve Yeowell, *Sebastian O,* issue 3 (New York: Vertigo, 1993), 7.

54. See, e.g., Phillip Wegner, "Alan Moore, 'Secondary Literacy,' and the Modernism of the Graphic Novel," *ImageText* 5, no. 3 (2010): n.p., www.english.ufl.edu/imagetext/archives/v5_3/wegner/.

55. Alan Moore and Kevin O'Neill, *The League of Extraordinary Gentlemen,* vol. 1 (La Jolla, CA: American's Best Comics, 2000). Jason B. Jones writes that the comic thus "firmly corrects the fateful decision [in *Dracula*] to exclude Mina from the vampire-hunters' planning." Jones, "Betrayed by Time," 102.

V.

Picturing Readers

NINE

Reading Victorian Valentines

Working-Class Women, Courtship, and the Penny Post in *Bow Bells* Magazine

JENNIFER PHEGLEY

> Young ladies should analyze their Valentine a little more
> closely before going into ecstacies [*sic*] on the receipt of
> those wild love effusions.
>
> —"The Morn of St. Valentine," *Bow Bells* (15 February 1865)

Writing love letters had a long, strong tradition prior to the nineteenth century, and by the 1850s there were thousands of advice books and letter-writing manuals that taught young lovers how to correspond with each other properly. Model letters for all courtship occasions were provided, and specific language was recommended to present oneself as both polite and passionate. A love letter not only expressed one's suitability as a husband or wife but also suggested that the writer was an appropriately literate person capable of attaining and/or maintaining middle-class status. Love letters were, then, the symbolic melding of private, romantic sentiments with a public display of respectability.[1] The introduction of the Penny Post in England in 1840 made letter writing easier and cheaper, thus precipitating an even greater reliance on courtship correspondence as a means of speeding up intimacy and forging appropriate marriages. Notably, postal reform put two new methods of courtship in the spotlight: matrimonial advertising and the exchange of valentines. The new accessibility of the postal service to the working classes fueled the explosion of matrimonial advertising, which was a phenomenon that took off in the penny press at midcentury and involved sending personal profiles to magazines as well as exchanging letters and cartes de visite—small, inexpensive photographic portraits—with suitors.[2] The Penny Post also made Valentine's Day a central part of courtship for all classes. The range and availability of commercial valentines rapidly expanded as the desire to exchange romantic sentiments through the mail reached its peak in the 1850s and '60s. These postal forms of courtship relied on visual images to convey their messages. Portraits taken in a studio provided realistic portrayals of individuals that could determine whether or not a romance would blossom, while ornate depictions of birds, flowers, butterflies, and hearts emblazoned on lace paper symbolically represented love. Both photographic calling cards and valentines reflected "a culture coming to terms simultaneously with romanticism and commodification, sentimentalism and consumption."[3] While advertising for love was a largely discredited form of courtship because it invited interactions among strangers, sending valentines was an acceptable, even de rigueur, way of connecting with a potential spouse. *Bow Bells* magazine exploited the iconic imagery of Valentine's Day by publishing its own special issues, attracting women eager to read illustrated stories and poems about this landmark occasion for courtship. Indeed, women readers were crucial to the magazine's Valentine's Day issues: they were both the target audience and the subjects of the illustrations.

The publication of Sally Mitchell's *The Fallen Angel: Chastity, Class, and Women's Reading, 1835–1880* (1981) and Kate Flint's *The Woman Reader, 1837–1914* (1993) helped launch an important new field of study examining women's reading practices.[4] Mitchell explores how working- and lower-middle-class women's reading of sentimental and sensational fiction in penny press magazines fueled their fantasies for romance and more financially stable lives (which were inextricably linked, since marriage was presumably a way to achieve both), whereas Flint analyzes representations of middle-class women's reading in middlebrow and high cultural works and paintings as a self-absorbed and private activity that potentially threatened domesticity and propriety. Returning to the same genre of working-class family periodicals that were Mitchell's focus, and borrowing Flint's approach to visual images of women readers, I turn my attention to illustrations of women reading valentines in *Bow Bells'* special issues during the 1860s. Susan Casteras notes that images of working-class women readers are rare in the nineteenth century, because it "is above all the middle- and upper-class female who reigns in art as a main consumer of books and almost a quasi-advertisement for reading itself."[5] Nevertheless, depictions of women readers regularly appear in *Bow Bells,* though the working- and lower-middle-class women in the magazine's illustrations do not lounge in chairs with novels in hand; instead, their reading is focused on courtship correspondence, particularly valentines.[6] These women do not read solely for pleasure or escape; rather, they read to achieve the goal of marriage, which is a major focus of *Bow Bells* generally.[7] Paul Goldman and Simon Cooke argue that midcentury magazine illustrations "go beyond the merely 'illustrative' and have a profound impact on the process of reading," amplifying particular elements of the text they accompany.[8] In what follows, I attend to the ways in which *Bow Bells'* illustrations work in tandem with articles, stories, and poems to emphasize the importance of working-class women's reading to their romantic endeavors, particularly when it comes to their reading of valentines.

Bow Bells and Working-Class Women Readers

Founded by publisher John Dicks, "a pioneer of cheap reading for the masses," *Bow Bells* (1862–97) was directed toward upwardly mobile lower-middle- and working-class readers, particularly women.[9] Dicks hoped his new magazine would capitalize on audiences already cultivated by previous penny weeklies, the *Family Herald* (1842–1939), the *London Journal* (1845–1906), *Reynolds's Miscellany* (1846–69), and *Cassell's Illustrated Family Paper* (1853–1932), whose readers included new city dwellers filling "clerical, technical, and supervisory jobs that hardly existed a generation earlier."[10] This was an audience "of changing aspirations, expectations, and opportunities" united by one "common denominator . . . the aspiration for respectability."[11] Magazines like *Bow Bells* offered readers a cheap means of entertainment, self-improvement, and a sense of community. By 1865, *Bow Bells* was a clear success, as it claimed an impressive circulation of 200,000.[12] In particular, *Bow Bells* offered material Louis

James characterizes as quintessentially suitable for female servants who were of "ambivalent social position," came from a wide range of backgrounds, and were "relatively mobile socially" if they left service.[13] While the housemaid was "subject to her employer ... she was also identified with the household in which she worked."[14] The ambivalent position occupied by "Betsy," as James calls her, was "shown in her periodical reading," which was "fiercely" improving but also escapist, romantic, and violent.[15] *Bow Bells* certainly appealed to this constituency as well as to a wide variety of other working- and lower-middle-class women readers.

Bow Bells regaled its Betsys with regular features on grammar, etiquette, cooking, and a variety of domestic pursuits. The Ladies' Pages included needlework and dress patterns as well as household advice and philosophical articles about women's roles. Articles and Notices to Correspondents columns were geared toward building properly domestic identities for women, even those who worked. They also provided advice about courtship and marriage for upwardly mobile women who were new to the city and looking to build their own families. These offerings were complemented by weekly installments of sensational and sentimental novels, usually two per issue, typically accompanied by one half-page illustration each. The illustrations were a key attraction, depicting scenes of action-packed adventure (sea voyages, shipwrecks, carriage chases, and daring rescues or escapes) or of emotional melodrama (fainting women, languishing invalids, deathbed scenes, and clandestine romantic rendezvous). The cover illustrations were particularly enticing, functioning as "a key part of the seduction of potential purchasers."[16] Robert Louis Stevenson's account of his own romance with illustrated penny papers reinforces this point. He tells of gazing into the windows of the shops that sold these periodicals in an effort to "fish out" the stories of adventure depicted on the covers: "Each new Saturday I would go from one news-vendor's window to another's, till I was master of the weekly gallery."[17] Working women (seamstresses, factory laborers, shop girls, and teachers among them) had little time to spare but were often eager to read for escape as well as for knowledge, and *Bow Bells* provided both at an affordable price.[18] The magazine's exciting fiction, plentiful illustrations, and needlework and dress patterns were all attention-getting marketing tools. Its special Valentine's Day issues (published in 1865 and 1867–69) were another means of increasing the value and attractiveness of the magazine that would make it stand out from its competitors.

Bow Bells' Valentine's Day Special Issues

The 8 February 1865 issue of *Bow Bells* devotes almost a full column of text to its debut Valentine's Day number under the bold headline "IMMENSE ATTRACTION!—UNPARALLELED NOVELTIES!"[19] The ad asserts that "it is universally conceded that *Bow Bells* is the most successful and popular periodical of the age. . . . That this is no empty boast, the following announcements will prove."[20] The editor goes on to preview "A Grand Valentine Number" with four tales, one poem, and abundant illustrations. This twelve-page special issue would include an additional eight-page supplement with needlework patterns, sheet music for an original Valentine's Day song, and colored woodcuts of Queen Victoria and Windsor Castle suitable for framing or collecting. The price for the entire package, including the standard weekly issue, was two pence. The special issue could also be purchased on its own for a penny. According to Marysa Demoor and Kate Macdonald, "seasonal supplements were published to provide extra reading during leisure time, when desire and need would be most easily tapped into."[21] Of course, Christmas issues were the most common means of adding "novelty, variety, and perhaps an element of a treat or extra pleasure" to boost reader loyalty, increase subscriptions, and attract new readers.[22] *Bow Bells'* Valentine's Day issues were probably not unique, but they were less common than Christmas issues and indicate that Dicks was positioning his publication as a woman's magazine.[23] During the 1850s and '60s, women's periodicals competed for attention via what Jolein De Ridder calls the key "experimental zones" of supplements, which helped them vie for readers.[24] For example, Samuel Beeton's supplementary fashion plates and needlework patterns in the *Englishwoman's Domestic Magazine* folded out of the bound pages and were hand painted, both lavish characteristics calculated to generate excitement.[25] Dicks certainly took notice of Beeton's tactics and aimed to provide similar, if more cheaply produced, features in *Bow Bells*. The Valentine's Day issues were a way to up the ante on his competitors.[26]

The success of the first Valentine's Day supplement is somewhat questionable given that Dicks retreated from it the following year, when the Valentine's Day material was folded into the regular issue. Although there is a brief advertisement for the 1866 "Valentine Number," it included only one Valentine's Day story, a novella called "Viola's Valentine"—which ran for five consecutive issues starting on 14 February—and a special waltz. Nevertheless, "Viola's Valentine" opened the issue, so that anyone glancing at it might think it signaled a collection of valentine-themed stories similar to those appearing in the 1865 special issue. The cover illustration features a woman reading a valentine (see fig. 9.1), further connecting it to the previous and future Valentine's Day supplements, which were replete with images of women holding their Valentine's Day epistles. Interestingly, Viola is one of the few truly leisured women readers depicted in the magazine, and she has much in common with women in higher cultural productions, as she lounges in a chaise while reading. However, her reading material, like that of more humble *Bow Bells* heroines, is in the form of a letter rather than a book.

Perhaps readers clamored for the return of the supplement, because it was relaunched in a new format for Valentine's Day 1867, when the announcement was made that *Bow Bells* would include an extra Valentine's Day issue edited by "Aunt Betsy."[27] This was a more carefully defined sixteen-page issue based on a specific concept: a Valentine's Day party hosted by Aunt Betsy of Valentine Cottage in Love Lane, at which each guest would tell a story appropriate for the occasion. Betsy Baker is a widow who met her beloved husband on Valentine's Day and married him on the same day a year later, only to have him die "with his head upon her breast" the next Valentine's Day.[28] Instead of being consumed by her loss, she channels her romantic impulses into the task of uniting others in matrimony. Although she is admired by many local farmers, Betsy does "not seek a husband for herself" but is "everlastingly engaged in the love affairs of her neighbors—making matches between couples, young and middle-aged, both, and afterwards tiring herself almost to death in dancing at their several weddings."[29] Aunt Betsy's special Valentine issue seems to have been a hit, as it continued for two more years with the same framework. The Valentine's Day issues were discontinued after February 1869, perhaps as a result of the magazine's merger with the more politically oriented and masculine publication *Reynolds's Miscellany,* also published by Dicks.

VIOLA CLIEFDEN INSPECTS THE MORNING'S POST-BAG

FIG. 9.1   "Viola Cliefden Inspects the Morning's Post-Bag." From "Viola's Valentine," *Bow Bells* 4, no. 81 (14 February 1866): 49. Reproduced with permission from an image produced by ProQuest LLC for its online product *British Periodicals.* www.proquest.com.

Given Aunt Betsy's cheerful disposition and formidable match-making skills, one might expect the stories included in her special issues to be uplifting tales of successful Valentine's Day courtship. However, they are not uniformly so. In fact, even those with happy endings often include a great deal of anxiety, suffering, and loss, like Aunt Betsy's own personal narrative. The first cover illustration for the 1867 Aunt Betsy issue previews the two sides of the Valentine's Day experience that are of concern in the stories featured in the special issues (see fig. 9.2). The top half of the illustration introduces us to "Mrs. Betsy Baker's Party," while the bottom half depicts a mob of women publicly competing for their valentines. In the upper frame, the party is assembled around a cozy fire to enjoy Aunt Betsy's Valentine's Day tale. This serene scene is framed by the standard iconography of Valentine's Day: a heart with two arrows through it accompanied by a pair of lovebirds and flanked on either side by poles covered in valentines. The posting of these intimate communications stands as a reminder that the valentine plays a public role. As a supposedly authentic expression of true emotion that was also "an incorporation of the terms of market exchange into the world of courtship itself," the

FIG. 9.2 "Mrs. Betsy Baker's Party." From "Aunt Betsy: Introduction" by Eliza Winstanley, *Bow Bells* Valentine Number (13 February 1867): 1. Reproduced with permission from an image produced by ProQuest LLC for its online product *British Periodicals*. www.proquest.com.

valentine presented both an opportunity and a risk.[30] The risk is dra-
matized in the second, rather frenzied, image of excited ladies lunging
toward Cupid, who is perched atop a pedestal and remains above
the fray as letters and cards fly out of his bag. These women lean in
more eagerly than their sisters gathered around Betsy's hearth. Some
women in the foreground of the picture seem to crouch to obtain a
better position from which to catch the soaring valentines or even in
preparation for leaping into the air. Those in the back of the crowd
wave their arms above their heads as they attempt to snatch valentines
before their rivals. These competing visions of Valentine's Day, one
quietly domestic and one raucously public, highlight what Elizabeth
White Nelson refers to as the two levels on which the valentine
story appealed to the woman reader: "[I]t fulfilled her desire for a
tale of requited love, and it addressed her concerns about the changing nature of courtship and the role of trifles in the serious business
of love."[31] This cover illustration also underscores *Bow Bells'* message
that Valentine's Day was a potentially pivotal moment in a woman's
quest for a suitable husband, because the reading of a valentine could
change the course of her life. The status of Valentine's Day as such a
crucial courtship event was, in large part, a result of the advent of the
Penny Post, which spawned "the heyday of lace-paper valentines in
England" from the 1840s to the 1860s.[32]

The Penny Post and the Promiscuous Exchange of Valentines

Universal Penny Postage was enacted on 10 January 1840 as part of
a series of postal reforms intended to make the national communication service more accessible, reliable, and far-reaching. As Laura
Rotunno points out, between 1812 and 1840, "British correspondents
faced the highest postal rates ever recorded," thus barring a substantial
portion of the population from communicating, especially across long
distances.[33] To make matters worse, recipients were expected to pay
the accrued postage fees, so expenses were often unexpected as well
as unaffordable. With the passage of the Postal Reform Act and the
introduction of the "Penny Black" stamp emblazoned with Queen
Victoria's head, postal fees were no longer calculated by distance delivered or charged to unwitting recipients but were prepaid with one
uniform and affordable form of postage. The Penny Post enabled a
new kind of free exchange among friends as well as strangers: in 1839,

before the advent of the Penny Post, 4,818,552 chargeable letters were sent through the postal service. Just two years later, the number had soared to 15,058,508.[34] By 1860, the General Post Office was serving many cities with six to twelve daily deliveries, depositing letters in as few as two to three hours.[35] Thus, the Penny Post revolutionized communication, especially among the working classes. David M. Henkin contends that cheap postage "exploited and emphasized the centrifugal, promiscuous, and anonymous features of a network that could bring any two people into direct contact."[36] Valentine's Day took full advantage of this postal anonymity, as most cards were left unsigned, leaving recipients to guess who sent their valentine.

In 1841, 400,000 valentines were mailed in England; by 1871, three times that number were sent in London alone.[37] While people still created their own valentines out of scraps of colored paper, lace, ribbon, beads, and other household items, increasingly elaborate cards were manufactured by stationery and perfume shops and sold in bundles for mass consumption. Barry Shank argues that "one of the important functions of valentines was to materialize the quality of the emotional relationships they represented" so that as high-quality embossed lace-paper valentines became more affordable at midcentury, they were the most desirable cards to send and receive.[38] Despite their commercial origins, these cards were usually assembled by hand and painted with cupids, hearts, flowers, birds, bows, or shells. They often featured multiple colorful layers of fancy paper and mechanical moving parts. A typical sentimental valentine reveals the layering of materials and visual icons (see fig. 9.3). At the center of the card—which is made of silver embossed lace paper covered with ribbons, paper flowers, and foil ornaments—floats a hand clasping a bouquet. Barely visible at the bottom of the card is a bow with the words "A Pledge" and "Of Love" printed on its tail ends. The visual impact of romantic valentines was more important than the clichéd text; even if one were to make a valentine at home, it was acceptable, even expected, that one would consult a "valentine writer," a manual that provided exemplary language appropriate for wooing a lover. Leigh Eric Schmidt claims that people "held fast to the customary" expressions of devotion; indeed, the "ever-growing abundance of sentiments available in the marketplace—rhymes to cover an expanding range of romantic feelings" made a personal message seem "quaint" or "obsolete."[39]

FIG. 9.3 "A Pledge of Love." Ornate valentine. © The Museum of London.

Some commercially produced valentines were infused with alluring scents. Eugene Rimmel's perfumery, known for introducing scented valentines, placed card advertisements in a variety of venues for every budget. Their products ranged from a "perfumed sensation valentine" for one shilling (featured in a *Sixpenny Magazine* ad) to more-elaborate satin, lace, and hand-painted Valentine's Day treasures selling for up to ten pounds (announced in an *All the Year Round* issue). Among the items sold at a higher price point were cards that played music, cards that held earrings, brooches, and charms, and cards that could be used as decorative fans.[40]

Not all valentines were romantic. Card companies popularized comic valentines as a way to encourage the wider distribution of their products. These valentines were cruelly critical of their recipients, who could be friends or acquaintances as well as lovers. These cheaply made cards often satirized one's class status, job, appearance, or behavior. Insulting valentines "took strategic advantage of the potential for anonymity that printed communication and the postal system offered" to ridicule recipients without consequence.[41] They "illustrated the humorous yet harsh capacities of inappropriate love," policing desire by mocking differences of class and gender within the "new and complex social conditions" in which "the exchange of these tokens took place."[42] Comic or insulting valentines boldly embodied anxieties about class and sexuality that were suppressed in their more sentimental counterparts. One comic valentine, for example, pokes fun at a sailor (see fig. 9.4), a vocation notorious for sexual promiscuity but nonetheless popular as an admirable character in *Bow Bells'* Valentine's Day issues.[43] This hapless sailor holds a wedding band in one hand and a net in the other, tools he will use to try to catch a wife. However, he is not considered a suitable valentine or a desirable husband, because he is untrustworthy (and he stinks of tar):

> A Jolly Jack Tar perhaps you may be, that has rambled over the briny sea,
> On land you seldom do resort, you find a wife in every port;
> I with a sailor cannot dwell, of tar I do not like the smell,
> Then go among the waves and wind, and seek some other Valentine.

Johnson, St. Martin's Lane.

A Jolly Jack Tar perhaps you may be, that has rambled over the briny sea,
On land you seldom do resort, you find a wife in every port ;
I with a sailor cannot dwell, of tar I do not like the smell,
Then go among the waves and wind, and seek some other Valentine.

FIG. 9.4 "Jolly Jack Tar." Comic valentine. © The Museum of London.

He is surrounded by a hideous border of Cupids fanning the flames of a rudimentary fire struck through with arrows. The standard valentine border of hearts and flowers is replaced by menacing torches and weeds that represent the dangers and displeasures of acquiescing to an inappropriate suitor. If you accept a sailor for a valentine, the iconography implies, you will surely get burned.

Women were not exempt from Valentine's Day ridicule. One comic valentine targeting feminine vanity features a lady whose fashion choice—an enormous crinoline skirt—has restricted her freedom of movement and will presumably prevent her from getting close to any potential beau (see fig. 9.5):

> [T]ell me if you think it wise
> To make yourself so huge a size?
> Perchance you make each smiling elf,
> Think you are ONE BESIDES YOURSELF.

Her absurd fashion choice would be considered even more egregious if she were a woman of the lower-middle or working classes. At midcentury these women were increasingly able to purchase clothing that imitated those above them in status, which may be the implication here. Crinolines received a great deal of attention in *Punch,* which sometimes associated the garments with romantic transgressions. For example, the large, unwieldy skirts were depicted as convenient places for men to hide from suspicious chaperones or as contraptions that could easily blow up in the wind, allowing men to see women's bare legs. In the case of this valentine, the man wielding the telescope in the background may be about to get a thrill if the woman lifts her skirt to hop the fence. In any case, comic valentines exposed the ugly truth that while the holiday promised to help secure love, marriage, and financial security, it could also produce less pleasant results. These sentimental and comic valentines depended on a reader's ability to construct a narrative—hopeful or tragic—from their aggregated iconic images as much as from the accompanying doggerel. This ability to interpret the valentine image-text, in turn, became the topic of *Bow Bells'* Valentine's Day narratives and illustrations.

Bow Bells suggested that reading valentines critically might help a woman avoid tragedy and achieve happiness. "Cupid's Letter Bag; or, St. Valentine's Day" is the opening feature of the first *Bow Bells*

FIG. 9.5   "However Shall I Get It In?" Comic valentine. © The Museum of London.

special issue in 1865. Its depiction of women actively pursuing their Valentine's Day cards hints at the potentially promiscuous qualities of postal courtship that made matrimonial advertising so distasteful.[44] The story takes place in a village nine miles away from the nearest railway station. Because of the distance, the letter carrier conveys the mailbag from the train to the village in a one-horse cart. When the mail delivery is delayed, five young ladies become impatient and take matters into their own hands:

> Perhaps on no other occasion might the matter have caused any alarm or produced any particular sensation, but as this just happened to be a day of all days on which the postman's knock was fraught with a special interest, it is no wonder if the protracted silence of each door-knocker excited impatience and engendered misgivings. . . . Conceive, gentle reader, how annoying—how *particularly* annoying it was to many . . . to be kept waiting for their letters on this special morning. Hearts that had been fluttering, were now pained with suspense: imaginations that had been picturing to themselves Cupids, and bows, and wings, and hearts, and bridal scenes, now cherished irate thoughts [against the postman].[45]

The schoolmaster's daughter, the rector's niece, the apothecary's daughter, a governess, and a farmer's daughter assemble at the railway omnibus determined to travel directly to the main station to find out what happened to the mail. When they find the overturned mail cart, they send the coachman to investigate. He reports that the postman is "dead," and in response "they gave a loud scream altogether—No, not exactly dead—but dead drunk!" (50). Once they have gotten over their shock at this revelation, they discover the mailbag and steal the key from the drunken man's pocket. The narrator explains that "we can scarcely undertake to explain what feeling of interest or curiosity now inspired the ladies; but as if animated with the same motive or thought" the five maidens "simultaneously plunged" into the bag: "[F]ive pairs of prettily gloved hands were quickly busied in picking up the letters, and as many pairs of bright eyes were engaged in glancing at the addresses. And then short ejaculations broke forth from five pairs of rosy lips. It was easy to distinguish the valentines from what may be termed the private letters; and it soon appeared that many of the former were addressed to persons whom the young ladies would not have suspected of being the objects of such attentions" (50). The bold colors and elaborate paper of the valentines make them visually discernable from the other pieces of mail, allowing the ladies to quickly take charge of their own "unmistakable valentines" in "creamy paper" with "gilt or blue edging" and many other "colours shining through" (50). The colors and textures in the paper entice the women as they scramble to rip open their envelopes and peruse their cards while also peering over each other's shoulders to compare their neighbors' valentines to their own. The mysterious origins of the letters make them as sensational as any serial novel featured in *Bow Bells,* and the women's physical involvement with the epistles marks them as intimate and perhaps even vaguely sexual. The tactile experience of the valentines is an inextricable part of what makes them so exciting; the words are almost an afterthought. While the women's reading of the cards is a communal courtship experience that is gendered feminine, they are also unmistakably in competition with each other for postal communication from anonymous men.

The illustration for the essay "The Morn of St. Valentine," included in the regular issue of *Bow Bells* for the same month, works in tandem with "Cupid's Letter Bag" (see fig. 9.6). In fact, the illustration could very well accompany the story, as it depicts five maidens pursuing Valentine's Day cards. While these women play with and even kiss the fluttering Cupids that surround them, "The Morn of St. Valentine" offers a darker view of valentines than the story of the women who commandeer the postman's bag. Not all of the cards distributed by the rogue cupids are what they seem. In fact, several fall into the category of the dreaded insult valentine, the one form in which words matter more than images. One unsuspecting lady reads the following message in her otherwise beautiful card: "My hope, my life, my love,—Oh! could you but fathom the recess of my heart, you would believe me sincere, when I tell you I am devotedly attached and a most sincere admirer of you—" and here the narrator interrupts to note that the young lady's "heart is in a flutter, as she turns over the leaf and gazes on the likeness of a female, by no means flattering to herself" and then rereads the final line: "—or any other *gal!*"[46] With this, the poor girl realizes she has received a false valentine, and her romantic dreams are crushed. Likewise, another young lady is dejected when she discovers that her letter contains a "serious charge against" her. It begins with the lines "I loved thee once, I'll love no more / Thine be the grief as is the blame; / Thou art not what thou wast before." The narrator concludes that she "has evidently jilted one of her lovers" and therefore "richly deserves her chastisement" (63). Not merely an insult, this is a punishing valentine that reprimands the recipient for her coquettish behavior. Continuing the dismal theme, the narrator criticizes the other valentines for their silly, unrealistic rhymes and their perpetuation of nonsensical romantic ideals, concluding that "young ladies should analyze their Valentine a little more closely before going into ecstacies [*sic*] on the receipt of those wild love effusions" (63). This command calls our attention to *Bow Bells'* emphasis on educating women in appropriate methods of courtship. The magazine's imagined and real women readers alike are presented with courtship challenges that remind them that life does not always have a romantic ending but inevitably includes disappointments that they must learn to navigate effectively. Reading *Bow Bells,* it is implied, will help them think more carefully about their courtship communications and, one hopes, have a more promising outcome than the ladies of "The Morn of St. Valentine," whose excitement over the immediate beauty of their cards is thwarted by a more careful reading of the accompanying text.

For Better or for Worse: *Bow Bells'* Valentine's Day Stories

The stories told at Aunt Betsy's Valentine's Day parties, and their accompanying illustrations, reflect the prevailing ambivalence toward the holiday as both a promising component of courtship and a harbinger of disappointment. For many of *Bow Bells'* readers—women who faced the financial challenges of supporting themselves—a happy ending was achieved by marrying a good man who could provide both emotional and financial fulfillment. Mitchell argues that stories about heroines who rise in class via marriage were popular in the penny press because they conveyed the idea that one's worth should be based on behavior rather than the circumstances of birth, certainly an appealing message for working-class women struggling to improve their lives. Such stories frequently hinge "on the perseverance and faithfulness of a woman who defies family and society and waits until her lover has earned his fortune and so removed the social bars [to marriage]. . . . But when the heroine succumbs to family pressure and makes a 'correct' marriage, the result is nearly always misery."[47] This message is conveyed in both word and image in *Bow Bells'* Valentine's Day issues.

FIG. 9.6 "The Morn of St. Valentine." *Bow Bells* 2, no. 29 (15 February 1865): 64. Reproduced with permission from an image produced by ProQuest LLC for its online product *British Periodicals.* www.proquest.com.

In "The Old Valentine," written by Eliza Winstanley (aka Aunt Betsy),[48] Constance Wargrave's financially unstable lover, Hubert Langly, is presumed to have died in a shipwreck, and a wealthy suitor, Mr. Oldbury, is forced upon her by her family and friends. The night before her wedding, Constance digs up an old valentine "written by Hubert—by his own dear hand—and sent . . . on Valentine's Day two years ago" (53). She sleeps with it under her pillow and dreams that Hubert is alive. When she awakens, she decides that she cannot marry Oldbury despite his status and the insistence of her mother: "It was the first time in her life that Constance Wargrave had ever had a fixed resolution; a resolution that nothing on earth would break, or even shake" (54). In the story's illustration, Constance clutches the "old worn valentine" with Hubert's handwritten message on it when she informs the women who have come to fetch her that she will not go to the altar as planned (see fig. 9.7). The valentine serves as a talisman of love for Constance. The illustration evokes Constance's valentine with its border of flowers and Cupids hovering above the ladies who assemble to make a marital decision. Whether or not the other women come under the spell of the valentine is a matter of speculation, though Mrs. Wargrave frets that Constance has "been poring over a dead lover's writing until it has driven [her] out of [her] sober senses" (53). Constance's devotion to both the valentine and the man who sent it is vindicated, however, as Hubert suddenly returns with a tale of his rescue by a ship sailing to Australia. Though he has a wooden leg, a blind eye, and no fortune, Constance is eager to marry him. When Hubert reveals that his handicaps were a ruse to test her devotion and that he struck gold while in Australia, Constance is rewarded, and her mother is cowed. Constance's devoted, almost telepathic reading of her old valentine is what gives her the courage to wait for Hubert even if it means struggling alone. The illustration reinforces the importance of Constance's reading even as it vindicates the valentine as an authentic form of communication.

Whereas the happy ending of "The Old Valentine" is welcome and even expected, there are a surprising number of tales of doomed love in *Bow Bells*. In her discussion of Valentine's Day stories in *Godey's Lady's Book,* Nelson argues that valentines served "as a test of love, but at great emotional cost. The stories often focused on negative aspects of valentine exchange: mysterious, cruel, and misunderstood valentines. The promises of emotional freedom that romantic love seemed to offer were, in many senses, hollow."[49] The poem and accompanying illustration for "A Legend of St. Valentine" by C. J. Rowe is emblematic of these negative outcomes. The poem opens with anticipation

CONSTANCE WARGRAVE REFUSES TO GO TO THE ALTAR.

FIG. 9.7   "Constance Wargrave Refuses to Go to the Altar." From "The Old Valentine" by Eliza Winstanley, *Bow Bells* 2, no. 29 (15 February 1865): 53. Reproduced with permission from an image produced by ProQuest LLC for its online product *British Periodicals.* www.proquest.com.

for the romantic holiday: "Tis Valentine's Day! Tis Valentine's Day! / When the eyes of maidens glisten" and "For the postman's knock they listen."[50] The fair maiden of this poem receives two deliveries: one valentine made with "an artist's cunning skill" was "decked with brave device, / And in the petals of each flower / Was placed a jewel of price"; the other had "but a simple flower," a blue forget-me-not with a "plain gold ring" nestled in its petals and the motto "Share my lot" written beneath it (lines 29–36). Instead of recognizing the handmade sincerity of the second missive,

> She kissed the first, and bid the last
> Go deck some other shrine;
> No simple, lowly, modest swain
> Should be her Valentine.
>
> (lines 37–40)

The verse conveys the skepticism with which some regarded the neatly packaged messages of prefabricated valentines. The humbler home-spun valentine, conversely, signals sincerity and devotion, qualities that the fortune-seeking heroine fails to see. Her disdain for modest but "truthful love" results in her near ruin when she is left by her "faith-less Valentine" without her "silken robe," "gaudy gems," and "painted boudoir" (all false trappings of wealth and indications that she is a kept woman) (lines 22–23, 39–40). Despite the heroine's lack of virtue or verbal repentance, she is saved by her "true valentine," who hears her "cry of misery" upon his return from honorably serving his country on the battlefield. He "raises her in his strong arms" and "draws her to his faithful heart" (lines 30–40). Although the heroine's reading of the valentines she receives is hampered by her greed and inability to distinguish between honesty and false seduction, she survives her bad decision. Yet whether she has really learned her lesson at the end of the poem is unclear.

The lack of moral resolution in the poem is reinforced by the emphasis on the tragic consequences of her misreading of valentines in the trio of scenes that illustrate the work (see fig. 9.8). We see the main character in the first scene reading; in the second, falling; and in the final scene, lying lifeless in the arms of the hero. We do not see her in a state of comfort or joy, though the narrative implies that she is mercifully given both in the end. The intertwining border of flowers, birds, and envelopes places the vignettes in the context of Valentine's Day and evokes feelings of hope and anticipation that are crushed by the main images of the illustration, which trace the progressively dire consequences of the heroine's misreading.

FIG. 9.8 "A Legend of St. Valentine." From "A Legend of St. Valentine" by C. J. Rowe, *Bow Bells* 10, no. 237, supp. (10 February 1869): 8. Reproduced with permission from an image produced by ProQuest LLC for its online product *British Periodicals.* www.proquest.com.

In Francis Derrick's "A Story of Love's Cruelty," from *Bow Bells'* 1869 Valentine's Day supplement, the absence of a valentine is the harbinger of death for the two main characters. Grace Glyn eagerly awaits a valentine from her beloved Ernest Drax year after year, but he never sends one despite the fact that he clearly loves her. Ernest is a brooding soul who washed ashore after a shipwreck and recovered in the Glyn family home while also attending to fellow sailors as the ship's doctor. Upon his recovery, he finds a job in London but continues to come to the shore to visit Grace, though he never professes his feelings for her. One Valentine's Day, Grace's sister Nora cruelly teases her about the situation when Nora receives a valentine from her beau. Grace insists that valentines are "senseless things" and she does not "wish anything half so silly" from Ernest, since if he had "anything to say to [her] of the sort usually said in valentines," he wouldn't "send it to [her] in silly verses among roses and Cupids."[51] Nora cattily replies that she "would rather have love told in a valentine, than not told at all" (5). The valentine's generic messages are, once again, seen as a somewhat suspect if still desirable part of courtship. Eventually

Ernest stops visiting, and Grace becomes ill, presumably of a broken heart. When Ernest finds out about Grace's condition, he seeks her out, but she dies before he arrives. The next day, Ernest's lifeless body is discovered by village children on the beach, and "the pistol with which he had done the deed was in his hand—the bullet in his heart" (7). Ernest's suicide note explains that he could not marry Grace as was already married to a woman who was sent to an asylum because of alcoholism. The tragic note stands in place of the absent valentine. While Ernest is honorable in his actions, his lack of communication proves deadly. The valentine, then, is held up as an important indicator of emotions that might otherwise go unexpressed.

The illustration accompanying the story features Ernest's suicide as the central image, surrounded by the sisters' Valentine's Day rivalry, Nora's minor quarrel with her beau, Ernest's brooding walks through town, and Grace's deathbed scene (see fig. 9.9). These bleak vignettes serve as a melodramatic reminder of the consequences of poor marital choices. Julia Thomas notes that deathbed scenes that were seen as morally edifying became "all too familiar in Victorian literary and visual culture. It could even be said that they were done to death."[52] Indeed, the visual tableau of dual deaths is reminiscent of the clichéd valentine itself, as the iconic imagery precludes the need for an explanation, telling the story of "Love's Cruelty" through visual cues with simple phrases printed on ribbons to convey key points. Here, too, the border of flowers, ribbons, and Cupids surrounding the images reinforces *Bow Bells'* insistence that tragedy is as much a part of Valentine's Day as the hoped-for happy ending. Yet the magazine sought to rein in the negative impact of the overly commercialized holiday while simultaneously capitalizing on it by using melodramatic tales to teach moral and practical lessons about proper courtship practices. Presented as complements to one another, the narratives and the illustrations enabled the magazine to convey conflicting messages—the hopeful and aspirational alongside the pessimistic and cautionary—and, thereby, trained its readers to analyze the mixed messages and hidden motives (their own and others') represented in real-life Valentine's Day exchanges.

According to Nelson's account of nineteenth-century Valentine's Day courtship, the "most vexing question was how to make romantic love consistent with its imperatives of financial stability and domestic

FIG. 9.9 "A Story of Love's Cruelty." From "A Story of Love's Cruelty" by Francis Derrick, *Bow Bells* 10, no. 237 (10 February 1869): 5. Reproduced with permission from an image produced by ProQuest LLC for its online product *British Periodicals.* www.proquest.com.

happiness. In other words, how to tame the dangerous possibilities of both passion and capitalism. The new manufactured valentine was a symbol of both; its role in the economy of the marriage market was necessarily complicated, holding out both possibility and threat by exposing the links between economic value and sentimental value."[53] *Bow Bells'* Valentine's Day special issues take the holiday as an occasion to equate good reading (of valentines and of the magazine itself) with the attainment of successful matrimonial matches. The magazine's sobering Valentine's Day fare points out the incredibly high stakes of courtship for its women readers and attempts to make them more sophisticated participants in the marriage market. The intense visuality of the valentine is replicated in the composition of *Bow Bells'* Valentine's Day issues. But, while visual forms such as valentines and the magazine's illustrations have their place, *Bow Bells* suggests that they fail to tell the whole story. Reading text and image together provides a more promising future.

Notes

I dedicate this essay to Sally Mitchell, whose generous mentorship has been crucial to my research and writing. I regret that she will be unable to share my delight in seeing this work in print.

Chapter epigraph: "The Morn of St. Valentine," *Bow Bells* 2, no. 29 (15 February 1865): 63.

1. Barry Shank, *A Token of My Affection: Greeting Cards and American Business Culture* (New York: Columbia University Press, 2004), 29–30.

2. For more information on matrimonial advertising, see Jennifer Phegley, *Courtship and Marriage in Victorian England* (Santa Barbara, CA: Praeger/ABC-Clio, 2012), chap. 3.

3. Leigh Eric Schmidt, *Consumer Rites: The Buying and Selling of American Holidays* (Princeton: Princeton University Press, 1995), 86.

4. Sally Mitchell, *The Fallen Angel: Chastity, Class, and Women's Reading, 1835–1880* (Bowling Green, OH: Bowling Green University Popular Press, 1981); Kate Flint, *The Woman Reader, 1837–1914* (Oxford, UK: Clarendon Press, 1993).

5. Susan P. Casteras, "Reader, Beware: Images of Victorian Women and Books," *Nineteenth-Century Gender Studies* 3, no. 1 (Spring 2007), para. 10, www.ncgsjournal.com/issue31/casteras.htm.

6. Illustrations of women readers in regular issues of *Bow Bells* also tend to depict the reading of correspondence. These letters bring sensational news of sudden death, betrayal, and forgery, as well as a wide variety of other criminal activities and legal troubles. Examples include "The Forgery" and "Ethel Appeals to Sibby for Help" from *The Home Angel*, in *Bow Bells* 2, no. 36 (5 April 1865): 225, and *Bow Bells* 2, no. 43 (24 May 1865): 400; "The Invitation" and "May Rivers Giving Amos the Letter" from *The Only Daughter*, in *Bow Bells* 2, no. 41 (10 May 1865): 357 and 2, no. 42 (17 May 1865): 381; "Madame Lishofsheim Reading Mrs. Marrington's Note" from [Eliza Winstanley], *Voices from the Lumber-Room*, in *Bow Bells* 3, no. 62 (4 October 1865): 229; "The Criminating Billet-Doux" from *Beyond His Income*, in *Bow Bells* 5, no. 119 (7 November 1866): 349; "A Struggle for the Letter" from *Carynthia: The Legend of Black Rock*, in *Bow Bells* 5, no. 127 (2 January 1867): 529; "Louisa Astonished at Her Mother's Letter" from "Home Duties," in *Bow Bells* 6, no. 154 (10 July 1867): 561; "Geraldine Reads the Realization of Her Fears" from *Captain Gerald*, in *Bow Bells* 7, no. 165 (25 September 1867): 193; "Comola Reads Captain Ormand's Letter" from *Astrutha*, in *Bow Bells* 7, no. 167 (9 October 1867): 241; and "News of Launcelot" from *Pansy Eyes*, in *Bow Bells* 9, no. 233 (13 January 1869): 601.

7. Casteras points out that courtship-related reading is often associated with letters rather than books ("Reader, Beware," para. 27). For more on *Bow Bells'* interest in the courtship practices of working- and lower-middle-class women, see Jennifer Phegley, "Victorian Girls Gone Wild: Matrimonial Advertising and the Transformation of Courtship in the Popular Press," *Victorian Review* 39, no. 2 (Fall 2013): 129–46; and Judith Rosen, "A Different Scene of Desire: Women and Work in Penny Magazine Fiction," *Pacific Coast Philology* 27 (September 1992): 102–9.

8. Paul Goldman and Simon Cooke, introduction to *Reading Victorian Illustration, 1855–1875: Spoils of the Lumber Room,* ed. Paul Goldman and Simon Cooke (Farnham, UK: Ashgate, 2012), 6.

9. Christopher Mark Banham, "Dicks, John (1818–1881)," in *Dictionary of Nineteenth-Century Journalism,* ed. Laurel Brake and Marysa Demoor (London: British Library, 2008), n.p., accessed through the ProQuest C19 Database. See also Guy Dicks, *The John Dicks Press* (Raleigh, NC: Lulu. com, 2013), a family account of the Dicks publishing empire.

10. Sally Mitchell, "The Forgotten Woman of the Period: Penny Weekly Family Magazines of the 1840s and 1850s," in *A Widening Sphere: Changing Roles of Victorian Women,* ed. Martha Vicinus (Bloomington: Indiana University Press, 1977), 33.

11. Ibid., 33–34.

12. Anne Humpherys, "*Bow Bells* (1862–1897)," in *Dictionary of Nineteenth-Century Journalism,* ed. Laurel Brake and Marysa Demoor (London: British Library, 2008), n.p., accessed through the ProQuest C19 Database. Sally Mitchell estimates that a penny magazine had to sell at least 30,000 copies to break even, so *Bow Bells'* circulation of 200,000 was a healthy readership that would have made the magazine profitable for Dicks. Mitchell, "Forgotten Woman," 37. Perhaps even more impressive is Andrew King's claim that the combination of the penny fiction weeklies the *London Journal, Cassell's Illustrated Family Magazine,* the *Family Herald,* and *Bow Bells* "cumulatively sold almost two million copies a week in the 1860s, their serial stories read or listened to by over 50% of the population of Britain." King, "'Killing Time,' or Mrs. Braby's Peppermints: The Double Economy of the *Family Herald* and the *Family Herald* Supplements," *Victorian Periodicals Review* 43, no. 2 (Summer 2010): 152.

13. Louis James, "The Trouble with Betsy: Periodicals and the Common Reader in Mid-Nineteenth-Century England," in *The Victorian Periodical Press: Samplings and Soundings,* ed. Joanne Shattock and Michael Wolff (Leicester: Leicester University Press, 1982), 353.

14. Ibid.

15. Ibid.

16. Andrew King, "A Paradigm of Reading the Victorian Penny Weekly: Education of the Gaze and the *London Journal*," in *Nineteenth-Century Media and the Construction of Identity*, ed. Laurel Brake, Bill Bell, and David Finkelstein (Basingstoke, UK: Palgrave Macmillan, 2000), 87.

17. Quoted in Patricia J. Anderson, "'Factory Girl, Apprentice and Clerk'—The Readership of Mass-Market Magazines, 1830–60," *Victorian Periodicals Review* 25, no. 2 (Summer 1992): 69.

18. *Bow Bells'* sensational and sentimental cover illustrations were balanced by the masthead of the magazine, which included images of women in classical robes engaged in various reading, writing, and artistic pursuits. These grand women lend the magazine a cultural cachet that would otherwise have been beyond the reach of its readers. They are arranged around the central image of the tower of St. Mary-le-Bow Church, which was the magazine's namesake and an identifying landmark of London's East End. In fact, the term "Cockney" originally referred to Londoners who lived within the range of "Bow's" bells. Thus, while the classical figures stand in sharp contrast to the magazine's contents and illustrations, they symbolize a kind of cultural identity that its core audience might have hoped to achieve. Positioning these ancient scholarly women as overseers of "a weekly magazine of general literature" also emphasized its educational purpose even while the serial fiction illustrations highlighted its entertaining qualities. Other magazines of the period such as the *Girls' Own Paper* and *Atalanta* also featured women in classical robes on their covers to convey their cultural importance. I thank Sally Mitchell for pointing this out.

19. Advertisement for *Bow Bells'* Valentine's Day issue, *Bow Bells* 2, no. 28 (8 February 1865): 35.

20. Ibid.

21. Marysa Demoor and Kate Macdonald. "Finding and Defining the Victorian Supplement," *Victorian Periodicals Review* 43, no. 2 (Summer 2010): 101.

22. Ibid., 103.

23. Many magazines featured Valentine's Day–themed material during February, but I am unaware of other special issues related to the holiday. As Demoor and Macdonald point out (ibid., 101), the terrain of periodical supplements has yet to be thoroughly charted. Laurel Brake likewise reminds us that supplements "were frequently lost, and many, perhaps most, remain unpreserved, unrecognized, unrecorded, uncatalogued." Brake, "Lost and Found: Serial Supplements in the Nineteenth Century," *Victorian Periodicals Review* 43, no. 2 (Summer 2010): 111. Andrew King

states that there is even less information on penny periodical supplements, which he colorfully describes as "genetically engineered mutants that may or may not live beyond a few issues." King, "Killing Time," 149.

24. Jolein De Ridder, "What? How? Why? Broadening the Mind with the *Treasury of Literature* (1868–1875), Supplement to the *Ladies' Treasury* (1857–1895)," *Victorian Periodicals Review* 43, no. 2 (Summer 2010): 187.

25. According to Koenraad Claes, such supplements "followed the tastes advocated in the women's magazine they were issued with, and affirmed its ideological positions," enabling "them to create and strengthen a clear profile for their ideal readership, which would . . . [forge] a link between the magazine and the reader's everyday life." Claes, "Supplements and Paratext: The Rhetoric of Space," *Victorian Periodicals Review* 43, no. 2 (Summer 2010): 206.

26. While the U.S. magazine *Godey's Lady's Book* did not have a Valentine's Day special issue, it did market itself as a suitable Valentine's Day gift. Elizabeth White Nelson, *Market Sentiments: Middle-Class Market Culture in Nineteenth-Century America* (Washington, DC: Smithsonian Books, 2004), 192–93.

27. Perhaps the name of the proprietress was a shout-out to all of the female servants who read the magazine. Advertisement for *Bow Bells'* Valentine's Day issue, *Bow Bells* 6, no. 132 (6 February 1867): 35.

28. [Eliza Winstanley], "Aunt Betsy: Introduction," *Bow Bells* 6, no. 133, supp. (6 February 1867): 2. Aunt Betsy was the alter ego of Mrs. Eliza Winstanley, who wrote regularly for *Bow Bells* and edited the weekly *Fiction for Family Reading,* also published by Dicks. Winstanley was born in England in 1818. She emigrated with her family to New South Wales in 1833. She married musician Henry Charles O'Flaherty in 1841 and returned to England with him in 1846. After her husband's death in 1854, she began a second career as a writer, publishing *Shifting Scenes in Theatrical Life* in 1859 and a novel titled *Bitter-Sweet—So Is the World* in 1860. By 1864 she had begun to devote herself to writing full time, publishing most of her novels serially in *Bow Bells* and in Dicks' English Novels series. N. M. Robinson, "O'Flaherty, Eliza (1818–1882)," in *Australian Dictionary of Biography,* National Centre of Biography, Australian National University, http://adb.anu.edu.au /biography/oflaherty-eliza-2520/text3411 (accessed 31 December 2013).

29. Winstanley, "Aunt Betsy," 2.

30. Nelson, *Market Sentiments,* 213.

31. Ibid., 203.

32. Ruth Webb Lee, *A History of Valentines* (London: B. T. Batsford, 1953), 136.

33. Laura Rotunno, *Postal Plots in British Fiction, 1840–1898: Readdressing Correspondence in Victorian Culture* (Basingstoke, UK: Palgrave Macmillan, 2013), 7.

34. Ibid., 7–8.

35. Catherine J. Golden, *Posting It: The Victorian Revolution in Letter Writing* (Gainesville: University Press of Florida, 2009), 107–8.

36. David M. Henkin, *The Postal Age: The Emergence of Modern Communications in Nineteenth-Century America* (Chicago: University of Chicago Press, 2006), 153.

37. Golden, *Posting It*, 223.

38. Shank, *Token of My Affection*, 56.

39. Schmidt, *Consumer Rites*, 62.

40. *Sixpenny Magazine* 2, no. 8 (February 1862): 218; *All the Year Round* 17 (January 1867): 123. Thanks to Troy Bassett for sharing his copies of Rimmel's ads with me.

41. Shank, *Token of My Affection*, 51. As Golden notes, "We cannot underestimate how the posting of romantic and insulting missives depended on anonymous collection and distribution of the mail. Secret admirers could declare love anonymously and disguise their handwriting. . . . Worse, a prankster could" send a card as a practical joke (*Posting It*, 225).

42. Shank, *Token of My Affection*, 51.

43. Indeed, this sailor may be suffering from syphilis, given his bandaged and disfigured nose.

44. Kate Thomas argues that the Penny Post allied "epistolary exchange to erotic transaction," combining both metaphorical and actual potential for promiscuity in its promotion of indiscriminate exchange between and among the sexes and across classes. Thomas, *Postal Pleasures: Sex, Scandal, and Victorian Letters* (Oxford: Oxford University Press, 2012), 25.

45. "Cupid's Letter Bag; or, St. Valentine's Day," *Bow Bells* 2, no. 29 (15 February 1865): 50. Emphasis in the original. Hereafter cited in text.

46. "Morn of St. Valentine," *Bow Bells*, 63. Emphasis in the original. Hereafter cited in text.

47. Mitchell, "Forgotten Woman," 40.

48. Eliza Winstanley, "The Old Valentine," *Bow Bells* 2, no. 29 (15 February 1865): 53–55. Hereafter cited in text.

49. Nelson, *Market Sentiments*, 203.

50. C. J. Rowe, "A Legend of St. Valentine," *Bow Bells* 10, no. 237, supp. (10 February 1869): 8. Hereafter cited in text. Linda Hughes offers

further discussion of the interaction of poems and their accompanying illustrations in chapter 7 of the present volume.

51. Francis Derrick, "A Story of Love's Cruelty," *Bow Bells* 10, no. 237, supp. (10 February 1869): 5–7. Hereafter cited in text.

52. Julia Thomas, "Happy Endings: Death and Domesticity in Victorian Illustration," in *Reading Victorian Illustration, 1855–1875: Spoils of the Lumber Room,* ed. Paul Goodman and Simon Cooke (Burlington, VT: Ashgate, 2012), 79. See also chapter 6 in the present volume.

53. Nelson, *Market Sentiments,* 173.

TEN

Picturing "Girls Who Read"

Victorian Governesses and Neo-Victorian Shōjo Manga

ANNA MARIA JONES

> All the same it is a pity, for the sake of young readers, that all
> the girls in novels, with so very rare exceptions—and Jane
> Eyre, if not pretty, probably was less plain than she thought,
> and certainly was *agaçante,* which is much more effective—
> should be beautiful and should have so much admiration
> and conquest. The girls who read are apt to wonder how it
> is that they have not the same fortune.
>
> —Margaret Oliphant, *Hester* (1883)

The fictional Victorian governess, as Margaret Oliphant's narrator observes, is a problem for "girls who read": socially mobile, independent yet vulnerable, romantically available, the
governess offers a compelling narrative that is likely to raise false hopes
in impressionable young women.[1] What does this narrative do to (or
for) girls who read in contemporary, transnational contexts? This
chapter undertakes a relational analysis across geographic, temporal,
and generic boundaries, taking as its topic a Japanese neo-Victorian
romance manga (comics) series, Moto Naoko's *Lady Victorian* (*Redī
Vikutorian,* 1999–2007), which spoofs the very same sensational and
romantic stories that it offers to readers.[2] Moto invokes the Brontëan
governess romance, Victorian serial fiction, and ladies' magazines, as

well as late Victorian *Japonisme,* to reimagine contemporary readers of *shōjo* (girls') manga vis-à-vis Victorian female readers and to explore the intersection between affective susceptibility and critical agency. It plays with the tension between the female reader's seemingly irreconcilable investments in sensational romance and in the critical sophistication that ostensibly inoculates against such generic susceptibilities. If, as Lauren Berlant argues, "'women's texts' are gendering machines, locating the ideality of femininity in fantasies of unconflicted subjectivity in an intimate world,"[3] then, I argue, *Lady Victorian* is like a skeleton watch with the gear works exposed, inviting the reader to appreciate the movements of its cogs and wheels.

In *Lady Victorian,* neo-Victorian content and the graphic form combine to reflect the contemporary reader uncannily back to herself (see fig. 10.1). Throughout the twenty-volume series, readers are invited to contemplate scenes of reading. We dwell on images of the manga's heroine, a penniless young governess living in late nineteenth-century England, as she dwells lovingly on pages from the *Lady's Magazine* depicting debutante balls and Queen Victoria's salons. The manga draws correspondences between anxieties about the contemporary reader of shōjo manga and Victorian debates about susceptible femininity, which crystallized around novel reading, with special reference to *Jane Eyre* (1847) and to 1860s sensation novels. It likewise evokes Victorian discussions of the effects of the "violent stimulus of serial publication," as Oliphant termed it, upon those impressionable readers.[4] The epigraph above, from Oliphant's 1883 novel *Hester,* may be taken as shorthand for the overlapping discourses of femininity and literary consumption that coalesced around the woman (or girl) reader in Victorian culture. Oliphant's novel uses the pain that its eponymous heroine feels upon perceiving the difference between herself and fictional heroines as an occasion to generalize about the perils and pleasures of readerly attachments. Because Oliphant was a professional writer in a male-dominated industry who produced both fiction and criticism that directly address the problem of "girls who read," she might be said to share many concerns with a contemporary *mangaka* (manga artist) like Moto:[5] about the ethical ramifications of addressing one's work to an audience of young women and girls who will form attachments to and identifications with one's characters, for good or ill; about the role of the professional woman writer

FIG. 10.1   Bell imagines being presented at court. Moto Naoko, *Lady Victorian,* vol. 2 (Tokyo: Akitashoten, 1999), 126. © Moto Naoko (Akitashoten), 1998–2007. Reproduced with permission.

as produced by and contributing to the market in which she and her products circulate; about the legitimacy of literature written for feminine mass consumption; about, in sum, the convergence of gender and genre. The contours of this Victorian debate materialize in the graphic form and conventions of the neo-Victorian manga. *Lady Victorian,* with its ability to represent visually shifting points of view and psychological states, allows readers to study scenes of reading and, thereby, to scrutinize the workings of their own textual attachments.

As is evident in the full-page montage in figure 10.1, which superimposes the heroine over images of her favorite periodical and the unrealistic fantasies it inspires, the manga is well suited to considering the Victorian trope of girls who read. Indeed, Kate Mitchell's description of the neo-Victorian as "a series of afterimages, still visible, in altered forms" becomes literalized in *Lady Victorian.*[6] As Thierry Groensteen describes, the comics form is fundamentally organized around "interdependent images that, participating in a series, present the double characteristic of being separated . . . and which are plastically and semantically over-determined by the fact of their coexistence *in praesentia.*"[7] I have argued elsewhere that this simultaneously serial and coexistent nature of comic images aids what Linda Hutcheon calls the "inherently palimpsestuous" nature of adaptation; that is, images both forward narrative progress and suspend the action in juxtaposed tableaux.[8] The iconic image of Queen Victoria; the layered volumes of the *Lady's Magazine,* with their English-language script; the dissolution of distinct frames in favor of hazily overlapping scenes; the interspersed sparkles and floral garlands; the frame of the heroine's ecstatic, blushing face superimposed over all: taken together, these images bring Victorian periodicals into the manga's present, simultaneously freezing the narrative progress to visualize the heroine's mindscape. The visual language of shōjo manga cues the reader's sentimental identifications with the heightened emotions that the scene represents, encouraging a desire to see Bell's story unfold, even as the tableaux, snapshots of her emotional state, invite close scrutiny of that with which the reader identifies.

Neo-Victorian studies scholars have tended to view "self-conscious" engagements with the Victorian past as distinct from the more sentimental and "nostalgic" adaptations that appeal to mass-market consumers, like the so-called heritage films or BBC adaptations of

Victorian novels, in which, as Louisa Hadley puts it, "the strangeness of the Victorians is not merely nostalgically mourned, but rather exoticized and fetishized."[9] And if, as is frequently the case, a particular neo-Victorian text might address both a critical and a popular readership, critics conceive of those readers as separate kinds of people: one "'ordinary,'" reading for plot and pleasure, and one "more 'knowledgeable,'" reading self-consciously and critically and, thus, attuned to the novel's metafictional "games-playing."[10] Moreover, these two kinds of readers are both posited as contemporary subjects encountering a text that reconstitutes, reforms, distills, or otherwise processes historical content for up-to-date sensibilities. Yet this formulation both flattens out the complexity of Victorian reading practices and elides the similarities between Victorian and contemporary readers. As Kate Flint points out, "[B]oth sensation and 'New Woman' fiction mock within themselves the belief that women read uncritically, unthoughtfully"; and even while "encouraging a sympathetic identificatory response on the part of their consumers . . . they stimulate[,] simultaneously, their readers' capacity for self-awareness and social analysis and judgment."[11] As Beth Palmer argues, it is precisely "sensation fiction's . . . self-consciousness about how the contemporary moment is constructed in and by print culture as it mediates the past" that is its "most significant and lasting legacy" and that particularly recommends it to neo-Victorian sensationalists, like Sarah Waters and Michel Faber, whose novels inherit rather than introduce a "self-reflexive interest in the materiality of print culture and the status of their novels in comparison with others."[12] Then, as now, self-reflexive treatments of readerly attachments in the texts that peddle those sensational pleasures allow us to consider the continuities both between Victorian and contemporary reading practices and between "passionate" readerly attachments and self-consciously critical and interpretive reading strategies.

It is worth thinking about neo-Victorianism, then, not just in terms of the repurposing of Victorian content for today's popular and critical readers but as part of an ongoing meditation on readerly subjectivity. In other words, the oft-noted spectral and uncanny nature of neo-Victorian texts may be about not only the simultaneous familiarity and strangeness of the reanimated past but also the tension between recognition and misrecognition of one's own readerly practices.

Just as Sigmund Freud describes the unsettling experience of seeing an "elderly gentleman" on a train whose appearance he "thoroughly disliked" and then realizing that it is his own reflection, so too the reader of the neo-Victorian text is invited to experience "the effect of meeting [her] image unbidden and unexpected" in the looking glass of the Victorian reader.[13]

What is more, if a manga like *Lady Victorian* invites its reader to consider her affective relationship to texts via the nineteenth-century past, it also presents the reader to herself through the lens of cultural alterity. After the opening of Japan's borders at midcentury, its cultural imports—decorative objects, fashion accessories, textiles, and artistic techniques—became ubiquitous in late Victorian Britain.[14] When *Lady Victorian* returns to this context in which Japan was aestheticized and objectified for British consumers, it does not just resurrect a Victorian "moment," fetishizing "exotic" England for Japanese readers, but turns this fetishization 180 degrees, showing its Victorian British characters consuming Japanese imports. Moto offers this ersatz Japonisme as a means through which to examine the interwoven dynamics of cultural consumption and identity formation. As such, the manga speaks to the necessity for Victorian and neo-Victorian scholars—to say nothing of comics studies scholars—to employ relational modes of investigation across linguistic and national boundaries and thereby to cultivate, in Mark Llewellyn and Ann Heilmann's words, a "more diverse awareness of the complicated cultural encounters with the nineteenth-century past."[15] As Rey Chow argues, speaking of what she calls "entangled" cross-cultural relationships, "The state of an intermixing, of a diminution of distances among phenomena that used to belong to a separate order of things, necessitates nothing short of a recalculation and redistribution of the normativized intelligibility of the world."[16] Texts like *Lady Victorian* call not just for the attention of Victorianist and neo-Victorianist scholars who might not ordinarily care much about girls' comics but for a reconsideration of the historical, geographical, and generic boundaries of "the Victorian."

Lady Victorian addresses itself across these boundaries to a "nonaggregate community" of readers, who are imagined, chimerically, as Victorian-shōjo.[17] Moto reflects the reader back to herself, doubly estranged, thus performing the sort of "terminological and epistemological displacement" that Llewellyn and Heilmann advocate for a global neo-Victorian studies.[18] In the pages that follow I discuss briefly the analogous discourses surrounding the Victorian woman reader and the contemporary shōjo consumer before turning my attention to *Lady Victorian*, focusing, firstly, on the manga's conjoined interrogations of gender and genre, and, secondly, on its transnational neo-Victorianism.

Victorian and Neo-Victorian Girls Who Read

The Victorian debates about women readers, while in many ways pathologizing those readers, also created a space in which to think about the intersections of gender and genre. As Jennifer Phegley describes, nineteenth-century anxieties about the woman reader grew in tandem with the rise of periodicals, literacy, and a burgeoning middle class whose women had increasing leisure to devote to pleasure reading: "Critics amplified fears that what women read (especially if it happened to be sensational or scandalous) and how they read (particularly if it was quickly and uncritically) would infect them with (at best) romanticized expectations that would leave them dissatisfied about their lives and (at worst) with immoral thoughts that could lead to immoral behavior."[19] These views of the susceptible woman reader were by no means the only ones; they were countered particularly by the family literary magazines of the latter half of the nineteenth century, which "placed [women readers] firmly in the center of the nineteenth-century literary marketplace as participants in a cultural debate rather than as subjects to be debated."[20] Moreover, as Flint argues, women readers' first-person accounts reveal that "the activity of reading was often the vehicle through which an individual's sense of identity was achieved or confirmed."[21] This is the dynamic that Oliphant's *Hester* critiques when the eponymous heroine comes to the conclusion that she is not like the heroines she reads about,[22] and the narrator regrets the unreality of novels on her behalf.

In Hester's case, the "sense of identity" achieved through reading is no simple matter of sentimental attachment or unthinking overidentification but instead a more complex negotiation of affect and cognition. Moto's adaptation of this Victorian debate in *Lady Victorian* does very similar work, but the problem that Oliphant poses in *Hester* of attempting to find one's self in fictional characters is rendered literal in the graphic format of the manga: readers of the manga, of course, actually can see the heroine without having to imagine her, and we can see what she sees, but even more than this, we can see *how* she sees. That is to say, the juxtaposition of what we might call plot-driven imagery, which shows us what is happening, and atmospheric or psychological imagery, which shows us what the heroine is thinking and how she is feeling, renders the conjoined affective and critical impulses in visual form, thereby offering a self-reflexive meditation on how genre and gender are coterminous and mutually constitutive productions.

There are many reasons, even aside from the current global vogue for "all things Victorian," that a twenty-first-century Japanese manga might look to nineteenth-century cultural antecedents to frame a consideration of its relationship to readers. Scholars in neo-Victorian studies are just beginning to think in transnational terms,[23] but there has been a rich tradition of non-Western adaption, translation, and appropriation of nineteenth-century British literature since the Meiji (1868–1912). In Japan, after the opening of its borders and with the social and political reforms of the Meiji, early engagements with the Western literary tradition were closely bound to discourses about national identity, gender roles, and modernity. As Eleanor Hogan and Inger Sigmund Brodey describe, the literary debate in the Meiji over the form of the novel was also "a thinly veiled political debate over national identity as well as over Japan's place in relation to its expanding world, particularly in relation to the 'West.'"[24] And as Rebecca Copeland argues, notions of modernity and national identity during the Meiji were always linked to women's literacy, such that "the Woman Question (*fujin mondai*) became the focal point for [Meiji] reformers' efforts to 'civilize' Japan."[25] Additionally, translations of myriad Western literary texts entered the literary marketplace; diverse titles such as Mary Braddon's *Lady Audley's Secret* (1862), Frances Hodgson Burnett's *A Little Princess* (serialized 1888; expanded and reissued 1905), and Louisa May Alcott's *Little Women* (1868)—which were first translated into Japanese in 1882, 1904, and 1906, respectively—offered diverse models of Anglo-American femininity to be contemplated and debated if not necessarily embraced wholeheartedly.[26]

Neo-Victorian manga like *Lady Victorian* looks back simultaneously to Japanese and British literary and cultural traditions. But it shares more than historical and geographic setting with its Victorian antecedents. Victorian mass-market literature and contemporary

Japanese manga also share some structural affinities in their modes of delivery and resultant narrative structures. Much like Victorian serials were, manga is marketed to all age, gender, and special-interest demographics, serialized in weekly or monthly installments, reissued in *tankōbon* (volume) form, and frequently adapted for drama CDs, anime, live-action TV and films, and even stage musicals. As Jennifer Prough puts it, "The manga culture industry has become the backbone of contemporary popular culture in Japan."[27] Shōjo and *josei* (ladies') manga represent a huge portion of the market and comprise a variety of subgenres: more or less realistic "slice-of-life" dramas, romantic comedies, supernatural romantic fantasies, and "boys' love," or *yaoi* stories, containing variously tame or graphic representations of male-male romantic and erotic relationships.[28]

Descriptions of susceptible Victorian women readers and today's female manga fans can likewise be seen as analogs of one another. Even sympathetic descriptions of female readers from shōjo manga industry insiders depend heavily on the conflation of generic tastes and gender identity: "At the most basic level, editors and artists used 'what girls like' to describe *shōjo manga* as a genre—always in relation to *shōnen manga* [boys' comics]. Here it is descriptive of content choices reliant on gender stereotypes such as 'girls like plots driven by human relations and romance while boys like adventure and violence' or 'girls want stories filled with interiority, intimacy, and emotions while boys want fast-paced action.'"[29] And as critics in fan studies have long acknowledged, much of the discussion (in both popular and critical discourse) of "what girls like" objectifies and pathologizes those ingénue-consumers. Representations of shōjo readers generally and *fujoshi*, or "rotting girl" (fans of *yaoi* or "boys' love"), in particular, often focus on how their tastes are both essentially feminine and also at odds with normative gender roles.[30] Indeed, the term *fujoshi* (腐女子) is a play on two different *kanji* with the same pronunciation (婦 and 腐) that mean, respectively, "pure femininity" (that is, lady, wife, or bride) and "rottenness," so the term *rotting girl,* with its implications of non-(re)productive desires, works because it blurs the lines between perverse and normative femininity.[31] I do not mean to suggest that Victorians and contemporary readers are identical.[32] Nor do I wish to conflate Western and Japanese female readers entirely.[33] There is, finally, a distinction to be made between the "reader" and the "fan," although the demarcations along any of these axes are not always clear. Regardless of how ethnographic or psychological studies of real readers and fans might address such cross-cultural and asynchronous comparisons, the slippage along these temporal, cultural, and affective axes forms the basis of Moto's conception of her Victorian-shōjo readers.

Lady Victorian's Victorian "Lady" Reader

Lady Victorian was serialized in monthly installments in the shōjo magazine *Princess Comics* and reissued in twenty volumes. It revives a familiar Victorian narrative in which the innocent young governess's precarious financial and social position and limited horizons are converted, against great odds, into romantic and economic opportunities, upward social mobility, personal fulfilment, and agency. And it reanimates Victorian rhetoric about the damaging effects of such romantic and improbable governess narratives on the minds of impressionable young female readers. The ingénue of *Lady Victorian,* the improbably named Bluebell Lily Everrose (Bell), is a sixteen-year-old daughter of a country vicar; she is also an avid, susceptible, sentimental reader of the *Lady's Magazine,* especially its serial installments of romance novels like the exciting *Governess Laura* (in which, à la *Jane Eyre,* a poor young governess wins the heart of her dashing, aristocratic boss). Bell's investments in *Governess Laura* and other stories of its ilk, and her aspirations to be a fine lady, propel her to the metropolis to seek her romantic and economic fortunes as a governess. Once in London, she discovers (like that other Brontë governess, Agnes Grey) that her job is unpleasant and her employers vulgar, but worse (unlike Agnes), she is mistakenly arrested and charged with murder, from which sensational predicament she is soon rescued by exciting new friends: Noel Scott, the handsome editor of Bell's beloved *Lady's Magazine,* and the beautiful, wealthy philanthropist Lady Ethel Constantia Westbury. Kate Flint's point about the intertextuality of Victorian sensation novels can apply to this neo-Victorian manga as well: "The references to shared reading material . . . function as a means of reinforcing the effect of the characters and readers occupying the same cultural space."[34] Moto's invocation of *Jane Eyre* and other governess novels like Anne Brontë's *Agnes Grey* (1847) and Henry James's *Turn of the Screw* (1898) as "shared reading material" creates a common "cultural space" that collapses temporal and geographic distances between readers and the Victorian past.[35] Or, to borrow Naoki Sakai's term, it might be more accurate to say that Moto frames a "nonaggregate community" through cultural antecedents that may or may not be known beforehand to her readers but that become familiar referents through her use of them.[36]

Given the limitations of space, I cannot do justice to Moto's entire series, but I will focus primarily on a few scenes in the first volume that set the terms of the reader's relationship to Bell and, through her, to the people and things that she reads (see fig 10.2). On this page, for example (read from right to left), we see Bell, newly established in her governess position, interrupting her tedious work upon discovering the latest issue of the *Lady's Magazine* among her mistress's possessions. As in figure 10.1, the panels, with their irregular sizes and shapes and incomplete gutters, convey emotional atmosphere as much as narrative progression. Here too Moto uses the visual tropes of shōjo manga to indicate the intensity of Bell's attachment to the magazine: her blushing face and the bubbles or sparkles in the background might, in another shōjo manga, indicate a girl's reaction to a romantic encounter rather than the excitement of discovering a magazine. Moto highlights the same stimulating nature of serial publication that Oliphant deplored, as Bell exclaims, "Thi— . . . this!! The latest issue of *The Lady's Magazine*!! It's out already!? Aaah . . . it's true, you can get things faster in London than in the country!!"[37] The scenario, with her furtive glances to make sure she is not observed, her fervent clasping of the magazine to her (heaving?) bosom, her ecstatic cries, goes to prove the Victorian naysayers right: it really is a bad idea to let "the help" read novels, not only because it will keep them from their work but also because it will fill their heads with unrealistic aspirations. She exclaims, "Argent Grey's serial novel, *Governess Laura*: the romance between a governess and her fascinating employer. Aaaah . . . if only I could have that kind of love!" (1:12; ellipses in original).[38] Clearly, the scene is played for comedy, but the shifting perspectives and distances—from an extreme closeup of Bell's face to a view of the magazine's pages from her perspective—also allow the reader to shift in and out of identification with our heroine. "We" may laugh at Bell, but we must also laugh at ourselves at the same time.

Throughout the manga, Bell blurs the distinctions between real people and the characters she reads about. She reads people for the

FIG. 10.2 Bell discovers the latest issue of her beloved *Lady's Magazine*. Moto
Naoko, *Lady Victorian*, vol. 1 (Tokyo: Akitashoten, 1999), 12. © Moto Naoko
(Akitashoten), 1998–2007. Reproduced with permission.

narrative pleasures they can provide, but she also uses both people and texts as models for her aspirations to ladyhood. For example, in the two-page spread in which she first meets her future benefactress, Lady Ethel, as a result of a fortuitous accident in Hyde Park, we see Lady Ethel through Bell's eyes, as fetishized fragments of an inhumanly perfect object (see fig. 10.3). On the verso (right-hand page),[39] the first, largest panel, cutting diagonally down two-thirds of the page, shows Lady Ethel as Bell sees her. "Is she human?" Bell wonders. "Silver hair . . . grey eyes, pure white skin: just like . . . just like a silver-work goddess" (1:16–17; ellipses in original).[40] Bell's blush and the sparkles that fill the space above her head in the following frame—an establishing "reaction shot," to borrow cinematic language—show the same sort of emotional response to Lady Ethel as that induced by the *Lady's Magazine* in the previous scene. The top frame of the recto brings home Bell's perspective even more forcefully when we see Lady Ethel, all eyes, hair, and veil, over the top of Bell's head in the foreground.

Moto's play with the reader's twinned impulses to objectify and to identify is true to the mode of the original nineteenth-century ladies' magazines to which she alludes. Bell's *Lady's Magazine* is presumably named for the British periodical of the same name, which ran from 1770 to 1847. This publication and others targeting the same demographic, like *Blackwood's Lady's Magazine* (1836–60), included reverent reports of royal salons and other aristocratic social events, alongside thrilling serial fiction and sumptuously colored fashion plates (see fig. 10.4). As Margaret Beetham describes, these periodicals' emphases on "amusement and instruction" fueled aspirations: "[W]hereas 'amusement' assumed this lady already existed and sought to address her pleasure, 'instruction' assumed that the reader was not yet the lady she ought to be and sought to make good the lack."[41] Thus, visually speaking, the plates offered the figures of fashionable young ladies as attractive, consumable objects: their gowns, hair, accessories, and even setting drawn in minute detail, down to the pattern in the carpet and the varied textures of the trim on the gowns. However, the plates were also meant to function as a means of constructing the self: they were meant to be copied. The rendering of details was useful for dressmakers charged with reproducing the fashions (some magazines included the actual sewing patterns), and the smooth, blank surfaces of the

FIG. 10.3   Bell meets her future benefactress, Lady Ethel Constantia Westbury, in Hyde Park. Moto Naoko, *Lady Victorian,* vol. 1 (Tokyo: Akitashoten, 1999), 16–17. © Moto Naoko (Akitashoten), 1998–2007. Reproduced with permission.

ladies' faces—indistinguishable from one another in the tableau—create screens onto which the reader can project her own image. The fashion plates, thus, offer consumable objects and powerful vehicles for imagining the self.[42]

When Moto adopts this fashion-plate tableau (see fig. 10.5), the dynamic of objectification and projection becomes even clearer. In a full-page spread remarkably like the *Blackwood's Lady's Magazine* fashion plate, we see the apotheosis of Bell's fantasies: with Lady Ethel's coaching, she attends her first ball. The tiny frame in the upper right shows Lady Ethel offering some last-minute instructions to her protégée. This frame is inset within a larger one that gives us a closeup of Bell's blushing, smiling face with the flowers and sparkles again signifying her excitement and pleasure. The remaining three-quarters of the page, however, presents Bell as fashion plate. Whereas she is most often drawn as the observer or reader, here Bell is displayed from head to toe. The flowers in her hair, the bows, flowers, and layered tiers on her gown, her fan and jewelry: all are rendered in detail. Her eyes are

LE BON TON

Journal de Modes

publié par la Société des Journaux de Modes réunis

On s'abonne aux Bureaux, rue St. Anne, 64, à Paris.

FIG. 10.4 Fashion plate from *Blackwood's Lady's Magazine* 40 (1857), between pages 32 and 33. Reproduced by kind permission of the Syndics of Cambridge University Library.

FIG. 10.5 Bell attends her first ball, under the tutelage of Lady Ethel. Moto Naoko, *Lady Victorian,* vol. 2 (Tokyo: Akitashoten, 1999), 156. © Moto Naoko (Akitashoten), 1998–2007. Reproduced with permission.

closed. She is, in this instance, there to be looked at rather than to serve as a proxy for the reader's point of view. To underscore this shift, the gloved hand of Bell's dance partner emerges from the foreground as if projecting from the reader herself. "We" have become the possessor of a masculine, proprietary gaze.

The gender bending that Moto encourages in the reader's sensibilities is also fundamental to the plot of *Lady Victorian*. Soon after her introduction to Lady Ethel, Bell discovers a secret that shōjo readers would be trained to expect: the "perfect silver lady" (*kanpeki na gin no redī*) is really the alter identity of Argent Grey, working-class male author of *Governess Laura*, among other best-selling serial romances. While the tropes of cross-dressing and gender bending have been staples of shōjo manga at least since the persistently popular *The Rose of Versailles* (*Berusaiyu no Bara*) debuted in 1972,[43] the revelation of Ethel-Argent's dual identity, like so much in *Lady Victorian*, forces the reader to question her own identifications, attachments, and readerly habits. In two sequential two-page spreads, Moto takes her reader from something like Hitchcockian voyeurism (see fig. 10.6), with Bell guiltily spying on what she thinks will be a romantic assignation between Noel and Lady Ethel, to a direct confrontation with the disrobed Argent Grey, who disturbingly returns the reader's gaze (see fig. 10.7).

In the first two pages, Bell, having fallen asleep on the sofa waiting for her friends, is concealed from them when they enter the room. From her hidden vantage point, Bell overhears Noel say, "That dress is very beautiful, but I want you to take it off quickly, Lady Ethel" (1:46).[44] The facing page shows Lady Ethel's compliance with Noel's wish, as panels fragmented longwise show her first from the front, clothed—a cloud of lacy veil, flowers, ruffles, and hair, as usual—and then from behind, in dishabille, her chemise and the lacings of her corset just emerging into view as she discards the dress. A small panel in the upper right, superimposed over the image of Lady Ethel, shows only an extreme closeup of Bell's wide-open eye, which image is repeated in the last frame of the page. As the fragmenting of the frames and closeup eye images on the second page suggest, Bell is viewing the scene from her place of hiding, so the largest panel on the previous page bears closer attention. This is a full-facing image of Noel as he urges Lady Ethel to disrobe. We can tell from the tiny image of the two at the top of the following page that Noel is lounging in a chair while Lady Ethel stands

FIG. 10.6 Bell spies on Noel Scott and Lady Ethel. Moto Naoko, *Lady Victorian*, vol. 1 (Tokyo: Akitashoten, 1999), 46–47. © Moto Naoko (Akitashoten), 1998–2007. Reproduced with permission.

FIG. 10.7 Bell discovers Lady Ethel's alternate identity, Argent Grey. Moto Naoko, *Lady Victorian*, vol. 1 (Tokyo: Akitashoten, 1999), 48–49. © Moto Naoko (Akitashoten), 1998–2007. Reproduced with permission.

before him, and Bell watches from behind the back of the sofa. But in this frame he is looking directly at the viewer, a perspective impossible from Bell's point of view in the actual layout of the scene but possible if the viewer (Bell? the manga's reader?) has projected herself into the figure of Lady Ethel as the object of Noel's desiring gaze.

In other words, Moto's reader is propelled, along with Bell, into a position of simultaneous identification with and objectification (arguably erotic fetishization) of the perfect Lady Ethel. The impact of the full-page panel on the verso of the second two-page spread is shocking, therefore, not because Lady Ethel is "really" a man—which revelation, as I have mentioned already, would not be unexpected to readers familiar with the genre—but because the image suddenly thwarts the identificatory projection that the previous pages have so skillfully encouraged. Argent, bare to the waist, legs spread with one arm suggestively between his legs, the other akimbo, faces the reader's gaze directly. And even more shocking information is revealed on the recto: Argent is planning innovations to his fiction that will challenge Bell's generic expectations, just as his dual identity challenges her gender expectations. "Now, Noel," Argent says, "Let's start this new production meeting. . . . Jeez, this current affair has brought images bubbling to the surface! The heroine this time is going to be a new type of gover . . . !!" (1:49; second set of ellipses in original).[45] The content of Argent's announcement—interrupted by Bell's shocked exclamation revealing her presence—is that Bell herself inspires his newest literary creation.

The ostensible sex scene has been revealed as an editorial consultation, but this, in its way, is as emotionally fraught and shocking to our reader-heroine. Indeed, once Argent and Noel explain Argent's secret, the sentimental, sensational aspects of Argent-Ethel's double life easily secure Bell's sympathy and complicity.[46] However, Bell does not become so readily attached to the fictionalization of her own story. Rather, meeting herself as a "new type" of heroine when she reads the first instalment of Argent's next serial, *Lady Bell* (*Redī Beru*),[47] she is dismayed. Argent's literary experiment combines, as he says, the "super-popular governess" with the "popular 'lady detective'" (1:99).[48] But the intrepid "Lady Bell" does not conform to Bell's notions of an ideal lady, and so, ironically, she has more trouble projecting herself into the figure that actually resembles herself than she did into the conventional romance and idealized fashion–plate ladies she had heretofore enjoyed in the *Lady's Magazine.*

Bell's pleasure in *mis*recognition and displeasure in recognition, then, mark a point of convergence between Moto's *Lady Victorian* and Oliphant's meditation on "girls who read" in *Hester.* The messages conveyed here, as in *Hester,* are not straightforward. On the one hand, Bell's initial attachments to the *Lady's Magazine* and to romances like *Governess Laura* are presented as naïve. Through her relationship to Argent-Ethel, she must learn to accommodate complex subjectivities rather than just admiring glittering surfaces and investing in clichéd romance plots. Significantly, the manga resists presenting Argent Grey as the "true" identity of Lady Ethel or vice versa but instead persists in viewing them both as legitimate, if conflicted, selves. Lady Ethel's sense of filial duty, her attractions for and to handsome, exciting men (Noel included), and the romantic possibilities those might entail are offset by Argent's literary aspirations and desires to give his readers true representations of real women rather than familiar formulas and idealized heroines.

Throughout the series, Bell continually forgets that Ethel and Argent are the same person; she is repeatedly surprised to discover one where she expected to meet the other. And, fascinatingly, Moto represents Bell's coming to terms with Ethel-Argent's liminality through what one might call neo-Japonisme (see fig. 10.8). On this page, from a scene toward the end of volume 1, Bell bursts into Lady Ethel's boudoir, overflowing with good news that she has, thanks to Lady's Ethel's intercession, secured a new governess position. Instead of finding her ladylike benefactress, however, to her horror Bell discovers a half-dressed Argent. He is displayed from head to foot, in a full-page image that is intermittently interrupted by smaller superimposed frames. Wearing a kimono that falls off one shoulder and exposes one leg to the upper thigh, Argent resembles nothing so much as an image of eroticized, Orientalized femininity from the late nineteenth-century European Cult of Japan. Indeed, Argent very much calls to mind the seminude female figure in James Tissot's *La Japonaise au Bain* (1864), with her artfully draped open kimono leaving little to the imagination. The page's text makes Argent's connection to European Japonisme explicit. Mortified by the social impropriety of the situation, Bell screams and then stammers an apology, but to smooth over the awkwardness, she offers Argent a compliment: "Tha—that's a lovely nightgown." "Thank you," he replies, unruffled. "My father bought it for me in Paris." And in tiny, barely legible script, Moto offers an authorial aside, "It's Japonisme, isn't it?" (1:97).[49] Argent embodies a particular moment of British cultural appropriation of Japanese aesthetics (by way of French Aestheticism), and in conjunction with this nod to Japonisme, he also invokes a particularly fetishized version of exotic femininity. That he is also a man performing the role makes his (Japanese neo-Japonisme) version of femininity arguably no more or less inauthentic than Tissot's Orientalist *Japonaise*. The breakdown of the distinction between an "authentic" and a "translated" cultural aesthetic, one of the signal features of late nineteenth-century Japonisme, likewise blurs the lines between "real" and "faux" femininity.

Thus, the scene forces Bell to confront again her investments in Lady Ethel's performance of perfect femininity. It reminds her that Ethel-Argent is more than a screen upon which her desires can be projected (Argent in dishabille is no perfect lady). But in shifting Bell's, and the reader's, attention from the display of Argent's body to the kimono, the scene shows how the consumption of material objects not only shapes individual subjectivities but also mediates affective, intersubjective relationships. Tellingly, the final frame on the page (which is demarcated by the drape of Argent's kimono on the right and bleeds off the left-hand and bottom edges of the page) shows Argent and Bell seated together on a chaise examining the fabric of the kimono. In other words, the scene replays the same tension between woman-as-object and woman-as-consumer-of-objects that we see at work in the fashion plates of the ladies' magazines, taking us from an unthinking sensational response to a quieter contemplation of the stuff of femininity. That this contemplation happens around the twice-imported Japanese-Parisian object enables Moto's readers to see their own consumption of the neo-Victorian manga as similarly mediated by overlapping global-historical contexts.

Moto's comment on her own Japonisme bears close attention. The authorial interjection, "It's Japonisme, isn't it?"—written in miniscule script over the top of Bell's back at the edge of the final frame—is easily overlooked (and is certainly not legible in the image reproduced here). *Japonisme* is rendered in *katakana*, thusly: ジャ ポニズム. One of two syllabary systems that, along with the kanji

FIG. 10.8 Bell finds Argent in dishabille in his Japanese kimono. Moto
Naoko, *Lady Victorian,* vol. 1 (Tokyo: Akitashoten, 1999), 97. © Moto Naoko
(Akitashoten), 1998–2007. Reproduced with permission.

characters, make up Japanese script, katakana is generally reserved for foreign or loan words, and so even the word's shape, quite aside from its actual meaning, signals its status as cultural import. And of course the original French term (which was readily adopted in late Victorian English parlance) designates a slippery practice of cultural and aesthetic appropriation, with all the attendant anxieties, projections, and pleasures. Further, to translate Moto's text into English for the purposes of this chapter, I might choose merely to transcribe the term back to its original form, *Japonisme* (as I have chosen, for the sake of convenience to call the manga by its anglicized title, *Lady Victorian*), or following transcription conventions, I might Romanize ジャポニズ ム literally as it is written, *Japonizumu,* and so retain the sense of the term as *re*translated. Frankly, the latter course seems more in keeping with the spirit of the manga's self-conscious treatment of its "entangled relationships" with its cultural antecedents.

The microreference to *Japonizumu* stands synecdochically for the manga's larger project of layering Victorian and contemporary reading practices. As such, it calls attention to the palimpsestuous investments—in objects, in texts, in people (and people-as-objects), in the past, in one's own self-fashioning—that accrue in the reading practices of a Victorian-shōjo reader. But the aside also calls attention to itself as commentary. That the aside is so tiny might suggest Moto's faith in her readers' ability to be attentive to such detail, rather than only reading for the sensational plot. It labels the space that it occupies on the page as the cognitive space for self-conscious reflection. Emerging literally in the interstices between frames, and atop the image of the manga's reader-heroine, the aside demonstrates the nascent possibilities for a thinking through of what "the Victorian" might mean, not just to critics and scholars in the "fuzzing-up of conventional classificatory categories . . . [and] the collapse of neatly maintained epistemic borders," as Rey Chow calls it,[50] but also in the fashioning of entangled gendered (and generic) readerly subjectivities.

This cultivated readerly subjectivity, finally, is what Moto offers as the payoff for *Lady Victorian*. In the resolution of the manga, Bell's ability to maintain her investments in romantic fictions, like Lady Ethel's perfect femininity, alongside her ability to reflect thoughtfully and compassionately on real-life situations, like Argent-Ethel's counterpoised desires, is what delivers the manga's happy ending:

Noel and Bell end up together (of course!), but even more importantly, Noel, who has sold the *Lady's Magazine,* will undertake a new
venture, a magazine for girls that will offer more-substantive content,
to which his new bride will be a regular contributor (see fig. 10.9).
Noel proposes that Bell write her own column, "Bell-Sensei's Governess Corner" (19:105).[51] As Noel explains, he will publish something that is "not a tedious manner book" but instead a magazine
that will enable "embryonic ladies to understand the world outside
their shells" (19:103).[52] Bell is perfectly suited to this project precisely
because she retains her pleasure in stories and in people and thus
can sympathize with young readers' tastes, even as she trains them to
become more-savvy readers. "You'll be everyone's sensei, Bell," Noel
asserts (19:105).[53] Bell demurs: "Wait a minute! Such a big job! To be
all the readers' lady-sensei? For that, one would truly have to be a
perfect lady, and I'm not equal to the task . . ." But upon reading affir-
mation in Noel's loving gaze, she assents: "Yes . . . I'm becoming one"

FIG. 10.9   Noel pitches his idea of a magazine column for girls, "Bell-Sensei's
Governess Corner." Moto Naoko, *Lady Victorian,* vol. 19 (Tokyo: Akitashoten,
1999), 104–5. © Moto Naoko (Akitashoten), 1998–2007. Reproduced with
permission.

(19:105–6; ellipses in the original).⁵⁴ It is worth noting that Moto's drawing style changes quite a bit over the course of the manga, so the later volumes show cleaner lines, less exaggerated facial features, and fewer frills, flowers, and sparkles; nevertheless, Bell's more restrained appearance here also indicates her maturation within the story.

The scene collapses the distinctions between romantic love and textual excitement: Noel lifts Bell in the air and embraces her. In this scene, too, Bell blushes, while sparkles light up the background, but whether the excitement is because of Noel or whether it refers to the idea of the column is not clear, for in center of the page, overflowing from their own gutterless frame into the adjacent frames, are the imagined "embryonic ladies" whom Bell will instruct. Though seven other frames on these two pages show either Bell or Noel, or both together, this central tableau of "girls who read" captures the gaze. These girls are one of the big narrative rewards for *Lady Victorian*'s readers. Bell, the "girl reader," becomes, through her reading—most of all through her ability to be entertained and affected by what (and whom) she reads—the ideal producer of reading material for girls. Girls' reading is reimagined not as a dangerous or frivolous pastime but as cultivating broad-reaching, ethically sound sensibilities.

Moto thus explores the interpenetration of generic form and gendered subjectivity, demonstrating that readerly affects, like texts, may be layered palimpsestuously. Just as one reads the neo-Victorian governess plot through the layers of its Victorian antecedents, so too does one experience the sensational pleasures of the manga's romance plot overlaid with the intellectual pleasures of its metafictional self-critique. It is precisely through acknowledging the entanglement of these seemingly divergent pleasures that *Lady Victorian* writes itself into the long history of girls who read.

Notes

1. Margaret Oliphant, *Hester,* ed. Philip Davis and Brian Nellist (1883; Oxford: Oxford University Press, 2003), 90.

2. The title of the manga in the original is written in *katakana* to spell "Lady Victorian" phonetically: "Redī Vikutorian" (レディー・ヴィク トリアン). For the sake of convenience, I have opted to use the English rendering of the title, rather than retaining the Romanized Japanese. Throughout I use the Japanese convention of surname first for authors

writing in Japanese; thus, Moto Naoko's surname is Moto, her given name Naoko. For writers with Japanese names writing in English, I have used the English convention of surname last.

3. Lauren Berlant, *The Female Complaint: The Unfinished Business of Sentimentality in American Culture* (Durham, NC: Duke University Press, 2008), 35.

4. [Margaret Oliphant], "Sensation Novels," *Blackwood's Edinburgh Magazine* 91 (May 1862): 568.

5. Likewise, in the shōjo manga industry, "the corporate editors are primarily men and the artists are all young women." Jennifer Prough, *Straight from the Heart: Gender, Intimacy, and the Cultural Production of Shōjo Manga* (Honolulu: University of Hawai'i Press, 2010), 6.

6. Kate Mitchell, *History and Cultural Memory in Neo-Victorian Fiction: Victorian Afterimages* (Basingstoke, UK: Palgrave Macmillan, 2010), 7.

7. Thierry Groensteen, *The System of Comics*, trans. Bart Beaty and Nick Nguyen (Jackson: University Press of Mississippi, 2007), 17–18.

8. Linda Hutcheon, *A Theory of Adaptation*, 2nd ed., with contributions by Siobhan O'Flynn (London: Routledge, 2013), 6; Anna Maria Jones, "'Palimpsestuous' Attachments: Framing a Manga Theory of the Global Neo-Victorian," in "Neo-Victorianism and Globalisation: Transnational Dissemination of Nineteenth-Century Cultural Texts," ed. Antonija Primorac and Monika Pietrzak-Franger, special issue, *Neo-Victorian Studies* 8, no. 1 (2015): 17–47.

9. Louisa Hadley, *Neo-Victorian Fiction and Historical Narrative: The Victorians and Us* (Basingstoke, UK: Palgrave Macmillan, 2010), 10.

10. Ann Heilmann and Mark Llewellyn, *Neo-Victorianism: The Victorians in the Twenty-First Century, 1999–2009* (Basingstoke, UK: Palgrave Macmillan, 2010), 17–18.

11. Kate Flint, *The Woman Reader, 1837–1914* (Oxford, UK: Clarendon Press, 1993), 15.

12. Beth Palmer, "Are the Victorians Still with Us? Victorian Sensation Fiction and Its Legacies in the Twenty-First Century," *Victorian Studies* 52, no. 1 (2009): 87, 92.

13. Sigmund Freud, "The Uncanny," in *An Infantile Neurosis and Other Works*, vol. 17 of *The Standard Edition of the Complete Psychological Works of Sigmund Freud,* ed. and trans. James Strachey with Anna Freud, Alix Strachey, and Alan Tyson (London: Hogarth Press, 1955), 248.

14. See Yoko Chiba, "Japonisme: East-West Renaissance in the Late 19th Century," *Mosaic* 31, no. 2 (1998): 1–20.

15. Mark Llewellyn and Ann Heilmann, "The Victorians Now: Global Reflections on Neo-Victorianism," *Critical Quarterly* 55, no. 1

(2013): 28. In fact, significant work has been done in comics studies to bridge linguistic and national boundaries. See, e.g., Jaqueline Berndt, ed., *Comics Worlds and the World of Comics: Towards Scholarship on a Global Scale* (Kyoto: Kyoto Seika University Press, 2010).

16. Rey Chow, *Entanglements, or Transmedial Thinking about Capture* (Durham, NC: Duke University Press, 2012), 10–11.

17. The term *nonaggregate community* comes from Naoki Sakai's provocative *Translation and Subjectivity: On "Japan" and Cultural Nationalism* (Minneapolis: University of Minnesota Press, 1997), 8. He defines it as a metaphorical space in which "we are together and can address ourselves as 'we' because we are distant from one another and because our togetherness is not ground [*sic*] on a common homogeneity" (7).

18. Llewellyn and Heilmann, "The Victorians Now," 28. I make this point at greater length elsewhere: see Jones, "'Palimpsestuous' Attachments," 37–38.

19. Jennifer Phegley, *Educating the Proper Woman Reader: Victorian Family Literary Magazines and the Cultural Health of the Nation* (Columbus: Ohio State University Press, 2004), 4.

20. Ibid., 7. See also Palmer, "Are the Victorians," 87. For a thorough account of Victorian serials, see Linda K. Hughes and Michael Lund, *The Victorian Serial* (Charlottesville: University of Virginia Press, 1991).

21. Flint, *Woman Reader*, 14.

22. Comparing herself to the fictional ideal, Hester "concluded that she was not pretty, and regretted it, though in her circumstances it mattered very little. . . . [S]he was never likely to produce the effect which heroines in novels—even though comparatively plain—did produce." Oliphant, *Hester*, 90.

23. See, e.g., Elizabeth Ho, *Neo-Victorianism and the Memory of Empire* (New York: Continuum, 2012); Ho, "Victorian Maids and Neo-Victorian Labour in Kaoru Mori's *Emma: A Victorian Romance*," *Neo-Victorian Studies* 6, no. 2 (2013): 40–63; Llewellyn and Heilmann, "Victorians Now"; Antonija Primorac and Monika Pietrzak-Franger, eds., "Neo-Victorianism and Globalisation: Transnational Dissemination of Nineteenth-Century Cultural Texts," special issue of *Neo-Victorian Studies* 8, no. 1 (2015): 1–206. See also chapter 2 in the present volume.

24. Eleanor J. Hogan and Inger Sigrun Brodey, "Jane Austen in Japan: 'Good Mother' or 'New Woman'?" *Persuasions* 28, no. 2 (2008), www.jasna.org/persuasions/on-line/vol28no2/index.html. For a good overview of the official Meiji policy regarding women—encapsulated in the Ministry of Education's official phrase "Ryōsai Kenbo" ("Good

Wife, Wise Mother")—see Sharon H. Nolte and Sally Ann Hastings, "The Meiji State's Policy toward Women, 1890–1910," in *Recreating Japanese Women, 1600–1945,* ed. Gail Lee Bernstein (Berkeley: University of California Press, 1991), 152. Imperfectly analogous to the Victorian "Angel in the House," the notion of the "Good Wife, Wise Mother" fitted woman into a subordinate role in a patriarchal culture but, at the same time, accorded her moral authority.

25. Rebecca Copeland, *Lost Leaves: Women Writers of Meiji Japan* (Honolulu: University of Hawai'i Press, 2000), 11.

26. For an account of "adaptive translations" of Western literature in Meiji Japan, see J. Scott Miller, *Adaptations of Western Literature in Meiji Japan* (New York: Palgrave, 2001); for a discussion of Alcott's *Little Women* in late Meiji Japan, see Hiromi Tsuchiya Dollase, "*Shōfujin* (Little Women): Recreating Jo for the Girls of Meiji Japan," *Japanese Studies* 30, no. 2 (2010): 247–62. Dollase stresses the ways that women's translation created space for female self-fashioning and identification in excess of the official Meiji restrictions on women's social agency. See also Hogan and Brodey, "Jane Austen in Japan"; Copeland, *Lost Leaves,* 99–158; Melek Ortabasi, "Brave Dogs and Little Lords: Thoughts on Translation, Gender, and the Debate on Childhood in Mid-Meiji," in *Translation in Modern Japan,* ed. Indra Levy (New York: Routledge, 2011), 186–212.

27. Prough, *Straight from the Heart,* 3.

28. Titles for women and girls range from "G-rated" to explicit and from idealized romance to "grittier" realism, so speaking broadly of the defining characteristics of shōjo or josei is difficult. Prough offers an excellent in-depth account of the shōjo industry. For a good overview of "boys' love" manga, especially its history, relation to Western slash fiction, and nuances of terminology, see Kumiko Saito, "Desire in Subtext: Gender, Fandom, and Women's Male-Male Homoerotic Parodies in Contemporary Japan," *Mechademia* 6 (2011): 171–91; see also Dru Pagliassotti, "Better Than Romance? Japanese BL Manga and the Subgenre of Male/Male Romantic Fiction," in *Boys' Love Manga: Essays on the Sexual Ambiguity and Cross-Cultural Fandom of the Genre,* ed. Antonia Levi, Mark McHarry, and Dru Pagliassotti (Jefferson, NC: McFarland, 2010), 59–83.

29. Prough, *Straight from the Heart,* 3.

30. As Prough describes in *Straight from the Heart,* the figure of the shōjo became emblematic of Japan's economic downturn: "[I]n the 1990s she not only represented contemporary social ills and consumption

itself . . . but she also became the symbol for the feminization and infantilization of postmodern Japan" (10).

31. Like the term *otaku,* which is most often applied to male fans, *fujoshi* is both a pejorative term and one that is used by fans to self-identify. For more on fujoshi, see Daisuke Okabe and Kimi Ishida, "Making *Fujoshi* Identity Visible and Invisible," in *Fandom Unbound: Otaku Culture in a Connected World,* ed. Mizuko Ito, Daisuke Okabe, and Izumi Tsuji (New Haven, CT: Yale University Press, 2012), 207–24; Patrick Gailbraith, "*Fujoshi*: Fantasy Play and Transgressive Intimacy among 'Rotten Girls' in Contemporary Japan," *Signs* 37, no. 1 (2011): 211–32; Matthew Thorn, "Girls and Women Getting Out of Hand: The Pleasures and Politics of Japan's Amateur Comics Community," in *Fanning the Flames: Fans and Consumer Culture in Contemporary Japan,* ed. William W. Kelly (Albany: SUNY Press, 2004), 169–86. Joli Jenson, speaking of English-language fans more broadly, sums up: "The literature on fandom is haunted by images of deviance," which are often taken to be indicative of a larger "social dysfunction." Joli Jenson, "Fandom as Pathology: The Consequences of Characterization," in *Adoring Audience: Fan Culture and Popular Media,* ed. Lisa A. Lewis (London: Routledge, 1992), 9.

32. Much fan studies scholarship does trace genealogies back to more or less distant pasts. For example, Henry Jenkins argues, with a nod to *Jane Eyre,* that representations of the pathologized "fan in the attic" can "no doubt trace their roots back to earlier representations of distracted or overidentified readers, such as *Don Quixote* or *Madame Bovary,* and enjoy a place in centuries-old debates about the dangers of consuming fiction." Henry Jenkins, *Textual Poachers: Television Fans and Participatory Culture,* 20th anniv. ed. (New York: Routledge, 2013), 14–15.

33. There has been a fair amount of scholarship drawing correspondences and distinctions between Japanese and Western women readers, particularly between *fujoshi* and slash-fiction fans. See Koichi Iwabuchi, "Undoing Inter-national Fandom in the Age of Brand Nationalism," *Mechademia* 5 (2010): 87–96; Pagliassotti, "Better than Romance?," 59–83; Saito, "Desire in Subtext," 171–91.

34. Flint, *Woman Reader,* 283.

35. The character names Bell and Argent Grey, to say nothing of the opening scene of the manga, in which Bell discovers that her new employers are vulgar parvenus, surely allude to *Agnes Grey* and its pseudonymous author, Acton Bell. Likewise, when Bell's second governess position leads her to a haunted house where she must protect her innocent young charge from the ghosts therein, it is hard not to think of James's novella.

36. Sakai, *Translation and Subjectivity*, 8. See note 17.

37. Moto Naoko, *Redī Vikutorian* [Lady Victorian], 20 vols. (Tokyo: Akitashoten, 1999–2007), 1:12 (ellipses in original): *"ko— . . . kore wa!! 'Redīzu magajin no saishingō!! Mō deteta no!?"* Hereafter cited in text. For this and all remaining quotations from Japanese text, I have provided English translations in the body of the essay with the Romanized transcription of the original, using Revised Hepburn conventions, in the notes. All translations are my own. Thanks to Kimiko Akita for checking my work. Any errors are entirely my own.

38. *"Āgento Gurei no rensai shōsetsu 'Govuanesu Rōra,' govuanesu to miryokuteki na yatoinushi to no rabu romansu. Aa . . . konna koi ga dekitara naa—"*

39. Verso and recto are reversed for Japanese texts. Hence, when I refer to *verso* and *recto*, I mean the right-hand and left-hand pages, respectively.

40. *"Ningen? Gin no kami . . . shiruba gurei no hitomi masshiro na hada. Marude . . . marude ginzaiku no megami-sama mitai."*

41. Margaret Beetham, *A Magazine of Her Own? Domesticity and Desire in the Woman's Magazine, 1800–1914* (London: Routledge, 1996), 24. See also chapter 9 in the present volume; for a discussion of fashion plates in particular, see Sharon Marcus, "Reflections on Victorian Fashion Plates," *Differences: A Journal of Feminist Cultural Studies* 14, no. 3 (2003): 4–33.

42. Scott McCloud suggests an inverse relationship between realistic detail and the reader's identification with a comics character; more-detailed characters are objectified, while more-iconic or simplified characters enable "masking," or the reader's projection into the character. McCloud, *Understanding Comics: The Invisible Art* (New York: HarperCollins, 1993), 42–44.

43. Ikeda Ryoko's *The Rose of Versailles* is one of the titles credited with ushering in the heyday of shōjo manga. It tells the story of a girl who is raised as a boy and becomes a royal guard to Marie Antoinette on the eve of the French Revolution.

44. *"Sono duresu wa totemo kirei dakedo hayaku nuide hoshī na Redī Eseru."*

45. *"Sā Noeru shinaku no uchiawase o hajimeyou ze. . . . Mō ore kondo no jiken de imēji wakimakuri da ze. Kondo no hiroin wa atarashī taipu no onnakateikyou . . ."* The "current affair" in question is Bell's recent brush with the law and subsequent vindication.

46. Argent, a workhouse orphan, was adopted as a child by the Westbury family because his uncanny resemblance to their dead daughter allowed him to be trained to inhabit her identity, thus saving the bereaved mother from her crippling grief. The mother does not know that Ethel is not really her daughter.

47. *Lady Bell* was actually the title of a historical novel serialized in *Good Words* in 1873. It begins with fourteen-year-old Lady Bell Etheredge at her first queen's drawing-room. Sarah Tytler [Henrietta Keddie], *Lady Bell: A Story of Last Century* (London: Strahan, 1873).

48. *"Motemote no onnakateikyōshi no ueryūkō no no 'onnatantei' demo aru."*

49. BELL: *"Su . . . suteki na o-nemaki desu ne."* ARGENT: *"Arigatō. O-tō-sama ga Pari de kattekite kudasatta no."* AUTHORIAL ASIDE: *"Japonizumu de yatsu desu ne."* Thanks to Clarissa Graffeo for help deciphering the microscopic script of this last quotation.

50. Chow, *Entanglements*, 10.

51. *"Beru-sensei no gavanesu cōnā."*

52. *"Katakurushii o-gyougihon [manābukku] jyanaku . . . jitsuyouteki na bakari de taikutsu na shinansho [gaido bukku] demo naku redī no tamago ga kara no soto no sekai o shirukoto ga dekiru yume no aru zasshi [hon]."* The quotation literally says "egg-ladies," so Noel's statement plays with the metaphor of girls "hatching" out of their shells into more-worldly sensibilities. The brackets in the transcription indicate places where the *furigana* diverges from the kanji glosses (e.g., where "o-gyougihon" is the pronunciation of the kanji but *manābukku* is the transliteration of the English "manner book").

53. *"Minna no sensei ni naru nda Beru."*

54. *"Ma . . . matte kudasai!! Sonna taiyaku!! Dokusha minna no sensei redī toshite ne. So . . . sore tte hontōni suteki na redī janai to tsutomarana . . . hai . . . narimasu sonna redī ni."*

AFTERWORD

Photography, Palimpsests, and the Neo-Victorian

KATE FLINT

Photography. Invented very early in Victoria's reign, it was used, from the start, both to tell and to illustrate stories. If *Drawing on the Victorians: The Palimpsest of Victorian and Neo-Victorian Graphic Texts* is predicated on the idea of the palimpsest—the present overwriting the past, yet the past still glimmering through—then the photograph claims a particular role in relation to this phenomenon. Anna Maria Jones and Rebecca N. Mitchell have brilliantly conceived of a volume that pays attention to graphic neo-Victorianism as well as to its written manifestation. In so doing, they bring together contributors who reveal the wide reach of transnational exchange not just within the Victorian period itself but in its later reinterpretations. Importantly, these contributors show how visual and verbal forms worked together to dramatize and interrogate cultural assumptions during Victoria's reign as well as subsequently. Graphic neo-Victorianism thus does not spring into unprepared territory: the volume demonstrates that, rather, for an author/artist to employ images as well as words is a further form of palimpsest, writing over an intermedial dialogue that Victorians themselves had put into place.

David Octavius Hill and Robert Adamson's scenes from Walter Scott, taken in the 1840s, exemplify the temporal complexities that are exhibited by so many of the subjects in this volume.[1] They use what was, at the time, a highly modern medium to illustrate a recent interpretation of a former period. By incorporating their own bodies, Hill and Adamson give these images a metareferentiality, the portrayer of the past appearing as one of the portrayed in a way that directly comments on the process of writing history and historical fiction: one can do so only from the immediacy of one's own moment. This collapsing of present and past, of live human with imaginary character, is a form of imaginative projection that bears significant similarities to Nigerian-born British artist Yinka Shonibare's series *Diary of a Victorian Dandy* (1998). How, these photographs ask, might someone behave when transplanted from their customary surroundings and given the opportunity to be "someone else" —or, rather, to "be themselves" in an unfamiliar place? Despite their nineteenth-century settings, these images are suspended somewhere between the tableau vivant and a Hogarth canvas—a painterly and moralizing influence that, as Brian Maidment's chapter in this volume attests, was still a powerful force in the early Victorian period. Hogarth's narratives, indeed, have seemed "like film stills" to Shonibare, who openly pays tribute to Hogarth's influence, as well as acknowledging the models of such practitioners of staged photography as Jeff Wall and Cindy Sherman. Shonibare borrows from his eighteenth-century predecessor to provoke us to think about history through an enactment of the counterfactual.

Victorian Dandy takes us through a Victorian aristocrat's day: his early morning, with four nubile maids and his valet; a spell in the well-furnished library, with four more young swells sycophantically applauding him, the valet/amanuensis, quill poised, at the desk, and the bevy of maids once again in attendance; a turn at the billiard table, with his companions looking ever more dissolute; being toasted, and fawned over, at an evening party; and the day ending in a wild sexual romp (see fig. A.1).[2] These settings and costumes, of course—the Indian rug, the rich silks—bear witness to the trade routes of empire, a point that Shonibare had already made in his 1996–97 installation piece, *The Victorian Philanthropist's Parlour*, with furniture upholstered in batik print (an Indonesian fabric printing technique industrialized by Dutch colonizers in the mid-nineteenth century and applied to cloth made in Manchester, producing a fabric that, while still exported to Africa for use in traditional dress, Shonibare bought in

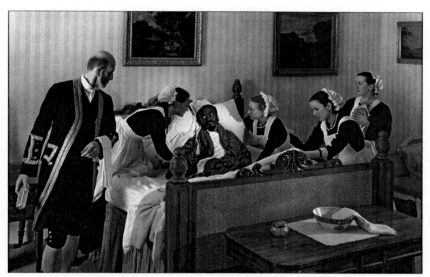

FIG. A.1   Yinka Shonibare, *Diary of a Victorian Dandy: 11:00 Hours* © Yinka Shonibare MBE. All rights reserved, DACS 2015. Reproduced with permission.

Brixton market) and walls covered in similar material, overprinted with images of black footballers.

Several things are at work in Shonibare's choice of the Victorian period—one he was to return to three years later in a series of photographs with himself as Dorian Gray. These factors link his work to the questions raised, in this volume, by Monika Pietrzak-Franger's and Anna Maria Jones's attention to transnational appropriation and adaptation. His interest in the period dates back to Mrs. Thatcher talking in the 1980s about returning to Victorian values, and he recalls, "I was thinking: Okay, so where do I stand? I live in England. I'm from Nigeria. Nigeria was colonized by the British. The Victorian era was the height of colonialism in Africa. How do I relate to the repressive Victorian regime? So Victorian for me actually means conquest and imperialism. And so, in a sense, it is actually my fear. So what I then decided to do was actually confront my fear and face my fear."[3] With this in mind, the images may be read in numerous ways. One can read the dandy (a repeatedly potent figure in neo-Victorian work) as someone who is using his dress, his style, and his wit to seem perfectly at home in a class and environment that he was not, most likely, born into—a commentary both on racial assimilation and, given the initial placement of this commissioned photograph as a poster on the

London Underground, on the operations of consumer society more generally. Indeed, Shonibare's work is thus a complex contemporary example of the breaking down of categories of high and mass art that is a recurrent theme in this volume. Or—and this suggestion comes from Shonibare—one can see the dandy as invoking parody and masquerade. The artist has pointed out the importance of carnival days in the Caribbean, both during the time of slavery and more recently: "If you were a slave or a poor person, you could dress up as an aristocrat. Carnival day was the one day the aristocrats were the working class. It was the one day you could be whatever you wanted to be."[4] Or one can note the autobiographical resonances in the work: the photographer translates his own privileged, servant-surrounded Nigerian upbringing into the surroundings of a self-regarding Victorian young man of leisure: a counterfactual version of where and how social power was possessed and made itself felt. Shonibare is creating what he calls "fantasies of empowerment in relation to white society, even if historically that equilibrium or equality really hasn't arrived yet."[5] At the same time, of course, he is interrogating the arrogance and the exploitation that so readily accompanies economic and social superiority. What runs throughout, and what helps makes this series irreducible to any one clear message (how *does* one find a stable ethical position from which to read this parodic enjoyment of hedonism by an African dandy?), is Shonibare's love of paradox. This is something that has been consolidated by the bestowal on him, in 2005, of an MBE—initials that he now flamboyantly flaunts as part of his name. "For me this is politically interesting because, of course, this is what I make my work about, and now I am actually a real member of the British Empire! And it's very important for my work, because it makes my name look like a performance on the page."[6]

Shonibare appropriates Victorian tropes to reject the ideology that they represent—a neo-Victorian strategy that runs close to the form of critique discussed by Heidi Kaufman and Jessica Straley in their chapters in this volume. Clare Strand's series *Gone Astray* (2002–3) offers a different type of interpretive challenge, one that—like the chapters by Anna Maria Jones and Jennifer Phegley herein—throws the onus back onto the role and responsibility of the reader.[7] Rather than costuming her subjects in Victorian clothes, Strand set up her actors, with carefully chosen props, as urban types—people whom, as she put it, "she would expect to find on any urban street (see fig. A.2). If they weren't there, I'd want to know why not."[8] They may look modern, but they are set against Victorian-style, incongruously pastoral backdrops. The series was made during a year's residency at the London College of Printing, when Strand took the opportunity to research various aspects of the city, reading William Blake, William Morris, Henry Mayhew, and, above all, Charles Dickens. The painted

FIG. A.2   Clare Strand, from *Gone Astray Portraits, 2001/2* © Clare Strand. Image courtesy Clare Strand and Grimaldi Gavin. Reproduced with permission.

backdrops that Mayhew mentions in his piece on photographers in *London Labour and the London Poor* (1851) provided a key starting point, and Strand melded these with the theatricality of the streets that Dickens writes about in his 1853 *Household Words* piece "Gone Astray." This article recalls the time when he was lost in the City as a boy, and while navigating the unfamiliar streets and the gigantic buildings through a combination of common sense and fairy tales, he found himself enjoying, up to a point, "the dismal dignity of being lost."[9]

Dickens perhaps had Mayhew's description of crafty beggars in mind when he looked back to himself as a small boy close up by St. Giles's Church and wrote, "I had romantic ideas in connection with that religious edifice; firmly believing that all the beggars who pretended through the week to be blind, lame, deaf and dumb, and otherwise physically afflicted, laid aside their pretenses every Sunday, dressed themselves in holiday clothes and attended divine service in the temple of their patron saint."[10] This passage was key for Strand, too. "Many times," she said, "I have moments wondering if people have been placed on the streets from central casting—as their being there is too expected, too clichéd."[11] These are the costumed subjects of her photographs: the woman who tries to look work-respectable but is betrayed by grubby sneakers, running mascara, and a Sainsbury's plastic bag; the smartly dressed figure apparently unaware of the hole and ladder in her tights; the muscly young guy in loose jeans, wrist bandages, and a pusillanimous stare; the young man wearing a hoody, with a possibly bloody nose, and something crumpled—a letter? a banknote?—in his right hand. The awkward, vulnerable poses suggest the latent violence (whether about to be performed or recently executed) that makes these images uncomfortable viewing. Although the images do not express—except possibly in the apparent lack of self-knowledge in the characters—the credulity of the boy Dickens, a bridge between the past and the present, between Dickens's piece and Strand's dressed-up portraits, is provided by a sentence in "Gone Astray" that hits home even harder today than it did when the photographs were made. "What did I know then," Dickens asked, "about the multitude who are always being disappointed in the City; who are always expecting to meet a party there, and to receive money there, and whose expectations are never fulfilled?"[12] Strand's portraits, moreover, of ostensibly unattractive people can be turned back into our general reading of Dickens, bringing home a basic interpretive and ethical point that tends to get lost through the compelling quirkiness of his prose and the weightiness of his specific targets for social reform: we would probably hurry on past a lot of his characters if we saw them in the street. Strand's series, with Dickens's "Gone Astray" as its foundational text, raises issues about how we make assumptions—now as in the Victorian period—about those who inhabit urban spaces: assumptions based on typology and the inherent assumptions on which it relies, a fleeting glance launching narratives in our imagination without us having any idea whether our surface reading of their appearance bears any true relation to what lies within.

The materiality of Victorian photographic conventions exists in these images in those incongruous, aspirational backdrops. But one encounters the force of materiality even more powerfully in my final example, Australian photographer Tracey Moffatt's *Laudanum* (1998).[13] This is a series of nineteen pictures, with one of these, the gothically gloomy overgrown exterior to a house, repeated three times. The images are in black and white: they are photogravure prints, many cut to resemble the shapes found in Victorian albums. Some are scratched and bear other blemishes, and this damage to the photos may be read as paralleling the physical and psychic damage that they seem to represent. For while this is a narrative sequence of a sort, it is an obscure, blurred, and unfocused one. We are left to decide whether the visual obscurity represents the passage of time and the illogicalities and gaps in historical transmission, or the unrecoverability of aspects of colonial, women's, and native history, or the swirled confusion of opium's effects.

Moffatt's opening shot shows a maid prostrate at the feet of her employer; on the opposite page is a brief extract from Jean Paulhan's preface to Pauline Réage's 1954 *Story of O*, her fictional account of masochistic heterosexual sexual submission and blissful humiliation. "It is only when you make me suffer that I feel safe and secure,"[14] reads one sentence here, and the photographs that follow show the maid bound by ropes and under constant scrutiny in her "punishment"; her hair being shorn; lying apparently satiated while it is the other woman's turn to seem exhausted; playing in some indecipherable way with branches or flowers on the dining room floor; bound in a cell—and then what?—as the mistress dances, wildly, in what looks like a show of flames or crazed ectoplasm; then dragging herself wearily up the stairs, with a large, striped, bolster or sack-like object, contents unknown, lying in the maid's place.

As well as generically referencing the appearance of nineteenth-century photography, the unsettling theme of knowledgeable inno-cence is reinforced by the similarity of some of the pictures of the maid to certain of Charles Dodgson's images, especially those of Xie Kitchin: images that in turn reference photographs as well as paintings of odalisques, and point forward to E. J. Bellocq's early twentieth-century scratched and battered plates of New Orleans prostitutes. The Oriental connection is important here. As any scholar of Wilkie Col-lins's *The Moonstone* (1868) knows, opium cannot be detached from the Oriental connotations of its origin and consumption.[15] Moreover, when Queensland's colonial government introduced the legislation in 1897 that confined its Aboriginal population to reservations and missions,[16] the fact that it also restricted the sale of opium suggests that Aboriginal use of this drug was a matter of concern—although in Moffatt's work, the white woman, not the maid, would seem to be the one who has taken the drug (although at times it seems to be the photographer or the spectator, too). As well as offering a commentary through this photo sequence on the pleasures (and dangers) of sexual submission and the exhausting effects on the dominatrix, the half-Aboriginal Moffatt is also, through her choice of an apparently native maid for this series, commenting on the possible pleasures—or at least the complicity—involved in colonial submission.

Yet Moffatt's photographs make us ask, whose pleasures, in the end? Those of the maid or of her mistress? The maid, after all, may simply have gotten up and walked off; the sequence may be an entire dream-fantasy based on the laudanum-taking mistress's habits (and is she taking it to escape pain or boredom?). And that pillow, or bolster—rather than being a damaged body, it may be just a pillow, perhaps the object onto which the older woman projected and en-acted some of her desires: its presence suddenly clear to her for what it is, signifying all that she crawls away from, naked and exhausted and abject, back up the stairs. In this context, the scratches on the image surfaces look less like a technique to signify the patina of age than an attempt to obliterate the shameful: they refer less to the damage a material object suffers through time than they suggest an individual act of destruction that nonetheless stops short of total obliteration.

This muted iconoclasm also speaks to the possible ambivalences that accompany the restrained mutilation of Bellocq's plates: shame and desire comingled. The refusal of the sequence to render up a clear meaning, additionally, produces the unstable borders between lust and abjection, between fantasy and acting on one's desires, between knowledge in the present and knowledge of the past. In allowing the viewer's imagination to enter in, to speculate about who what might be doing what to whom and gaining what kind of pleasure from it, *Laudanum* blurs the ground between acting and reality when it comes to sexual role playing in general. We are invited to project our own responses onto a sequence to make sense of it, and hence, as with so many of the works discussed in this volume, our reading produces only the most fragile of distinctions between a "then" and a "now."

These photographers rely on their viewers' interpretive imagination to think not only about connections between the experience of the past and now but also between earlier and current practices of representation. They are animated not so much by an idea of a human, sensory and emotional continuum that makes the past as close as yesterday, personalizing it, but by the very practices and conventions of photography, and indeed photographs and paintings themselves and their material and compositional forms. They participate in the disruption of temporal boundaries and in the creation of what Katie King has termed "pastpresents . . . quite palpable evidences that the past and the present cannot be purified from each other."[17] By playing with material continuities, and also with artificiality, incongruity, hallucination, and the imagination, they enact, in their varied forms, the central premise that Jones and Mitchell bring out through this splendid collection of essays: the richness and variety of historical interpretation and reinvention that resides within the interplay of image and text in neo-Victorian imaginative work.

Notes

1. See Jordan Bear, "'The Experienced Eye of the Antiquary': Hill and Adamson's Medieval Revival," *PhotoResearcher* 20 (2013): 46–55.

2. Examples of Yinka Shonibare's *Diary of a Victorian Dandy* series can be seen in the artist profile "Yinka Shonibare" on the Victoria and Albert Museum website, www.vam.ac.uk/content/articles/s/yinka–shonibare/ (accessed on 10 March 2015).

3. Yinka Shonibare MBE, interview by Chris Boyd, *The Morning After: Performing Arts in Australia*, 30 September 2008, http://chrisboyd. blogspot.com/2008/09/yinka-shonibare-1-mad-world.html.

4. Yinka Shonibare MBE, interview by Richard Lacayo, *Time*, 7 July 2009, http://lookingaround.blogs.time.com/2009/07/07/more-talk-with -yinka-shonibare/.

5. Yinka Shonibare MBE, interview by Anthony Downey, *Bomb* 93 (Fall 2005), www.bombsite.com/issues/93/articles/2777.

6. "Interview with Yinka Shonibare MBE," by Bernard Müller, in *Garden of Love*, by Yinka Shonibare MBE (Paris: Flammarion, 2007), 22.

7. See www.clarestrand.co.uk/works/?id=100 (accessed on 10 March 2015).

8. "Interview: Clare Strand in Conversation with Chris Mullin," in *Clare Strand: A Photoworks Monograph*, by Rebecca Drew (Brighton, UK: Photoworks, 2009), 95.

9. [Charles Dickens], "Gone Astray," *Household Words* 13 August 1853, 553.

10. Ibid., 553.

11. Strand, "Interview . . . with Chris Mullin," 95.

12. Ibid., 554–55.

13. See the artist profile "Tracey Moffatt" on the Roslyn Oxley9 Gallery website, www.roslynoxley9.com.au/artists/26/Tracey_Moffatt/61/ (accessed on 10 March 2015).

14. Jean Paulhan, "Happiness in Slavery," in *The Story of O*, by Pauline Réage, trans. Sabine d'Estrée (New York: Ballantine Books, 1992), xxi–xxxvi.

15. See, among other sources, Virginia Berridge and Griffith Edwards, *Opium and the People: Opiate Use in Nineteenth-Century England* (London: Allen Lane, 1981); and Alethea Hayter, *Opium and the Romantic Imagination* (Berkeley: University of California Press, 1968).

16. The Aboriginals Protection and Restriction on the Sale of Opium Act, 1897.

17. Katie King, "Historiography as Reenactment: Metaphors and Literalizations of TV Documentaries," *Criticism* 46, no. 3 (2004): 459.

Bibliography

"1837/1897;Journalist—Then/Journalist—Now." *Punch*, 19 June 1897, 293.

Abbott, Edwin A. *Flatland: A Romance of Many Dimensions.* London: Seeley, 1884.

Adams, Jack [Alcanoan O. Grigsby and Mary P. Lowe]. *Nequa, or the Problem of the Ages.* Topeka, KS: Equity Publishing, 1900.

Advertisement for *Bow Bells'* Valentine's Day Issue. *Bow Bells* 2, no. 28 (8 February 1865): 35; 4, no. 80 (7 February 1866): 35; 6, no. 132 (6 February 1867): 35; 8, no. 184 (5 February 1868): 35; 10, no. 236 (3 February 1869): 35; 10, no. 237 (10 February 1869): 59.

Advertisement for Rimmel's Valentines. *Sixpenny Magazine* 2, no. 8 (February 1862): 218; *All the Year Round* 17 (January 1867): 122–24.

Altick, Richard. *The Shows of London.* Cambridge, MA: Harvard University Press, 1978.

American McGee's Alice. Culver City, CA: Electronic Arts, 2000. Video game.

American McGee's Alice: Madness Returns. Culver City, CA: Electronic Arts, 2011. Video game.

"Among the Tombs." Text by Henry Newbolt, illustrations by Patten Wilson. *Pall Mall Magazine* 19 (September 1899): 68–69.

Anderson, Patricia J. "'Factory Girl, Apprentice and Clerk'—The Readership of Mass-Market Magazines, 1830–60." *Victorian Periodicals Review* 25, no. 2 (Summer 1992): 64–72.

———. *The Printed Image and the Transformation of Popular Culture, 1790–1860.* Oxford, UK: Clarendon Press, 1991.

Antal, Frederick. *Hogarth and His Place in European Art.* London: Routledge and Kegan Paul, 1962.

Arias, Rosario, and Patricia Pulham, eds. *Haunting and Spectrality in Neo-Victorian Fiction: Possessing the Past.* Basingstoke, UK: Palgrave Macmillan, 2010.

Armour, George Denholm. "Past and Present, A Sportsman's Diary." *Punch,* 19 June 1897, 297.

Armstrong, Nancy. *Fiction in the Age of Photography: The Legacy of British Realism.* Cambridge, MA: Harvard University Press, 2002.

Artmann, H. C. *Frankenstein in Sussex.* Illustrated by Hans Arnold. Munich: Lenz, 1974.

Astrutha. Bow Bells 7, nos. 166–78 (9 October–25 December 1867): 241–45, 277–80, 289–93, 325–28, 337–41, 373–76, 385–89, 421–24, 439–42, 473–76, 509–12, 521–24.

Bailey, J. O. Introduction to *Symzonia: A Voyage of Discovery,* by Captain Adam Seaborn. 1820; reprint, Gainesville, FL: Scholars' Facsimiles and Reprints, 1965.

"A Ballad of a Shield." Text by Cosmo Monkhouse, illustration by Charles Ricketts. *Magazine of Art* (January 1892): 421–22.

"Ballad of the Page and the King's Daughter (Translated from Giebel [*sic*])." Text by E[llen] C[ook], illustration by Edward J. Poynter, engraving by Joseph Swain. *Once a Week,* 6 June 1863, 656–58.

Banham, Christopher Mark. "Dicks, John (1818–1881)." In *Dictionary of Nineteenth-Century Journalism,* edited by Laurel Brake and Marysa Demoor, n.p. London: British Library, 2008. Accessed through the ProQuest C19 Database.

Banta, Martha. *Barbaric Intercourse: Caricature and the Culture of Conduct, 1841–1936.* Chicago: University of Chicago Press, 2003.

Barber, Suzanne, and Matt Hale. "Enacting the Never-Was: Upcycling the Past, Present, and Future in Steampunk." In *Steaming into a Victorian Future: A Steampunk Anthology,* edited by Julie Anne Taddeo and Cynthia Miller, 165–84. Plymouth, UK: Scarecrow Press, 2013.

Barnes, Julian. *Arthur & George.* New York: Vintage, 2005.

Bauduin, Tessel. "Occulture and Modern Art." *Aries: Journal for the Study of Western Esotericism* 13 (2013): 1–5.

Beale, Charles Willing. *The Secret of the Earth.* New York: F. Tennyson Neely, 1899.

Bear, Jordan. "'The Experienced Eye of the Antiquary': Hill and Adamson's Medieval Revival." *PhotoResearcher* 20 (2013): 46–55.

Beazley, David. *Images of Angling.* Haslemere, UK: Creel Press, 2010.

Beetham, Margaret. *A Magazine of Her Own? Domesticity and Desire in the Woman's Magazine, 1800–1914.* London: Routledge, 1996.

Benjamin, Walter. "Thesis on the Philosophy of History." In *Illuminations: Essays and Reflections,* 253–64. Edited by Hannah Arendt. Translated by Harry Zohn. New York: Harcourt Brace Jovanovich, 1968.

———. "The Work of Art in the Age of Mechanical Reproduction." In *Illuminations: Essays and Reflections,* 217–52. Edited by Hannah Arendt. London: Fontana, 1986.

Bennett, Bridget. *Transatlantic Spiritualism and Nineteenth-Century American Literature.* Basingstoke, UK: Palgrave Macmillan, 2007.

Bennett, Tony. *The Birth of the Museum: History, Theory, Politics.* London: Routledge, 1995.

Berlant, Lauren. *The Female Complaint: The Unfinished Business of Senti-mentality in American Culture.* Durham, NC: Duke University Press, 2008.

Berndt, Jaqueline, ed. *Comics Worlds and the World of Comics: Towards Scholarship on a Global Scale.* Kyoto: Kyoto Seika University Press, 2010.

Berridge, Virginia, and Griffith Edwards. *Opium and the People: Opiate Use in Nineteenth-Century England.* London: Allen Lane, 1981.

Besant, Walter. *The Inner House.* New York: Harper, 1888.

Best, Stephen, and Sharon Marcus. "Surface Reading: An Introduction." *Representations* 108, no. 1 (2009): 1–21.

———, eds. "The Way We Read Now." Special issue, *Representations* 108, no. 1 (2009).

Beyond His Income. Bow Bells 5, nos. 114–22 (3 October–28 November 1866): 217–21, 253–56, 265–68, 301–4, 313–16, 349–52, 361–64, 397–400, 423–24.

Bivona, Daniel. "Alice the Child-Imperialist and the Games of Wonder-land." *Nineteenth-Century Literature* 41, no. 2 (1986): 143–71.

Blum, Hester. "John Cleves Symmes and the Planetary Reach of Polar Exploration." *American Literature* 84, no. 2 (2012): 243–71.

"Book Illustrations." *All the Year Round* (10 August 1867): 151–55.

Bowser, Rachel A., and Brian Croxall. "Introduction: Industrial Evolu-tion." Special issue, *Neo-Victorian Studies* 3, no. 1 (2010): 1–45.

Braddon, Mary Elizabeth. *Lady Audley's Secret.* London: Tinsley, 1862.

Bradshaw, William R. *The Goddess of Atvatabar, Being the History of the Discovery of the Interior World and Conquest of Atvatabar.* New York: J. F. Douthitt, 1892.

Brake, Laurel. "Lost and Found: Serial Supplements in the Nineteenth Century." *Victorian Periodicals Review* 43, no. 2 (Summer 2010): 111–18.

———. *Print in Transition, 1850–1910: Studies in Media and Book History.* Basingstoke, UK: Palgrave, 2011.

———. "'Time's Turbulence': Mapping Journalism Networks." *Victorian Periodicals Review* 44, no. 2 (Summer 2011): 115–27.

Brake, Laurel, and Marysa Demoor, eds. *Dictionary of Nineteenth-Century Journalism in Great Britain and Ireland.* Ghent, Belgium: Academia Press, 2009.

"The Bride of Rozelle: A Jersey Legend." Text by Eleanora L. Hervey, illustration by Arthur Boyd Houghton, engraving by the Swain School. *Once a Week,* 8 June 1867, 662–64.

Bristow, Joseph. "Whether 'Victorian' Poetry: A Genre and Its Period." *Victorian Poetry* 42, no. 1 (2004): 81–109.

Britten, Emma Hardinge. *Modern American Spiritualism: A Twenty Years Record of the Communion between Earth and the World of the Spirits.* New York: privately published, 1870.

Bronfen, Elisabeth. *Over Her Dead Body: Death, Femininity and the Aesthetic.* Manchester: Manchester University Press, 1992.

Brontë, Emily. *Wuthering Heights.* 1847. Edited by Pauline Nestor. London: Penguin Books, 2003.

Burnett, Frances Hodgson. *Sara Crewe; or, What Happened at Miss Minchin's.* 1887–88. New York: Charles Scribner's Sons, 1888.

Cadwallader, Jennifer. "Spirit Photography and the Victorian Culture of Mourning." *Modern Language Studies* 37, no. 2 (2008): 8–31.

Campbell, Matthew. "Thomas Moore, Daniel Maclise and the New Mythology: The Origin of the Harp." In *The Voice of the People: Writing the European Folk Revival, 1740–1914,* edited by Matthew Campbell and Michael Perraudin, 65–86. London: Anthem Press, 2012.

Captain Gerald. Bow Bells 7, nos. 161–74 (28 August–27 November 1867): 97–101, 121–24, 145–48, 169–72, 193–96, 217–20, 253–56, 265–68, 301–4, 313–16, 349–52, 361–64, 397–400, 409–12.

Carlyle, Thomas. "On History." In *Historical Essays,* 3–14. Edited by Chris R. Vanden Bossche. Berkeley: University of California Press, 2003.

Carroll, Lewis. *Alice's Adventures in Wonderland.* In *The Annotated Alice: The Definitive Edition,* 3–127. Edited by Martin Gardner. London: Norton, 2013.

———. *Alice's Adventures in Wonderland.* London: Macmillan, 1866.

———. *Through the Looking-Glass and What Alice Found There.* In *The Annotated Alice: The Definitive Edition,* 129–274. Edited by Martin Gardner. London: Norton, 2013.

Carter, Angela. *The Sadeian Woman and the Ideology of Pornography.* New York: Pantheon Books, 1978.

Carynthia: The Legend of Black Rock. Bow Bells 5, nos. 123–30 (5 December 1866–23 January 1867): 434–38, 457–60, 481–85, 505–8, 529–32, 553–56, 577–81, 601–4; 6, nos. 131–32 (30 January–6 February 1867): 1–4, 25–28.

Casteras, Susan P. "Reader, Beware: Images of Victorian Women and Books." *Nineteenth-Century Gender Studies* 3, no. 1 (Spring 2007). www.ncgsjournal.com/issue31/casteras.htm.

Chaplow, Lester. "Tales of a Hollow Earth: Tracing the Legacy of John Cleves Symmes in Antarctic Exploration and Fiction." Master's thesis, University of Canterbury, New Zealand, 2011.

"Charles Keenesque Croquet Period." *Punch,* 19 June 1897, 312.

Chéroux, Clément, ed. *The Perfect Medium: Photography and the Occult.* New Haven, CT: Yale University Press, 2005.

Cherry, Brigid, and Maria Mellins. "Negotiating the Punk in Steampunk: Subculture, Fashion, and Performance Identity." *Punk & Post-Punk* 1, no. 1 (September 2011): 5–25.

Cheshire, Jim, ed. *Tennyson Transformed: Alfred Lord Tennyson and Visual Culture.* Aldershot, UK: Lund Jeffries, 2009.

Chiba, Yoko. "Japonisme: East-West Renaissance in the Late 19th Century." *Mosaic* 31, no. 2 (1998): 1–20.

Chow, Rey. *Entanglements, or Transmedial Thinking about Capture.* Durham, NC: Duke University Press, 2012.

Christians, Karen. "Steampunk: Future Past." *Metalsmith* 31, no. 3 (August 2011): 18–19.

Chute, Hillary. "Comics as Literature? Reading Graphic Narrative." *PMLA* 123, no. 2 (2008): 452–65.

———. *Graphic Women: Life Narrative and Contemporary Comics.* New York: Columbia University Press, 2010.

Chute, Hillary, and Marianne DeKoven. "Introduction: Graphic Narrative." Special issue, *MFS: Modern Fiction Studies* 52, no. 4 (Winter 2006): 767–82.

Cioffi, Frank L. "Disturbing Comics: The Disjunction of Word and Image in the Comics of Andrzej Mleczko, Ben Katchor, R. Crumb, and Art Spiegelman." In *The Language of Comics: Word and Image,* edited by Robin Varnum and Christina T. Gibbons, 97–122. Jackson: University Press of Mississippi, 2001.

Cioran, E. M. *Vom Nachteil Geboren zu Sein.* Frankfurt: Suhrkamp, 1979.

Claes, Koenraad. "Supplements and Paratext: The Rhetoric of Space." *Victorian Periodicals Review* 43, no. 2 (Summer 2010): 196–210.

Clayton, Jay. *Dickens in Cyberspace: The Afterlife of the Nineteenth Century in Postmodern Culture.* New York: Oxford University Press, 2006.

Cohen, I. Bernard. "A Brief History of the *Principia.*" In *The Principia: Mathematical Principles of Natural Philosophy,* by Isaac Newton, 11–25. Translated by I. Bernard Cohen and Anne Whitman. Berkeley: University of California Press, 1999.

Colbert, Charles. *Haunted Visions: Spiritualism and American Art.* Philadelphia: University of Pennsylvania Press, 2011.

Colville, W. J. "Ode to Spirit Art." *Gallery of Spirit Art: An Illustrated Quarterly Magazine Dedicated to Spirit Photography, Spirit Painting, the Photographing of Materialized Forms and Every Form of Spirit Art* 1, no. 1 (August 1882): 1–14.

Conant, Mrs. J. H. *Flashes of Light from the Spirit-Land*. Boston: William White, 1872.

Copeland, Rebecca. *Lost Leaves: Women Writers of Meiji Japan*. Honolulu: University of Hawai'i Press, 2000.

Corbett, David Peters. *The World in Paint: Modern Art and Visuality in England, 1848–1914*. Manchester: Manchester University Press, 2004.

Corbett, David Peters, and L. Perry, eds. *English Art, 1860–1914: Modern Artists and Identity*. Manchester: Manchester University Press, 2001.

Cox, Robert. *Body and Soul: A Sympathetic History of American Spiritualism*. Charlottesville: University of Virginia Press, 2003.

Crane, Ben. *The Before and After Trade Card*. Schoharie, NY: Ephemera Society of America, 1995.

Crary, Jonathan. *Techniques of the Observer: On Vision and Modernity in the Nineteenth Century*. Cambridge, MA: MIT Press, 1992.

Crowell, Ellen. "Scarlet Carsons, Men in Masks: The Wildean Contexts of *V for Vendetta*." *Neo-Victorian Studies* 2, no. 1 (2008/2009): 17–45.

Csicsery-Ronay, Istvan Jr. *The Seven Beauties of Science Fiction*. Middletown, CT: Wesleyan University Press, 2008.

"Cupid's Letter Bag; or, St. Valentine's Day." *Bow Bells* 2, no. 29 (15 February 1865): 49–50.

Curl, James Stevens. *The Victorian Celebration of Death*. Thrupp, UK: Sutton Publishing, 2000.

Dauber, Jeremy. "Comic Books, Tragic Stories: Will Eisner's American Jewish History." In *The Jewish Graphic Novel: Critical Approaches*, edited by Samantha Baskind and Ranen Omer-Sherman, 22–42. New Brunswick, NJ: Rutgers University Press, 2008.

Davenport, Reuben Briggs. *The Death-Blow to Spiritualism: Being the True Story of the Fox Sisters, as Revealed by the Authority of Margaret Fox Kane and Catherine Fox Jencken*. New York: G. W. Dillingham, 1888.

Davies, Norman. *God's Playground: A History of Poland*. New York: Columbia University Press, 1982.

Davis, Andrew Jackson. *Answers to Ever-Recurring Questions from the People: A Sequel to the Penetralia*. New York: A. J. Davis, 1862.

———. *The Diakka and Their Earthly Victims: Being an Explanation of Much That Is False and Repulsive in Spiritualism*. New York: A. J. Davis, 1873.

———. *The Magic Staff: An Autobiography of Andrew Jackson Davis*. 1857. 13th ed. Boston: Colby and Rich, 1885.

———. *A Stellar Key to the Summer Land*. 5th rev. ed. Boston: Colby and Rich, 1867.

Davis, Paul. *The Lives and Times of Ebenezer Scrooge.* New Haven, CT: Yale University Press, 1990.

Davys, George. *A Volume for a Lending Library.* 2nd ed. London: J. G. F. and J. Rivington, 1840.

De Camp, L. Sprague, and Willy Ley. *Lands Beyond.* New York: Rinehart, 1952.

Delaney, J. G. P. *Charles Ricketts: A Biography.* Oxford, UK: Clarendon Press, 1990.

Demoor, Marysa, and Kate Macdonald. "Finding and Defining the Victorian Supplement." *Victorian Periodicals Review* 43, no. 2 (Summer 2010): 97–110.

De Quincey, Thomas. "The Palimpsest." In *Suspiria de Profundis: Being a Sequel to the Confessions of an English Opium Eater,* pt. 1. *Blackwood's Edinburgh Magazine* 57, no. 356 (June 1845): 739–43.

De Ridder, Jolein. "What? How? Why? Broadening the Mind with the *Treasury of Literature* (1868–1875), Supplement to the *Ladies' Treasury* (1857–1895)." *Victorian Periodicals Review* 43, no. 2 (Summer 2010): 174–95.

Derrick, Francis. "A Story of Love's Cruelty." *Bow Bells* 10, no. 237, supp. (10 February 1869): 5–7.

[Dickens, Charles]. "Gone Astray." *Household Words,* 13 August 1853, 553–57.

Dickens, Charles. *The Old Curiosity Shop.* 1841. Edited by Norman Page. London: Penguin, 2000.

———. *Oliver Twist.* 1837–39. Edited by Kathleen Tillotson. Oxford: Oxford University Press, 1999.

Dicks, Guy. *The John Dicks Press.* Raleigh, NC: Lulu.com, 2013.

Di Liddo, Annalisa. *Alan Moore: Comics as Performance, Fiction as Scalpel.* Jackson: University of Mississippi Press, 2009.

Dillon, Sarah. "Reinscribing De Quincey's Palimpsest: The Significance of the Palimpsest in Contemporary Literary and Cultural Studies." *Textual Practice* 19, no. 3 (2005): 243–63.

Dirge, Roman. *Lenore* animated shorts. Sony Entertainment, 2002.

———. "Lenore in 'The Macabre Malevolence of Mortimer Fledge.'" *Roman Dirge's Lenore,* vol. 2, no. 1. London: Titan Publishing Group, 2009.

———. *Roman Dirge's Lenore: Cooties.* London: Titan Publishing Group, 2010.

———. *Roman Dirge's Lenore: Noogies, Collecting "Lenore," Issues 1–4.* San Jose, CA: Slave Labor Graphics, 1999.

Disraeli, Benjamin. *The Wondrous Tale of Alroy.* London: Saunders and Otley, 1833.

Dollase, Hiromi Tsuchiya. "*Shōfujin* (Little Women): Recreating Jo for the Girls of Meiji Japan." *Japanese Studies* 30, no. 2 (2010): 247–62.

Doyle, Arthur Conan. *The History of Spiritualism.* London: Cassel, 1926.

Drews, Jörg. "Die neuesten Kunststücke des H. C. Artmann." In *Über H. C. Artmann,* edited by Gerald Bisinger, 83–86. Frankfurt: Suhrkamp, 1972.

Duffey, Mrs. E. B. *Heaven Revised: A Narrative of Personal Experiences after the Change Called Death.* Manchester, UK: Two Worlds, 1909.

Du Maurier, George. "Frustrated Social Ambition." *Punch,* 21 May 1881, 229.

Eaton, Marcia Muelder. "Laughing at the Death of Little Nell: Sentimental Art and Sentimental People." *American Philosophical Quarterly* 26, no. 4 (October 1989): 269–82.

"An Echo from Willowwood." Text by Christina G. Rossetti, illustrations by Charles Ricketts. *Magazine of Art* (January 1890): 385.

Eisner, Will. *Comics and Sequential Art: Principles and Practices from the Legendary Cartoonist.* 1985. Rev. ed., New York: W. W. Norton, 2008,

———. *Fagin the Jew.* 2nd ed. Milwaukie, OR: Dark Horse Comics, 2013.

———. *Graphic Storytelling and Visual Narrative: Principles and Practices from the Legendary Cartoonist.* 1996. Reprint, New York: W. W. Norton, 2008.

Elliott, Kamilla. "Tie-Intertextuality, or, Intertextuality as Incorporation in the Tie-in Merchandise to Disney's *Alice in Wonderland* (2010)." *Adaptation* 7, no. 2 (2014): 191–211.

Encyclopædia Britannica Online Academic Edition. S.v. "Alboin." Encyclopædia Britannica, 2013. www.britannica.com/EBchecked/topic/13066/Alboin (accessed 11 August 2013).

Endelman, Todd M. *The Jews of Georgian England, 1714–1830: Tradition and Change in a Liberal Society.* Philadelphia: Jewish Publication Society of America, 1979.

"Extremes Meet; or, Some Victorian Contrasts, II." *Punch,* 19 June 1897, 308.

"Extremes Meet; or, Some Victorian Contrasts, III." *Punch,* 19 June 1897, 310.

"Faint Heart Never Won Fair Ladye." Text by Astley H. Baldwin, illustration by M. J. Lawless, engraver unidentified. *Once a Week,* 18 July 1863, 97–98.

Fara, Patricia. "Hidden Depths: Halley, Hell and Other People." *Studies in History and Philosophy of Science* 38, no. 3 (2007): 570–83.

Felsenstein, Frank. *Anti-Semitic Stereotypes: A Paradigm of Otherness in En-glish Popular Culture, 1660–1830*. Baltimore, MD: Johns Hopkins University Press, 1995.

Felsenstein, Frank, and Sharon Liberman Mintz. *The Jew as Other: A Century of English Caricature, 1730–1830; An Exhibition, April 6–July 31, 1995, The Library of the Jewish Theological Seminary of America*. New York: Library of the Jewish Theological Seminary of America, 1995.

Ferguson, Christine. *Determined Spirits: Eugenics, Heredity, and Racial Regeneration in Anglo-American Spiritualist Writing, 1848–1930*. Edinburgh: Edinburgh University Press, 2012.

———. "Neo-Victorian Presence: Tom Phillips and the Non-hermeneutic Past." *Australasian Journal of Victorian Studies* 18, no. 3 (2013): 22–57.

———. "Surface Tensions: Steampunk, Subculture, and the Ideology of Style." *Neo-Victorian Studies* 4, no. 2 (2011): 66–90.

———. "Victoria-Arcana and the Misogynistic Poetics of Resistance in Iain Sinclair's *White Chappell Scarlet Tracings* and Alan Moore's *From Hell*." *LIT: Literature, Interpretation, Theory* 20, nos. 1–2 (2009): 45–64.

Flint, Kate. *The Victorians and the Visual Imagination*. Cambridge: Cambridge University Press, 2000.

———. *The Woman Reader, 1837–1914*. Oxford, UK: Clarendon Press, 1993.

Foucault, Michel. *The History of Sexuality*. Vol. 1. Translated by Robert Hurley. New York: Vintage, 1990.

Freeman, Marc. "Death, Narrative Integrity, and the Radical Challenge of Self-Understanding: A Reading of Tolstoy's 'Death of Ivan Ilyich.'" *Aging and Society* 17, no. 4 (2000): 373–98.

Freud, Sigmund. "The Uncanny." In *An Infantile Neurosis and Other Works*, 219–52. Vol. 17 of *The Standard Edition of the Complete Psychological Works of Sigmund Freud*. Edited and translated by James Strachey, in collaboration with Anna Freud and with the assistance of Alix Strachey and Alan Tyson. London: Hogarth Press, 1955.

"From a Ruined Tower." Text by Lewis Morris, illustrations by E. F. Skinner, Swantype engraving. *Pall Mall Magazine* 7 (November 1895): 321–25.

Gailbraith, Patrick. "*Fujoshi*: Fantasy Play and Transgressive Intimacy among 'Rotten Girls' in Contemporary Japan." *Signs* 37, no. 1 (2011): 211–32.

Gaiman, Neil. Introduction to *Roman Dirge's Lenore: Cooties*, by Roman Dirge, 6. London: Titan Publishing Group, 2010.

Gardner, Martin. *Fads and Fallacies in the Name of Science*. New York: Dover, 1957.

Gaskell, Elizabeth. *Mary Barton*. 1848. Edited by Jennifer Foster. Toronto: Broadview Press, 2000.

Gaunt, Paul J. "Henry Bielfeld (1802–1892)." *PsyPioneer Journal* 6, no. 7 (2010): 171–78.

Genette, Gérard. *Introduction à l'architexte*. Paris: Editions du Seuil, 1979.

———. *Palimpsests: Literature in the Second Degree*. Translated by Channa Newman and Claude Dubinsky. Lincoln: University of Nebraska Press, 1997. Published in French in 1982.

Gill, Stephen. Introduction to *Oliver Twist*, by Charles Dickens, vii–xxv. Edited by Kathleen Tillotson. Oxford: Oxford University Press, 1999.

Gilman, Sander. *The Jew's Body*. New York: Routledge, 1991.

Girouard, Mark. *The Return to Camelot: Chivalry and the English Gentleman*. New Haven, CT: Yale University Press, 1981.

Golden, Catherine J. "Cruikshank's Illustrative Wrinkle in *Oliver Twist*'s Misrepresentation of Class." In *Book Illustrated: Text, Image, and Culture, 1770–1930*, edited by Catherine J. Golden, 117–46. New Castle, DE: Oak Knoll Press, 2000.

———. *Posting It: The Victorian Revolution in Letter Writing*. Gainesville; University Press of Florida, 2009.

Goldman, Paul. *Victorian Illustration: The Pre-Raphaelite, the Idyllic School and the High Victorians*. Aldershot, UK: Scolar Press, 1996.

Goldman, Paul, and Simon Cooke, eds. *Reading Victorian Illustration, 1855–1875: Spoils of the Lumber Room*. Farnham, UK: Ashgate, 2012.

Good, Joseph. "'God Save the Queen, for Someone Must!': *Sebastian O* and the Steampunk Aesthetic." *Neo-Victorian Studies* 3, no. 1 (2010): 208–15.

Gorey, Edward. *The Gashlycrumb Tinies; or, After the Outing*. 1963. Reprint, Boston: Harcourt, 1991.

———. *The Hapless Child*. 1961. Reprint, San Francisco, CA: Pomegranate Communications, 1989.

Gray, Valerie. *Charles Knight: Educator, Publisher, Writer*. Aldershot, UK: Ashgate, 2006.

"Great Queens of History." *Punch*, 19 June 1897, 289.

Green-Lewis, Jennifer. *Framing the Victorians: Photography and the Culture of Realism*. Ithaca, NY: Cornell University Press, 1996.

Gregory, Raven, Daniel Leister, and Nei Ruffino. *Return to Wonderland*. Fort Washington, PA: Zenescope Entertainment, 2009–11.

Griffin, Duane. "Hollow and Habitable Within: Symmes's Theory of Earth's Internal Structure and Polar Geography." *Physical Geography* 25, no. 5 (2004): 382–97.

———. "What Curiosity in the Structure: The Hollow Earth in Science." Unpublished manuscript, 1–43. Bucknell University Department of Geography. www.facstaff.bucknell.edu/dgriffin/Research /Griffin-HE_in_Science.pdf.

Grimm, Jacob, and Wilhelm Grimm. "Mother Hulda." In *Household Stories from the Brothers Grimm Translated from the German by Lucy Crane,* 128–31. London: Macmillan, 1882.

Groensteen, Thierry. *Comics and Narration.* Translated by Ann Miller. Jackson: University Press of Mississippi, 2013.

———. *The System of Comics.* Translated by Bart Beaty and Nick Nguyen. Jackson: University Press of Mississippi, 2007.

Gunning, Tom. "Phantom Images and Modern Manifestations: Spirit Photography, Magic Theater, Trick Films, and Photography's Uncanny." In *Fugitive Images: From Photography to Video,* edited by Patrice Petro, 42–71. Bloomington: Indiana University Press, 1995.

Gutleben, Christian. *Nostalgic Postmodernism: The Victorian Tradition and the Contemporary British Novel.* Amsterdam: Rodopi Press, 2001.

———. "Palinodes, Palindromes and Palimpsests: Strategies of Deliberate Self-Contradiction in Postmodern British Fiction." *Miscelánea: A Journal of English and American Studies* 26 (2002): 11–20.

Hadley, Louisa. *Neo-Victorian Fiction and Historical Narrative: The Victorians and Us.* Basingstoke, UK: Palgrave Macmillan, 2010.

Halley, Edmond. "An Account of the Cause of the Change of the Variation of the Magnetical Needle; With an Hypothesis of the Structure of the Internal Parts of the Earth: As It Was Proposed to the Royal Society in One of Their Late Meetings." *Philosophical Transactions* 16 (1692): 563–78.

Hannavy, John. *Encyclopedia of Nineteenth-Century Photography.* New York: Routledge, 2008.

Harben, Will N. *The Land of the Changing Sun.* New York: Merriam, 1894.

Hare, Robert. *Experimental Investigations of the Spirit Manifestations.* New York: Partridge and Brittan, 1856.

Hawthorne, Nathaniel. "P's Correspondence." *United States Magazine and Democratic Review* (April 1845): 337–45.

Hayter, Alethea. *Opium and the Romantic Imagination.* Berkeley: University of California Press, 1968.

Heilmann, Ann, and Mark Llewellyn. *Neo-Victorianism: The Victorians in the Twenty-First Century, 1999–2009.* Basingstoke, UK: Palgrave Macmillan, 2010.

Heinrich, Anselm, Katherine Newey, and Jeffrey Richards, eds. *Ruskin, the Theatre, and Victorian Visual Culture.* Basingstoke, UK: Palgrave Macmillan, 2009.

Helsinger, Elizabeth. *Poetry and the Pre-Raphaelite Arts: Dante Gabriel Rossetti and William Morris.* New Haven, CT: Yale University Press, 2008.

Henkin, David M. *The Postal Age: The Emergence of Modern Communications in Nineteenth-Century America.* Chicago: University of Chicago Press, 2006.

Hervey, Eleanora L. *The Feasts of Camelot, with the Tales That Were Told There.* London: Bell and Daldy, 1863.

———. *Our Legends and Lives: A Gift for All Seasons.* London: Trübner, 1869.

Hewitt, John. "The Poster in England in the 1890s." *Victorian Periodicals Review* 35, no. 1 (Spring 2002): 37–62.

Heywood, Ian, and Barry Sandywell. "Introduction: Critical Approaches to the Study of Visual Culture." In *The Handbook of Visual Culture,* edited by Ian Heywood and Barry Sandywell, 1–56. London: Berg, 2010.

"Highland Officer in the Crimea." *Punch,* 12 January 1856, 20.

Ho, Elizabeth. *Neo-Victorianism and the Memory of Empire.* New York: Continuum, 2012.

———. "Victorian Maids and Neo-Victorian Labour in Kaoru Mori's *Emma: A Victorian Romance.*" *Neo-Victorian Studies* 6, no. 2 (2013): 40–63.

Hoffman, A. Robin. "G Is for Gorey Who Kills Children." *Studies in Weird Fiction* 27 (Spring 2005): 23–32.

Hogan, Eleanor J., and Inger Sigrun Brodey. "Jane Austen in Japan: 'Good Mother' or 'New Woman'?" *Persuasions* 28, no. 2 (2008). www.jasna .org/persuasions/on-line/vol28no2/index.html.

Hogarth, William. *The Harlot's Progress. Saturday Night.* Vol. 2, 129, 162, 193, 226, 257, 305. London: Hodgson, 1824.

———. *Hogarth: The Complete Engravings.* Edited by Joseph Burke and Colin Caldwell. London: Alpine Fine Arts Collection, 1989.

———. *The Idle and Industrious Apprentices. Saturday Night.* Vol. 1, 193, 225, 258, 299, 322, 354, 385, 417, 449; vol. 2, 1, 17, 49. London: Hodgson, 1824.

———. *Industry and Idleness.* In *A Volume for a Lending Library.* Edited by George Davys. 2nd ed. London: J. G. F. and J. Rivington, 1840.

———. *Industry and Idleness.* In *The Thief: A London, Edinburgh and Dublin Journal of Literature and Science.* London: W. Strange, 1832–33.

———. *The Rake's Progress. Saturday Night.* Vol. 2, 338, 354, 369, 402, 414, 433, 449, 465. London: Hodgson, 1824.

Hogarth and His Works. Penny Magazine of the Society for the Diffusion of Useful Knowledge. Vol. 3 (1834), 121–28, 209–16, 249–56, 287–89, 329–30, 377–84, 401–2, 481–82; (1835), 29–30, 81–88, 113–14, 145–46, 172–76, 193–95, 209–15. London: Charles Knight, 1834–35.

Hollander, John. *Vision and Resonance: Two Senses of Poetic Form.* New York: Oxford University Press, 1975.

Holubetz, Margarete. "Death-Bed Scenes in Victorian Fiction." *English Studies* 67, no. 1 (1986): 14–34.

The Home Angel. Bow Bells 2, nos. 30–45 (22 February–7 June 1865): 81–84, 106–8, 129–32, 152–56, 177–80, 201–4, 225–28, 261–64, 285–88, 309–12, 333–36, 353–54, 376–78, 400–402, 424–36, 448–50.

"Home Duties." *Bow Bells* 6, no. 154 (10 July 1867): 560–62.

Hotz, Mary Elizabeth. *Literary Remains: Representations of Death and Burial in Victorian England.* Albany: State University of New York Press, 2009.

Hughes, Linda K., and Michael Lund. *The Victorian Serial.* Charlottesville: University of Virginia Press, 1991.

Humpherys, Anne. "*Bow Bells* (1862–1897)." In *Dictionary of Nineteenth-Century Journalism,* edited by Laurel Brake and Marysa Demoor, n.p. London: British Library, 2008. Accessed through the ProQuest C19 Database.

"Hunting Ladies." *Saturday Review,* 6 May 1865, 533–34.

"The Huntress of Armorica: A Tale of St. Michael's Mount." Text by Eleanora L. Hervey, illustration by Paul Gray, engraving by Swain. *Once a Week,* 29 December 1866, 706–8.

Hutcheon, Linda. "Historiographic Metafiction: Parody and the Intertextuality of History." In *Intertextuality and Contemporary American Fiction,* edited by Patrick O'Donnell and Robert Con Davis, 3–32. Baltimore, MD: Johns Hopkins University Press, 1989.

———. *A Poetics of Postmodernism.* New York: Routledge, 1988.

———. *The Politics of Postmodernism.* New York: Routledge, 1989.

———. *A Theory of Adaptation.* 2nd ed. With contributions by Siobhan O'Flynn. London: Routledge, 2013.

"Industry and Idleness." *Cottager's Monthly Visitor* (October 1839): 342–44.

Israel, Kali. "Asking Alice: Victorian and Other Alices in Contemporary Culture." In *Victorian Afterlife: Postmodern Culture Rewrites the Nineteenth Century,* edited by John Kucich and Dianne F. Sadoff, 252–87. Minneapolis: University of Minnesota Press, 2006.

Iwabuchi, Koichi. "Undoing Inter-national Fandom in the Age of Brand Nationalism." *Mechademia* 5 (2010): 87–96.

Jalland, Pat. *Death and the Victorian Family.* Oxford: Oxford University Press, 1999.

James, Louis. "The Trouble with Betsy: Periodicals and the Common Reader in Mid-Nineteenth-Century England." In *The Victorian*

Periodical Press: Samplings and Soundings, edited by Joanne Shattock and Michael Wolff, 349–66. Leicester: Leicester University Press, 1982.

Jameson, Fredric. *Postmodernism; or, The Cultural Logic of Late Capitalism.* Durham, NC: Duke University Press, 1991.

Jenkins, Henry. *Textual Poachers: Television Fans and Participatory Culture.* 20th anniv. ed. New York: Routledge, 2013.

Jenson, Joli. "Fandom as Pathology: The Consequences of Characterization." In *Adoring Audience: Fan Culture and Popular Media,* edited by Lisa A. Lewis, 9–29. London: Routledge, 1992.

"Joan of Arc." Text by G. A. Simcox, illustration by George Du Maurier, engraving by Swain. *Cornhill Magazine* 16 (November 1867): 584–88.

Jones, Anna Maria. "'Palimpsestuous' Attachments: Framing a Manga Theory of the Global Neo-Victorian." In "Neo-Victorianism and Globalisation: Transnational Dissemination of Nineteenth-Century Cultural Texts," edited by Antonija Primorac and Monika Pietrzak-Franger. Special issue, *Neo-Victorian Studies* 8, no. 1 (2015): 17–47.

———. *Problem Novels: Victorian Fiction Theorizes the Sensational Self.* Columbus: Ohio State University Press, 2007.

Jones, Jason B. "Betrayed by Time: Steampunk & the Neo-Victorian in Alan Moore's *Lost Girls* and *The League of Extraordinary Gentlemen.*" *Neo-Victorian Studies* 3, no. 1 (2010): 99–126.

Joyce, Simon. Review of *Victorian Afterlife: Postmodern Culture Rewrites the Nineteenth Century,* by John Kucich and Dianne F. Sadoff, eds. *Victorian Studies* 44, no. 3 (Spring 2002): 555–57.

———. *The Victorians in the Rearview Mirror.* Athens: Ohio University Press, 2007.

"Just Think of It." *Punch,* 19 June 1897, 312.

Kaplan, Cora. *Victoriana: Histories, Fictions, Criticism.* New York: Columbia University Press, 2007.

Kaplan, Louis. *The Strange Case of William Mumler, Spirit Photographer.* Minneapolis: University of Minnesota Press, 2008.

Kennedy, Victor. "Mystery! Unraveling Edward Gorey's Tangled Web of Visual Metaphor." *Metaphor and Symbolic Activity* 8, no. 3 (1993): 181–93.

King, Andrew. "'Killing Time,' or Mrs. Braby's Peppermints: The Double Economy of the *Family Herald* and the *Family Herald* Supplements." *Victorian Periodicals Review* 43, no. 2 (Summer 2010): 149–73.

———. *The London Journal, 1845–83.* Aldershot, UK: Ashgate, 2004.

———. "A Paradigm of Reading the Victorian Penny Weekly: Education of the Gaze and the *London Journal.*" In *Nineteenth-Century Media and the Construction of Identity,* edited by Laurel Brake, Bill Bell, and David Finkelstein, 77–92. Basingstoke, UK: Palgrave Macmillan, 2000.

King, Katie. "Historiography as Reenactment: Metaphors and Literalizations of TV Documentaries." *Criticism* 46, no. 3 (2004): 459–76.

"King Goll." Text by W. B. Yeats, illustration by Jack Yeats. *Leisure Hour* (September 1887): 636–37.

"King Sigurd, the Crusader." Text by William Forsyth, illustration by Edward Burne-Jones, engraving by Dalziel. *Good Words* 3 (December 1862): 247–49.

Kiššová, Mária. "The Twenty-First Century Wonderland and What a Reader Finds There: Mytho-Geo-Graphical Landscape of Brian [*sic*] Talbot's *Alice in Sunderland.*" *Çankaya University Journal of Humanities and Social Sciences* 9, no. 1 (May 2012): 59–73.

Kneale, Matthew. *English Passengers: A Novel.* New York: Anchor, 2000.

Köhler, Harriet. "Das Buch meines Lebens: Harriet Köhler über E. M. Ciorans 'Vom Nachteil, geboren zu sein.'" *Der Spiegel* 10 (3 March 2008). www.spiegel.de/spiegel/print/d-56047457.html.

Kohlke, Marie-Luise. "Introduction: Speculations in and on the Neo-Victorian Encounter." *Neo-Victorian Studies* 1, no. 1 (2008): 1–18.

Kohlke, Marie-Luise, and Christian Gutleben, eds. *Neo-Victorian Tropes of Trauma: The Politics of Bearing After-Witness to Nineteenth-Century Suffering.* Amsterdam: Rodopi Press, 2010.

Kokkinen, Nina. "Occulture as an Analytical Tool in the Study of Art." *Aries: Journal for the Study of Western Esotericism* 13 (2013): 7–36.

Kooistra, Lorraine Janzen. *The Artist as Critic: Bitextuality in Fin-de-Siècle Illustrated Books.* Aldershot, UK: Scolar Press, 1995.

———. *Christina Rossetti and Illustration: A Publishing History.* Athens: Ohio University Press, 2002.

———. *Poetry, Pictures, and Popular Publishing: The Illustrated Gift Book and Victorian Visual Culture, 1855–1875.* Athens: Ohio University Press, 2011.

Koven, Seth. *Slumming: Sexual and Social Politics in Victorian London.* Princeton: Princeton University Press, 2004.

Krebs, Katja, ed. *Translation and Adaptation in Theatre and Film.* New York: Routledge, 2014.

Kubrin, David. "'Such an Impertinently Litigious Lady': Hooke's 'Great Pretending' vs. Newton's *Principia* and Newton's and Halley's Theory of Comets." In *Standing on the Shoulders of Giants: A Longer View of Newton and Halley,* edited by Norman J. W. Thrower, 55–90. Berkeley: University of California Press, 1990.

Kucich, John. "Death Worship among the Victorians: *The Old Curiosity Shop.*" *PMLA* 95, no. 1 (January 1980): 58–72.

Kucich, John, and Dianne F. Sadoff, eds. *Victorian Afterlife: Postmodern Culture Rewrites the Nineteenth Century.* Minneapolis: University of Minnesota Press, 2000.

Kuhn, Thomas S. *The Copernican Revolution: Planetary Astronomy in the Development of Western Thought.* Cambridge, MA: Harvard University Press, 1957.

Kunzle, David. "Between Broadsheet Caricature and *Punch:* Cheap Newspaper Cuts for the Lower Classes in the 1830s." *Art Journal* 43, no. 4 (Winter 1983): 339–46.

———. *The History of the Comic Strip: The Nineteenth Century.* Berkeley: University of California Press, 1990.

"The Lady of Shalott." Illustration by Dante Gabriel Rossetti, text by Alfred Lord Tennyson in *Poems* by Alfred Lord Tennyson, 75. London: Edward Moxon, 1857.

Lamb, Charles. "On the Genius and Character of Hogarth, with Some Remarks on a Passage in the Writings of the Late Mr. Barry." *Reflector* 2, no. 3 (March 1811): 61–77.

Lane, Mary E. Bradley [Mary E. Bradley]. *Mizora: A World of Women.* 1880–81. New York: G. W. Dillingham, 1890.

Lang, Hans-Joachim, and Benjamin Lease. "The Authorship of *Symzonia:* The Case for Nathaniel Ames." *New England Quarterly* 48, no. 2 (1975): 241–52.

Larew, Karl G. "Planet Women: The Image of Women in Planet Comics, 1940–1953." *Historian* 59, no. 3 (1997): 591–612.

Larson, Barbara Jean, and Fae Brauer, eds. *The Art of Evolution: Darwin, Darwinisms, and Visual Culture.* Hanover, NH: Dartmouth College Press, 2009.

Lauster, Martina. *Sketches of the Nineteenth Century: European Journalism and Its "Physiologies," 1830–1850.* Basingstoke, UK: Palgrave Macmillan, 2007.

"Law of Deterioration as Applied to Spiritual Phenomena." *Psychological Review* (June 1882): 339–43.

Lear, Edward. *Nonsense Songs, Stories, Botany, and Alphabets.* Boston: James R. Osgood, 1871.

Leary, Patrick. "Googling the Victorians." *Journal of Victorian Culture* 10, no. 1 (Spring 2005): 72–86.

———. *The Punch Brotherhood: Table Talk and Print Culture in Mid-Victorian England.* London: British Library, 2010.

Lee, Ruth Webb. *A History of Valentines*. London: B. T. Batsford, 1953.

Leighton, Mary Elizabeth, and Lisa Surridge. "Making History: Text and Image in Harriet Martineau's Historiettes." In *Reading Victorian Literature, 1855–1875: Spoils of the Lumber Room*, edited by Paul Goldman and Simon Cooke, 137–58. Farnham, UK: Ashgate, 2012.

———. "The Plot Thickens: Toward a Narratological Analysis of Illustrated Serial Fiction in the 1860s." *Victorian Studies* 51, no. 1 (2008): 65–101.

———. "The Transatlantic *Moonstone*: A Study of the Illustrated Serial in *Harper's Weekly*." *Victorian Periodicals Review* 42, no. 3 (2009): 207–43.

Leitch, Thomas. "Twelve Fallacies in Contemporary Adaptation Theory." *Criticism* 45, no. 2 (Spring 2003): 149–71.

Lessing, Gotthold Ephraim. *Laocoon: An Essay on the Limits of Painting and Poetry*. Translated by E. C. Beasley. London: Longman, Brown, Green, and Longmans, 1853.

Levine, Caroline. "Scaled Up, Writ Small: A Response to Carolyn Dever and Herbert F. Tucker." *Victorian Studies* 49, no. 1 (2009): 100–105.

Llewellyn, Mark, and Ann Heilmann. "The Victorians Now: Global Reflections on Neo-Victorianism." *Critical Quarterly* 55, no. 1 (2013): 24–42.

Lloyd, John Uri. *Etidorpha*. Cincinnati: Robert Clarke, 1895.

Longfellow, Henry Wadsworth. "Resignation." *Literature Online*. http://lion.chadwyck.co.uk.

MacWilliam, Suzanne. *Remote Viewing*. London: Black Dog Publishing, 2008.

"Madame La Mode Reviews a Few of Her Vagaries during the Last Sixty Years." *Punch*, 19 June 1897, 291.

Mahler, Nicolas. *Alice in Sussex*. Berlin: Suhrkamp Verlag, 2013.

Maidment, Brian. *Comedy, Caricature and the Social Order, 1820–1850*. Manchester: Manchester University Press, 2013.

———. "A Draft List of Published Book and Periodical Contributions by Robert Seymour." Digital annex to vol. 38 of *Victorians Institute Journal* (2011). *NINES (Nineteenth-Century Electronic Scholarship Online)*. www.nines.org/exhibits/Robert_Seymour.

———. "The Mysteries of Reading: Text and Illustration in the Fiction of G. W. M. Reynolds." In *G. W. M. Reynolds: Nineteenth-Century Fiction, Politics, and the Press*, edited by Ann Humpherys and Louis James, 227–46. Aldershot, UK: Ashgate, 2008.

———. *Reading Popular Prints, 1790–1870*. Manchester: Manchester University Press, 1996.

Malory, Sir Thomas. *The birth, life, and acts of King Arthur, of his noble knights of the Round Table, their marvelous enquests and adventures, the achieving of the San Greal, and in the end, Le morte Darthur with the dolorous death and departing out of this world of them all.* Illustrated by Aubrey Beardsley. London: J. M. Dent, 1893–94.

Mancoff, Debra. *The Arthurian Revival in Victorian Art.* New York: Garland, 1990.

Marcus, Sharon. "Reflections on Victorian Fashion Plates." *Differences: A Journal of Feminist Cultural Studies* 14, no. 3 (2003): 4–33.

Maudsley, Henry. *Natural Causes and Supernatural Seemings.* London: Kegan, Paul, Trench, 1886.

Maxwell, Richard, ed. *The Victorian Illustrated Book.* Charlottesville: University of Virginia Press, 2002.

Mayer-Deutsch, Angela. "'Quasi-Optical Palingenesis': The Circulation of Portraits and the Image of Kircher." In *Athanasius Kircher: The Last Man Who Knew Everything*, edited by Paula Findlen, 102–29. London: Routledge, 2004.

Mayhew, Henry. *London Labour and the London Poor.* 3 vols. London: George Woodfall and Sons, 1851.

Mays, Kelly J. "Looking Backward, Looking Forward: The Victorians in the Rearview Mirror of Future History." *Victorian Studies* 53, no. 3 (Spring 2011): 445–56.

McBride, James. *Symmes's Theory of Concentrix Spheres, Demonstrating That the Earth Is Hollow, Habitable Within, and Widely Open about the Poles.* Cincinnati: Morgan, Lodge and Fisher, 1826.

McCarthy, Patrick J. "The Curious Road to Death's Nell." *Dickens Studies Annual* 20 (1991): 17–34.

McClintock, Anne. *Imperial Leather: Race, Gender, and Sexuality in the Colonial Contest.* New York: Routledge, 1995.

McCloud, Scott. *Understanding Comics: The Invisible Art.* New York: HarperCollins, 1993.

McGarry, Molly. *Ghosts of Futures Past: Spiritualism and the Cultural Politics of Nineteenth-Century America.* Berkeley: University of California Press, 2008.

Meadows, Kenny. *Heads from Nicholas Nickleby.* London: Robert Tyas, 1839–40.

———. *The Heads of the People.* 2 vols. London: Robert Tyas, 1840–41.

Melville, Herman. *Moby-Dick; or, The Whale.* 1851. New York: Penguin Books, 2013.

Merrill, Linda. *A Pot of Paint: Aesthetics on Trial in Whistler v. Ruskin.* Washington, DC: Smithsonian, 1993.

Miller, Andrew H. "'A Case of Metaphysics': Counterfactuals, Realism, *Great Expectations*." *ELH* 79, no. 3 (2012): 773–96.

Miller, J. Scott. *Adaptations of Western Literature in Meiji Japan*. New York: Palgrave, 2001.

Milliken, E. J., ed. *Mr. Punch's Victorian Era: An Illustrated Chronicle of Fifty Years of the Reign of Her Majesty the Queen*. 3 vols. London: Bradbury, Agnew, 1888.

Mintz, Sharon Liberman, Havva Charm, and Elka Deitsch. *Image and Impression: Rare Prints from the Collection of the Library of the Jewish Theological Seminary of America*. New York: Library of the Jewish Theological Seminary of America, 2002.

Mitchell, Kate. *History and Cultural Memory in Neo-Victorian Fiction: Victorian Afterimages*. Basingstoke, UK: Palgrave Macmillan, 2010.

Mitchell, Sally. *The Fallen Angel: Chastity, Class, and Women's Reading, 1835–1880*. Bowling Green, OH: Bowling Green University Popular Press, 1981.

———. "The Forgotten Woman of the Period: Penny Weekly Family Magazines of the 1840s and 1850s." In *A Widening Sphere: Changing Roles of Victorian Women,* edited by Martha Vicinus, 29–51. Bloomington: Indiana University Press, 1977.

Mochizuki Jun. *Pandora Hātsu*. 24 vols. Tokyo: Square Enix, 2006–15. Published in English as *Pandora Hearts*. 24 vols. New York: Yen Press, 2009–16.

Mogensen, Jannie Uhre. "Fading into Innocence: Death, Sexuality and Moral Restoration in Henry Peach Robinson's *Fading Away*." *Victorian Review* 32, no. 1 (2006): 1–17.

Moore, Alan, and Eddie Campbell. *From Hell*. Marietta, GA: Top Shelf, 1989–96.

Moore, Alan, and Melinda Gebbie. *Lost Girls*. Atlanta, GA: Top Shelf Productions, 2006.

Moore, Alan, and Kevin O'Neill. *The League of Extraordinary Gentlemen*. Vol. 1. La Jolla, CA: American's Best Comics, 2000.

Moore, R. Laurence. *In Search of White Crows: Spiritualism, Parapsychology, and American Culture*. Oxford: Oxford University Press, 1977.

Mori Kaoru. *Ema*. 10 vols. Tokyo: Enterbrain, 2002–6. Published in English as *Emma*. 10 vols. New York: CMX Comics, 2006–9.

Morley, John. *Death, Heaven, and the Victorians*. Pittsburgh: University of Pittsburgh Press, 1971.

"The Morn of St. Valentine." *Bow Bells* 2, no. 29 (15 February 1865): 63–64.

Morrison, Arthur, and J. A. Shepherd. *Zig Zags at the Zoo*. *Strand Magazine* 4 (July 1892): 13–20, 165–75, 245–53, 38–97, 635–44; 5 (January 1893): 35–43, 127–37, 248–57, 407–14, 464–72, 593–600; 6 (July 1893): 139–147, 288–95, 342–52, 501–8, 693–702; 7 (January 1894): 33–40, 141–48, 374–82, 457–64, 599–605; 8 (July 1894): 22–28, 148–54.

Morrison, Grant, and Steve Yeowell. *Sebastian O*. New York: Vertigo, 1993. Reprinted 2004.

Morrison, Mark. *Modern Alchemy: Occultism and the Emergence of Atomic Theory*. Oxford: Oxford University Press, 2007.

Moto Naoko. *Redī Vikutorian* [Lady Victorian]. 20 vols. Tokyo: Akitashoten, 1999–2007.

Mulford, Prentice. *Der Unfug des Lebens und Der Unfug des Sterbens*. Stuttgart: Stuttgarter Hausbücherei, 1955.

———. *Your Forces and How to Use Them*. New York: F. J. Needham, 1888–92.

Mulholland, Tara. "More Than Words: Britain Embraces the Graphic Novel." *New York Times*, 22 August 2007, E8.

Murphy, Gretchen. "*Symzonia, Typee*, and the Dream of U.S. Global Isolation." *ESQ* 49, no. 4 (2003): 249–83.

Mussell, Jim, ed. "Teaching and Learning in the Digital Humanities Classroom." Special issue, *Victorian Periodicals Review* 45, no. 2 (Summer 2012): 200–238.

Natsume Fusanosuke. "Pictotext and Panels: Commonalities and Differences in Manga, Comics and BD." Translated by Jessica Bauwens-Sugimoto. In *Comics Worlds and the World of Comics: Towards Scholarship on a Global Scale*, edited by Jaqueline Berndt, 40–54. Kyoto: Kyoto Seika University Press, 2010.

Nelson, Elizabeth White. *Market Sentiments: Middle-Class Market Culture in Nineteenth-Century America*. Washington, DC: Smithsonian Books, 2004.

Nelson, Victoria. *The Secret Life of Puppets*. Cambridge, MA: Harvard University Press, 2001.

Nemesvari, Richard, and Lisa Surridge, eds. Appendix A in *Aurora Floyd*, by Mary Elizabeth Braddon, 551–59. Peterborough, ON: Broadview, 1998.

Nevins, Jess. "Introduction: The 19th-Century Roots of Steampunk." In *Steampunk*, edited by Ann VanderMeer and Joe R. Lansdale, 3–12. San Francisco: Tachyon, 2008.

———. "It's Time to Rethink Steampunk." *io9*. Posted January 27, 2012. http://io9.com/5879231/its-time-to-rethink-steampunk.

"A New Elaine." Text by Sarah Doudney, illustration by M. Kerns, engraver unidentified. *Quiver* 11 (January 1876): 561–62.

Newton, Isaac. *The Principia: Mathematical Principles of Natural Philosophy.* Translated by I. Bernard Cohen and Anne Whitman. Berkeley: University of California Press, 1999.

Nolte, Sharon H., and Sally Ann Hastings. "The Meiji State's Policy toward Women, 1890–1910." In *Recreating Japanese Women, 1600–1945,* edited by Gail Lee Bernstein, 151–74. Berkeley: University of California Press, 1991.

Novak, Daniel. *Realism, Photography, and Nineteenth-Century Fiction.* Cambridge: Cambridge University Press, 2008.

Oberter, Rachel. "Esoteric Art Confronting the Public Eye: The Abstract Spirit Drawings of Georgina Houghton." *Victorian Studies* 48, no. 2 (2005): 221–32.

———. "'The Sublimation of Matter into Spirit': Anna Mary Howitt's Automatic Drawings." In *The Ashgate Research Companion to Nineteenth-Century Spiritualism and the Occult,* edited by Tatiana Kontou and Sarah Willburn, 333–58. Farnham, UK: Ashgate, 2012

Okabe, Daisuke, and Kimi Ishida. "Making *Fujoshi* Identity Visible and Invisible." In *Fandom Unbound: Otaku Culture in a Connected World,* edited by Mizuko Ito, Daisuke Okabe, and Izumi Tsuji, 207–24. New Haven, CT: Yale University Press, 2012.

Okabe, Tsugumi. "From Sherlock Holmes to 'Heisei' Holmes: Counter Orientalism and Post Modern Parody in Gosho Aoyama's *Detective Conan* Manga Series." *International Journal of Comic Art* 15, no. 1 (2013): 230–50.

Oliphant, Margaret. *Hester.* 1883. Edited by Philip Davis and Brian Nellist. Oxford: Oxford University Press, 2003.

[———]. "Sensation Novels." *Blackwood's Edinburgh Magazine* 91 (May 1862): 564–84.

"One Day." Text by Ella Wheeler Wilcox, illustrations by Herbert Cole, Swantype engraving. *Pall Mall Magazine* 19 (September 1899): 1–3.

The Only Daughter. Bow Bells 2, nos. 41–52 (10 May–26 July 1865): 357–60, 381–84, 405–8, 453–56, 495–98, 519–22, 543–46, 567–70, 591–94, 613–15.

Ortabasi, Melek. "Brave Dogs and Little Lords: Thoughts on Translation, Gender, and the Debate on Childhood in Mid-Meiji." In *Translation in Modern Japan,* edited by Indra Levy, 186–212. New York: Routledge, 2011.

Pagliassotti, Dru. "Better Than Romance? Japanese BL Manga and the Subgenre of Male/Male Romantic Fiction." In *Boys' Love Manga:*

Essays on the Sexual Ambiguity and Cross-Cultural Fandom of the Genre, edited by Antonia Levi, Mark McHarry, and Dru Pagliassotti, 59–83. Jefferson, NC: McFarland, 2010.

Palmer, Beth. "Are the Victorians Still with Us? Victorian Sensation Fiction and Its Legacies in the Twenty-First Century." *Victorian Studies* 52, no. 1 (2009): 86–94.

Pansy Eyes. Bow Bells 9, nos. 230–34 (23 December 1868–20 January 1869): 533–37, 557–60, 581–84, 599–602, 622–26.

Patten, Robert L. *Charles Dickens and "Boz": The Birth of the Industrial Age Author.* Cambridge: Cambridge University Press, 2012.

———. *George Cruikshank's Life, Times, and Art.* Vol. 2, *1835–1878.* New Brunswick, NJ: Rutgers University Press, 1996.

Paulhan, Jean. "Happiness in Slavery." In *The Story of O,* by Pauline Réage. Translated by Sabine d'Estrée, xxi–xxxvi. New York: Ballantine Books, 1992.

Pearce, Joseph. *The Unmasking of Oscar Wilde.* San Francisco, CA: Ignatius Press, 2004.

"Personal and Art Intelligence." *Photographic and Fine Art Journal* 7 (July 1855): 223–24.

Peter, William. *The Maid of Orleans, and Other Poems.* Cambridge, UK: John Owen, 1843.

Phegley, Jennifer. *Courtship and Marriage in Victorian England.* Santa Barbara, CA: Praeger/ABC-Clio, 2012.

———. *Educating the Proper Woman Reader: Victorian Family Literary Magazines and the Cultural Health of the Nation.* Columbus: Ohio State University Press, 2004.

———. "Victorian Girls Gone Wild: Matrimonial Advertising and the Transformation of Courtship in the Popular Press." *Victorian Review* 39, no. 2 (Fall 2013): 129–46.

Picker, John M. *Victorian Soundscapes.* Oxford: Oxford University Press, 2003.

Pietrzak-Franger, Monika. "Envisioning the Ripper's Visions: Adapting Myth in Alan Moore and Eddie Campbell's *From Hell.*" *Neo-Victorian Studies* 2, no. 2 (2009/2010): 157–85.

Plender, Olivia. *Cult Fiction.* London: Southbank Centre, 2007.

———. *The Masterpiece.* 2002–6. Graphic novel.

———. *A Stellar Key to the Summerland.* London: Book Works, 2007.

Plotz, Judith. "Literary Ways of Killing a Child." In *Aspects and Issues in the History of Children's Literature,* edited by Maria Nikolajeva, 1–26. Westport, CT: Greenwood Press, 1995.

Portela, Manuel. "A Portrait of the Author as an Author." Reprint of essay in *Novas Histórias Literárias/New Literary Histories,* edited by Isabel Caldeira, 357–71. Coimbra, Portugal: Minerva, 2004. *Manuelporte-laweb,* www1.ci.uc.pt/pessoal/mportela/arslonga/MPENSAIOS /a_portrait_of_the_author.htm#[N].

Porter, Roy. *The Making of Geology: Earth Science in Britain, 1660–1815.* Cambridge: Cambridge University Press, 1977.

"Practice and Precept." *Punch,* 2 November 1904, 302.

Preface to *The Scrapbook of Literary Varieties.* London: John Reynolds, n.d.

Prettejohn, Elizabeth. *After the Pre-Raphaelites: Art and Aestheticism in Victorian England.* Manchester: Manchester University Press, 1999.

———. *Art for Art's Sake: Aestheticism in Victorian Painting.* New Haven, CT: Yale University Press, 2007.

Primorac, Antonija. "Other Neo-Victorians: Neo-Victorianism, Translation and Global Literature." In "Neo-Victorianism and Globalisation: Transnational Dissemination of Nineteenth-Century Cultural Texts," edited by Antonija Primorac and Monika Pietrzak-Franger. Special issue, *Neo-Victorian Studies* 8, no. 1 (2015): 48–76.

Primorac, Antonija, and Monika Pietrzak-Franger, eds. "Neo-Victorianism and Globalisation: Transnational Dissemination of Nineteenth-Century Cultural Texts." Special issue, *Neo-Victorian Studies* 8, no. 1 (2015): 1–206.

"Prospectus for *The Yellow Book* 1." April 1894. Mark Samuels Lasner Collection, on loan to the University of Delaware Library, Newark. In *The Yellow Nineties Online,* edited by Dennis Denisoff and Lorraine Janzen Kooistra. Ryerson University, 2011. www.1890s.ca/HTML .aspx?s=YBV1_prospectus.html.

"Proud Princess." Text by Lydia Busch, illustration by Herbert Cole. *Pall Mall Magazine* (December 1910): 1046–48.

Prough, Jennifer. *Straight from the Heart: Gender, Intimacy, and the Cultural Production of Shōjo Manga.* Honolulu: University of Hawai'i Press, 2010.

Raven-Hill, Leonard. "Early Du Maurier Crinoline Period." *Punch,* 19 June 1897, 312.

Reed, E[dward] T. "Design for a Parliamentary Car for the Queen's Procession." *Punch,* 19 June 1897, 294.

———. "A Prehistoric Jubilee." *Punch,* 19 June 1897, 311.

Reed, William. *The Phantom of the Poles.* New York: W. S. Rockey, 1906.

Rhodes, Kimberly. *Ophelia and Victorian Visual Culture: Representing Body Politics in the Nineteenth Century.* Aldershot, UK: Ashgate, 2008.

Richards, Thomas. *The Commodity Culture of Victorian England: Advertising and Spectacle, 1851–1914.* Palo Alto, CA: Stanford University Press, 1991.

Robinson, H[enry] P[each]. *The Elements of a Pictorial Photograph.* Bradford, UK: Percy Lund, 1896.

———. *Pictorial Effect in Photography: Being Hints on Composition and Chiaroscuro for Photographers.* London: Piper and Carter, 1869.

Robinson, N. M. "O'Flaherty, Eliza (1818–1882)." In *Australian Dictionary of Biography.* National Centre of Biography, Australian National University. http://adb.anu.edu.au/biography/oflaherty-eliza-2520/text3411 (accessed 31 December 2013).

Romero-Jórdan, Andrés. "A Hammer to Shape Reality: Alan Moore's Graphic Novels and the Avant-Gardes." *Studies in Comics* 2, no. 1 (2011): 39–56.

"Rosamond, Queen of the Lombards." Text by C. J. E., illustration by Frederick Sandys, engraving by Swain. *Once a Week,* 30 November 1861, 630–31.

Rose, Clare. *Making, Selling, and Wearing Boys' Clothes in Late-Victorian England.* Farnham, UK: Ashgate, 2010.

Rose, Margaret. "Extraordinary Pasts: Steampunk as a Mode of Historical Representation." *Journal of the Fantastic in the Arts* 20, no. 3 (January 2009): 319–33.

Rosen, Judith. "A Different Scene of Desire: Women and Work in Penny Magazine Fiction." *Pacific Coast Philology* 27 (September 1992): 102–9.

Rosenthal, Jesse. "The Large Novel and the Law of Large Numbers; or, Why George Eliot Hates Gambling." *ELH* 77, no. 3 (2010): 777–811.

Rossetti, Dante Gabriel. "Of Life, Love, and Death: Sixteen Sonnets." *Fortnightly Review* 5 (March 1869): 266–73.

Rotunno, Laura. *Postal Plots in British Fiction, 1840–1898: Readdressing Correspondence in Victorian Culture.* Basingstoke, UK: Palgrave Macmillan, 2013.

Round, Julia. "Visual Perspective and Narrative Voice in Comics: Redefining Literary Terminology." *International Journal of Comic Art* 9, no. 2 (Fall 2007): 316–29.

Rowe, C. J. "A Legend of St. Valentine." *Bow Bells* 10, no. 237, supp. (10 February 1869): 8.

Ruby, Jay. *Secure the Shadow: Death and Photography in America.* Cambridge, MA: MIT Press, 1995.

Rusch, Mark T. "The Deranged Episode: Ironic Dissimulation in the Domestic Scenes of Edward Gorey's Short Stories." *International Journal of Comic Art* 6, no. 2 (Fall 2004): 445–55.

Ruskin, John. *Notes on Some of the Principal Pictures Exhibited in the Rooms of the Royal Academy.* Vol. 5. London: Smith, Elder, 1855.

Saatchi Gallery. *The Masterpiece,* pt. 4, *A Weekend in the Country,* by Olivia Plender. www.saatchigallery.com/artists/olivia_plender.htm (last updated 2016).

Saito, Kumiko. "Desire in Subtext: Gender, Fandom, and Women's Male-Male Homoerotic Parodies in Contemporary Japan." *Mechademia* 6 (2011): 171–91.

Sakai, Naoki. *Translation and Subjectivity: On "Japan" and Cultural Nationalism.* Minneapolis: University of Minnesota Press, 1997.

Sanders, Julie. *Adaptation and Appropriation.* London: Routledge, 2006.

Schaffer, Simon. "Halley's Atheism and the End of the World." *Notes and Records of the Royal Society* 32, no. 1 (1977): 17–40.

Schmidt, Leigh Eric. *Consumer Rites: The Buying and Selling of American Holidays.* Princeton: Princeton University Press, 1995.

Schönthan, Gaby. *Angenehme Müdigkeit.* Hamburg: Marion von Schröder, 1965.

Schuchard, Ronald. *The Last Minstrels: Yeats and the Revival of the Bardic Arts.* Oxford: Oxford University Press, 2008.

Schürzer, Rudolf. *Schwankende Gestalten.* Vienna: Burgverlag, 1926.

Schuster, Marc-Oliver. "'Bei allem, was weiß ist': Intertextuelle Komplexität und implizite Ästhetik in H. C. Artmanns *Frankenstein in Sussex.*" In *Aufbau wozu. Neues zu H. C. Artmann,* edited by Marc-Oliver Schuster, 185–220. Würzburg: Königshausen und Neumann, 2010.

———. "Einleitung." In *Aufbau wozu: Neues zu H. C. Artmann,* edited by Marc-Oliver Schuster, 7–18. Würzburg: Königshausen und Neumann, 2010.

Seaborn, Captain Adam. *Symzonia: A Voyage of Discovery.* 1820. Reprint, New York: Arno, 1975.

Seed, David. "Breaking the Bounds: The Rhetoric of Limits in the Works of Edgar Allan Poe, His Contemporaries and Adaptors." In *Anticipations: Essays on Early Science Fiction and Its Precursors,* edited by David Seed, 75–97. Syracuse: Syracuse University Press, 1995.

Seymour, Robert. *Sketches by Seymour.* 5 vols. London: G. S. Tregear, 1834–36?

Seymour, Robert, and "Crowquill" [Albert Forrester]. *Seymour's Humorous Sketches.* London: Henry Bohn, 1841. Reprinted 1843.

Seymour, Robert, and R. B. Peake. *An Evening's Amusement; or, The Adventures of a Cockney Sportsman.* London: privately printed, 1846.

Sfar, Joann, and Emmanuel Guibert. *The Professor's Daughter.* Translated by Alexis Siegel. New York: First Second, 1997.

Shank, Barry. *A Token of My Affection: Greeting Cards and American Business Culture.* New York: Columbia University Press, 2004.

Sherlock. Created by Mark Gatiss and Steven Moffat. London: Hartswood Films and BBC Wales for Masterpiece Theatre, 2010–. Television series.

Sherlock Holmes. Directed by Guy Ritchie. 2009; DVD, Burbank, CA: Warner Home Video, 2009.

Sherlock Holmes: A Game of Shadows. Directed by Guy Ritchie. 2011; DVD, Burbank, CA: Warner Home Video, 2012.

Shonibare, Yinka MBE. Interview by Chris Boyd. *The Morning After: Performing Arts in Australia,* 30 September 2008. http://chrisboyd .blogspot.com/2008/09/yinka-shonibare-1-mad-world.html.

———. Interview by Anthony Downey. *Bomb* 93 (Fall 2005): n.p. www.bombsite.com/issues/93/articles/2777.

———. Interview by Richard Lacayo. *Time Magazine,* 7 July 2009. http://lookingaround.blogs.time.com/2009/07/07/more-talk -with-yinka-shonibare/.

———. "Interview with Yinka Shonibare MBE." By Bernard Müller. In *Garden of Love,* by Yinka Shonibare MBE, 22. Paris: Flammarion, 2007.

Shorter, Thomas [T. S.]. "Death and the Afterlife." *Spiritual Magazine* 5, no. 11 (September 1870): 418–21.

Siemann, Catherine. "'But I'm Grown Up Now': *Alice* in the Twenty-First Century." *Neo-Victorian Studies* 5, no. 2 (2012): 175–201.

Simanek, Donald E. "Turning the Universe Inside-Out: Ulysses Grant Morrow's Naples Experiment." *Myths and Mysteries of Science: Removing the Mystery.* Maintained by Donald E. Simanek. www.lhup .edu/~dsimanek/hollow/morrow.htm (accessed 4 May 2013).

Simmonds, Posy. *Tamara Drewe.* New York: Houghton Mifflin, 2007.

Simpson, Roger. *Camelot Regained: The Arthurian Revival and Tennyson, 1800–1849.* Cambridge, UK: D. S. Brewer, 1990.

Sinnema, Peter W. "10 April 1818: John Cleves Symmes's 'No. 1 Circular.'" *BRANCH: Britain, Representation, and Nineteenth-Century History.* Edited by Dino Franco Felluga. Extension of Romanticism and Victorianism on the Net. www.branchcollective.org/ (accessed 13 June 2012).

"Sir Dinadan's Death." Text by unidentified poet, illustration by E. Wagner, engraver unknown. *Belgravia* 37 (February 1879): 75–78.

Sitwell, Sacheverell. *Narrative Pictures: A Survey of English Genre and Its Painters.* London: B. T. Batsford, 1936. Reprinted 1969.

Slater, Michael. *The Composition and Monthly Publication of Nicholas Nickleby*. Menston, UK: Scolar Press, 1973.

Smith, Dan. "New Maps of Heaven." *Art Monthly* 338 (July–August 2010): 11–14.

Smith, Jonathan. *Charles Darwin and Victorian Visual Culture*. Cambridge: Cambridge University Press, 2006.

Smith, Lindsay. "The Shoe-Black to the Crossing Sweeper: Victorian Street Arabs and Photography." In *The Politics of Focus: Women, Children and Nineteenth-Century Photography*, 111–32. Manchester: Manchester University Press, 1998.

Speidel, Klaus. "Can a Single Still Picture Tell a Story? Definitions of Narrative and the Alleged Problem of Time with Single Still Pictures." *Diegesis* 2, no. 1 (2013): 173–294.

"St. Cecilia." Illustration by D. G. Rossetti, to "The Palace of Art," in *Poems* by Alfred Lord Tennyson, 113. London: Edward Moxon, 1857.

Standish, Peter. *Hollow Earth: The Long and Curious History of Imagining Strange Lands, Fantastical Creatures, Advanced Civilizations, and Marvelous Machines Below the Earth's Surface*. Cambridge, MA: Da Capo, 2006.

Stasinski, Robert. "Olivia Plender: I'll Give You Television." *Flash Art* 42, no. 267 (2009): 52–54.

Steiner, Wendy. *Pictures of Romance: Form against Context in Painting and Literature*. Chicago: University of Chicago Press, 1988.

Stewart, Garrett. *Death Sentences: Styles of Dying in British Fiction*. Cambridge, MA: Harvard University Press, 1984.

Strand, Clare. "Interview: Clare Strand in Conversation with Chris Mullin." In *Clare Strand: A Photoworks Monograph*, by Rebecca Drew, 95. Brighton, UK: Photoworks, 2009.

"The Strife Song." Text by John Kindred, illustration by Gilbert James, Swantype engraving. *Pall Mall Magazine* 21 (August 1900): 482–83.

Symmes, Americus. *The Symmes Theory of Concentric Spheres, Demonstrating That the Earth Is Hollow, Habitable Within, and Widely Open about the Poles*. Louisville, KY: Bradley and Gilbert, 1885.

Symmes, John C[leeves]. "No. 1 Circular." 1818. In *Hollow Earth Theory*. Oliver's Bookshelf, http://olivercowdery.com/texts/1818symm.htm#item1 (accessed 10 May 2007).

"Symmes and His Theory." *Harper's New Monthly Magazine* 65 (October 1882): 740–44.

Szyłak, Jerzy, and Jarowsław Gach. *Alicja po Drugiej Stronie Lustra* [Alice through the looking glass]. Warsaw: Timof i cisi wspólnicy, 2008.

Szyłak, Jerzy, and Mateusz Skutnik. *Alicja* [Alice]. Warsaw: Timof i cisi wspólnicy, 2006.

Talbot, Bryan. *Alice in Sunderland: An Entertainment.* Milwaukie, OR: Dark Horse Comics, 2007.

Tamara Drewe. Directed by Steven Frears. 2010; DVD, Culver City, CA: Sony Pictures Classics, 2011.

Tay, Johny. "*Seven Years in Dog-Land:* An Overview." *All My Things: The Website for Johny Tay's Stuff,* http://johnytay.net/2013/10/overview-seven-years-in-dog-land/ (accessed 15 December 2014).

Teed, Cyrus Reed, and Ulysses Grant Morrow. *The Cellular Cosmogony, or the Earth a Concave Sphere.* Chicago: Guiding Star, 1898.

"A Tennysonian Study." Text by Alfred Lord Tennyson, design and engraving by Frank Godart. *London Society* 48, no. 283 (July 1885): v.

Teukolsky, Rachel. *The Literate Eye: Victorian Art Writing and Modernist Aesthetics.* Oxford: Oxford University Press, 2009.

Thackeray, William Makepeace. *The Newcomes.* 1855. Edited by David Pascoe. London: Penguin Books, 1996.

"Thalia and Melpomene, Assisted by Mr. Punch, Hold a Reception of Notable Histrions of the Past Sixty Years." *Punch,* 19 June 1897, 299.

Thomas, Julia. "Happy Endings: Death and Domesticity in Victorian Illustration." In *Reading Victorian Illustration, 1855–1875: Spoils of the Lumber Room,* edited by Paul Goodman and Simon Cooke, 79–96. Burlington, VT: Ashgate, 2012.

Thomas, Kate. *Postal Pleasures: Sex, Scandal, and Victorian Letters.* Oxford: Oxford University Press, 2012.

Thorn, Matthew. "Girls and Women Getting Out of Hand: The Pleasures and Politics of Japan's Amateur Comics Community." In *Fanning the Flames: Fans and Consumer Culture in Contemporary Japan,* edited by William W. Kelly, 169–86. Albany, NY: SUNY Press, 2004.

Toboso Yana. *Kuroshitsuji.* 23 vols. to date. Tokyo: Square Enix, 2007–. Published in English as *Black Butler.* 22 vols. to date. New York: Yen Press, 2010–.

Tolstoy, Leo. *The Death of Ivan Ilyich.* New York: Bantam Books, 1985.

"Transformation Scenes in Real Life." *Graphic,* 16 January 1875, 64.

Treister, Suzanne. *Hexen 2.0.* London: Black Dog Publishing, 2012

Trusler, John. *Hogarth Moralized.* London: S. Hooper, 1768.

Tytler, Sarah [Henrietta Keddie]. *Lady Bell: A Story of Last Century.* London: Strahan, 1873.

Voigts-Virchow, Eckart. "Anti-Essentialist Versions of Aggregate Alice: A Grin without a Cat." In *Translation and Adaptation in Theatre and Film,* edited by Katja Krebs, 63–79. New York: Routledge, 2014.

Vollrath, Lisa. "I See Dead People: Victorian Post-Mortem Photography." *Bad Influence: From the Studio of Lisa Vollrath* (October 2006): 12–14.

Voltaire [François-Marie Arouet]. *Candide.* New York: Bantam Books, 1959.

Walkowitz, Judith. "Urban Spectatorship." In *City of Dreadful Delight: Narratives of Sexual Danger in Late Victorian London,* 15–40. Chicago: University of Chicago Press, 1992.

Wallace, Irving. *The Square Pegs: Some Characters Who Dared to Be Different.* London: Hutchinson, 1958.

Wallis, Henry. "Obituary for Robert Seymour." *Seymour's Sketches— Angling.* Back cover. London: Thomas Fry, 1836.

Waters, Sarah. *Fingersmith.* New York: Riverhead, 2002.

Wegner, Phillip. "Alan Moore, 'Secondary Literacy,' and the Modernism of the Graphic Novel." *ImageText* 5, no. 3 (2010). www.english.ufl .edu/imagetext/archives/v5_3/wegner/.

Weig, Heidi. "'Rebuilding Yesterday to Ensure Our Tomorrow': An Overview of Steampunk Aesthetics and Literature." *Inklings: Jahrbuch für Literatur und Ästhetik* 30 (2012): 135–50.

Westfall, Richard S., and Gerald Funk. "Newton, Halley, and the System of Patronage." In *Standing on the Shoulders of Giants: A Longer View of Newton and Halley,* edited by Norman J. W. Thrower, 3–13. Berkeley: University of California Press, 1990.

Whistler, James McNeill. *Mr. Whistler's Ten O'Clock.* Cambridge, MA: Riverside Press, 1896.

Willburn, Sarah. "Viewing History and Fantasy through Victorian Spirit Photography." In *The Ashgate Research Companion to Nineteenth-Century Spiritualism and the Occult,* edited by Tatiana Kontou and Sarah Willburn, 359–81. Farnham, UK: Ashgate, 2012.

"William Hogarth: Painter, Engraver, and Philosopher." *Cornhill.* Vol. 1 (London: Smith Elder, 1860): 177–93, 264–82, 417–37, 561–81, 716–35; vol. 2 (London: Smith Elder, 1860): 97–112, 225–41, 354–69, 438–61.

Winchester, J. "Spirit Art." *Gallery of Spirit Art: An Illustrated Quarterly Magazine Dedicated to Spirit Photography, Spirit Painting, the Photographing of Materialized Forms and Every Form of Spirit Art* 1, no. 1 (August 1882): 3–5.

Wingerden, Sophia A. van. *The Woman's Suffrage Movement in Britain, 1866–1929.* London: Macmillan, 1999.

[Winstanley, Eliza.] "Aunt Betsy: Introduction." *Bow Bells* 6, no. 133, supp. (13 February 1867): 2.

———. "The Old Valentine." *Bow Bells* 2, no. 29 (15 February 1865): 53–55.

———. *Voices from the Lumber Room. Bow Bells* 2, nos. 46–52 (26 July 1856): 477–80, 525–28, 549–52, 573–76, 597–600, 615–18; 3, nos. 46–72 (9 August–13 December 1865): 37–40, 61–64, 85–88, 133–36, 157–60, 181–84, 205–8, 229–33, 277–80, 301–4, 325–38, 349–52, 373–76, 397–400, 421–24, 439–42, 488–90.

Wolfreys, Julian. "Notes towards a Poethics of Spectrality: The Examples of Neo-Victorian Textuality." In *Reading Historical Fiction: The Revenant and Remembered Past,* edited by Kate Mitchell and Nicola Parsons, 153–72. Basingstoke, UK: Palgrave Macmillan, 2013.

Wood, Mrs. J. *Pantaletta: A Romance of Sheheland.* New York: American News, 1882.

Yan, Shu-chuan. "'Politics and Petticoats': Fashioning the Nation in *Punch* Magazine, 1840s–1880s." *Fashion Theory* 15, no. 3 (September 2011): 345–72.

Yaszek, Lisa. "Democratising the Past to Improve the Future: An Interview with Steampunk Godfather Paul Di Filippo." *Neo-Victorian Studies* 3, no. 1 (2010): 189–95.

Young, Art. "On the Ledge." In *Sebastian O,* by Grant Morrison and Steve Yeowell, no. 1 (May 1993): 28.

Zubrzycki, Genvième. "Polish Mythology and the Traps of Messianic Martyrology." In *National Myths: Constructed Pasts, Contested Presents,* edited by Gérard Buchard, 110–32. New York: Routledge, 2013.

Contributors

CHRISTINE FERGUSON is professor in English literature at the University of Sterling. She is the author of *Language, Science, and Popular Fiction at the Victorian Fin-de-Siècle: The Brutal Tongue* (2006) and *Determined Spirits: Eugenics, Heredity, and Racial Regeneration in Anglo-American Spiritualist Writing, 1848–1930* (2012), as well as articles and book chapters in *Australasian Journal of Victorian Studies; Neo-Victorian Studies; Studies in English Literature, 1500–1900; LIT: Literature, Interpretation, Theory; PMLA; ELH;* and *Teaching the Graphic Novel* (2009).

KATE FLINT is Provost Professor of Art History and English at the University of Southern California. Her books include *The Transatlantic Indian, 1776–1930* (2008), *The Victorians and the Visual Imagination* (2000), *The Woman Reader, 1837–1914* (1993), and *Dickens* (1985). She is the general editor of the *Cambridge History of Victorian Literature* (2012), a coeditor, with Howard Morphy, of *Culture, Landscape and the Environment* (2000), and the editor of *Victorian Love Stories* (1996), as well as numerous works by Charles Dickens, Virginia Woolf, D. H. Lawrence, and Anthony Trollope for Penguin Classics and Oxford World's Classics. Recent articles by her have appeared in *Victorian Studies, Novel: A Forum on Fiction, European Romantic Review, Romanticism and Victorianism on the Net,* and *Journal of Victorian Culture.*

LINDA K. HUGHES, Addie Levy Professor of English at Texas Christian University, is a Victorian specialist with interests in historical media (poetry and print culture, periodicals, serial fiction), gender studies, and transnationality. Her monographs include *Graham R.: Rosamund Marriott Watson, Woman of Letters* (2005), *The Cambridge Introduction to Victorian Poetry* (2010), and, coauthored with Michael Lund, *The Victorian Serial* (1991) and *Victorian Publishing and Mrs. Gaskell's Work* (1999). She is a coeditor, with Sarah R. Robbins, of *Teaching Transatlanticism: Resources for Teaching Nineteenth-Century Anglo-American Print Culture* (2015) and, with Sharon M. Harris, of the four-volume *A Feminist Reader: Feminist Thought from Sappho to Satrapi* (2013). She has recently published book chapters on poetry and the visual arts in the work of Michael Field (2013), William Morris, and D. G. Rossetti (2011). Her recent articles have appeared in *Victorian Poetry*, *Victorian Review*, and *Victorian Periodicals Review*.

ANNA MARIA JONES is associate professor of English at the University of Central Florida, where she teaches Victorian and neo-Victorian literature, literary theory, and Japanese manga and anime. She is the author of *Problem Novels: Victorian Fiction Theorizes the Sensational Self* (2007). Recent articles and book chapters by her have appeared in *BRANCH: Britain, Representation, and Nineteenth-Century History*, *Neo-Victorian Studies*, *Criticism*, *Victorian Literature and Culture*, *European Romantic Review*, *Cambridge Companion to Victorian Culture* (2010), and *A Companion to Sensation Fiction* (2011). Her current research explores transnational and transmedial engagements with and appropriations of the Victorians.

HEIDI KAUFMAN teaches nineteenth-century literature at the University of Oregon. She is the author of *English Origins, Jewish Discourse, and the Nineteenth-Century British Novel: Reflections on a Nested Nation* (2009) and a coeditor of *Fear, Loathing, and Victorian Xenophobia* (2013) and *An Uncomfortable Authority: Maria Edgeworth and Her Contexts* (2004). Articles by her have appeared in *Victorian Literature and Culture*, *Nineteenth Century Studies*, *Shofar*, and *Partial Answers*. Her current research focuses on archival theory, digital humanities, and writing from the nineteenth-century East End.

BRIAN MAIDMENT is professor of the history of print at Liverpool John Moores University. He is the author of *Comedy, Caricature and the Social Order, 1820–1850* (2013), as well as *Reading Popular Prints, 1790–1870* (1996) and *Dusty Bob—A Cultural History of Dustmen, 1790–1870* (2007). He is a coeditor, with Keith Hanley, of *Persistent Ruskin: Studies in Influence, Assimilation, and Effect* (2013). Recent articles by him have appeared in *Victorian Poetry*, *Dickens Quarterly*, and *Victorian Periodicals Review*. He is contributing a chapter on illustration to the forthcoming *Routledge Companion to Victorian Periodicals*. He is a member of the executive board of the Research Society for Victorian Periodicals and a member of the editorial boards of *Victorian Periodicals*

Review and *Victorians Institute Journal*. He was also an associate editor for the *Dictionary of Nineteenth-Century Journalism* (2009), to which he contributed many entries on artists and illustrated journals.

REBECCA N. MITCHELL is senior lecturer in Victorian literature at the University of Birmingham (UK). She is the author of *Victorian Lessons in Empathy and Difference* (2011), a coeditor of the anniversary edition of George Meredith's *Modern Love and Poems of the English Roadside, with Poems and Ballads* (2012), and a coauthor, with Joseph Bristow, of *Oscar Wilde's Chatterton: Literary History, Romanticism, and the Art of Forgery* (2015). Articles by her have appeared in *Nineteenth-Century Literature, Victorian Literature and Culture, Fashion Theory,* and *Victorian Periodicals Review,* among other journals.

JENNIFER PHEGLEY is professor of English at the University of Missouri–Kansas City. She is the author of *Educating the Proper Woman Reader: Victorian Family Literary Magazines and the Cultural Health of the Nation* (2004) and *Courtship and Marriage in Victorian England* (2012). She is a coeditor, with John Barton and Kristin Houston, of *Transatlantic Sensations* (2012); with Andrew Maunder, of *Teaching Nineteenth-Century Fiction* (2010); and, with Janet Badia, of *Reading Women: Literary Figures and Cultural Icons from the Victorian Age to the Present* (2005). Recent articles by her have appeared in *Victorians Institute Journal, Victorian Review, Victorian Periodicals Review,* and *American Periodicals.*

MONIKA PIETRZAK-FRANGER is visiting professor of English at Hamburg University. She is the author of *The Male Body and Masculinity: Representations of Men in the British Visual Culture of the 1990s* (2007) and the forthcoming *Spectres of Syphilis: Medicine, Knowledge and the Spectacle of Victorian (In)Visibility* (2017), as well as the editor of *Women, Beauty, and Fashion* (2014). She is also a coeditor, with Martha Stoddard Holmes, of "Disease, Communication and the Ethics of (In)Visibility," a special symposium issue of the *Journal of Bioethical Inquiry* 11, no. 4 (2014); with Eckart Voigts and Barbara Schaff, of *Reflecting on Darwin* (2014); and, with Eckart Voigts-Virchow, of *Adaptations—Performing across Media and Genres* (2009). With Antonija Primorac, she was a coeditor of "Neo-Victorianism and

Globalisation: Transnational Dissemination of Nineteenth-Century Cultural Texts," a special issue of *Neo-Victorian Studies* 8, no. 1 (2015). She is the book review editor for the journal *Adaptation*.

PETER W. SINNEMA is professor of English at the University of Alberta. He is the author of *Dynamics of the Printed Page: Representing the Nation in the* Illustrated London News (1998) and *The Wake of Wellington: Englishness in 1852* (2006). He has edited scholarly editions of Samuel Smiles's *Self-Help* (2002) and Edward Bulwer-Lytton's *The Coming Race* (2008). His articles have appeared in such journals as *Victorian Review, Victorian Periodicals Review,* and *Oxford Art Journal,* as well as in *BRANCH: Britain, Representation, and Nineteenth-Century History.*

JESSICA STRALEY is associate professor of English at the University of Utah. She is the author of *Evolution and Imagination in Victorian Children's Literature* (2016). She has also published articles on Victorian literature's engagements with evolutionary theory and vivisection in *Victorian Studies* and *Nineteenth-Century Literature.* Her current research explores the function of animals as both pedagogical objects and fantastical subjects in Victorian culture.

Index

Page numbers in italics refer to illustrations on those pages.

INDEX

Wallis, Henry, 53–54, 66n22
Waterhouse, Alfred, 255
Waters, Sarah: *Fingersmith*, 5
webcomics, 6
Wegner, Phillip, 266n54
Weig, Heidi, 261n3
Westfall, Richard S., and Gerald Funk, 118n19
Whistler, James McNeill, 14–15, 18
Wilde, Oscar, 6, 26, 176, 177, 183, 253, 257; Dorian Gray (character), 333; Wildean dandy (*see* dandy)
Wilson, Patten, "Among the Tombs," 226
Winchester, J., 122–23
Wingerden, Sophia van, 236n43
Winstanley, Eliza ("Aunt Betsy"), *276*, 287–88, *289*, 297n28
women: activism of, 209; death of, 181–87; depiction of, 214, 219–20, 224–25, 282, 250–60, 271–77, 282, 286–94, 294n6, 296n18, 303, 312–16; education of, 209, 225; gender roles of, 208–9, 211–25, 228–30, 248–60, 272, 301, 316–18; as hero, 78, 215–17, 220, 230, 233n22, 286–90, 301;

periodicals for, 273, 297n25; photography of, 179–82, 337; as readers (*see under* reader, the); suffrage of, 132, 214, 219, 230; translations by, 327n26; "Woman Question" (*fujin mondai*), 307
Wood, Mrs. J., 117n11
wood engraving, 9, 12, 44, 46, 235n34, 273
working class, 269–94; depictions of, 27, 58, 271, 285, 316; readers, 27, 271–76, 286. *See also* class
World War II, legacy of, 71, 76, 152
Wow!, 156

Yan, Shu-chuan, 265n51
yaoi. See manga
Yaszek, Lisa, 260n1
Yeats, Jack, 224, 234n28
Yeats, W. B., 224, 234n28
Yellow Book, The, 15, 34n49, 257
Yeowell, Steve, and Grant Morrison: *Sebastian O*, 6, 240, 253–57, *254*, *256*
Young, Art, 263n18

Zig Zags at the Zoo, 15–17, *16*, 25